AN ECONOMIC STUDY OF THE CITY OF LONDON

AN ECONOMIC STUDY OF THE CITY OF LONDON

by the Economists Advisory Group

Directors and Editors of Study
John H. Dunning
E. Victor Morgan

University of Toronto Press

First published in 1971

First published in Canada and the United States
by University of Toronto Press, Toronto and Buffalo

ISBN 0-8020-1842-4
ISBN microfiche 0-8020-0174-2

Printed in Great Britain
in 10 on 11 Times Roman type
by Alden & Mowbray Ltd
at the Alden Press, Oxford

AN ECONOMIC STUDY OF THE CITY OF LONDON
was prepared by
The Economists Advisory Group

The members of the Group are:
Professor J. H. Dunning, Professor D. S. Lees
Professor E. V. Morgan, Professor J. Wiseman
Professor A. T. Peacock

Studies are normally undertaken under the
direction of one member of the Group, but all
members participate in the preparation of each
Study and accept responsibility for the material
used and the conclusions reached. This Study was
directed by Professors J. H. Dunning and E. V.
Morgan

The E.A.G. staff engaged upon this study were:
Mr J. D. Carmichael, Mr J. M. Jefferson, Mr J. A. Woodman and
Mr I. Haferkost

The Study was Commissioned by the
Corporation of the City of London

Foreword

The contribution made by the City to our country's balance of payments position is often mentioned in the press and on radio and television, and usually is referred to as 'invisible exports'.

I have had doubts whether there has been sufficient public knowledge about these 'invisible' earnings or of the proportion of these attributable to the relatively few people in the Square Mile.

I was therefore greatly pleased when the Common Council of the City of London decided in 1966 to commission the Economists Advisory Group to carry out an exhaustive survey and to report on the whole complicated and esoteric subject of the financial activities carried on in the City – its innumerable facets; how they function and interlock and overlap; of great importance, what we, the Corporation, could do so as best to nurture this vital work, particularly in our role of local planning authority.

After many months of labour by highly skilled people, this survey was completed. Subsequently, the Corporation have decided to give a much wider circulation to this work and have agreed to its publication. I am delighted to have been asked to write this brief introduction. Like most technical works it is not light reading, but to all those who seek information on which to base policy decisions it will, I am sure, be of inestimable value.

Peter Studd.
Lord Mayor of London
70/71.

Preface

The Economists Advisory Group wish to express their sincere appreciation to all who have contributed to this Study.

Many personalities of the academic world as well as representatives of the professions and commerce of the City of London have given valuable help and have been generous with their time. Some were deeply involved in the day-to-day life of the City, while others had no links with the Square Mile.

It is impossible for the Group to give acknowledgement to everyone concerned, but our thanks go especially to the Chief Architect, Mr E. Chandler, his colleagues and staff at Guildhall. We are also grateful to Professor J. Parry Lewis of the Department of Town and Country Planning, University of Manchester, for his advice and contribution to several sections of our work, particularly that concerned with traffic flows and transport problems.

Other papers have been contributed by Mr M. Barron, Mr F. J. B. Stilwell, and Mr G. N. Yannopoulos (University of Reading); Professor G. Rees (University College of Aberystwyth); Mr K. Hartley (University of York); Dr D. Singh and Mr A. Traill (University of Manchester); Mr J. Goddard (London School of Economics); Mr D. Massey (University of Cambridge); Professor J. Bird (University of Southampton); and Mr Brian Anstey. We are also very grateful to Mrs Gillian Barron for compiling the index.

Many other individuals gave liberally of their time, expertise and experience both in interviews and replies to our letters. About a thousand persons co-operated in completing our sampling questionnaires. Without their very full co-operation, and that of the trade associations represented in the City, this report could not have been written.

This study was originally completed in the latter part of 1967 and was the product of twelve months' research. As far as possible, we have sought to update our statistics and take account of the more important developments since 1966, but the structure of the study remains essentially as we prepared it for the Corporation of London.

J. H. DUNNING

E. V. MORGAN

September 1970.

11

Contents

CONTENTS

Tables

Figures

Précis of Terms of Reference given to the Economists Advisory Group by the Corporation of the City of London

'The study is required in order to provide background information for the preparation of the City Development Plan. It should, therefore, cover all economic matters which are relevant to the use of land and the types of activity and of building which will be provided in the Plan.

The future of the City should be considered both in relation to its place in international trade and to the expansion of the domestic economy.

The study is to lead to a statement of the economic obstacles to the expansion of the City; the economic advantages and disadvantages of further expansion; the possibilities of planned dispersion; and the likely effects of such dispersion on the interests concerned, on the efficiency of the City as a whole and its contribution to the national economy.

In particular the study will cover the following:

(a) The Present Economic Functions of the City

A general assessment of its importance in the national and international economy. A classification of the activities carried on in the City. The relevant characteristics of each activity to be described, special attention being paid to the number and size of firms. The links with other economic activities, both within and outside the City and special needs in the way of type of building, proximity to one another or access to transport or other facilities.

(b) Employment

For each activity distinguished under (a) figures to be compiled for employment, distinguishing, so far as possible, between managerial, clerical and manual workers and between male and female adults and juveniles.

(c) Land Use

As much information as possible to be obtained regarding land use in order to show the amount of space occupied by each activity and the tendency for certain activities to be concentrated in particular parts of the City. The study will also consider the relative importance of owner-occupation and renting of premises with particular regard to the availability of premises for new and expanding firms.

(d) Transport

(i) For passenger traffic, information is needed about the place of residence of those who work in the City, their normal means and route of travel and their walking distance at the end of the journey.

(ii) For goods traffic, to distinguish so far as possible between traffic originating and/or terminating in the City, and through traffic with points of origin and destination.

(iii) For each means of transport, to ascertain the present degree of congestion and the limitations on the future expansion of capacity.

(e) Prospective Growth

For the main activities carried on in the City, to examine the growth trend in the country as a whole and factors affecting increasing (or decreasing) concentration in the City. This should lead to consideration of the future demand for resources within the City and in particular:

(i) *Labour.* Taking account of the effects of mechanization; the use of computers; and government measures on the types of labour employed in the City.

(ii) *Land and premises.* Including the influences of rising land values, building costs and public policies on various forms of activity.

(f) Centralization and Decentralization

Consideration with respect to the main activities of the City of the advantages and disadvantages of concentration in a small area. To consider both the concentration of a number of firms in a particular activity, and of a number of related activities. Similarly in considering dispersion, to consider various methods, e.g. the removal from the City of particular forms of activity or only of certain parts of them, such as the keeping of managerial and technical members of a firm in London with the bulk of the clerical staff outside.'

Introduction

We have entitled this report 'An economic study of the City of London'. This is exactly what it is. In the chapters which follow, we seek to give an account – in varying depth and detail – of all the major economic activities carried on in the City today and their prospects for the future. We also look at the role of the City in the economic life of the nation and examine its contribution both to the national output and the balance of payments.

The study is divided into two parts. The first, which runs from Chapters 1 to 4, sets out the present economic characteristics of the City. The first chapter outlines the recent historical development of the Square Mile, paying particular attention to its increasing specialization as a financial centre. Chapter 2 analyses, in very considerable detail, the main activities now carried out in the City and their spatial distribution. Chapter 3 outlines the role of the City in the national and international economy and emphasizes a number of distinctive features about its workings. Chapter 4 surveys the present use made of land and buildings, and describes the structure of land values and rentals.

The second part of our study does two things. First, it examines, at some length, a number of the more important activities in the City. Second, it looks into the future prospects of these activities. Chapter 5 contains a brief account of the alternative methods of forecasting the future: it stresses the difficulties (and the dangers) of making precise predictions from national statistics or past trends, and concludes that a study of the prospects of individual industries is more likely to be 'approximately' right than 'precisely' wrong.

Chapter 6 is a long and very important chapter. It looks into the main economic factors likely to influence the shape of the City's economy in future years. Some of these affect the demand for the products and services which City firms are, at present, producing; others concern the costs and opportunities of operating in the City. Chapter 7 looks at some wider issues. It seeks to answer the questions 'What are the costs and benefits, to the national economy, of the present level and pattern of economic activity in the City? 'Can one say anything about the relative advantages of centralization and decentralization? 'What do we mean when we talk about the 'social' costs of traffic congestion or the 'social' benefits to the balance of payments?

Chapters 8 to 11 deal with each of the main financial, trading and manufacturing activities carried on in the City. We start with a discussion of the banks, the money and capital markets, and other financial institutions (Chapter 8) and then move on to insurance activities (Chapter 9). The trading function of the City which covers the Port of London, commodity and produce markets is covered in Chapter 10, while the following chapter discusses the last remaining manufacturing industry of any importance in the City – namely, paper, printing and publishing.

Chapter 12 turns to examine the implications of the pattern of economic activity, described in the previous chapters, on the flow of traffic in and through the City. It also looks into the type of transport problems which are likely to face the City in future years. Chapter 13 deals with a variety of miscellaneous services provided by City firms and concludes with a brief discussion of retail, catering and other consumer services.

The final chapter attempts to bring together the findings of the earlier chapters, and to give a thumb-nail sketch of the probable shape of the City's economy during the next decade or so.

Chapter 1

HISTORICAL REVIEW

INTRODUCTION

Perhaps the most obvious change in the City of London since pre-war days is its physical appearance. Although a few areas escaped serious bomb damage, the devastation was widespread, affecting about a third of the City's accommodation and a quarter of its rateable value. It was estimated in 1935 that, in spite of some important redevelopments since 1919, three-quarters of the buildings in the City were over thirty years old. Of the 77 million sq. ft of floor-space available in 1968, compared with 84·4 million sq. ft in 1939, more than 20 million sq. ft had been erected in the previous twenty years.

The exterior of these new buildings quickly reveals the most significant trend in the post-war economy of the City, viz. the rapid expansion of all kinds of office activities. In 1939, as Table 1.1 shows, office accommodation accounted for 45 per cent of the floor-space in the City; by 1957, this had risen to 59 per cent and by 1968 to 62 per cent. By contrast, the area of floor-space occupied by warehouses and industry has fallen dramatically, both in absolute and relative terms. In 1939, these activities were spread over an estimated 32 million sq. ft, or 38 per cent of the total floor-space in the City; by 1968, this area had more than halved to 15·5 million sq. ft, i.e. just over one-fifth of the floor-space. It was the areas of warehousing, particularly along the river between Blackfriars and Southwark Bridges and north to the Barbican and Aldersgate, which suffered most from the war. Some of these latter areas are now being replaced by offices, and in the Barbican, by new residential development as well.

The war was an economic watershed in the life of the City. A few months of intensive bombing accomplished what normally would have taken many years of reconstruction and redevelopment to achieve. The City is no longer so important as a place where goods

31

Table 1.1. Distribution of Floor-space in the City 1939–68
(millions of sq. ft)

Floor-space standing	Offices	Warehouses	Industry	Shops	Public Houses	Public buildings	Residential	Miscellaneous	Total
1939	37·6	22·3	9·9	4·1	1·2	6·5	1·0	1·8	84·4
1949	31·5	10·3	4·9	2·7	0·8	5·6	0·7	0·1	56·6
1957	37·8	10·4	5·0	2·8	0·9	5·8	0·7	0·9	64·2
1958	39·7	10·4	5·0	2·9	0·9	5·9	0·7	1·0	66·4
1959	40·7	10·4	5·2	2·9	0·9	6·2	0·7	1·2	68·1
1960	42·0	10·5	5·3	2·9	0·9	6·4	0·7	1·3	70·1
1961	42·9	10·6	5·3	3·0	0·9	6·8	0·7	1·4	71·6
1962	43·7	10·4	5·3	3·0	0·9	7·2	0·7	1·3	72·6
1963	44·7	10·2	5·3	3·0	0·9	7·2	0·7	1·3	73·4
1964	46·0	10·2	5·2	3·1	0·9	7·2	0·7	1·3	74·6
1965	46·5	10·1	5·3	3·2	0·9	7·3	0·8	1·3	75·3
1966	46·9	10·3	5·3	3·2	0·9	7·4	0·8	1·3	76·0
1967	47·8	10·3	5·3	3·2	0·9	7·4	0·8	1·3	77·0
1968	47·9	10·3	5·2	3·2	0·9	7·5	0·8	1·3	77·0

Notes

1. The basis of all post-war calculations is the amount of floor-space standing in 1949 as measured from Goad's Insurance Maps, which are brought up to date each year by adding the actual floor-space in new major building projects, and deducting the decrease in floor-space which has been demolished, taken from the 1949 figure.

2. The amount of floor-space in new major building projects is calculated on the plot ratio basis – i.e. measured over external walls, but excluding car parking, loading and unloading and bank strongrooms. Consequently these figures are not strictly comparable to those analysed from the Land Use Survey, which include car parking, loading and unloading, and bank strongrooms. Moreover, changes of use within a building cannot be ascertained by this method.

3. 'Shops' includes restaurants. 'Public Buildings' includes livery halls and multi-storey car parks.

4. Floor-space figures for the Inner and Middle Temples are not included since the Temples are not part of the City for the purpose of Planning.

Source: City Corporation.

are bought and sold; its business is almost entirely confined to the transfer of rights and titles and to taking decisions which make possible the exchange of goods and services, not only in this country but throughout the world. Behind these functional changes fundamental economic and social forces have been at work. It is the purpose of this chapter to examine the more important of these.

THE CHANGING CHARACTER OF THE CITY OF LONDON

One hundred years ago, this complete specialization of the City did not exist; neither were its firms and institutions so completely dependent on a commuting labour force as they are today. In 1851, the residential population of the City was 128,000, probably the same as its daytime working population – though, even at this date, there was some commuting. Whole areas in the City – particularly those adjacent to its northern boundaries – which are now given over to commercial activities, were still very largely occupied by dwellings of one kind or another; its churches, shops and schools were in full use. To be born within the sound of Bow Bells was not unusual.

In the course of the next half-century, the situation dramatically changed. By 1901, as Table 1.2 reveals, the residential population of the City had fallen to 27,000 while its commuting labour force had risen to well over 300,000. This transformation of the City into an industrial and commercial work-place by day, but an abandoned shell by night and at weekends, was essentially the result of two forces – economic change and the revolution in London's transport and communications system.

The pressure on land use in the City for commercial purposes soared with the growth of Britain as an international economic power. Earlier in the nineteenth century, she had become the world's leading industrial nation; by 1875 she was not only supplying between one-third and one-half of the world's trade in manufactures, but the facilities which made possible most of the rest of trade and investment. City banks advanced large sums of short-term credit to importers and exporters and arranged the finance of long-term investments overseas. The Stock Exchange was the centre of the world's capital market; and London's insurance companies had no serious international competitors.

By 1850, already half of Britain's trade passed through the Port of London. Now it developed as the world's premier entrepôt port.

Table 1.2. Population Trends in the City and Greater London
1801–1966
Population (thousands)

	Greater London	City of London Residential	Day*	City of London day population as a percentage of Greater London
1801	1,115	129	—	
1811	1,139	120	—	
1821	1,380	124	—	
1831	1,656	122	—	
1841	1,949	124	—	
1851	2,681	128	—	
1861	3,223	112	—	
1866	3,555	93(c)	170(a)	4·8
1871	3,886	75	200(c)	5·1
1881	4,767	51	261(a)	5·5
1891	5,634	38	301(a)	5·3
1901	6,581	27	332(c)	5·0
1911	7,251	20	364(a)	5·0
1921	7,480	14	437(b)	5·8
1931	8,204	11	482(a)	5·9
1935	8,475	10	500(a)	5·9
1939	8,728	8·7		
1946	7,835	5·1		
1951	8,351	5·3	339(b)	4·0
1961	7,997	4·8	390(b)	4·8
1966	7,671	4·9	361	4·7

* The daytime population is defined as those resident and working in the City, plus those working in the City but resident outside.
(a) Census by Corporation of London.
(b) Census by Registrar General.
(c) Interpolated.

This enormously strengthened the role of the City's commodity markets and merchanting activities, and increased the demand for warehousing and industrial accommodation. By 1886 the nucleus of each of the five dock systems of the port had been created.

Though the leading institutions in the City were already well established – the Stock Exchange, the Bank of England and Lloyd's all date back to the seventeenth century, and the Baltic to the eighteenth century – it was the City's ability to supply such a comprehensive range of financial and trading services which was largely responsible for its emergence as a centre of international repute.

34

No other city could offer such a 'package deal' of interrelated activities.

In addition to these international developments, a number of manufacturing industries, which had earlier found the City an attractive location, now expanded to meet the demands of domestic markets.[1] The publishing industry, originally established around St Paul's in medieval times, was joined by the newspaper industry which evolved westwards along Fleet Street. Jobbing and commercial printing followed a similar pattern and spread to the Barbican and Bishopsgate areas. The clothing industry was active in various parts of the City. The back lanes of St Giles and Holborn housed the out-workers supplying orders for the army clothiers of Pall Mall, while in the Cornhill area, export and shipping clothiers sold light clothing to plantations, shippers and sea captains. The Houndsditch district was the centre of a flourishing secondhand clothes trade and ware-housing. Furniture shops and makers were prominent in the St Paul's, Cheapside, and Shoreditch vicinity. Like the activities already described, they were attracted to the City by market considerations and the ready accessibility of ancillary firms. The precision instrument industries began to cluster in the Fleet Street area in the eighteenth century, while Hatton Garden became the leading centre of the jewellery trade around 1850. Numerous small waterside businesses existed associated with the river trace – flour mills, timber yards, etc. – but, in time, these moved downstream.

The effect of these new demands for labour and land in the City was to raise both wages and rents. This forced certain activities to decentralize and encouraged the immigation of day labour. The price of land and of freehold property rose spectacularly. Sites that were only partly built on or occupied by low buildings were re-developed with higher buildings. At least sixteen churches and many historic buildings and antiquities were demolished to make way for commerce and finance. Rates in the City increased faster than the national average. The number of clerical and administrative workers multiplied five-fold in the second half of the nineteenth century.

Associated with these developments were the improvements in transport and communications. Prior to 1851, most people employed in the City, but living outside, had either to walk to work or travel by horse bus. But, between 1861 and 1874, five new railway termini were built within the City, viz. Cannon Street, Broad Street, Fen-

[1] P. G. Hall, *The Industries of London since 1861*, Hutchinson University Library, 1962.

church Street, Blackfriars and Liverpool Street, and these were quickly followed by a labyrinth of tube connections. The last link of the Inner Circle was completed in 1884; while the Waterloo and City line, opened in 1898, together with the City and South London, opened in 1890, connected the City with the South Bank. But not until the Edwardian era of tube construction were the main line termini of the West End fully linked with the City. New routes like the Northern further emphasized the twin functions of Central London with its West End and City branches.

The railway companies were instrumental in dispersing the work force from the City in two ways. First, the termini were built in the centre of the main residential area of the City; acres of dwellings were demolished to provide space for Liverpool Street and Broad Street. New housing developments and the labour force followed the radial pattern of rail communication closely. And with improvements in roads and road transport, the commuting belt widened.

Secondly, the railways enabled the new surburban population and, in particular, the working class, to travel to the City cheaply and speedily. To obtain parliamentary approval to demolish working-class homes for their Broad Street extensions in 1861, the North London had to agree to provide special workmen's trains at low fares. In 1864, to get into Liverpool Street the Great Eastern had to do the same. By the 1880s, a journey from Enfield to Liverpool Street by workmen's train cost 2d return. Even today, a larger proportion of City workers live in north-east London and Essex than in any other part of the commuting belt.

By the same token, the railways enabled the prosperous commercial classes to migrate to the rural areas of Kent, Surrey and Middlesex and still be within forty minutes of their work. Street improvements, the building of new road bridges across the Thames, and the intro-duction of the London bus complemented these trends. By 1889, the two main bus companies in London were carrying 133 million passengers a year.

By the turn of the century, the City of London had become a specialist supplier of two fairly distinct groups of services. One, centred on the Port of London and arising out of Britain's premier position in international trade, was provided by the banking, finance and insurance world; the other was met by a group of industries and services supplying mainly domestic markets, which had a par-ticular and special need to be located in the centre of London, e.g. the newspaper industry and certain sections of the clothing and precision instrument trades.

A third class of activity – the operation of head or central offices of firms producing goods and services elsewhere in the country (or indeed the world) – did not become important in the City until after the First World War, by which time the Square Mile had little space for further building, and what there was tended to be along its western perimeter. In 1968, twice the number of large U.K. companies had their Head Offices in the West End as had them in the City.

There are very few reliable statistics of the City's economic role prior to 1939. All occupational and industrial data available in the annual *Censuses of Population*, prior to 1951, were classified by place of residence rather than place of work, and the annual Ministry of Labour *Employment Statistics* which, in any event, are subject to considerable error when compiled at Employment Exchange level, date back only to 1939. Data collected by H.M. Inspector of Factories are more reliable for assessing employment trends in manufacturing industry; but again, these have been published only since 1938. We know of no continuous series of statistics on income, earnings or productivity in the City and only a limited amount on rateable values and rents. Indeed, the only published pre-1941 information on economic activity we have been able to find is that of the distribution of factory employment in 1907. This is presented in Table 1.3 which shows that 39,524 people were then employed in 1,058 City factories, and 25,547 of these in the paper and printing industry.

Since that date, manufacturing activity in the City has become steadily less important. Some industries have simply died; others, as we know from trade and street directories, have gradually moved out, first to a manufacturing belt immediately to the north and north-east, and later further afield to the southern and western parts of Middlesex and eastwards to the Lea Valley in Essex.[2] Few twentieth-century industries find it attractive to be located in the centre of a City, mainly because of the prohibitive costs of land. A further decentralizing force has been the wider choice of location made possible by more efficient forms of transport and communications and new sources of energy and power. Only those industries or services already located in the City, and with long leases at well below current rents, have found it economic to remain.

The same picture is typical of other large cities of the world. In his analysis of the New York metropolitan region, Raymond Vernon

[2] P. G. Hall, 'Industrial London: a General View', in *Greater London*, ed. J. T. Coppock and H. C. Prince, Faber & Faber, London, 1964.

37

Table 1.3. Distribution of Factory Employment in the City of London 1907

	Number of factories	Male	Female	Total	%
			Employment		
Metals	124	2,122	91	2,213	5·6
Paper and printing	653	19,734	5,813	25,547	64·6
Food, drink and tobacco	68	1,307	598	1,905	4·8
Wood and wooden articles	41	1,047	326	1,373	3·5
Dress	75	1,008	4,069	5,077	12·8
Chemicals and drugs	28	723	65	788	2·0
Gas and electricity supply	11	120	0	120	0·3
Stone, brick and glass	(a)	99	2	101	0·3
Fine instruments	(a)	158	0	158	0·4
Skins and leather	(a)	45	24	69	0·2
Textiles	14	194	260	454	1·1
Jewellery and plate	6	130	12	142	0·4
Other	38	596	981	1,577	4·0
Total	1,058	27,283	12,241	39,524	100·0

(a) Included in 'Other'.
Source: 'Census of Factory Employees', published in London Statistics, Vol. XXII, pp. 56/65.

classified the manufacturing industries which still value a city location into three types:

(a) those which are communications-oriented and need to be in close and personal proximity with suppliers and customers – the newspaper and publishing industry comes within this group;
(b) those which supply products for which the demand is uncertain and unpredictable, and need to be close to knowledge of current trends – for example, job-printing and high-class dressmaking; and
(c) those which draw heavily on a pool of common facilities which only a City complex can provide – again such as newspapers and publishing.[3]

In each instance, Vernon points out, the advantages of speed, flexibility and the external economies of agglomeration outweigh

[3] E. M. Hoover and R. Vernon, Anatomy of a Metropolis and R. Vernon, Metropolis, 1985, Harvard University Press, 1958 and 1960.

the savings in rents, labour, costs and traffic congestion which might be achieved by decentralization. Similarly, apart from newspapers, plants tend to be small and their technology simple, and products differentiated and continually changing. In each case, the scope for intensive mechanization and improvements in productivity is limited.

As it has become cheaper to transport people rather than goods to and from the City of London, transport-oriented industries have increasingly decentralized their activities. But less obvious forces have also been shaping the City's economy over the last half-century. The decline in riverside and warehousing activities is due partly to a shift of the Port of London's operations downstream, and partly to a reduction in entrepôt trade, as the City's commodity markets have dealt increasingly in rights of titles to goods rather than in the goods themselves. The increase in the size of vessels entering the Port, and the growing congestion of the road approaches to the river, has further reduced the function of the wharves and jetties within the City. Furthermore, goods now entering the Port of London are often dispatched direct to inland wholesalers and/or retailers and by-pass riverside warehouses.[4]

In contrast to the decline in the industrial and warehousing functions of the City, the last half-century has seen a rapid growth of all kinds of office activities. How many people were actually employed in offices before the war is not known. Between 1951 and 1961, the number of office workers rose from 219,446 to 263,770 and by 1966 to around 289,000. This latter figure is probably little different from that of 1939, in spite of a 25 per cent increase in office space, and is largely the result of increased labour productivity associated with mechanization and rationalization.

The following chapter will analyse the present structure of the City's office activities in detail, but such evidence as we have on recent trends would suggest two things. First, that the growth of offices has been concentrated very strongly in two sectors, viz. insurance, banking and finance; and business services, e.g. accountants, lawyers, managerial consultants, etc. Second, that, within these (and other) sectors, there have been structural and institutional changes at work.

This growth in office activity follows the national pattern. For some years, the City has had a more than proportionate share of growth industries. This means that many activities in the City have expanded simply because of national and international trends. There

_____
[4] For further details see Chapter 10.

39

is, for example, a close statistical association in advanced economies between the growth of national real income and the value of new insurance premiums. The sector which is the largest single employer in the City – insurance, banking and finance – is the second fastest growing employer of labour in the country as a whole.

There is also a 'built-in' impetus to the expansion of a variety of services supplied to international markets. For example, the City's invisible earnings are an important and growing contribution to the U.K. balance of payments. Their prosperity is closely linked with the level and direction of world trade, with the role of sterling as a reserve currency and, more particularly in the last decade or so, with international capital movements.

Perhaps the most interesting aspect of these trends, from the viewpoint of this particular study, is that the activities which have been most affected are those which consider it important to have, at least, part of their operations centred in the City, because of important linkages with other activities located there. This has had far-reaching effects on the pattern of land use. Before 1939, the most striking feature of land use was the congregation of different types of activity in fairly well-defined clusters, with office accommodation largely centred in and around the Bank of England. Today, offices have moved much wider afield, both within and outside the City. In some lines of activity, e.g. insurance, there has been much decentralization; in others, e.g. stockbroking, comparatively little.

SPATIAL INTERDEPENDENCE AND THE CITY

The City of London is part of the Central Business District (C.B.D.) of the capital, and although we know something of its network of activities we are still awaiting a satisfactory theory to explain our observations. Perhaps the most promising approach is that of Folke Kristensson who has likened the dynamics of localization in a city to a gravity model in which bodies of different masses interact in conformity with the laws of gravitation.[5] The feature which primarily attracts activities towards the core of the city (that is, its centre of gravity) is their need for *contact*, sometimes among themselves, and sometimes with their source of inputs and/or markets. As a city

[5] *People, firms and regions. A structural economic analysis*, The Economic Research Institute, Stockholm School of Economics, 1967, See particularly Chapter 4. For a U.K. analysis see P. Haggett, 'The spatial structure of city regions' – paper presented to Conference on 'The future of the city region', organized by Social Science Research Council and Centre for Environmental Studies, London, July 1968.

grows, there is a tendency for these activities to increase the pressure of demand for resources, leading to an intensification of building use and a rise in both labour and land prices. Those activities which are the most sensitive to these prices and have the least need to be in a central area then disperse, making room for activities with a high average employee/space density content and a higher frequency of contact per employee. Eventually, the city core becomes reserved for enterprises with a low price-sensitivity but with the greatest need for each other, yet allowing free movement of business traffic. These are likely to be the high-order business activities.[6]

To distinguish this from other theories of urban spatial structure,[7] let us call it the *interdependence* theory. To some extent, of course, extreme specialization and interdependence go hand in hand. But there is no reason for the related activities to be spatially linked. The City of London supplies a limited number of highly specialized activities. As Chapter 2 shows, more than three-fifths of its employment is within those industries which nationally account for only 8 per cent of the labour force. They are complementary to each other; they need to use each others' products and be in close communication to function efficiently. They also create a demand for satellite consultancy services, so much so that the sellers of information and ideas are the third largest employers in the City. In some instances, the external economies of being in the same location are obvious; for example, access to a common pool of services, though this is probably less important than once it was as a result of improved transport and communication facilities. Spatial interdependence implies accessibility and the minimization of the costs of space between a group of firms or institutions. It makes possible the easy and speedy flow of goods, people, and information.

To some extent, the need for spatial contact is implicit in the organization of certain markets in the City. While most large cities operate local capital markets, none operates, in addition to a stock exchange, an insurance exchange, an exchange for air and shipping freight and several commodity and produce markets where buyers and sellers physically congregate to do business. If the Stock Exchange, Lloyds and the wholesale and produce markets were removed from the Square Mile, upwards of 80,000 jobs would go with them. Partly, too, it is a matter of tradition, particularly in the banking

[6] Kristensson, op. cit.
[7] Such as the *central place* and the *ecological* theories. See *inter alia*, B. J. Berry and A. Pred, *Central Place Studies; a bibliography of Theory and Applications*, Regional Research Institute, Philadelphia, 1965.

world, that so many visits are made in person to settle things which could quite easily be done by letter or telephone. But perhaps, most of all, City institutions feel they need to be near each other because of the character of their inputs and outputs. Here, the most striking change which has taken place over the last half-century has been a gradual shifting of functions from the exchange of *goods* and *services* to the exchange of *rights* or *titles* to goods and services.

There are very few goods which are either produced in the City today or even handled there. Apart from the printing and publishing of newspapers and books, and a small amount of specialized clothing on the eastern boundaries, there is no manufacturing industry. Most of this had already disappeared before the First World War. The trading function of the City, namely, wholesaling and commodity dealing, still remains very important but its locational requirements have changed as the Port's operations have shifted downstream, due partly to a reduction in its entrepôt trade and partly to the increased size of vessels now entering the Thames. Moreover, goods imported are now usually dispatched direct to inland wholesalers and, since the introduction of containerization, increasingly to manufacturers. Changing world trading relationships, the development of wholesale markets in producing countries, the innovation of new materials, particularly the various synthetics, have reduced the need to handle goods at the wholesaling stage. Some physical trade persists; for example, furs are still stored above the Fur Exchange at Beaver House; while other commodities, notably tea and wool, are auctioned by sample. But the great majority of commodity markets (of which there are over forty) deal with transactions of contracts in unseen commodities and in prices, such as terminal futures trading.[8] Even the world-famous produce markets of Billingsgate, Smithfield, and Spitalfields deal mostly in samples. Once again, this reflects changes in both supply and demand conditions for the goods in question, especially the impact of modern freezing and packaging techniques and direct marketing.

Most high-order commercial activities nowadays involve the transfer of rights – to goods, to services and to assets – and the provision of specialized services in supplying those rights. From the consumers' viewpoint, rights are often jointly demanded and there is some convenience in their suppliers being located close to each other. Not only can the congregation of insurance and shipping companies to the east of the City be explained by this need; sometimes quite different activities may make up the package of services bought.

<hr>

[8] For further details see Chapter 10.

Spatial interaction may be both complementary and competitive: the consignment of goods abroad from the City, for example, involves not only the services of a shipping company and of forwarding agents, but, like as not, of export merchants, warehousers, insurance brokers, underwriters and possibly banking and discount houses as well.

The sellers of these rights also find it desirable to be in close touch with each other. One reason for this is that the market conditions of trading in rights are often unstable; the price of a share, of an insurance policy, of a commodity in world trade are all affected by expectations of the future; and on these prices, which might fluctuate hourly, many vital decisions are taken. It is necessary, not only for businesses to know *when* prices change, but to be able to anticipate such price changes. Only by being in the closest touch with market trends and the expertise necessary to predict these trends will this be possible. It is this need for 'knowledge in a hurry' – a phrase coined by Robbins and Terleckyj[9] – which is the main centralizing force of the 'rights' industry in the Square Mile

Over the years, too, the City has not only become more specialized in the services it provides, but in the *functions* performed by firms supplying these services. Side by side with the centralizing forces mentioned earlier, have been the powerful decentralizing agents of increasing space and labour costs. Initially, these forced out the residential and manufacturing activities from the City and later, the handling of goods as well. This left the provision of services connected with trade or finance. But now a centrifugal force is at work which is splitting up these activities. In the last decade, in particular, offices have increasingly decentralized certain of their operations. The findings of our own study accord with those of the New York Metropolitan Study mentioned earlier. It is becoming too expensive to run office 'factories' in the C.B.D. The routine and repetitive tasks; those involving the least external contacts; those which are either space- or labour-intensive, are moving out to the provinces. Recent changes in the organizational structure of firms; in the mechanization of operations; in the recording and processing of information; in the standardization and streamlining of office procedures; and in communication techniques – have facilitated the separation of high-order from low-order office activities. What remains in the urban core is the top of the hierarchy – an elite group of co-ordinators, decision-takers and policy-makers, with their supporting staff: those

[9] S. M. Robbins and N. E. Terleckyj, *Money Metropolis*, Harvard University Press, 1960.

who need to be in close physical proximity to others so as to negotiate, to converse, to gain or pass on information and ideas. The C.B.D. has been described as a point of confrontation for those who need to produce answers to non-standardized problems, and as a machine for producing, processing and trading specialized intelligence between a group of highly skilled professionals engaged in decision-taking and strategy formulation.[10]

This is certainly happening in the City of London and the process is a continuing one. One result is that the income per head is very much higher for City workers than for U.K. workers as a whole. The differential is increasing as routine operations are being dispersed. The number of contacts between firms in the City is far greater than elsewhere. So are the buying and selling operations. The average size of establishments is kept small – of the 8,500 privately owned office establishments in the City in 1966, 6,642 employed a staff of twenty-five or under and only fifty-four more than 500 people.

Over the years, the City has also had to face the challenge of institutional and technical change. The Baltic Exchange, for example, has widened its services to include dealings in air freight. Merchant bankers have added domestic industry to their widespread international interests, especially mergers and industrial reorganization. The role of the foreign exchange market has altered with the evolution of several new activities, as for example, the Euro-dollar market, and with the demise of others. Fifty years ago, the City offices of the leading joint stock banks made only a minor contribution to the finance of foreign trade; now these interests predominate. As business has become more international, more foreign banks and financial institutions have set up branches in London. The increasing volume and complexity of government legislation, both national and international, relating to the behaviour of companies have led to more demand for the services of specialist consultants and so on.

THE IMPACT OF GOVERNMENT POLICY ON THE CITY'S DEVELOPMENT

The influence of national or local government policy on the pace and pattern of City development has been increasingly marked in recent years. In general, it has had a restraining effect on the City's growth. A detailed examination of the effects of government regulations and planning controls on office development is given in Chapter 6. For

[10] Kristensson, op. cit., pp. 4.8 to 4.12.

the moment, we propose to sketch the broad evolution of these trends.

Before 1939, such constraints on development were largely those introduced by the local planning authority (the Corporation of London) to safeguard building and accommodation standards and to promote the free movement of goods and people into and out of the City. In 1936, a comprehensive survey of the accommodation in the City was undertaken by the Corporation; this contained certain recommendations about the future pattern of land use, but action had hardly been taken on these before war broke out. With the widespread destruction in the City, it was clear that the time was opportune for a reappraisal of resources, and, in 1941, the Corporation commissioned Mr C. J. Forty, the City Engineer, to carry out investigations and prepare draft proposals on the post-war reconstruction of the City. The report was submitted in 1944, and was followed by two important events:

(a) In that year a Parliamentary Act was passed giving local authorities powers to acquire war-damaged areas and any property enclosed by or on the edge of them in order to ensure improvements in their layout. Something like a third of the City's area was 'declared subject to compulsory purchase' by the Corporation of London.
(b) With this Act in mind, the Corporation asked two planning consultants, Mr C. H. Holden and Professor W. G. Holford, to prepare a redevelopment plan 'to obtain a good balance between the amount of accommodation space and the amount of circulation space in the City.' Their proposals, published in 1947, formed the basis of all subsequent planning in the City.

An important aspect of post-war locational planning of Central Government policies has been to control the growth of London. In 1940, the Barlow Commission had stressed the need to contain the capital's growth, and in 1943 the Abercrombie Plan was published, which proposed the dispersal of a million people from Greater London in the post-war period. With these sentiments in mind, the Holden and Holford report[11] – commissioned by the Court of Common Council in 1945 – recommended that the Corporation should plan for an eventual daytime population of the City of not more than 472,000. They considered that this could be achieved within a total accommodation of about 82 million sq. ft, spread over

[11] C. H. Holden and W. G. Holford, *The City of London: a record of destruction and survival*, Corporation of London, 1947.

a smaller area of land than that used before the war. Since this figure represented an area five times that of the building sites in the City – after allowing for improvements in roads and open spaces – the consultants recommended that, for a standard office building, the floor area should not exceed five times the area of the plot on which it was situated. This became known as the *plot ratio*. This method of controlling floor space has been adopted by the Corporation with some rigidity in the last twenty years: together with a gradual improvement in the conditions of office accommodation, it has helped to contain the growth of employment in the City to well below the limit envisaged by Holden and Holford.

Indeed, in the three most important areas of the City where the Corporation has acquired and developed land previously occupied by private industry, there has been a considerable reduction in both commercial floor space and the daytime population. Table 1.4 presents the relevant figures. A more detailed account of the changing pattern of land use and tenure in the City is given in Chapter 4. Throughout the post-war period, the Corporation, by acquiring land and not renewing the leases of old and derelict properties, has influenced the pattern and quality of land use and of building standards.

Superimposed on local planning controls, have been attempts by successive national Governments to influence the level and structure of economic activity in London and elsewhere. Up to 1963, these had little effect on the City. Control was mainly exercised through the various Town and Country Planning Acts, 1962 and 1963, and selective granting of Industrial Development Certificates, which had to be obtained by manufacturing firms if they wanted to build factories of 5,000 sq. ft or more. The latter legislation affected a few printing, engineering and clothing firms in the City but not the pattern of economic activity as a whole. When, however, these regulations were extended to cover office activities under the Control of Office Industrial Development Act, 1965, the City became very much involved. Since this time, government pressures for office decentralization from the London area have been very strong indeed. The effects of these controls, and the operations of the Location of Offices Bureau, set up by the Government in 1963 to assist firms in their dispersal plans, are traced in Chapter 6.

Statistical Data on the City

It is extremely difficult to quantify the various propositions put forward in this chapter due to the paucity of statistical data. More-

Table 1.4. Changes in Daytime Population in Three Areas of the City 1939–66

	1939			1966–7	
	Gross floor-space, all uses (sq. ft)	Daytime population (at average 170 sq. ft per person)		Gross floor-space, all uses (sq. ft)	Daytime population, actual or estimated
Barbican Area (including commerce space north of Barbican)	8,113,400	44,600	Completed or retained	1,816,000	7,702*
			Under construction	1,057,200	6,218
			Vacant	308,200	1,813
			Projected	484,400	2,076
			Totals	3,665,800	17,809
Paternoster Area and St Paul's South and East (including Bank of England, Gateway House Ralli House and Financial Times)	3,726,800	20,624	Completed	2,099,300	9,412*
			Under construction	344,000	2,024
			Projected	56,750	326
			Totals	2,500,050	11,762
Tower Hill Area	1,204,100	7,083	Completed or retained	547,600	2,448*
			Projected approx.	120,000	706
			Totals	867,600	3,154
Total for three areas	13,044,300	72,307		7,033,450	32,727

Note: 1966–7 daytime population figures marked with an asterisk are actual and show a high ratio of floor-space per person (about 225 sq. ft per person). Remaining figures are calculated at 170 sq. ft per person (the Holford pre-war figure), to show the highest likely density of workers.
Source: Corporation of London.

47

over, such data as have been published are rarely comparable with each other, as they are either derived from completely different sources or based on different definitions. However, to conclude this chapter, it might be useful to summarize the main sources of information which are available.

1. *Resident Population.* This is one area where reasonably reliable statistics are regularly published. As set out in Table 1.2, the population, which is chiefly made up of service workers and their families,[12] fell continuously between 1931 and 1961 (except perhaps for the war years) but, over the last five years, has been stable at around 4,800.[13]

2. *Working Population.* Various estimates have been made of the numbers employed in the City since 1866 and these are given in Table 1.2. It is fairly clear from this table that the working population reached its peak somewhere between 450,000 and 500,000 in the inter-war period and then fell markedly during the war and its immediate aftermath. The 1951 *Census of Population* put the daytime population of the City as 338,787,[14] nearly 100,000 less than in 1921, when the last similar count was taken. Between 1951 and 1961, during which time the industrial and commercial floor-space of the City increased by about one-third, the working population rose by 15·5 per cent to 390,410.

In the 1960s the working population in the City fell slightly due both to advances in office technology and decentralization of activities. The 1966 Census revealed a total working population of 360,680, made up of 2,740 people resident in the City and 357,940 daytime commuters. Further details are given in Chapter 2.

3. *Structure of Employment.* The data in Table 1.1 reveal that the City has become a more specialized office and commercial centre since 1939. The industry and occupational tables of the *Censuses of Population* for 1951, 1961 and 1966, presented in Chapter 2, confirm this trend. In 1966, 167,310 of the 360,680 workers in the City were classified as clerical workers; and another 95,470 as professional and sales workers, managers and administrators. Three industries – insurance; banking and finance; paper, printing and publishing;

[12] For further details see Appendix 3 to Chapter 2.

[13] With the new housing developments in the Barbican area of the City, this figure is now rising again.

[14] Made up of people resident and working in the City, plus those working in the City but resident outside.

and miscellaneous services (e.g. consultant engineers, architects, lawyers, business services) accounted for more than 90 per cent of the total increase in employment in the period 1951 to 1966. A quick examination of these activities reveals that these are 'core type' industries which gain most by being linked with each other and other communication-oriented services in the City. At the same time, the City's share of the *national* employment in these industries has remained about the same over the period; there is no evidence that the concentration of these activities in the City is increasing. Further particulars of the changing structure of employment in factories are given in Table 1.5 These portray an even stronger concentration of

Table 1.5. Distribution of Factory Employment in the City 1954–66

	1954	1957	1966
Food, drink and tobacco	827	909	138
Chemical and allied industries	28	31	52
Engineering (electrical goods)	1,024	549	231
Textiles	134	146	27
Leather, leather goods and fur	644	748	361
Clothing and footwear	3,660	3,501	1,919
Paper, printing and publishing	12,031	11,949	16,069
Woodworking	262	303	62
Other industry (including service industry)	1,162	1,195	2,336
All industry	19,772	9,331	21,195

Source: H.M. Inspector of Factories.

communication-oriented industries in 1966 than in 1954, the only previous date for which comparable data are available.

4. *Land Use.* Several land-use surveys have been undertaken by various planning bodies since the war – notably in 1949, 1957, 1962 and 1966, by the Corporation of London. We understand, however, that the coverage and reliability of these surveys varies a great deal and, for this reason, we have not analysed them in any detail. Table 1.1 presents the broad picture and this, it can be seen, confirms the changing pattern of activity already described. The results of the 1966 Land Survey will be dealt with in Chapter 4.

5. *Rateable Values.* Details of trends in rateable values of property in the City compared with the rest of London and England and

Wales are presented in Tables 1.6 and 1.7. It can be seen that values in the City have broadly kept pace with those in other parts of the capital and have moved upwards rather more rapidly than the rest of England and Wales. This is partly explained by the unusual structure of accommodation in the City; Table 1.7 again confirms the extremely high dependence of the City on office activities of one kind or another.

Table 1.6. Rateable Values in the City and London Administrative County 1871–1968

Rateable Values (£ thousand)

Year	(a) City of London	(b) London AC[1]	(a) as % of (b)
1871	2,354	19,963	12.7
1881	3,479	27,629	12·6
1891	4,084	33,005	12·4
1901	4,858	39,644	12·3
1911	5,658	44,555	12·7
1921	6,230	48,383	12·9
1931	8,685	59,146	14·7
1935	8,981	61,205	14·7
1941	8,291	60,175	13·8
1946	6,134	54,383	11·3
1951	6,491	56,730	11·4
1956	14,032	105,343	13·3
1961	13,898	109,115	12·7
1963	43,760	332,908	13·1
1966	44,418	635,532	7·0†
1967	46,370	646,031†	7·2
1968	46,520	653,919†	7·1

[1] Administrative County.
† Refers to the new G.L.C. area rather than London Administrative County.
Source: *Rates and Rateable Values in England and Wales*—Ministry of Housing and Local Government, except where specified, and from Report on Reconstruction in the City of London 1944.

6. *Income.* We have detailed data on earned incomes in the City only for 1954–5 and 1959–60. These are given in Table 1.8 which reveals not only that the average taxable earnings in the City are about two-fifths higher than the U.K. as a whole, but that the differential is widening. This confirms our earlier proposition that it is the less-skilled workers who are most likely to be affected by dispersal policies

Table 1.7. Rateable Values in the City, Greater London (G.L.C. Area) and England and Wales 1963–9

Type of hereditament	1963–4									1968–9								
	City of London			Greater London			England and Wales			City of London			Greater London			England and Wales		
	Rateable value £ thousand	% of total	% of total excl. Dom.	Rateable value £million	% of total	% of total excl. Dom.	Rateable value £million	% of total	% of total excl. Dom.	Rateable value £ thousand	% of total	% of total excl. Dom.	Rateable value £million	% of total	% of total excl. Dom.	Rateable value £million	% of total	% of total excl. Dom.
Domestic	171·4	0·4	—	257·5	42·6	—	967·35	47·4	—	176·8	0·4	—	270·7	41·4	—	1,113·52	48·1	—
Shops	2,150·3	4·9	5·0	67·4	11·1	19·4	209·76	10·3	19·6	1,875·8	4·0	4·1	66·7	10·2	17·4	216·58	9·4	18·1
Offices	34,130·6	78·0	78·3	92·5	15·3	26·6	119·07	5·8	11·1	35,107·5	75·5	75·8	102·1	15·6	26·6	137·16	5·9	11·4
Other commercial	3,752·6	8·2	8·2	52·7	8·7	15·2	147·22	7·2	13·7	3,002·7	6·5	6·5	54·6	8·3	14·2	166·28	7·2	13·9
Industrial	1,254·8	2·9	2·9	75·5	12·5	21·7	312·16	15·3	29·1	1,227·1	2·6	2·6	72·4	11·0	18·9	322·30	13·9	26·9
Crown property	880·8	2·0	2·0	10·7	1·8	3·1	32·53	1·6	3·0									
Other	1,596·7	3·6	3·7	48·7	8·0	14·0	251·88	12·3	23·5	5,130·3	11·0	11·1	87·4	13·4	22·8	357·85	15·5	29·8
Total	43,766·3	100·0	100·0	605·0	100·0	100·0	2,039·98	100·0	100·0	46,520·2	100·0	100·0	653·9	100·0	100·0	2,313·68	100·0	100·0

Note: Values for Crown property and Other property were not given separately 1968–9.
Source: Rates and Rateable Values in England and Wales – Ministry of Housing and Local Government.

Table 1.8. Personal Pre-tax Incomes in the City and the U.K. 1954/5–1959/60

| | 1954-5 | | | | | | 1959-60 | | | | | | Percentage increase in average incomes 1954-5: 1959-60 | |
| | City | | | U.K. | | | City | | | U.K. | | | | |
	Total £million	Number of Cases (thousands)	Average £	Total £million	Number of Cases (thousands)	Average £	Total £million	Number of Cases (thousands)	Average £	Total £million	Number of Cases (thousands)	Average £	City	U.K.
Total Net income	338·6	367·1	922	11,073·6	20,279·8	546	409·5	353·4	1,159	15,332·9	20,954·4	732	25·7	34·1
Profits and professional earnings (schedule D)	40·2	17·7	2,268	1,019·6	1,546·6	659	35·4	12·8	2,766	1,191·3	1,604·7	742	22·0	12·6
Employment income (schedule E)	239·9	350·4	685	8,628·2	18,155·2	475	304·8	319·3	952	11,809·8	18,310·7	645	39·0	35·8

Source: 100th and 106th Reports o the Commissioners of H.M. Inland Revenue.

and that the value-added per employee (i.e. labour productivity) in City institutions today, relative to that in the U.K. as a whole, is higher than before the war.[15]

7. *Location of Offices.* In an article published in *Urban Studies*[16] in 1968, John Goddard examined the changing location of a group of office activities in London between 1918 and 1966.

Goddard did not specifically define the City in his analysis, but the postal districts E.C.2 to E.C.4 may be taken as a rough and ready approximation for this purpose. Table 1.9 presents his findings of the changes in the location of three of the activities analysed – advertising agents, publishers and architects – between 1938 and 1966. It can be seen that in all cases there has been a marked westward and/or outward movement over the years in question. A later analysis of the location of the head offices of public companies and chartered accountants between 1950 and 1967 reveals a similar pattern. Goddard concludes from this analysis that many types of office activity are much less tied to particular parts of the centre than in the past. Inner parts of the core are crossed by a much more diverse mix of activities than those areas with a long history of commercial occupation. Older activities with formerly more restricted location choices and newly developed activities are both contributing to this new pattern. An additional analysis of the location of firms in the rapidly expanding field of business consultancy (in 1966 there were 160 management consultants listed in the current *Kelly's P.O. Directory* compared with 8 in 1951) indicated a strong preference for prestige West End addresses, but otherwise a completely random location pattern.

SUMMARY

In the course of the last century, the City has evolved from being a general-purpose commercial and industrial centre to a highly specialized supplier of a group of closely interrelated financial and trading services, each of which is primarily located in the City because of the presence of the other. Once largely self-supporting in its labour supply, the City now relies almost exclusively on a commuting work force.

[15] See also J. H. Dunning, 'The Efficiency of the City', in Committee on Invisible Exports, *Britain's Invisible Earnings*, London, 1968.

[16] J. Goddard, 'Changing office location patterns in Central London', *Urban Studies*, Vol. 4, 1968, pp. 276–285.

Table 1.9. Location of Selected Services in Central London 1938-66

Central London	Advertising agents				Publishers				Architects			
	1938		1966		1938		1966		1938		1966	
	A	B	A	B	A	B	A	B	A	B	A	B
W.1	48	10·1	151	38·0	189	21·3	203	25·7	56	7·3	285	49·5
S.W.1	40	8·4	30	7·6	184	20·7	52	6·5	51	6·7	88	15·3
W.C.1	63	13·2	54	13·6	230	25·9	133	16·7	141	18·5	143	24·8
W.C.2	153	32·1	71	17·9	130	14·6	141	17·7	155	20·3	60	10·4
E.C.1	17	3·6	14	3·5	13	1·5	48	6·0	26	3·4	20	3·5
E.C.2	29	6·1	15	3·8	36	4·1	23	2·9	24	3·1	15	2·6
E.C.3	11	2·3	2	0·3	15	1·7	7	0·9	13	1·7	10	1·7
E.C.4	111	23·0	58	14·6	73	8·2	168	21·1	273	35·7	29	5·0
S.E.1	5	1·0	2	0·5	18	2·0	19	2·4	25	3·3	6	1·0
Total	477	100	397	100	888	100	795	100	764	100	576	100
Fringe	3		33		30		69		17		70	
Rest of London	20		43		111		112		24		131	
Total	500		473		1032		981		805		777	
Percentage in Centre	95.4		83·9		86·0		81·0		94·9		74·1	

Key: Col. *A*, Number of firms; Col *B*, Percentage of Central Area total; Fringe—S.W.3, S.W.7, W.2, N.W.1, N.1, E.1 and E.2.
Source: *Kelly's Post Office Directory*; John Goddard 'Changing Office Location Patterns in Central London', *Urban Studies*, Vol. 4, 1968.

During this time, national and international forces shaping both the demand for goods and services and the supply of resources, have combined to promote both centripetal and centrifugal forces, the result of which has been that those activities which now remain in the City are those which produce a high net output per employee and are strongly dependent on financial and market expertise, speedy and efficient communication, and face-to-face contacts.

These events are reflected in land-use patterns and employment trends, although such data do not always show the important changes which have occurred *within* particular activities, some of which have had important effects on locational choice. Rationalization and mergers of firms have also aided the decentralization of certain routine and repetitive activities.

This means that the economic role of the City is not confined to the activities conducted *within* its boundaries (if indeed this ever was the case). Without the supporting activities of decentralized activities in other parts of the country, many City offices could not function. The numbers employed by the banks and insurance offices in the geographical area of the City considerably underestimate the true importance of the functional role played by these institutions in the City.

Both the land occupied by buildings and the number employed in the City are less than before the war. This is due partly to the post-war plot ratio laid down by the Corporation, partly to the improvement in standards of office accommodation, partly to the needs of increasing mechanization, and partly due to the changing land-use pattern between activities. In the last few years, the pace of new building has slowed down and the numbers employed have increased only very slightly—if at all. Coupled with the reduction in activities involving goods transport, this has tended to ease slightly the flow of *intra*-City transport in the City.

An investigation into the changing locational pattern of a group of activities suggests that while the 'core' activities have continued to cluster around each other in the City, others have moved to other parts of Central London or outside Central London altogether.

Chapter 2

THE PRESENT ECONOMIC STRUCTURE OF THE CITY

INTRODUCTION

This chapter analyses the current economic structure of the City in some detail. It attempts to do two things—first to assess the importance of different kinds of activity in the City, drawing mainly on employment statistics; and second, to evaluate the relevance of spatial linkages between these activities.

SOURCES OF STATISTICAL DATA

Quite early on in our investigation, we found that none of the published sources of material could help us very much: they were either out of date, insufficiently detailed, not wide enough in coverage, or unreliable in some way or the other. Data from the 1966 *Census of Population* and the 1966–7 *G.L.C. Employment Survey* were not available at the time. Where possible, we have used the results of the Land Use, Employment and Social Surveys undertaken by the Corporation of London in recent years, but, for most purposes, these were not classified in sufficient industrial detail. Had we been conducting a national economic survey, we would have naturally turned to Ministry of Labour employment figures. But at the Employment Exchange level of disaggregation, these are sometimes subject to a large degree of error. The latest information available on the value of the City's output of manufactured goods was that contained in the 1958 *Census of Production*, and apart from the structure of retail sales given in the 1961 *Census of Distribution*, there was virtually nothing published on the contribution of the service industries to the City's economy

The statistical data for this chapter were largely obtained from two sources; first that collected by the Corporation of London from most non-manufacturing establishments in accordance with the Offices, Shops and Railway Premises Act 1963 (O.S.R.P. returns)

56

and secondly that derived from the records of H.M. Inspector of Factories (H.M.I.F. returns). Neither is entirely satisfactory for our purposes as, in both cases, the information was collected at various points of time between mid-1964 and December 1966.

THE CENSUSES OF POPULATION 1951 AND 1961

Before turning to analyse these two sets of data, it might be helpful to take a brief look at some of the more important findings of the 1951 and 1961 *Censuses of Population*.[1] Table 2.1 presents the distribution of employment by industry in the City, the rest of Central London, and England and Wales, in 1961.

The intensely specialized character of the City's economy is highlighted by the fact that four activities – insurance, banking and finance; wholesale distribution; printing and publishing; and posta

Table 2.1. Employment by Industry in the City, other Central London areas and England and Wales 1961*

	City of London		Other Central London areas		England and Wales	
Agriculture, forestry, fishing	1		40		72,692	(3·5)
Mining and quarrying	9		257	(0·3)	63,591	(3·0)
Total Extractive	10	(0·0)	297	(0·3)	136,283	(6·5)
Food, drink and tobacco	442	(1·1)	1,480	(1·5)	62,090	(2·9)
Chemicals and allied trades	569	(1·5)	1,770	(1·7)	46,341	(2·2)
Engineering, electrical goods and vehicles	651	(1·6)	5,651	(5·4)	267,643	(12·7)
Metal goods not elsewhere specified	174	(0·4)	1,362	(1·4)	50,284	(6·4)
Textiles, clothing and footwear	730	(1·9)	4,617	(4·5)	120,968	(5·8)
Printing, publishing	4,018	(10·3)	5,961	(5·7)	35,645	(1·7)
Other paper, printing, publishing	310	(0·8)	584	(0·6)	19,189	(0·9)
Other manufacturing	452	(1·2)	2,792	(2·7)	164,640	(7·8)
Total Manufacturing	7,346	(18·8)	24,217	(23·5)	766,800	(40·4)

[1] Separate details of the 1966 Sample Census are given in Appendix 3 to this chapter.

Table 2.1.—contd.

	City of London		Other Central London areas		England and Wales	
Construction	626	(1·6)	4,922	(4·9)	142,570	(6·8)
Gas, electricity and water	143	(0·4)	915	(0·9)	34,756	(1·6)
Railways	582	(1·5)	3,442	(3·4)	40,771	(1·9)
Sea transport	1,236	(3·2)	329	(0·3)	7,568	(0·3)
Postal and telecommunication	2,266	(5·8)	3,594	(3·5)	32,224	(1·5)
Other transport and communication	1,902	(4·8)	3,556	(3·5)	69,128	(3·3)
Wholesale distribution	3,756	(9·6)	5,669	(5·4)	45,888	(2·2)
Other distributive trades	1,838	(4·7)	9,845	(9·6)	241,225	(11·4)
Insurance, banking and finance	12,178	(31·2)	5,005	(4·9)	52,942	(2·5)
Accountancy	1,374	(3·5)	977	(1·0)	7,744	(0·4)
Legal	921	(2·4)	1,346	(1·3)	8,873	(0·4)
Other professional and scientific services	897	(2·3)	7,987	(7·8)	174,029	(8·2)
Miscellaneous services	2,882	(7·4)	19,368	(19·0)	211,242	(10·0)
Public administration and defence	968	(2·5)	10,570	(10·3)	130,577	(6·2)
Total Services	31,569	(80·9)	77,525	(75·8)	1,199,537	(56·7)
Industry inadequately described	132	(0·3)	395	(0·4)	6,962	(0·3)
Total All Industry	39,057	(100·0)	102,434	(100·0)	2,109,582	(100·0)

Source: *Census of Population 1961.*
* Since the census was a 10 per cent sample the data should be multiplied by a factor of ten.
Figures in parentheses refer to the percentage of total employment.

and telecommunications – accounted for 56·9 per cent of its total labour force in 1961, whereas these same industries in England and Wales accounted for only 7·9 per cent. A large proportion of those engaged in manufacturing and extractive industry in the City also worked in offices; occupational tables of the 1961 Census reveal that only 27,340 (37·2 per cent) of the 73,460 workers in manufacturing were factory operatives.

Table 2.2 sets out the occupational structure of the labour force in the City by the main industrial groups and Table 2.3 compares this structure and the growth of employment since 1951 with that in

Table 2.2. Distribution of Employment in the City by Occupation and Industry 1961

Occupation	Agriculture, etc. Mining and quarrying	Manufacturing	Construction	Gas, electricity and water	Transport and communication	Distributive trades	Insurance, banking and finance	Professional and scientific services	Miscellaneous services	Public administration and defence	Total, all industries
Operatives	2	2,734	395	45	676	751	205	40	138	40	5,026
Office (1)	3	794	98	21	623	352	845	1,107	225	178	4,246
(2)	–	562	23	8	214	21	1,513	56	192	15	2,604
(3)	3	2,273	82	60	2,612	2,442	8,430	1,517	930	498	18,847
(4)	–	71	–	2	64	31	425	11	43	33	680
Office Total	6	3,700	203	91	3,513	2,846	11,213	2,691	1,390	724	26,377
Transport	1	191	4	1	1,462	113	42	1	35	5	1,856
Sales	–	378	7	1	41	1,681	63	21	596	2	2,700
Other	1	475	17	5	294	203	655	439	722	197	3,008
Total, all occupations	10	7,478	626	143	5,986	5,594	12,178	3,192	2,882	968	39,057

* Office (1) – Office, administrative and professional workers, sedentary.
  (2) – Office, administrative and professional workers who travel.
  (3) – Office, clerical workers, sedentary.
  (4) – Office, clerical workers who travel (e.g. messengers).

Source: *Census of Population 1961.*

N.B. The figures shown are the Census returns since the census was a 10 per cent sample the data should be multiplied by a factor of ten. Also it should be noted that sampling error may be considerable in groups with small numbers.

Table 2.3. Percentage of Employment in the City, Other Central London* and England and Wales by Selected Occupational Groups 1951–61

Industry	Area	Percentage of employment 1961				Growth of employment 1951–61 (1951 = 100)			
		Operatives	Office workers	Other workers	All workers	Operatives	Office workers	Other workers	All workers
Manufacturing and extractive	City	7·0	9·5	2·7	19·2	101·6	110·5	156·1	111·5
	O.C.L.	10·2	10·7	3·4	24·3	na	na	na	90·5
	E. & W.	31·8	7·6	3·7	43·1	89·0	129·1	171·7	98·5
Transport and communication	City	1·7	9·0	4·6	15·3	136·8	143·6	74·7	112·0
	O.C.L.	1·5	4·7	4·4	10·7	na	na	na	107·4
	E. & W.	1·5	1·7	3·9	7·1	117·0	133·3	83·8	98·2
Distributive trades	City	1·9	7·3	5·1	14·3	148·3	67·1	169·3	94·4
	O.C.L.	3·0	5·2	6·9	15·1	na	na	na	102·2
	E. & W.	2·5	2·2	8·9	13·6	211·6	86·4	115·9	119·6
Insurance, banking and finance	City	0·5	28·7	1·9	31·2	138·2	132·4	90·0	128·7
	O.C.L.	0·2	4·2	0·5	4·9	na	na	na	127·6
	E. & W.	0·1	2·3	0·2	2·5	94·2	136·3	101·2	131·5

Table 2.3.—contd.

Professional and scientific services	City	6·9	1·2	8·2	100·0	105·5	69·2	98·0
	O.C.L.	5·9	3·9	10·1	na	na	na	107·0
	E. & W.	2·0	6·5	9·0	135·9	140·2	140·6	140·3
Other services	City	6·2	4·1	11·8	96·6	273·1	100·9	149·0
	O.C.L.	17·9	12·1	34·9	na	ba	na	105·7
	E. & W.	5·1	9·7	24·6	117·0	152·6	80·4	103·5
All services	City	58·0	16·9	80·8	125·2	122·0	99·0	116·5
	O.C.L.	38·0	27·8	75·7	na	na	na	105·7
	E. & W.	13·2	29·3	56·9	127·5	129·7	100·0	112·1
Total	City	12·9	19·6	100·0	111·1	120·2	104·2	115·5
	O.C.L.	20·1	31·2	100·0	na	na	na	101·5
	E. & W.	46·2	33·0	100·0	98·2	129·5	105·1	105·8

* The definition of Other Central London (O.C.L.) used in the first part of this table is as shown in Table 2.1, but in the second part the definition is slightly different, being the boroughs of Westminster, Holborn, Finsbury, St Marylebone and St Pancras.
na = not available.
Source: *Censuses of Population 1951 and 1961.*

Table 2.4. Percentage Distribution of Office Workers in the City, other Central London and England and Wales by Grades* 1961

	City			Other Central London			England and Wales		
	Male	Female	Total	Male	Female	Total	Male	Female	Total
Office (1)	25·8	1·9	16·1	38·0	3·8	22·5	38·6	2·8	22·5
(2)	15·5	1·7	9·9	13·1	3·3	8·7	16·9	2·9	10·6
(3)	54·5	96·3	71·5	46·1	92·7	67·2	43·5	94·2	66·3
(4)	4·2	0·1	2·6	2·8	0·2	1·6	1·1	0·1	0·7
Total	100·0	100·0	100·0	100·0	100·0	100·0	100·0	100·0	100·0

* For definition of grades, see Table 2.2.
Source: *Census of Population 1961*.

Central London and England and Wales. Table 2.4 presents a distribution of office workers by grade of workers.

The main conclusions to be drawn from the data in these tables are as follows:

1. The City of London depends absolutely and, in relation to other areas, more completely on all kinds of office employment. This is partly because its economic structure is heavily weighted towards financial and commercial activities and also because in other industries, e.g. manufacturing, and transport and communication, the proportion of office workers to non-workers is much higher than the national average.
2. Compared to the rest of Central London, the City's office employment is much more concentrated; indeed two sectors of activity, viz. professional services and insurance, banking and finance, account for just over one-half of its office workers. But the rest of Central London has a slightly larger and growing share of office workers in manufacturing and extractive industries. These data confirm that it is the West End of London rather than the City which is becoming the main centre of the Head Offices of enterprises outside the finance and trade sector.
3. The proportion of administrative and professional office workers, relative to all office workers, is somewhat lower than elsewhere; relative to all workers it is somewhat higher than in the rest of Central London (17·6 per cent as against 15·1 per cent) and very much higher than in England and Wales (17·6 per cent as against 6·9 per cent).

To estimate, more precisely, the degree of economic specialization in the City of London, use may be made of the statistical device known as *Location Quotient* (L.Q.).[2] Table 2.5 classifies the distribution of employment in the City and elsewhere by the (national) rate of growth of employment between 1951 and 1961. It also derives the City's L.Q. for each industry, both in relation to Central London (including the City) and to England and Wales.

The results of this table are very illuminating. First, it is clear that the City's economic structure in 1961 was very growth-oriented – considerably more so than either Central London as a whole or England and Wales. Second, the extent of its specialization is clearly shown by the very large range of its L.Q.s (*vis-à-vis* England and Wales) from zero through to 12·4. Indeed, there is hardly an activity, the relative importance of which is the same in the City as in England and Wales. In this sense, the economic structure of the City is quite unique.

The *Census of Population* also gives some information about the distribution of employment by males and females. We confine our analysis here to classifying the more important industrial groups by occupation and sex. Table 2.6 shows that the ratio of female to total employment is slightly higher in the City than in England and Wales as a whole. This is not because this ratio is higher in any particular activity or occupation in the City, but rather because the City specializes in activities and occupations with a higher female/total employment ratio.

Finally the Census sheds some useful light on the relationship between *income-creating* and *income absorbing* activities. We define the former as those activities which mainly sell their products or services outside the region in which they are produced; the latter cater for the spending needs of the local inhabitants or working population. There is no completely clear-cut distinction between these two types of activity. But, because of the unusual structure of the City's economy, we would be not far wrong in assuming that all activities, except retail distribution, education and medical services, entertainment and sport, and catering and hotels are *income-creating*. On this criteria, 92 per cent of the employment of the City in 1966 was generated by demands outside the City's boundaries. Such an exceptionally high proportion is almost entirely a reflection of the

---

[2] The Location Quotient for a particular activity is obtained by dividing the proportion of the total members which are in a particular activity in one area by the same proportion in another (usually a larger) area. For example, if Area A has 40 per cent of its total employment in chemicals compared with Area B's 20 per cent, then the location quotient of the chemical industry in Area A (relative to that of Area B) is 2 – i.e. it is twice as important in terms of employment.

Table 2.5. Percentage distribution of employment in the City, England and Wales and Central London* 1961

Industry	Percentage employment in the City 1961	Percentage employment in E. & W. 1961	Location quotient of the City cf. E. & W.	Percentage employed in C.L. 1961	Location quotient of the City cf. C.L.	Annual average rate of growth E. & W. 1951-61
(a) *Fast growing industries†*						
Professional and scientific services	8·2	9·0	(0·9)	9·5	(0·9)	3·3
Insurance, banking and finance	31·2	2·5	(12·4)	12·1	(2·6)	2·8
Other manufacturing	0·3	1·3	(0·3)	0·6	(0·6)	2·3
Engineering and electrical goods	1·6	8·9	(0·2)	4·2	(0·4)	2·2
Paper, printing and publishing	11·1	2·6	(4·3)	7·7	(1·4)	1·8
Vehicles	0·1	3·8	(0·0)	0·3	(0·4)	1·8
Other distributive trades	4·7	11·4	(0·5)	8·3	(0·6)	1·7
Chemicals	1·5	2·2	(0·7)	1·7	(0·9)	1·6
Total: Fast-growing industries	58·6	41·8	(1·4)	44·3	(1·3)	2·2
(b) *Slow-growing industries*						
Construction	1·6	6·8	(0·2)	3·9	(0·4)	1·3
Metal goods (n.e.s.)	0·4	2·4	(0·2)	1·1	(0·4)	1·2
Food, drink and tobacco	1·1	2·9	(0·4)	1·4	(0·8)	0·9
Metal manufacture	0·2	2·7	(0·1)	0·4	(0·6)	0·8
Wholesale distribution	9·6	2·2	(4·4)	6·7	(1·4)	0·8
Gas, electricity, and water	0·4	1·6	(0·2)	0·8	(0·5)	0·5
Bricks, pottery and glass	0·1	1·4	(0·1)	0·3	(0·3)	0·4
Total: Slow-growing industries	13·5	20·0	(0·7)	14·5	(0·9)	1·0

Table 2.5.—contd.

(c) *Declining industries*

Transport/communication	15·3	7·1	(2·2)	12·0	(1·3)	−0·1
Timber, furniture	0·2	1·3	(0·2)	0·5	(0·4)	−0·3
Public administration, defence	2·5	6·2	(0·4)	8·2	(0·3)	−0·3
Miscellaneous services	7·4	10·0	(0·7)	15·7	(0·5)	−0·5
Shipbuilding	0·1	0·8	(0·1)	0·1	(1·2)	−1·2
Mining, quarrying	0·0	3·0	(0·0)	0·2	(0·1)	−1·3
Clothing and footwear	1·3	2·5	(0·5)	3·3	(0·4)	−1·6
Textiles	0·6	3·3	(0·2)	0·5	(1·1)	−1·9
Leather and fur	0·2	0·3	(0·8)	0·4	(0·5)	−2·0
Agriculture, forestry and fishing	0·0	3·5	(0·0)	0·0	(−)	−2·2
Total: Declining industries	27·6	37·9	(0·7)	40·9	(0·7)	−1·1

* Including the City in this instance.

† Classified by national rate of growth 1951–61.

Source: *Census of Population 1961.*

C

Table 2.6. Percentage of Female to Total Employment in the City and England and Wales 1961. (Classified by industry and occupation)

Occupation / Industry		Manufacturing (incl. industry n/s)	Construction	Gas, electricity and water	Transport and communication	Distributive trades	Insurance, banking and finance	Professional and scientific services	Miscellaneous services	Public administration and defence	Total
Operatives	City	15	0	2*	2	9	2	25*	12	3*	10
	E. & W.	28	0	0	2	20	2	13	10	3	18
Office (1)	City	7	2	0*	5	7	3	3	9	7	5
	E. & W.	5	3	1	5	12	6	6	12	7	6
(2)	City	16	9*	25	5	10*	2	4	15	7*	7
	E. & W.	9	5	9	9	17	8	31	24	16	12
(3)	City	59	55	40	45	59	54	57	73	33	55
	E. & W.	66	60	39	47	78	60	75	79	49	64
(4)	City	1	0*	0*	6	0*	0	0*	19*	3*	2
	E. & W.	15	0*	0*	5	5	1	7	8	4	6
Office total	City	40	24	29	35	52	41	34	53	25	41
	E. & W.	40	27	26	39	71	41	51	60	38	45
Transport	City	4	0*	0*	6	6	43*	0*	8*	0*	7
	E. & W.	1	0	0	5	3	28	5	6	3	4
Sales	City	16	14*	100*	54*	16	89	86*	70	50*	30
	E. & W.	27	46	55	56	51	90	96	58	55	52
Other	City	41	24*	80*	36	35	44	51	52	20	43
	E. & W.	46	19	36	27	65	57	66	69	17	54
Total	City	29	9	22	24	34	41	36	54	23	35
	E. & W.	31	4	11	13	47	41	60	53	20	33

* Based on a sample of less than 50 persons.

Source: Census of Population 1961.

66

very low ratio of the resident to daytime population. It does mean, however, that the prosperity of the City is almost completely determined by extraneous forces, and that such local industries as there are depend more on the daytime population for their market than on those who actually live in the City. This latter point will be further emphasized when we look at the pattern of retail distribution in the City in Chapter 13.

THE STRUCTURE OF OFFICE ACTIVITIES IN THE CITY

We now turn to examine the data supplied to us by the Corporation of London. This part of our analysis is confined to those employed in *independent* offices, shops and warehouses, and excludes those working in national and local government undertakings. Between mid-1964 and December 1966, during which returns under the Offices, Shops and Railway Premises Act were submitted by 8,500 establishments, employment totalled 261,452. This figure, we believe, represented 90 per cent and 95 per cent of those actually employed in these activities, and, apart from where the very small firm is an important component, the coverage was a comprehensive one.

We classified these data both by type of activity and location within the City: concerning the former, the analysis of activities in this chapter is largely confined to the twelve main groups of office activities, set out in Table 2.7 and a selection of the 86[3] sub-groups. We use the sub-group data more fully in Chapters 8 to 12 in our discussion of the main activities of the City.

Employment in each establishment was also coded by 216 street blocks and thirteen 500-metre Ordinance Survey map quadrants. Since, however, for most types of spatial analysis, 250 statistical units is an unnecessarily large number, while thirteen units, nine of which are cut by the City boundary, are too few, the street blocks were used to build fifty-four 'super-blocks', or sub-districts. These are marked out in Figure 2.1. The boundaries of the blocks and the numbers used have no particular significance; they simply provide a convenient framework for our statistical analysis. Finally, on the basis of the patterns of economic activity revealed by these sub-districts, we amalgamated these into eleven functional regions or districts, distinguished by the names of the major streets or institutions in them. These are shown in Figure 2.2.

The functional districts were derived in the following way.

[3] A list of these sub-groups and their respective code numbers (which are used later in this chapter) are set out in Appendix 1 to this chapter.

67

Table 2.7. Employment in Offices in the City by Activity and District 1964-6

District / Activity	(1) Banking	(2) Other finance	(3) Insurance	(4) Wholesale markets	(5) Commodity markets	(6) Shipping	(7) Professional services	(8) Printing and publishing	(9) Central offices	(10) Transport	(11) Income absorbing	(12) Others	(13) All types of activity
1 Fleet St	1,140	2,729	2,531	2,323	772	248	7,901	9,852	2,273	77	3,016	2,747	35,609
2 Smithfield	152	402	50	4,467	313	167	409	139	1,196	76	514	1,860	9,745
3 Barbican	1,840	2,527	3,176	975	681	229	3,930	173	2,163	45	1,048	116	16,903
4 Thames St	666	545	1,204	1,248	1,673	1,190	3,210	1,101	1,565	314	1,303	760	14,779
5 The Bank	30,351	4,504	14,659	442	1,504	1,028	6,175	1,083	647	59	2,567	196	63,215
6 Finsbury Circus	5,779	10,318	2,490	383	683	133	4,523	247	1,945	366	1,708	24	28,599
7 Houndsditch, Billingsgate	2,044	1,111	6,042	3,304	2,286	4,358	3,520	332	1,097	629	2,766	555	28,044
8 Lloyd's	1,626	387	9,266	592	861	2,459	954	58	167	20	1,071	23	17,484
9 Baltic	3,183	621	6,324	1,173	1,470	7,644	1,271	145	396	4,258	850	154	27,489
10 Fenchurch St	3,224	1,135	4,080	705	3,788	3,491	942	47	926	44	1,116	87	19,585
11 All districts	50,005	24,279	49,822	15,612	14,031	20,947	32,835	13,177	12,375	5,888	15,959	6,522	261,452

Source: Corporation of London.

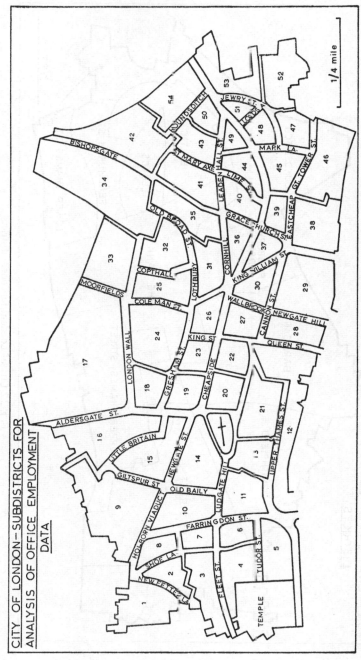

Fig. 2.1. City of London: Sub-districts for analysis of office employment data

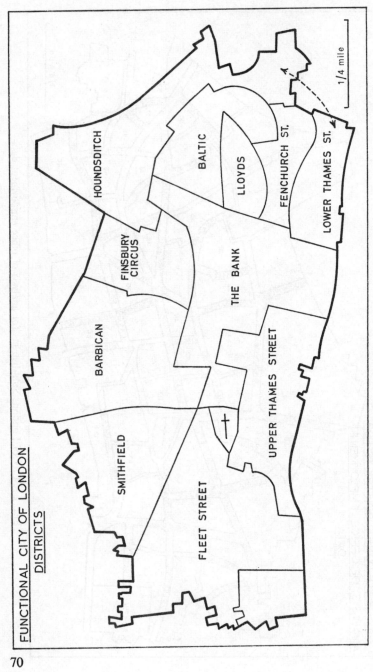

FUNCTIONAL CITY OF LONDON
DISTRICTS

HOUNDSDITCH

BALTIC

LLOYDS

FENCHURCH ST.

LOWER THAMES ST.

1/4 mile

FINSBURY CIRCUS

THE BANK

BARBICAN

UPPER THAMES STREET

SMITHFIELD

FLEET STREET

Fig. 2.2 City of London: functional districts

First, we calculated the number of workers in each office activity in each sub-district, surplus to those necessary to produce the goods and services in that area for local consumption. We assumed this latter ratio to be the same as the share of that activity's total employment in the national economy. We then expressed the number of surplus workers in each of the ten main office groups as a percentage of the total number of surplus workers in all activities in these districts. Figure 2.3 portrays the groups with the highest percentages. It shows both the extent to which a sub-district is dominated by one or more activities, and which activities tend to be associated with each other in their locational patterns. This was the basis for the eleven districts presented in Figure 2.2 and the starting point of our analysis.

Tables 2.7 to 2.10 summarize the spatial distribution of employment of the leading office and shopping activities in the City. In general, they confirm the structure revealed by the *Censuses of Population* although only the leading activities of the City are considered here. These statistics largely speak for themselves, but the following points are worth emphasizing.

1. Financial activities, e.g. banking, finance and insurance, account for just under one-half of the total office, etc., employment in the City. Commercial and trading activities, e g. wholesale distribution, export and import merchants, commodity dealers, shipping and services incidental to the Port of London, employ about one-fifth of the labour force.
2. The ancillary services to these two main activities are the third largest employers of labour. Accountancy, legal services, consultancy and advertising employ 32,835 people between them – an eighth of the total labour force.
3. Printing and publishing apart, office employment of companies with their main activities elsewhere (classified under Central Offices) is comparatively unimportant and accounts for probably not more than 5 per cent of total employment.
4. There is fairly distinct spatial delineation of most kinds of activities. The Bank is clearly the centre of the financial district. Printing and publishing is largely concentrated along Fleet Street, and shipping and transport services around the Baltic and Fenchurch Street. Commodity trading and wholesale distribution are rather more widely dispersed as are the central offices of firms, income-absorbing and professional services. Lloyds (insurance), Bank (banking), Smithfield (wholesale markets), and Finsbury Circus (banking and other finance) are particularly specialized.

71

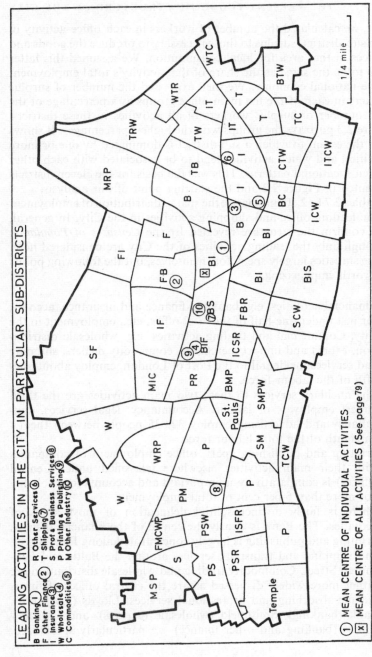

LEADING ACTIVITIES IN THE CITY IN PARTICULAR SUB-DISTRICTS

B Banking ①   R Other Services ⑥
F Other Finance ②   T Shipping ⑦
I Insurance ③   S Prof. & Business Services ⑧
W Wholesale ④   P Printing & Publishing ⑨
C Commodities ⑤   M Other Industry ⑩

① MEAN CENTRE OF INDIVIDUAL ACTIVITIES
☒ MEAN CENTRE OF ALL ACTIVITIES (See page 79)

1/4 mile

Fig. 2.3 Leading activities in the City by particular sub-districts

Table 2.8 Percentage Distribution of Employment in Offices in Particular Activities in the City by District 1964–6

District	Banking (1)	Other finance (2)	Insurance (3)	Wholesale markets (3)	Commodity markets (5)	Shipping (6)	Professional services (7)	Printing and publishing (8)	Central offices (9)	Transport (10)	Income absorbing (11)	Others (12)	All types of activity (13)
1 Fleet St	2·28	11·24	5·08	14·88	5·50	1·18	24·06	74·77	18·37	1·31	18·90	42·12	13·62
2 Smithfield	0·30	1·66	0·10	28·61	2·23	0·80	1·25	1·05	9·66	1·29	3·22	28·52	3·73
3 Barbican	3·68	10·41	6·37	6·25	4·85	1·09	11·97	1·31	17·48	0·76	6·57	1·78	6·47
4 Thames St	1·33	2·24	2·42	7·99	11·92	5·68	9·78	8·36	12·65	5·33	8·16	11·65	5·65
5 The Bank	60·70	18·55	29·42	2·83	10·72	4·91	18·81	8·22	5·23	1·00	16·08	3·01	24·18
6 Finsbury Circus	11·56	42·50	5·00	2·45	4·87	0·63	13·77	1·87	15·72	6·22	10·7	0·37	10·94
7 Houndsditch, Billingsgate	4·09	4·58	12·13	21·16	16·29	20·8	10·72	2·52	8·86	10·68	17·33	8·51	10·73
8 Lloyd's	3·25	1·59	18·60	3·79	6·14	11·74	2·91	0·44	1·35	0·34	6·71	0·35	6·69
9 Baltic	6·37	2·56	12·69	7·51	27·08	36·49	3·87	1·10	3·20	72·72	5·33	2·36	10·50
10 Fenchurch St	6·45	4·67	12·69	4·52	27·08	16·64	2·84	0·36	7·48	0·75	6·99	1·33	7·49
11 All districts	100·0	100·0	100·0	100·0	100·0	100·0	100·0	100·0	100·0	100·0	100·0	100·0	100·0

Source: Corporation of London.

Table 2.9. Percentage Distribution of Employment in Offices in Particular Districts in the City by Activity 1964–6

District	Banking (1)	Other finance (2)	Insurance (3)	Wholesale markets (4)	Commodity markets (5)	Shipping (6)	Professional services (7)	Printing and publishing (8)	Central offices (9)	Transport (10)	Income-absorbing (11)	Other (12)	All types of activity (13)
1 Fleet St	3·20	7·66	7·11	6·52	2·17	0·70	22·19	27·67	6·38	0·22	8·47	7·71	100·0
2 Smithfield	1·56	4·13	0·51	45·84	3·21	1·71	4·20	1·43	12·27	0·78	5·27	19·09	100·0
3 Barbican	10·89	14·95	18·79	5·77	4·03	1·35	23·25	1·02	12·80	0·27	6·20	0·69	100·0
4 Thames St	4·51	3·69	8·15	8·44	11·32	8·05	21·72	7·45	10·59	2·12	8·82	5·14	100·0
5 The Bank	48·01	7·12	23·19	0·70	2·38	1·63	9·77	1·71	1·02	0·09	4·06	0·31	100·0
6 Finsbury Circus	20·21	36·08	8·71	1·34	2·39	0·47	15·82	0·86	6·8	1·28	5·97	0·08	100·0
7 Houndsditch, Billingsgate	7·29	3·96	21·54	11·78	8·15	15·54	12·55	1·18	3·91	2·24	9·86	1·98	100·0
8 Lloyd's	9·30	2·21	53·0	3·39	4·92	14·06	5·46	0·33	0·96	0·11	6·13	0·13	100·0
9 Baltic	11·58	2·26	23·01	4·27	5·35	27·81	4·62	0·53	1·44	15·49	3·09	0·56	100·0
10 Fenchurch St	16·46	5·80	20·83	3·60	19·34	17·82	4·81	0·24	4·73	0·22	5·7	0·44	100·0
11 All districts	19·13	9·29	19·06	5·97	5·36	8·01	12·56	5·04	4·73	2·26	6·10	2·49	100·0

N.B. Some rows do not add up to exactly 100; this is due to rounding errors.   Source: Corporation of London.

Table 2.10. Number of Office Establishments in the City by Activity and District 1964–6

District	Banking (1)	Other finance (2)	Insurance (3)	Wholesale markets (4)	Commodity markets (5)	Shipping (6)	Professional services (7)	Printing and publishing (8)	Central offices (9)	Transport (10)	Income absorbing (11)	Other (12)	All types of activity (13)
1 Fleet St	23	30	21	111	53	10	329	230	81	4	267	19	1,178
2 Smithfield	8	6	3	249	28	8	45	13	59	6	69	17	511
3 Barbican	28	49	22	44	34	5	82	5	49	2	76	6	402
4 Thames St	17	36	32	95	176	27	160	40	72	4	126	19	804
5 The Bank	156	197	122	45	118	47	249	27	52	7	265	15	1,300
6 Finsbury Circus	72	309	35	21	62	13	195	16	44	2	161	6	936
7 Houndsditch, Billingsgate	28	52	69	235	171	132	181	17	75	16	314	34	1,324
8 Lloyd's	18	29	272	29	58	72	58	4	25	2	123	4	694
9 Baltic	33	34	103	45	109	214	76	10	42	10	101	14	791
10 Fenchurch St	21	29	56	52	173	63	56	4	30	2	68	6	560
11 All districts	404	771	735	926	982	591	1,431	366	529	55	1,570	140	8,500

Source: Corporation of London.

75

By contrast, most activities are well represented in Thames Street/ Houndsditch/Billingsgate and the Baltic districts.

While the spatial distribution of *establishments* in the City is broadly the same as that of the labour force, there are significant differences. Broadly speaking, the average size of establishment is lowest in the central districts (banking and insurance in the Bank district are a notable exception) and highest on the peripheries of the City. This reflects both the structure of economic activity and the functions undertaken by particular enterprises.

HOW CONCENTRATED ARE ACTIVITIES IN THE CITY?

So much for broad description. Once again, it is possible to be more specific about the extent to which particular activities are spatially concentrated or dispersed in the City, by use of the Location Quotient (L.Q.).[4] In Table 2.11 we divide each district's percentage share of the City's total employment of each main activity by its percentage share of all employment, to give an index of concentration for that activity. The results largely speak for themselves. Printing and publishing is an example of a very concentrated activity: the L.Q. for Fleet Street is 5·49, while in other districts (apart from Thames Street) it is never higher than 0·34. Transport and communications and wholesale markets are other examples of highly localized activities. By contrast, L.Q.s for income absorbing activities range only from 0·51 to 1·62. We also calculated, for each of the ten industrial groups, the L.Q. by the fifty-four sub-districts: the broad picture is mapped in Figures 2.4 to 2.13 and described in the following section of this chapter.

From these data, the *Coefficient of Localization* (C.L.) may be derived, which portrays, in a single statistic, the extent to which employment in a particular industry is localized or dispersed over a particular area. In our analysis, we calculated the C.L. by adding together all the positive (or negative) differences between the percentage share of a district's (or sub-district's) employment in a given activity and that of its share of employment in the City as a whole, and then dividing the result by 100. Complete industrial concentration (all employment in one district or sub-district) would give an index of 1·0. A completely even distribution (each district or sub-district having the same percentage of employment in that activity as all employment) would give an index of zero.

4 See footnote 2, p. 63 for definition.

Table 2.11. Employment Location Quotients by Main Activity and District in the City

District	Activity	(1) Banking	(2) Other finance	(3) Insurance	(4) Wholesale markets	(5) Commodity markets	(6) Shipping	(7) Professional services	(8) Printing and publishing	(9) Central offices	(10) Transport	(11) Income absorbing	(12) Other
1	Fleet St	0·17	0·83	0·37	1·09	0·40	0·09	1·77	5·49	1·35	0·10	1·39	3·09
2	Smithfield	0·08	0·45	0·03	7·67	0·60	0·21	0·34	0·28	2·59	0·33	0·86	7·63
3	Barbican	0·57	1·61	0·99	0·97	0·75	0·17	1·85	0·20	2·70	0·12	1·02	0·28
4	Thames St	0·24	0·40	0·43	1·42	2·11	1·01	1·73	1·48	2·24	0·94	1·44	2·06
5	Bank	2·51	0·77	1·22	0·12	0·44	0·20	0·78	0·34	0·22	0·04	0·67	0·12
6	Finsbury Circus	1·06	3·89	0·46	0·22	0·45	0·06	1·26	0·17	1·44	0·57	0·98	0·03
7	Houndsditch, Billingsgate	0·38	0·43	1·13	1·97	1·52	1·94	1·00	0·24	0·83	1·00	1·67	0·79
8	Lloyd's	0·49	0·24	2·78	0·57	0·92	1·76	0·44	0·07	0·20	0·05	1·00	0·05
9	Baltic	0·61	0·24	1·21	0·72	1·00	3·48	0·37	0·11	0·31	6·89	0·51	0·23
10	Fenchurch St	0·86	0·62	1·09	0·60	3·61	2·23	0·38	0·05	1·00	0·10	0·93	0·18

Source: Derived from data in Table 2.7.

The Coefficients of Localization (C.L.s) for the ten main activity groups by district and sub-district are presented in Table 2.12. This confirms the results of Table 2.11; printing and publishing, central offices, and shipping are seen to be the most concentrated of activities; insurance, income-absorbing services, and professional services the least. It will be observed that the coefficients are universally higher for the sub-districts than the districts.

Table 2.12. Coefficients of Localization (C.L.) and Standard Distance Indices (S.D.) for Main Activities in the City

	C.L.				S.D.	
	(a) For 11 districts		(b) For 54 sub-districts		For 54 sub-districts	
Banking	0·37	(6)	0·43	(5)	0·73	(1)
Other finance	0·36	(5)	0·47	(6)	0·57	(3)
Insurance	0·21	(2)	0·33	(2)	0·61	(2)
Wholesale markets	0·39	(7)	0·50	(7)	0·30	(7)
Commodity markets	0·31	(4)	0·39	(4)	0·39	(5)
Shipping	0·50	(9)	0·55	(9)	0·54	(4)
Professional services	0·23	(3)	0·35	(3)	0·33	(6)
Printing and publishing	0·64	(10)	0·71	(10)	0·15	(10)
Central offices in manufacturing	0·40	(8)	0·53	(8)	0·28	(8)
Income-absorbing services	0·15	(1)	0·29	(1)	0·26	(9)

N.B. Rankings (in parentheses) are in order of *ascending* concentration.
Source: Corporation of London.

Although describing spatial distributions, neither the L.Q. nor the C.L. fully takes into account the distance separating the employees in a given activity. It is quite possible, for example, for a group of banking enterprises at the periphery of one district to be closer to those in an adjacent district than those in another part of the same district. This means that values of L.Q.s and C.L.s are inevitably effected by the pattern and number of units used. To overcome this particular problem, we made use of a technique which attempts to measure the extent to which employment in a particular activity is concentrated or dispersed around its centre of gravity or mean centre. Imagine, for example, the area of the City to be a plane over which the employed population is distributed: the centre of gravity would be the point on which the plane, differentially weighted by the population, would balance.[5] As each activity has a different distribution over the City, this will be reflected in different balancing points.

In our present exercise, we derived this point in the following way. The employment in each of the fifty-four districts and sub-districts was assumed to be located at the mid-point of the area of that district; these local mid-points were then given longitude and latitude values, numbered, by convention, from the south-west corner of the City. To find the longitude and latitude of the centre of gravity, the longitudes and latitudes of each district were each weighted by the employment in the district; and the mean longitude and latitude was obtained by summing both sets of products and dividing each by the total employment for all areas. The centre of each activity can then be plotted on a map. The mean centres of employment of ten of the twelve main industrial groups and employment in the City as a whole are given in Figure 2.3. The most striking feature here is that all but one of the centres of gravity are within 700 yards of the Bank of England.

The spatial spread of employment around these mean centres may be expressed in terms of the sum of the weighted and squared distance deviations of each district from these centres. This measure of scatter is termed the *Standard Distance* (S.D.). Referring again to the system of longitudes and latitudes, the dispersion or each of these axes can be obtained by summing the squared deviations from the mean as already defined; the overall dispersion is then computed as the square root of the sum of the longitudinal and latitudinal dispersions. The more dispersed the distributions of employment, the greater is the value for standard distance, and vice versa. By comparing the standard distances of each activity with that for all employment, these can be expressed as an index of relative dispersion, ranging from zero to 1·0 – the latter coefficient indicating an activity as dispersed as the total population.

S.D. coefficients provide us with a useful complementary measure of industrial concentration to the C.L. measure. Nevertheless, the technique has one major disadvantage. Where there is more than one concentration of employment of a particular activity in a certain region, i.e. there are two or more centres of gravity, the formula can

---

[5] Using this analogy it will be seen that employment located on the edge of the plane will exert the greatest influence on the centre of gravity.

give misleading results. The mean centre of an activity concentrated exclusively at diagonally opposite ends of the City would be in the centre and hence the S.D. would be very high. Had the City been split down the middle into two units, quite a different result would have emerged. This measure should thus be used with some caution and only where high L.Q.s are confined to only one district (or cluster of districts).

Table 2.12 sets out the S.D. coefficients for each of the ten main activity groups both by district and sub-district. These are compared with the relevant C.L.s. In general, the rankings of the two indices are very close but there are one or two awkward exceptions, the most serious of these being 'other services'.

THE LOCATIONAL PATTERN OF THE MAIN ACTIVITIES

Next, we briefly summarize the pattern of spatial distribution of the ten main activities in the City. The numbers in parentheses refer to the coding of the sub-groups of activity listed in Appendix 1.

Banking

Banking is the leading economic activity in the City, and accounts for 19·5 per cent of the total office employment. Banking establishments are found throughout the Square Mile: Table 2.12 reveals that it is the fifth or sixth most dispersed group in terms of its C.L. and the most dispersed in terms of its S.D. Nevertheless, Figure 2.4 shows clearly that this sector consists of a well-defined core centred on the Bank of England – around which banking employment declines in all directions. Sub-districts 30, 35 and 36 contain one-third of all employment in banking: adding in the remaining areas shaded on Figure 2.4 accounts for a further third.

Table 2.13 sets out the numbers employed in the main banking sectors – which broadly correspond to the same locational pattern. It is the ordinary branch offices of the London clearing banks (48) that are most dispersed in the City (C.L. = 0·55 and S.D. = 0·61); other banks not on the Bank of England list of recognized foreign exchange dealers are slightly less dispersed (C.L. = 0·58 and S.D. = 0·26). However, whereas ordinary branch office employment rises sharply in the banking core sub-district 35, where its L.Q. is 7·85, those banks not recognized by the Bank of England have concentrations outside the financial core – sub-districts 17 and 18 recording L.Q.s of 4·67 and 5·38 respectively.

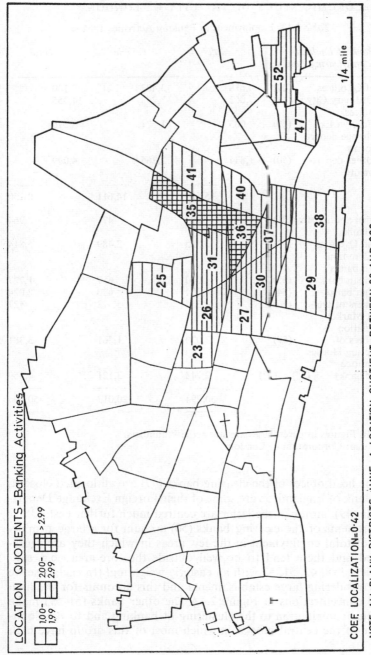

LOCATION QUOTIENTS – Banking Activities

LOCATION QUOTIENTS – Banking activities

LOCATION QUOTIENTS BETWEEN 00 AND 0·99

1·00–1·9,9

2·00–2·99

>2·99

COEF. LOCALIZATION=0·42

NOTE: ALL BLANK DISTRICTS HAVE A LOCATION QUOTIENT BETWEEN 00 AND 0·99

Fig. 2.4 Location quotients – Banking activities

1/4 mile

81

Table 2.13. Employment in Banking Activities 1964–6

Bank of England – London Clearing Banks		Male	Female	Total
(a) H.Q. offices	(47)	4,618	3,482	8,100
(b) Ordinary City offices	(48)	7,062	7,293	14,355
(c) Foreign Exchange departments	(49)	2,005	1,571	3,576
(d) Other departments	(50)	1,834	2,265	4,099
		15,519	14,611	30,130
Scottish and North Irish banks	(51)	493	471	964
British Overseas and Commonwealth banks	(52)	3,325	2,489	5,814
American banks	(53)	1,070	657	1,727
Foreign banks	(54)	1,394	630	2,024
Members of Discount Market Association	(56)	355	72	427
Members of Accepting Houses Committee	(57)	2,020	1,361	3,381
Other banks (55)	(77)	2,748	2,121	4,869
		30,294	20,012	50,306

N.B. Figures in parentheses are sub-activity numbers.
Source: Corporation of London.

The head offices of the clearing banks (47) are all located close to the Bank of England, as are some of their Foreign Exchange Departments (49), although the latter are centred much further east. Other departments of the clearing banks (50) account for a large proportion of total employment in the few areas in which they are represented and these tend to be well outside the core area – e.g. subdistricts 1, 8, 47, 51, 52 with an easterly weighting. (In each case we are considering large establishments and this accounts for the high local concentrations in Figure 2.4.) The other banks (51–57) make a major contribution to the clustering of banking and to the dominance of the central blocks, in which most of this group have high

L.Q.s. Foreign banks and their affiliates (54) are the most dispersed of all (C.L. = 0·61) and the members of the discount market most concentrated (C.L. = 0·86), the latter being strongly concentrated around Lombard Street (sub-district 36) with an L.Q. of 14·85.

These well-defined patterns are also related to the pattern of land values in the City (see Chapter 4). Those activities most frequently involved with the working of the money market and dominating the financial core are prepared to pay high rents for a central location in view of savings in essential communication costs, while the other sub-activities of this group, particularly those with a large amount of 'back office' employment, are forced to the periphery.

Other Financial Activities

This sector is a tier below the dominant activities of banking, insurance and professional services, and accounts for 8·0 per cent of all employment in the City. As can be seen from Table 2.14 and

Table 2.14. Employment in Other Financial Activities 1964–6

		Numbers employed		
		Male	Female	Total
Members of Finance Houses Association	(58)	426	441	867
Stock Exchange; stock brokers and jobbers	(59)	10,403	4,668	15,071
Investment and unit trust companies	(60)	497	352	849
Other finance, including Building Societies, foreign exchange dealers	(61)	3,719	3,773	7,492
		15,245	9,234	24,279

Source: Corporation of London.

Figure 2.5 the group is overshadowed by the stock market; not surprisingly, then, it shows a strong agglomeration in the sub-districts bounded by Coleman Street, Old Broad Street, Lothbury and London Wall: this area, in fact, contains one-third of all the employment in the group. But, as with most other activities, expansion is taking place outwards from this core, particularly north and west, away

84

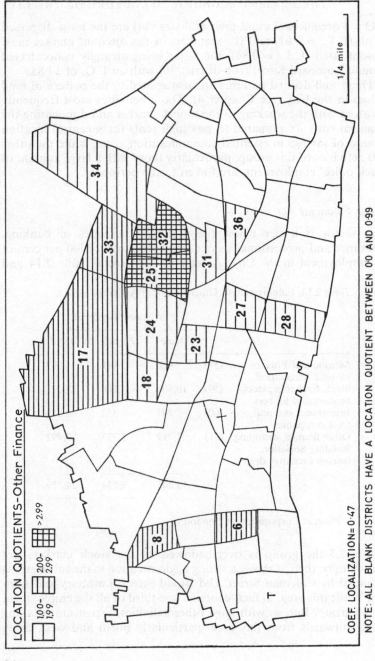

LOCATION QUOTIENTS-Other Finance

LOCATION QUOTIENTS

	1·00- 1·99
	2·00- 2·99
	> 2·99

1/4 mile

COEF. LOCALIZATION= 0·47

NOTE: ALL BLANK DISTRICTS HAVE A LOCATION QUOTIENT BETWEEN 0·0 AND 0·99

FIG. 2.5 Location quotients – Other finance

from those areas dominated by the banking sector. It is one of the few groups scoring high in the Barbican sub-district (17). When the distribution throughout the City is considered, this appears as a well-dispersed group.

Stockbrokers and jobbers (59) and investment and unit trusts (60) have similar location patterns, although the latter group is centred somewhat further west. Stockbroking ranks high as a dispersed activity (C.L. = 0·60, S.D. = 0·60). Investment and unit trusts appear equally dispersed in terms of their C.L. but concentrated in terms of their S.D. – this is a difficult anomaly to explain. Other finance (61) is so poorly represented in our data that no conclusions about its location can be drawn.

Insurance

The classification of insurance activities is presented in Table 2.15. These activities, like banking, are found throughout the City. It is

Table 2.15. Employment in Insurance Activities 1964–6

| | | Numbers employed | | |
		Male	Female	Total
Life assurance companies	(40)	4,349	3,610	7,959
Non-life insurance companies	(41)	3,412	2,481	5,893
Life and non-life companies at the same address	(42)	7,179	5,148	12,327
Lloyd's insurance brokers	(43)	10,938	7,554	18,492
Other insurance brokers	(44)	1,075	815	1,890
Underwriters and underwriters' agents	(45)	691	521	1,212
Other insurance activities (insurance agents, etc.)	(46)	1,115	934	2,049
Total		28,759	21,063	49,822

Source: Corporation of London.

the second most dispersed industrial group in terms of its C.L. and S.D. However, unlike the groups previously considered, it does not have such a well-defined core about which employment consistently declines. As can be seen from Figure 2.6 the group is centred well

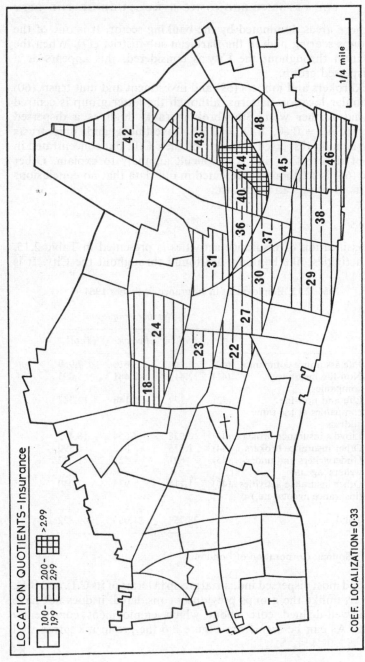

LOCATION QUOTIENTS—Insurance

1.00–1.99 ☐   2.00–2.99 ▦   >2.99 ▓

COEF. LOCALIZATION=0.33

NOTE: ALL BLANK DISTRICTS HAVE A LOCATIONAL QUOTIENT BETWEEN 0.0 AND 0.99

Fig. 2.6 Location quotients – Insurance

1/4 mile

into the end of the City with high L.Q.s to the south of Leadenhall Street in the blocks surrounding Lloyd's. In addition, some blocks in the middle of the City bordering Gresham Street also have relatively high L.Q.s

When we examine the distribution of the component activities that make up this sector, this pattern is partly explained. The principal activities concerned show similar high levels of dispersion but have particular concentrations in slightly different parts of the City: the life insurance companies (40) and life and non-life companies (42) are more important in western areas, while the non-life companies (41) and Lloyd's insurance brokers (43) are centred further east.

The rest of the insurance business appears to be more clustered. The non-Lloyd's brokers (44) are centred further west than the Lloyd's brokers, with certain sub-districts recording particularly high concentrations (16's L.Q. = 6·30; 37 = 9; 47 = 10·05), giving an overall C.L. of 0·65. The underwriters (45) are more firmly established around Lloyd's, the block adjacent to the Exchange having an L.Q. of 15·03.

Other insurance activities (46) appear to be slightly more dispersed (C.L. = 0·64) except for two particular areas of agglomeration, the first north of London Wall and along the north-east boundary of the City; and the second in the heart of the insurance/shipping area.

Although problems of classification arise in distinguishing between life and non-life insurance, especially since a large number of firms participate in both, our evidence suggests that the more 'risk-oriented' insurance firms concentrate in the core of the insurance area while others occupy peripheral locations. This pattern in many ways repeats, within the City, the earlier tendency for life insurance companies to leave the financial core altogether.[6]

Wholesaling

Although still accounting for 6 per cent employment in the City, wholesaling is considerably less important than once it was. Table 2.16 presents details of its present employment structure. This activity is now only dominant in the Smithfield area and along the eastern boundary of the City, making it a relatively concentrated function, ranking seventh according to both of our indices. Figure 2.7 shows that the belt of wholesaling activities, which previously extended from Smithfield to the river and then along the length of

[6] S. M. Robbins and W. E. Terleckyj, *The Money Metropolis*, Harvard University Press, 1960.

Lower Thames Street, is still weakly represented. However, although redevelopment may have priced out that part of wholesaling which requires extensive warehouse accommodation, many wholesalers still retain offices in these historic parts of the City.

Most component activities within this functional group show broadly similar spatial patterns; of these, food and textile wholesaling are most important. Wholesale distribution of provisions (31) has its main concentration in the vicinity of the Baltic Exchange (sub-district 50 has an L.Q. of 44·3); other food wholesaling (32) covers the Smithfield and Billingsgate markets which both generate a considerable amount of office employment in the immediate vicinity.

Table 2.16. Employment in Wholesaling Activities 1964–6

| | | Numbers employed | | |
		Male	Female	Total
Grocery and provisions, confectionery and drink	(31)	1,307	478	1,785
Other food	(32)	4,099	449	4,548
Tobacco	(33)	73	34	107
Textiles and footwear	(34)	1,327	717	2,044
Paper, stationery and books	(35)	1,216	675	1,891
Petroleum products	(36)	378	215	593
Other non-food goods	(37)	1,597	993	2,590
General wholesale merchants	(38)	1,192	862	2,054
Total		11,189	4,423	15,612

Source: Corporation of London.

Textile wholesaling (34) – together with offices of manufacturers in this field (10, 11, 12) – is still concentrated in the old textile quarter focused on Aldersgate. The wholesale distribution of paper, stationery and blocks (35) is, not surprisingly, localized in the press area west of St Paul's. A large number of paper wholesaling firms are to be found in the region of Upper Thames Street, together with the offices of the paper manufacturers themselves (15). Companies concerned with non-food goods tend to cluster and are largely in the northern part of the City and in the heart of the commodity trading area, where all the employment in activity 37 is concentrated. Finally, in contrast to these wholesaling activities, general merchants (38) are more widely dispersed (C.L. = 0·60), though, again, employment in this group rises sharply along the eastern City boundary.

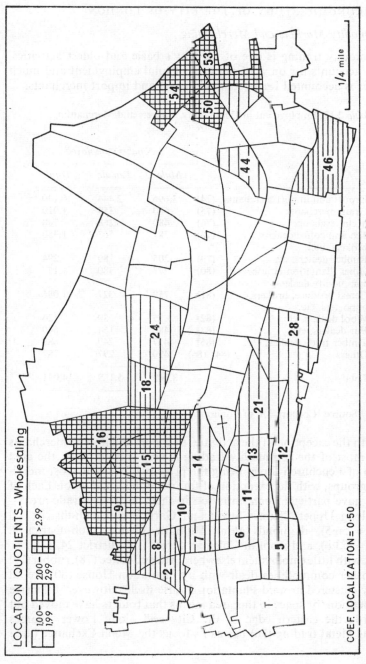

LOCATION QUOTIENTS – Wholesaling

1·00– 1·99
2·00– 2·99
>2·99

COEF. LOCALIZATION = 0·50

NOTE: ALL BLANK DISTRICTS HAVE A LOCATION QUOTIENT BETWEEN 0·0 AND 0·99

Fig. 2.7 Location quotients – Wholesaling

1/4 mile

Commodity Markets and Merchanting

Commodity trading is one of the City's basic and oldest activities, yet it accounts for only 5·5 per cent of total employment and much of this is accounted for by general export and import merchants.

Table 2.17. Employment in Commodity Markets and Merchanting
1964–6

		Numbers employed		
		Male	Female	Total
Export and import merchants	(74)	3,696	2,444	6,140
Grain merchants	(75)	660	359	1,019
Metal exchange	(76)	480	268	748
Tea and coffee dealers, brokers, etc.	(78)	787	563	1,350
Rubber dealers, etc.	(79)	205	89	294
Other Plantation House commodity dealers	(80)	777	380	1,157
Cereal produce, brokers, importers, etc.	(81)	759	327	1,086
Wool dealers, etc.	(82)	85	39	124
Fur dealers, etc.	(83)	486	154	640
Timber trade dealers, etc.	(85)	437	249	686
Others	(84) (86)	490	297	787
Total		8,862	5,169	14,031

Source: Corporation of London.

With the exception of the activities of export and import merchants (74), most of the commodity trading is very concentrated, the area south of Fenchurch Street being the principal focus for most individual groups, with the exception of fur, diamonds, and wool. Each of these have particular concentration in their respective trade areas – fur along Upper Thames Street and Garlick Hill (sub-district 12, L.Q. = 56·5), diamonds along Holborn Viaduct (sub-district 8, L.Q. = 73·8), and wool in Coleman Street (sub-district 24, L.Q. = 10·0), with little employment elsewhere. Tea and coffee (78), rubber (79) and other commodities dealt with by Plantation House (80) are all firmly clustered around Plantation House itself. However, intensive competition for space in this area means that traders have moved out towards the eastern edge of the City and along Lower Thames Street. Metal trading (76) has as its focus the Metal Exchange (area

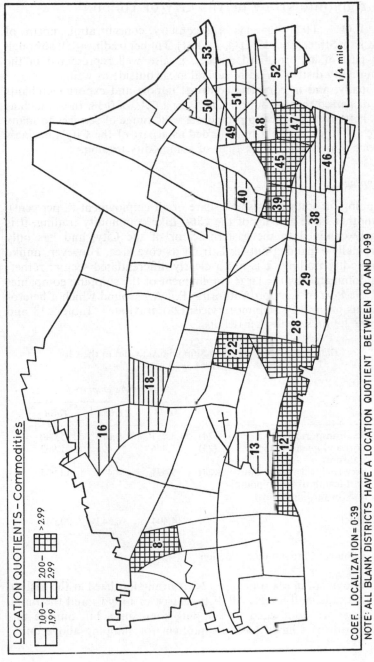

LOCATION QUOTIENTS – Commodities

1·00 – 1·99 2·00 – 2·99 >2·99

COEF. LOCALIZATION = 0·39

NOTE: ALL BLANK DISTRICTS HAVE A LOCATION QUOTIENT BETWEEN 0·0 AND 0·99

FIG. 2.8 Location quotients – Commodities

1/4 mile

40, L.Q. = 11·1) but has a secondary concentration north of Gresham Street (area 18, L.Q. = 26·1). Timber trading (85), although not part of an organized market, is also well represented in the commodity district – and in several areas outside as well.

Finally, and in complete contrast, import and export merchants are dispersed throughout the City with a C.L. of 0·38. In as much as this heterogeneous group provides a wide range of services to many City activities, it could be regarded as a part of the City's business service population, rather than of commodity trading.

Shipping

Shipping, in spite of its small share of all employment (8 per cent), is another basic activity of the City. Like commodity trading, it is largely confined to the eastern sector of the City, and has only marginally expanded outwards from its core area. However, unlike commodity trading, it is not a clearly differentiated sector: rather, it is dominated by the large employment of the shipping companies and the Port of London Authority (P.L.A.) around which a heterogeneous group of shipping services (28) gravitates. Table 2.18 and Figure 2.9 present further details.

Table 2.18. Employment in Shipping Activities in the City
1964–6

		Numbers employed		
		Male	Female	Total
Sea transport	(24)	3,467	1,613	5,080
Port and inland water transport	(25)	1,466	496	1,962
Services incidental to transport (shipbrokers, shipping and forwarding agents)	(28)	9,471	4,434	13,905
Total		14,404	6,543	20,947

Source: Corporation of London.

Employment in sea transport (24) is firmly localized at the eastern end of Leadenhall Street. All districts east of Lloyd's and the Baltic Exchange are dominated by shipping companies, but outside this area, no district has a location quotient for shipping above unity.

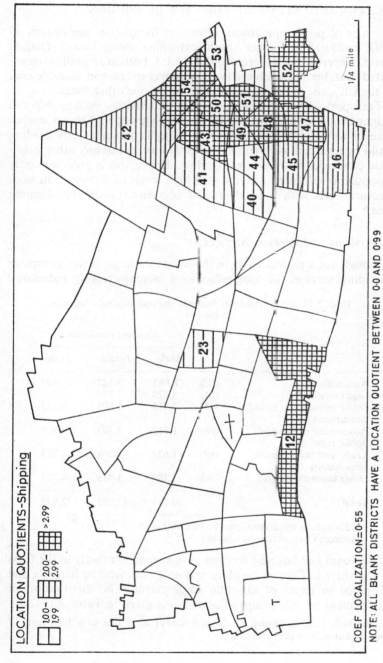

LOCATION QUOTIENTS—Shipping

	1.00– 1.99
	2.00– 2.99
	>2.99

COEF LOCALIZATION=0.55

NOTE: ALL BLANK DISTRICTS HAVE A LOCATION QUOTIENT BETWEEN 0.0 AND 0.99

FIG. 2.9 Location quotients – Shipping

¼ mile

The axis of port employment, obviously focused on sub-district 47 (L.Q. = 23·61), is further south, extending along Lower Thames Street. Nevertheless, in terms of their C.L.s, both are equally concentrated; but, because each is a large employer over a considerable area of the City, they rank as well-dispersed on our other index.

Transport services include a diversity of activities, such as ship and freight brokers, shipping and forwarding agents, and travel agents. Like import and export merchants, many firms under this heading could be regarded as providing essential business to any other enterprise concerned with overseas trading. Hence, this is predominantly a population-oriented activity with high levels of dispersal on both measures, but with some degree of concentration in the shipping area.[7]

Professional and Business Services

Although not a basic activity in the sense that firms in this group are providing services for long-established income-creating industries,

Table 2.19. Employment in Professional and Business Services 1964–6

		Numbers employed		
		Male	Female	Total
Accountancy	(62)	8,085	3,322	11,407
Legal services*	(64)	3,220	3,546	6,766
Other services (including consultancy)	(65)	2,315	1,808	4,123
Advertising agents and public relations	(68)	1,612	1,307	2,919
Trade and professional associations	(69)	1,622	1,261	2,883
Other business services	(70)	3,289	1,448	4,737
Total		20,143	12,692	32,835

* Excluding those employed in Inns of Court.
Source: Corporation of London.

professional and business services have expanded rapidly in the City, as elsewhere in Central London, and now rank next to banking and insurance in terms of absolute employment. The distribution of employment by sub-groups of activities is given in Table 2.19. As a

[7] The high L.Q. in Figure 2.8 for sub-district 12 is due to a high level of employment in transport services.

population-oriented activity, we can expect a fairly widespread distribution throughout the City, and this is, in fact, seen to be the case from its low C.L. (0·23).

However, it is clear from Figure 2.10 that professional and business services are largely excluded from the core of the well-established trade areas already recognized. Although nowhere strikingly pre-eminent, the map shows that this element is well represented around the periphery of the financial core from Liverpool Street, Barbican and the west-central City to Upper Thameside. The only area of marked agglomeration is, in fact, Fleet Street. The distribution of the constituent activities is broadly similar to that of the whole group. There are no particular trading areas for accountancy (62) and legal services (64) although both have pronounced concentrations in the northern part of the City.

Other professional services (65), which consist of a great variety of specialized forms of consultancy, are the most dispersed element in the group, followed by employers' trade and professional associations (69). The dispersal of the latter group is hardly surprising as associations play an important part in regulating and organizing the operations of numerous activities throughout the City. Other business services (70) including employment agencies, translating services, etc., are equally dispersed, although there is some clustering of these enterprises along Fleet Street and Liverpool Street.

Most of the service activities are also well represented in the Fleet Street area, although, of this group, only advertising and public relations (68), with the most well-pronounced westerly component in its centre of gravity, is located solely west of St Paul's. Advertising, then, clearly belongs to the press group.

Printing and Publishing

Our data give us only partial coverage of this sector, as they include only office staff in establishments not attached to premises where printing and publishing takes place. Some of the major newspaper enterprises are therefore excluded and this accounts for the unusual blanks for sub-districts 6 and 8 in Figure 2.11. Nevertheless, it is clear that this forms another concentrated and tightly-knit trade area radiating out from just east of St Paul's to the western edge of the City: of the major functional groups recognized, it is easily the most concentrated according to both indices (Table 2.12). As has already been indicated, the press concentration includes a number of additional activities with obvious functional linkages, e.g. paper manu-

95

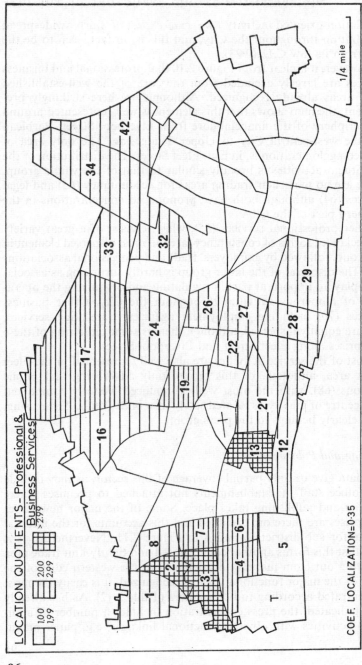

LOCATION QUOTIENTS – Professional & Business Services

1·00 1·99	
2·00 2·99	
>2·99	

COEF. LOCALIZATION=0·35

NOTE: ALL BLANK DISTRICTS HAVE A LOCATION QUOTIENT BETWEEN 0·0 AND 0·99

Fig. 2.10 Location quotients – Professional and business services

1/4 mile

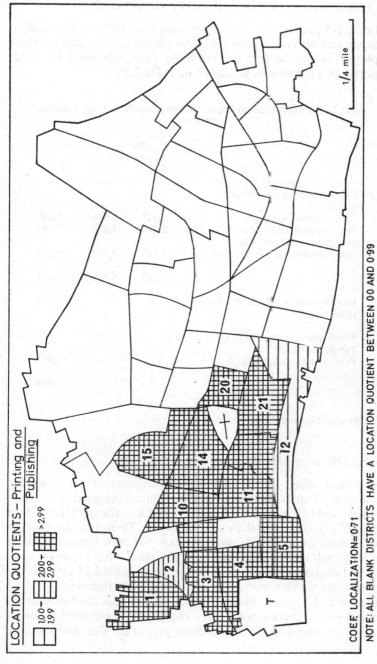

LOCATION QUOTIENTS – Printing and Publishing

	1,00– 1,99
	2,00– 2,99
	>2.99

NOTE: ALL BLANK DISTRICTS HAVE A LOCATION QUOTIENT BETWEEN 0·0 AND 0·99

COEF. LOCALIZATION=0·71

FIG. 2.11 Location quotients – Printing and publishing

D

facturers (18), advertising agents (68) and the wholesale distribution of paper, stationery and books (13). An estimate of the *total* numbers employed in this sector, i.e. including data submitted to H.M. Inspector of Factories, is presented in Table 2.20.

Table 2.20. Employment in Paper, Printing and Publishing Activities 1964–6

| | | Numbers employed | | |
		Male	Female	Total
1	Employment in independent offices			
	Paper, board, etc. (15)	1,025	816	1,841
	Printing and publishing of (16) newspapers and periodicals	2,743	3,056	5,799
	Other printing and publishing (17)	3,145	2,392	5,573
		6,913	6,264	13,177
2	Employment in offices attached to factories			6,750
3	Employment in factories Paper, board, etc. Printing and publishing			16,067
				35,994

Source: Corporation of London.

Central Offices of Manufacturing Firms

The central offices of manufacturing firms account for a similar proportion of the City's total employment as commodity trading, yet they would seem to be far less integrated into the spatial structure of the City's economy than are the latter. There are no obvious trading areas or similar repeated location patterns. Some industries are localized in a few districts while others have employment scattered over various non-contiguous areas. Table 2.21 sets out the employment of office workers in each of the main industries.

Figure 2.12 suggests that most industrial offices cannot afford a location within the financial core. The principal industrial concentrations are, therefore, to the northern part of the City and adjacent

Table 2.21. Employment in Central Offices in the City 1964–6

		Numbers employed		
		Male	Female	Total
Mining and quarrying	(2)	1,098	652	1,750
Food, drink and tobacco	(3)	980	1,046	2,026
Chemical and allied trades	(4)	647	376	1,043
Metal manufacturing	(5)	547	136	683
Engineering and electrical goods	(6)	1,412	508	1,920
Vehicles	(8)	398	104	502
Textiles	(10)	593	339	932
Clothing and footwear	(12)	158	127	285
Timber, furniture, etc.	(14)	327	131	458
Other industries (1) (7) (9) (11) (13) (18)		655	519	1,174
Central offices of companies operating abroad	(71)	164	125	289
Central offices of companies engaged in more than one activity	(73)	781	532	1,313
Total		7,780	4,595	12,375

Source: Corporation of London.

to, and beyond, St Paul's. When examining the distribution of industrial activities, it must be remembered that since many of the activities have a very small total employment, a high L.Q. can be produced, although in absolute terms very few people may be employed in the particular district. The scattering of industrial mean centres is indicative of the lack of cohesion within this sector, although it is possible that the use of the broad S.I.C. orders may miss important similarities of locations within activities.

Income-Absorbing Activities

A concentration of office workers inevitably creates a demand for essential consumer services (such as retail outlets, catering facilities), just as the offices themselves require specialized business services. However, while business services constitute the third most important activity within the City, consumer services account for only 6 per cent of the total employment. Further details of employment in this sector

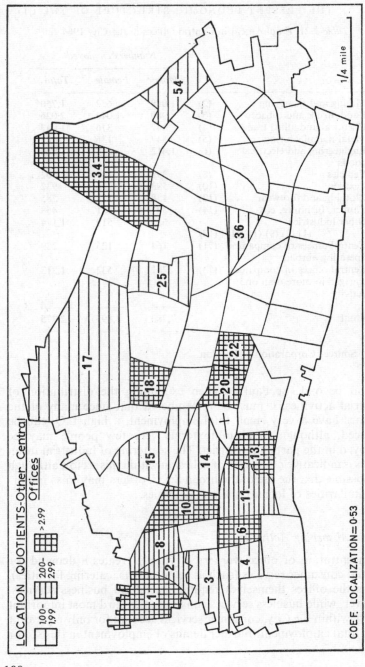

LOCATION QUOTIENTS–Other Central Offices

1·00- 1·99

2·00- 2·99

>2·99

COEF. LOCALIZATION=0·53

NOTE: ALL BLANK DISTRICTS HAVE A LOCATIONAL QUOTIENT BETWEEN 0·0 AND 0·99

Fig. 2.12 Location quotients – Other central offices

1/4 mile

Table 2.22. Employment in Income-Absorbing Services in the City
1964–6

		Numbers employed		
		Male	Female	Total
Retail distribution	(39)	2,808	2,264	5,072
Catering and hotels	(66)	2,965	5,572	8,537
Education, medical and religious*	(63)	343	474	817
Personal services (laundry, hairdressing, etc.)	(67)	391	539	930
Miscellaneous services	(72)	265	338	603
Total		6,772	9,187	15,979

* Excluding those employed at St Bartholomew's Hospital, estimated at 3,110.
Source: Corporation of London.

are given in Table 2.22 and Figure 2.13. Like professional and business services, this entirely income-absorbing sector can be expected to mirror the distribution of total employment throughout the City, with a particular emphasis on the major thoroughfares. A wide dispersal of consumer services is indicated by the lowest C.L. (0·29), and mean centres adjacent to that of total employment. Catering (66) is the most widely dispersed element within this sector. In addition, our separate tabulation of catering employment *within* other establishments suggests that this is as important as independent catering. Retail employment is similarly dispersed, with particular emphasis on the major street lines.

THE MEASUREMENT OF ACTIVITY LINKAGES[8]

So much for a broad assessment of the economic structure of the City. We now turn to examine ways of assessing (a) the extent to which activities or functions are linked with one another, and (b) the character of the linkages. How far, for example, is there a tendency

[8] This section draws substantially on articles by J. Goddard, 'Multivariate Analysis of Office Location Patterns in the City Centre: a London Example', *Regional Studies*, Vol. 2, No. 1, September 1968; and J. H. Dunning 'The City of London: a case study in urban economics', *Town Planning Review*, Vol. 40, No. 3, October 1969. John Goddard was a consultant to E.A.G. on the City of London project.

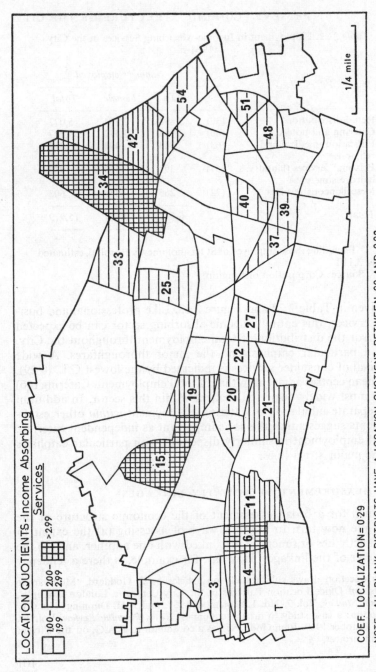

LOCATION QUOTIENTS-Income Absorbing
Services

LOCATION QUOTIENTS
☐ 1.00 – 1.99
▤ 2.00 – 2.99
▦ > 2.99

COEF. LOCALIZATION = 0.29

NOTE: ALL BLANK DISTRICTS HAVE A LOCATION QUOTIENT BETWEEN 0.0 AND 0.99

1/4 mile

Fig. 2.13 Location quotients – Income-absorbing services

for certain activities and functions to cluster together in different parts of the City, and how far do different parts of the City tend to specialize in particular types or complexes of activity? Is it possible to identify financial and/or trading complexes or patterns of spatial association, and the reasons for them?

The idea of a network of interdependent offices constituting a city-centre activity system, which contains a number of interrelated sub-systems, has been put forward by various writers,[9] and is now generally accepted as a planning precept by consultants working on urban renewal and growth in Britain. Clearly any appreciation of the form and extent of linkages, and the delineation of different types of office complexes, depends ultimately on the data which are available both as regards the input–output transactions between firms and the acquisition and transmission of information.

There have been few multivariate analyses of locational patterns along these lines. Most studies of the structure of the C.B.D. (for example, Morgan's of London, Rannells's of Philadelphia, Davies's of Cape Town and Schacher's of Tel Aviv),[10] using various geo-statistical and mapping techniques, have described the characteristics of individual activities and their relation to each other, but have not attempted systematically to delineate complexes or groupings of activity. Studies by other writers of linkages of activities outside the C.B.D. have gone somewhat further and in at least one of these,[11] use was made of input–output data to help identify types of possible linkages.

In our attempt to assess the extent to which groups of activities in the City are spatially linked, we first calculated, for each *pair* of 80 sub-industries and over the 216 street blocks, the coefficient of correlation. The 216×80 data matrix was normalized: first, by expressing employment in each activity as a percentage of all employment in the street block to allow for differences in the size of the areal unit; secondly, since the distributions were, in general, highly skewed, by transforming the percentage figures into logarithms; and thirdly, for the purposes of subsequent analysis, by converting the

[9] See, for example, F. S. Chapin, 'The Analysis of Urban Activity Systems' in *Urban Land Use Planning*, Illinois, University of Illinois Press, 1965.

[10] W. T. W. Morgan, 'A Functional Approach to the Study of Office Distributions', *Tijdschrift voor Economische en Sociale Geografie*, Vol. 52, 1961; J. Rannells, *The Core of the City*, New York, University of Columbia Press, 1965; D. H. Davies, *Land Use in Central Capetown*, Longmans, Capetown, 1965; A. Schacher, 'Geostatistical Techniques in Urban Research,' *Regional Science Association Papers*, 1967.

[11] See M. Streit, cited on p. 104.

data to standard scores – that is, positive or negative deviations about a zero mean, to give each variable a variance of one.[12]

Of the 3,160 interrelationships considered, using a log linear estimating equation, 206 proved to be significant at the 0·1 per cent confidence level. These activities we regarded as being *prima facie* spatially linked, although strictly speaking, to eliminate the possibility that they are associated with each other due to some general locational advantage, an additional variable relating each pair of activities to the volume and distribution of all activities should be added.[13] It should be further observed that these correlations reflect a complex set of historical, institutional and economic forces. They do not necessarily reflect the *need* of firms to be located near one another; simply the extent to which they are.

The relationships obtained are portrayed diagrammatically in Figure 2.14. This sets out nine main activities, and the associations between 73 sub-groups of activities within and between these activities. It can be seen that the correlation 'bonds' so drawn reveal a highly complex structure. Of the functional groups illustrated, only 'industries' and 'wholesaling' do not have strong internal bonds. However, besides these intra-activity bonds, there are also important inter-activity linkages. The most significant of these are between shipping (24 and 28), commodities (75, 80, 81) and insurance. There are also various connections between insurance and banking, and between banking and other finance. Wholesaling, with few internal bonds, would appear to be a subsidiary element within several other groups, notably commodities, rather than a functional group in its own right The self-contained press group also has external links with a number of service and industrial activities. The only cluster within the 'industries' sector represents the remnants of a textile trading function (10, 11, 12).

Given this pattern of relationships, our next task was to try to identify the character of the more important *groups* of associations. For while correlation analysis may tell us that Stock Exchange jobbers are spatially linked with accepting houses, and export merchants with ship brokers and forwarding agents, it cannot tell us how significant these linkage complexes are in explaining variations in employment

[12] Even this procedure, however, does not get over the fundamental problems associated with the autocorrelation of variables, and the delineation of areas (the coefficients are slightly different when the 54 sub-groups are used as observations), particularly as clusters of activities may well be linked rather than divided by street boundaries.

[13] M. E. Streit, 'Spatial Associations and Economic Linkages between Industries', *Journal of Regional Science*, 1969, Vol. 9, No. 2, pp. 5 ff.

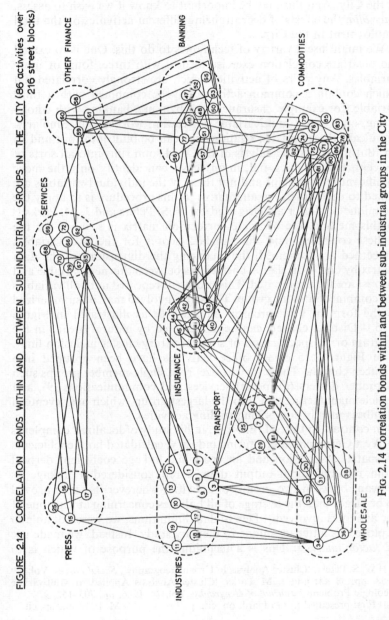

FIGURE 2.14 CORRELATION BONDS WITHIN AND BETWEEN SUB-INDUSTRIAL GROUPS IN THE CITY (86 activities over 216 street blocks)

Fig. 2.14 Correlation bonds within and between sub-industrial groups in the City

in the City. And this may be important to know if we wish to assess, *inter alia*, the effects of decentralizing different activities on the total employment in the City.

We might use a variety of techniques to do this. One is to extend the bivariate correlation exercise to deal with three, four, or more variables. Any pairs of activities which are strongly correlated but which contain a common activity may be combined with a third variable (for example, insurance with banking, banking with wholesaling, etc.) and a multivariable correlation worked out. Similarly, significant three-variable relationships can be built into four and so on. But multivariate analysis of this kind soon runs into all sorts of conceptual difficulties and, in any case, can identify only the more significant relationships and not the way the individual variables are linked to each other. An alternative to this procedure is to apply the technique of cluster analysis used by W. S. Peters and J. M. Parks.[14] In this method, the bivariate correlation matrix is scanned for the highest coefficient and the standard scores for the two variables concerned are combined, thus reducing the dimensions of the data matrix by one. Correlation coefficients between this new variable and the rest are then computed. This process is repeated until all variables are combined into one group. The steps involved may be summarized in the form of a hierarchical linkage tree as illustrated in Figure 2.15.[15] Distinct clusters can be demarcated by natural breaks in the diagram or by specification of some arbitrary cluster inclusion limit.

In Figure 2.15 eighty office activities have been grouped into eighteen clusters. These vary in size from single-member groups such as timber dealers (6), postal services and communications (9), and vehicle manufacturers (17) to the largest group, which has seventeen members mostly comprising trading activities.

In contrast to this, M. E. Streit, in his study of localized complexes in West German manufacturing industry, calculated both coefficients of spatial association and an economic linkage coefficient derived from regional input–output data. Streit considered a linkage as relevant between two groups of activities wherever its value proved to be larger than the average of all linkages concerning at least one of the activities involved.[16] Due to data limitations, we were not able to explore this latter technique in the City study. Instead, we made use of *factor analysis*. This is a technique the purpose of which is to

[14] W. S. Peters, 'Cluster Analysis in Urban Geography', *Social Forces*, Vol. 37, 1958, pp. 38–44; and J. M. Parks, 'Cluster Analysis Applied to Multivariate Geologic Problems,' *Journal of Geography*, Vol. 74, 1966, pp. 703–15.
[15] First presented in Goddard, op. cit., p. 76.   [16] M. E. Streit, op. cit.

identify from a large number of relationships between activities those patterns or groups of activities which are the most important.[17] The methods used to do this in the City study are rather complicated and are described in some detail by Goddard in his article. Here we simply present the conclusions of our exercise.

In the City, we found that six factors, or groups of variables, were of particular importance in explaining variations in employment, within which 50 of the 80 activities were contained. Five of these are illustrated in Table 2.23: between them, they accounted for about one-third of the total variations in employment. Factor 1 is composed of the closely interrelated activities of commodity trading, risk insurance and shipping. These follow the pattern of the correlation bond diagram and cluster analysis described earlier, and serve to confirm their conclusions. It represents one of the principal functions of the City, namely, the provision of services through which the production, transfer and marketing of goods and produce throughout the world is facilitated. Factor 2 contains the capital and investment side of finance and is here termed the financial 'ring' factor. The activities found in the financial core factor (Factor 5) are principally those involved in the daily operations of the money market. Factor 3 consists of those offices whose interests focus on the activities of Fleet Street and the press. Factor 4 isolates textile trading from the international trading activities of Factor 1; this factor also contains some other manufacturing elements which, by chance, are found in similar parts of the City.

What of the activities not represented in Table 2.23? The failure to represent all the variables may have been due to a lack of linearity in the data. Because of the large number of variables and observations, many of the cells in the raw data matrix were empty. To remove this distorting influence, a second data matrix was generated consisting of 'zeros' and 'ones', that represented the presence or absence of a particular type of office in any block. This was subjected to the same analytical procedure to produce an almost identical factor structure – which suggests that the relationships are largely of this binary nature and need not be considered in terms of similarity varying levels of employment. From these results it might be concluded that the unrepresented office types are not fully integrated into the City's activity system and might well be decentralized without serious diseconomies.

[17] R. Cattell, 'Factor Analysis: An Introduction to Essentials', *Biometrics*, Vol. 21, March and June 1965.

FIGURE 2.15

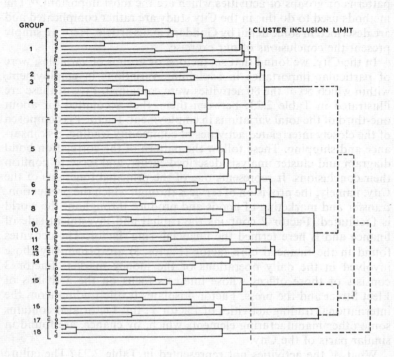

FIGURE 2.15 CLUSTER ANALYSIS: LINKAGE TREE OF ACTIVITIES IN THE CITY

Key to Fig. 2.15

Group 1

a, Other banks (77); b, Mining companies (1); c, Investment and unit trusts (60); d, Stockbrokers and jobbers (59); e, Foreign banks (53); Life and non-life insurance (42); g, Life insurance (40); h, Head offices of firms interested in more than one activity (73); i, Finance Houses (58); j, General wholesale merchants (38).

Group 2

a, Wool dealers (82); b, Construction (19).

Group 3

a, Employers', trade and professional associations (69); b, Other business services (70).

Group 4

a, Grain dealers (75); b, General produce merchants (81); c, Shipping companies (24); d, Non-life insurance (41); e, Other insurance – reinsurance (46); f, Tea and coffee merchants (78); g, Miscellaneous commodity dealers (86); h, London Clearing banks – foreign exchange departments (49); i, Metal dealers (76).

Group 5

a, Lloyd's insurance brokers (43); b, Transport services (28); c, Dealers in other Plantation House commodities (80); d, Port and Inland water transport (25); e, Food, drink and

108

tobacco manufacturers (3); f, Wholesale distribution – grocery and provisions (31); g, Rubber merchants (79); h, Wholesale distribution – tobacco (33); i, Shipbuilding (7); j, Any other transport services (29); k, Underwriters and underwriters' agents (45); l, Chemical manufacturers (4); m, Wholesale distribution – other foods (32); n, Storage associated with transport (30); o, Other insurance brokers (44); p, Import and export merchants (74).

Group 6
a, Accepting houses (57); b, Other registered banks (55); c, London Clearing Banks – other departments (50).

Group 7
a, Timber dealers (85).

Group 8
a, Other finance – building societies, etc. (61); b, Accountants (62); c, Legal services (64); d, London Clearing Banks – ordinary City branches (48); e, Education, medical and religious services (63); f, Retail distribution (39); g, Catering (66).

Group 9
a, Postal services and telecommunications (27).

Group 10
a, Metal manufacturers (5); b, Engineering and electrical goods (6).

Group 11
a, Bricks, pottery and glass (13); b, Metal goods not elsewhere specific (9); Consumer services (67).

Group 12
a, Diamond merchants (84).

Group 13
a, Gas, electricity and water (20).

Group 14
a, Head offices of firms operating overseas (71); b, Wholesale distribution – non-food goods (36); c, Fur dealers (83).

Group 15
a, Paper and board manufacturers (15); b, Wholesale distribution – paper, stationery and books (35); c, Advertising and public relations (68); d, Other publishing (books) (17); e, Publishing of newspapers and periodicals (16); f, Other professional services – consultancy (65); g, Other miscellaneous services (72).

Group 16
a, Other manufacturing industry (18); b, Textile manufacturers (10); c, Leather, leather goods and fur (11); d, Timber and furniture manufacturers (14); e, Clothing and footwear manufacturers (12); f, Wholesale distribution – clothing and footwear (34).

Group 17
a, Vehicle manufacture (8).

Group 18
a, Members of the Discount Market (56); b Scottish and Northern Irish banks (51); c, British Overseas and Commonwealth banks (52); d, London Clearing Banks – Head Offices (47).

THE SPATIAL DISTRIBUTION OF LINKED ACTIVITIES

Finally, what of the spatial distribution of the linked activities just described? To help answer this question, we used the standard scores of the 216 street blocks on all 80 variables to estimate each block's score on each of the factors. The spatial structure of the City's economy may then be summarized in a 215 × 6 matrix of factor scores; although, in doing this, a lot of the original detail is lost. Plotting the scores for each factor enables us to pinpoint those street blocks in which the particular groupings of offices are to be found. Figures 2.16 to 2.19 illustrate the distribution of the top-scoring blocks for four separate factors – trading, the financial core, the financial ring, and publishing and professional services.

Table 2.23. Basic Factors Underlying the Spatial Variation of Employment in the City

Primary variable (No.)	Factor loading
Factor 1. The trading factor	
General produce merchants (81)	−0·65
Transport services (28)	−0·63
Grain dealers (75)	−0·61
Tea and coffee merchants (78)	−0·60
Dealers in other Plantation House commodities (80)	−0·58
Miscellaneous commodity dealers (86)	−0·55
Lloyd's insurance brokers (33)	−0·52
Food, drink and tobacco manufacturers	−0·47
Port and inland water transport (25)	−0·47
Wholesale distribution – grocery and provision (31)	−0·47
Rubber merchants (79)	−0·47
Shipping companies, airlines (24)	−0·45
Other insurance brokers (44)	−0·45
Other insurance – reinsurance (46)	−0·45
Shipbuilding (7)	−0.42
Wholesale distribution – tobacco (33)	−0·39
Metal dealers (76)	−0·39
Import and export merchants (74)	−0·38
Underwriters and underwriters' agents (45)	−0·38
Non-life insurance (41)	−0·37
Factor 2. The financial 'ring' factor	
Stockbrokers and jobbers (59)	0·60
Other finance – building societies, etc. (61)	0·55
Other banks (77)	0·53
Foreign banks (53)	0·53
Investment and unit trusts (60)	0·52
Accountants (62)	0·49
Finance Houses (58)	0·48
Mining companies (1)	0·47
Factor 3. Publishing and professional services factor	
Printing and publishing of newspapers and periodicals (16)	−0·60
Advertising and public relations (68)	−0·59
Other professional services – consultancy (65)	−0·58
Paper and board manufacturers (15)	−0·45
Other business services (70)	−0·41
Wholesale distribution – paper, stationery, books (35)	−0·41
Miscellaneous services (72)	−0·37
Factor 4. Textile trading and other manufacturing factor	
Wholesale distribution – clothing and footwear (34)	0·71
Leather, leather goods and fur (11)	0·60
Textile manufacturers (10)	0·58

Table 2.23.—contd.

Primary variable (No.)	Factor loading
Clothing and footwear manufacturers (12)	0·51
Wood dealers (82)	0·43
Other manufacturing industries (18)	0·43
Construction (19)	0·43
Wholesale distribution – other non-food goods (36)	0·39
Factor 5. The finanacial core factor	
British Overseas and Commonwealth banks (52)	0·74
Scottish and Northern Irish banks (51)	0·68
Members of the Discount Market (56)	0·68
Life and non-life insurance companies (42)	0·50
London clearing banks – head offices (47)	0·42
Non-life insurance (41)	0·41
Other banks (77)	0·41
Life insurance (40)	0·34

Figure 2.16 shows that the City's *trading* activities are mainly grouped east of a line down Bishopsgate to London Bridge and are centred on one of the leading institutions on the City, viz. Lloyd's. The map of the *publishing and professional services factor* (Figure 2.17) depicts the expected localization on Fleet Street, but a number of dispersed blocks with large professional service elements, have lower scores on this factor. The *financial core* (Figure 2.19) activities form an almost continuous zone around the Bank of England; their concentration is strongest to the east of the Bank, and weakest to the north of the Stock Exchange. *Financial ring* activities (Figure 2.18) fill the gap adjacent to the Stock Exchange and then fan out to the north-west of the Bank, around the financial core. The major concentration follows London Wall and Gresham Street, although there are high-scoring blocks scattered elsewhere. These maps confirm the generally held opinion that groups of closely linked activities can be found similarly spaced in particular parts of the City. But to what extent do these activities create activity 'enclaves', from which other types of business are excluded? Visual comparisons of the mapped distributions of factor scores suggests some degree of overlap. But accurate comparison is only possible with multi-dimensional analysis which permits exact measurement of the degree of similarity between blocks with respect to all six basic patterns of variation simultaneously. Once the degree of similarity between each pair of blocks is

111

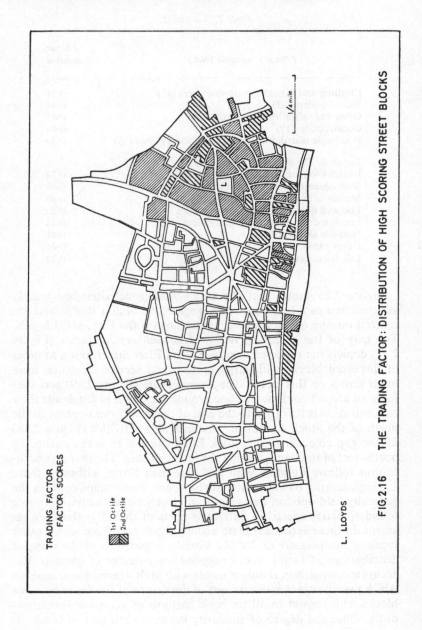

TRADING FACTOR
FACTOR SCORES

1st Octile
2nd Octile

L. LLOYDS

FIG. 2.16   THE TRADING FACTOR: DISTRIBUTION OF HIGH SCORING STREET BLOCKS

¼ mile

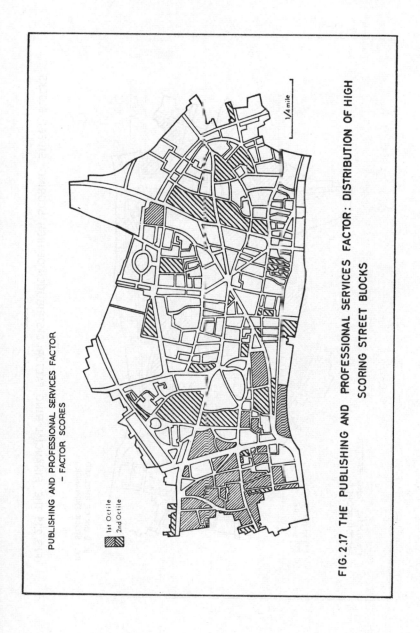

PUBLISHING AND PROFESSIONAL SERVICES FACTOR
– FACTOR SCORES

1st Octile
2nd Octile

1/4 mile

FIG. 2.17 THE PUBLISHING AND PROFESSIONAL SERVICES FACTOR: DISTRIBUTION OF HIGH
SCORING STREET BLOCKS

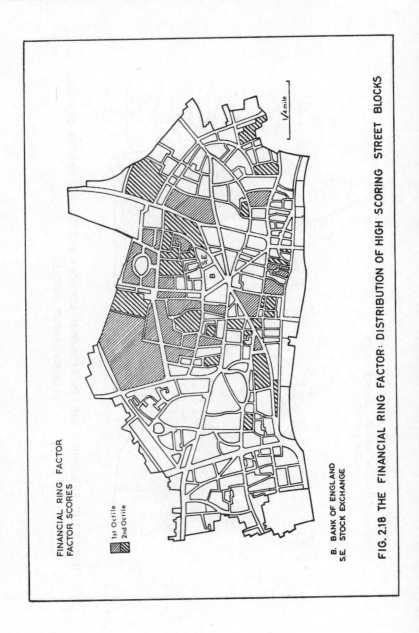

FINANCIAL RING FACTOR
FACTOR SCORES

1st Octile
2nd Octile

B. BANK OF ENGLAND
S.E. STOCK EXCHANGE

1/4 mile

FIG. 2.18 THE FINANCIAL RING FACTOR: DISTRIBUTION OF HIGH SCORING STREET BLOCKS

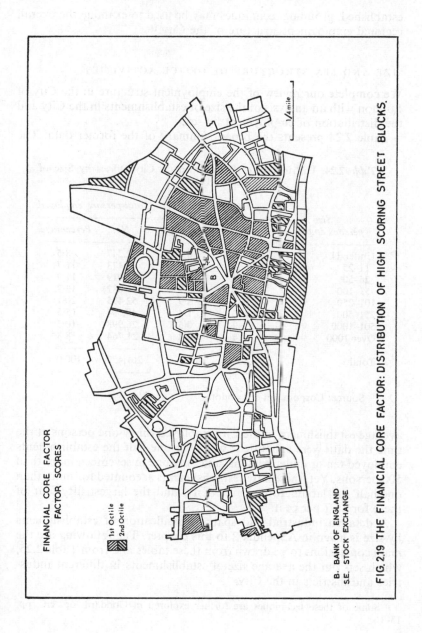

FINANCIAL CORE FACTOR
FACTOR SCORES

1st Octile
2nd Octile

B. BANK OF ENGLAND
S.E. STOCK EXCHANGE

FIG. 2.19 THE FINANCIAL CORE FACTOR: DISTRIBUTION OF HIGH SCORING STREET BLOCKS.

1/4 mile

established, grouping techniques may be used to examine the overall regional employment structure of the City.[18]

SIZE AND SEX STRUCTURE OF OFFICE ACTIVITIES

We complete our review of the employment structure in the City of London with an analysis of the size of establishments in the City and the distribution of employment by sex.

Table 2.24 presents the broad summary of the former data. The

Table 2.24. Distribution of Employment in City Offices by Size of Office 1964–6

Size (persons employed)	Establishments		Total persons employed	
	No.	Percentage	No.	Percentage
Under 11	4,810	56·6	22,247	8·5
11–25	1,832	21·5	30,473	11·7
26–50	853	10·0	31,019	11·9
51–100	500	5·9	35·882	13·7
101–250	335	3·9	52·475	20·1
251–500	116	1·4	40,594	15·5
501–1000	40	0·5	26,998	10·3
Over 1000	14	0·2	21,764	8·3
Total	8,500	100·0	261,452	100·0

Source: Corporation of London.

average establishment in the City employed thirty-one persons at the time the data were submitted; well over one-half the establishments employed ten or under persons, and only one in seventeen more than 500 persons. Yet, these latter establishments accounted for more than one-half the labour force in the City, and the largest fifty-four of these for 18·7 per cent.

A detailed industrial and spatial classification of establishments by size is given in Appendix 2 to this chapter. The following are the main conclusions to be drawn from these tables and from Table 2.25, which sets out the average size of establishments in different industries and districts in the City.

[18] Some of these techniques are further explored in Goddard, op. cit., pp. 13–16.

Table 2.25. Average Size of Office and Other Establishments in the City by Industry and District 1964–6

		Persons employed			*Persons employed*
1	Fleet St	30	1	Banking	124
2	Smithfield	19	2	Other finance	32
3	Barbican	42	3	Insurance	68
4	Thames St	18	4	Wholesale markets	17
5	The Bank	49	5	Commodity markets	14
6	Finsbury Circus	31	6	Shipping	35
7	Houndsditch, Billingsgate	21	7	Professional services	23
			8	Printing and Publishing	36
8	Lloyd's	25			
9	Baltic	35	9	Central offices	23
10	Fenchurch St	35	10	Transport and communication	107
	Average for all	—	11	Income-absorbing	10
	districts	31	12	Others	47
				Average for all industry	— 31

Source: Corporation of London.

1. Apart from the unusual size distribution of establishments in the transport and communications industry – where one office accounts for more than 70 per cent of the total employment – the insurance and banking sectors are the most dominated by large establishments; while the proportion of small establishments is above average in commodity and wholesale markets, professional services and income-absorbing activities. These differences in size structure largely reflect the type of operations undertaken in these sectors.

2. As one would expect from this conclusion and our analysis earlier in this chapter, large establishments tend to be geographically concentrated in the Bank district; indeed, of the fifty-four establishments employing more than 500 people, twenty-two are in this district. The Barbican and Baltic districts also have more than their share of large offices. By contrast more than 95 per cent of the establishments in the Smithfield, Thames Street, and Houndsditch and Billingsgate districts employ 50 people or less.

Finally, our data reveal some interesting information on the sex

117

structure of establishments in the City. Table 2.26 shows that, on average, women account for two-fifths of all workers in City offices and shops, and that this ratio holds, at least approximately, for most of the main activities. The chief exceptions are income-absorbing activities (which includes catering and retail establishments) and, to a lesser extent, insurance where the proportion of women employed is above the average. The proportion is less than the average in transport and communications, wholesale markets and shipping.

Table 2.26. Distribution of Employment by Sex and Industry in City Offices 1964–6

		Male	Female	Total	Percentage female
1	Banking	27,985	22,020	50,005	44·0
2	Other finance	15,370	8,909	24,279	36·7
3	Insurance	25,303	24,519	49,822	49·2
4	Wholesale markets	11,048	4,564	15,612	29·2
5	Commodity markets and merchanting	8,935	5,096	14,031	36·3
6	Shipping	14,525	6,422	20,947	30·7
7	Professional and business services	20,435	12,400	32,835	37·5
8	Printing and publishing	6,911	6,266	13,177	47·6
9	Central offices of manufacturing firms	7,589	4,786	12,375	38·7
10	Transport and communication	5,451	437	5,888	7·4
11	Income-absorbing	6,870	9,089	15,959	57·0
12	Others	4,249	2,273	6,522	34·9
	Total	154,671	106,781	261,452	40·8

Table 2.26 confirms the findings of the Censuses of Population. The City employs a slightly higher proportion of female labour than does the national economy, but this is principally because it accounts for a larger proportion of activities most dependent on female labour. But, *within* particular enterprises, the City usually employs less female labour than the national average. In insurance, banking and finance, for example, from information given to us by individual firms and trade associations, it would seem this percentage is declining.

CROWN OFFICES

Data on the numbers employed in Crown Offices were made available to us by H.M. Inspector of Factories. There are 123 of these offices, which at the time the statistics were submitted (between May 1964 and December 1966) employed 24,481 people in the City. Some 16,028 of these work for the General Post Office. Two other Government departments – Customs and Excise and the Board of Trade (which also has oversight of the Export Credit Guarantees Department) – employ more than 1,000 each. A breakdown of the labour force of Crown Offices is given in Table 2.27. These figures largely speak for themselves but it is interesting to observe that the six largest Crown Office Establishments account for nearly one-half of all Crown Office employment. The G.P.O. is by far the largest single employer in the City.

These figures do not, of course, include employment in public corporations or other nationalized undertakings. Neither do they take account of the labour force in local authority undertakings. These latter data, which have been provided for us separately by the relevant authorities, are given in Table 2.28. In addition, the number at railway stations and British Rail offices within the City is 862.

When all these figures are added together, employment in publicly owned undertakings in the City is seen to be just over 31,000, between 8 and 10 per cent of our estimate of the total employment in the City in 1966.

FACTORY EMPLOYMENT

The final set of data we wish to briefly analyse in this chapter is that obtained from H.M. Inspector of Factories records. Like the data collected under the Offices, Shops and Railway Premises Act, H.M.I.F. statistics are collected, not at a particular moment of time, but over a period of time – in this case, mostly between 1964 and 1966.

Table 2.29 presents a fairly detailed breakdown of factory employment in the City. The total figure of 21,195 is some 1,864 more than in 1957. This increase is entirely due to a rise in employment in paper, printing and publishing: the rest of the labour force in manufacturing industry has remained stable or is falling slightly. Apart from the clothing and footwear industry, no other manufacturing industry in the City now employs more than 400 people.

There are 596 factories in the City. The most numerous are in

119

Table 2.27. Distribution of Crown Office Employment in the City 1964-6

	G.P.O.	H.M. Customs and Excise	Inland Revenue	Treasury	Board of Trade	Ministry of Labour	Export Credit Guarantee	Ministry of Social Security	Other	Total
Fleet St	2,926	15	44	169	1,444				379	4,977
Smithfield	6,099	5	133	26		114			900	7,118
Barbican	3,369	476	28				720		19	4,267
Thames St	1,913		23						39	2,456
The Bank	388		230		15		364		508	1,298
Finsbury Circus	936	54	102					64		1,284
Houndsditch	225	894						108	55	1,384
Billingsgate										
Lloyd's	47								25	72
Baltic	95		82				28			205
Fenchurch St	30	1,285	68		37					1,420
Total	16,028	2,729	710	195	1,496	114	1,112	172	1,925	24,481

Source: H.M. Inspectorate of Factories.

Table 2.28. Distribution of Local Authority Employment in the City 1967

Corporation of London	1,193
Ambulance Service	44
Fire Service	78
Salvage Corps	95
St Bartholomew's Hospital	3,110
Central Criminal Court	265
Police, wardens, civilians and cadets	1,035
	5,820

Source: Corporation of London.

Table 2.29. Distribution of Factory Employment in the City 1966

S.I.C. order

III	Food, drink and tobacco	138
VI	Engineering and electrical goods	231
XI	Leather, leather goods and fur (of which fur 332)	361
XII	Clothing and footwear (of which women's and girls' outerwear 592, dresses, lingerie, etc. 839)	1,919
XV	Paper, printing and publishing (of which printing, publishing of newspapers and periodicals 12,429; Bookbinding, engraving 3,474)	16,067
IV, VII, IX, X, XIV, XVI	Other manufacturing industry	371
	All manufacturing industry	19,087
XVII	Construction	39
XVIII	Gas, electricity and water	52
XIX	Transport and communications	450
XX	Distributive trades (of which wholesale distribution 577)	468
XXI	Insurance, banking and finance	615
XXII, XXIII, XXIV	Other service trades	484
	All service trades	2,108
	Total	21,195

Source: H.M. Inspectorate of Factories.

121

paper, printing and publishing (157) and in clothing and footwear (120). The average number employed in an establishment is 36 – about the same as in offices: this varies considerably from 102 in paper and publishing, to 6 in engineering and electrical goods. There are 416 establishments which employ 10 people or under and only 22 that employ more than 100. The furniture trade, which was at one time quite important in the City, now employs only 64 people in 12 plants.

Spatially, the distribution of factory operatives is strongly concentrated in the Fleet Street district which houses 14 of the 22 establishments employing 100 or more people. In terms of the numbers of establishments, Fleet Street also heads the list with 182; the Houndsditch/Billingsgate area is second with 138 followed by Thames Street (85) and Smithfield (75). Table 2.30 also shows some interesting geographical concentrations *within* particular industries. Apart from the paper, printing and publishing industry which is strongly localized in the Fleet Street district, clothing establishments strongly favour the Houndsditch/Billingsgate district; and engineering and electrical establishments the Fleet Street/Smithfield district. All the other industries (apart from the 'hotchpotch' of miscellaneous services) are pretty well dispersed in the City.

There are no obvious linkages between different types of factory establishments, except perhaps between paper, printing, publishing, and the engineering and electrical industries both localized in the Fleet Street district. Some of the latter factories, and probably some of those classified under miscellaneous services as well, are little more than maintenance or repair shops for the publishing business or for service industries (e.g. advertising agencies, etc.) associated with this business. As between factory and non-factory trades, the closest links are (a) the paper, printing and publishing and miscellaneous services, sectors with professional and business services and central offices (in the Fleet Street district); (b) clothing establishments with shipping, commodity markets and income-absorbing activities in the Houndsditch/Billingsgate district; and (c) the leather and fur industry with commodity markets in the Thames Street district.

CONCLUSIONS AND SUMMARY

Our statistical review of the economy of the City is now virtually complete but there are certain activities in the City about which we have not been able to obtain detailed data. These are:

122

Table 2.30. Distribution of Factory Establishments by S.I.C. Orders and District 1964-6

	III	VI	XI	XII	XV	XVI*	XVII	XVIII	XIX	XX	XXI	XXII	XXIII	XXIV	Total
Fleet St	1	15	5	11	88	14	2	2	2	8	1		33		182
Smithfield	2	7	17	17	11	9			2	5		1	4		75
Barbican				2	2				1	3	1		6	2	19
Thames St	2	6	19	10	15	7	2		2	16		1	6		85
The Bank		2		6	8	3	2			4	9		3		38
Finsbury Circus		1			1		1				3		2		10
Houndsditch, Billingsgate	4	4	9	62	19	11	3	2	5	11	1	1	8		138
Lloyd's	1			6	2					1			1		12
Baltic	2	1	1	5	7	3	2			4					26
Fenchurch St	1			1	4					4			1		11
Total	12	38	51	120	157	48	12	5	13	56	15	2	64	3	596

S.I.C. orders

* Including IV, VII, IX, X and XIV.
Source: as for Table 2.29.

(i) the distribution of employment in offices attached to factory premises,

(ii) the non-operative workers employed in factories,

(iii) employment in warehouses belonging to the owners, trustees or conservators of docks, wharves or quays.

According to information supplied to us by the Corporation of London category (i) employed 6,750 in 1966, the great majority of which were in paper, printing and publishing. There is no way of estimating the numbers involved in category (ii). We suspect them to be small, as most publishing firms operate independent offices in close proximity to the factories. We do not think employment would exceed 1,000; it may be much less. As regards category (iii), we know from the employment survey of the City Corporation that there are 10,270 employed in warehousing activities. Our own estimates based on Offices, Shops and Railway Premises data show a figure of 9,034; in addition those employed in warehousing activities attached to factories will have been included in H.M.I.F. statistics: we do not, however, think these to be large. It might be fair to assume that 1,250 are employed in dock warehouses.

Finally, as we have pointed out earlier, the O.S.R.P. returns do not represent a complete census of every office activity. But when considered in the light of the Corporation's own Survey and the occupational tables of the 1961 Census, we do not think that a 'grossing up' to cover errors and omissions of more than 10 per cent would be justifiable.

Our final estimate of the level and distribution of the City's employment for the 1964–6 period is presented in Table 2.31. At 349,410, it is about 10 per cent less than the estimate given in the Census of Population for 1961 and 5·5 per cent less than that of the Census for 1966. There are various reasons for this difference; it is, for example, important to remember that both the 1961 and the 1966 'place of work' tables were derived from a 10 per cent sample only. Also, our figure is largely based on the number of people working in the City at a given moment of time; it does not allow for shift-working as the Census does.

It would be impossible to give an adequate summary of this chapter but we would underline the following four points.

1. The City is a highly specialized and closely interwoven network of commercial and financial activities.
2. Its occupational structure is strongly biased towards high-grade office employment and a high value added per employee; there is

124

evidence that this occupational specialization is becoming even more marked with the passing of time.

3. There are very considerable spatial linkages between many industries and sub-industries in the City. This results in a number of separate clusters of activities, the value of each individual activity being highly dependent on the close proximity of other activities.

Table 2.31. Estimated Total Employment in the City 1964–6

1. *Offices, Shops and Railway Premises Return*
   - (a) Independent Offices   252,418
   - (b) Warehousing and canteens   9,034
   - (c) Crown offices   24,481
   - (d) Offices attached to factories   6,750

        292,693
   - (e) Estimated errors and omissions of (a),   26,840
     (b) and (d)

        319,533

2. *Public Authority Employment*
   - (a) Office   1,193
   - (b) Railway premises   862
   - (c) Other   4,627

        6,682

3. *H.M. Inspector of Factories Returns*   21,195

4. Estimates of employment in dock warehouses
   and of non-operatives in factories   2,000

        349,410

4. The average size of most establishments in the City is small. This chiefly reflects the function of the activities carried out. Increasingly the City is becoming the hub of decision-taking in most financial and commercial activities. The routine operations are gradually being dispersed. Since it is in precisely this area where the need for close linkages is most strongly felt, this increases the 'package deal' value of the City still further

125

Appendix 1

CLASSIFICATION OF OFFICE ACTIVITIES IN THE CITY BY SUB-ACTIVITY

1. Agriculture, forestry, fishing, mining and quarrying.
3. Food, drink and tobacco.
4. Chemical and allied industries.
5. Metal manufacture.
6. Engineering and electrical goods.
7. Shipbuilding and marine engineering.
8. Vehicles.
9. Metal goods not elsewhere specified.
10. Textiles.
11. Leather, leather goods and fur.
13. Bricks, pottery, glass and cement.
14. Timber, furniture, etc.
15. Paper and board manufacture.
16. Printing, publishing of newspapers and periodicals.
17. Other printing and publishing (books).
18. Other manufacturing industries.
19. Construction.
20. Gas, electricity and water.
21. Rail transport, road passenger transport and road haulage.
24. Sea and air transport – shipping companies and airlines.
25. Port and inland water transport (Port of London Authority).
27. Postal services and telecommunications.
28. Transport services – ship and freight brokers, shipping and forwarding agents.
29. Any other transport services – travel agents.
30. Storage associated with transport – bonded warehouses.
31. Wholesale distribution – grocery and provisions.
32. Wholesale distribution – other food.
33. Wholesale distribution – tobacco.
34. Wholesale distribution – footwear and textiles.
35. Wholesale distribution – paper, stationery and books.
36. Wholesale distribution – other non-food goods.

38. Wholesale distribution – general wholesale merchants.
39. Retail distribution.
40. Life insurance.
41. Non-life insurance.
42. Life and non-life insurance combined.
43. Lloyd's insurance brokers.
44. Other insurance brokers.
45. Underwriters and underwriters' agents.
46. Other insurance (reinsurance brokers, insurance agents).
47. London Clearing Banks – headquarters offices.
48. London Clearing Banks – ordinary City branches.
49. London Clearing Banks – foreign exchange departments.
50. London Clearing Banks – any other departments.
51. Scottish and N. Irish banks.
52. British Overseas and Commonwealth banks.
53. Foreign banks.
55. Other banks registered with the Bank of England.
56. Members of the Discount Market.
57. Accepting houses.
58. Finance houses.
59. Stockbrokers and jobbers.
60. Investment and unit trusts.
61. Other finance – building societies, property companies.
62. Accountants.
63. Education, medical and religious services.
64. Legal services.
65. Other professional services – consultancy.
66. Catering and hotels.
67. Consumer services.
68. Advertising agents and public relations consultants.
69. Employers', trade and professional associations.
70. Any other business services – employment agencies, typing, etc.
71. Head offices of firms operating abroad.
72. Miscellaneous services not elsewhere specified.
73. Head offices of firms interested in more than one activity.
74. Import and export merchants.
75. Grain dealers.
76. Metal dealers.
77. All other banks.
78. Tea and coffee merchants.
79. Rubber merchants.
80. Dealers in other commodities handled by Plantation House.

81. General produce merchants.
82. Wool dealers.
83. Fur dealers.
84. Diamond merchants.
85. Timber dealers.
86. Miscellaneous commodity dealers.

(N.B. The terms 'merchant' or 'dealer' are used loosely to cover all firms concerned with the product, including brokers and importers.)

Appendix 2

SUPPLEMENTARY STATISTICAL TABLES
(All derived from O.S.R.P. data)

Table 2.32. Total Office Employment in the City by Size Group and Sub-activity

Sub-activity No.	Size group – employment										Total
	1–10	11–25	26–50	51–75	76–100	101–250	251–500	561–750	751–1,000	1,001+	
1	6										6
2	29	52				294	454		921		1,750
3	48	88	175	75		874	766				2,026
4	108	177	106	74	88	490					1,043
5	61	31			180	411					683
6	256	297	281	258		298		530			1,920
7	54	67									121
8	2						500				502
9	53	40									93
10	249	194	141	129		219					932
11	38	14									52
12	114	48	123								285
13	43	43				101					187
14	57	55	88	174	84						458
15	292	120	308				318		803		1,841
16	264	305	691	494	619	1,383	1,008	1,035			5,799
17	446	654	620	710	256	1,282	749		820		5,537
18	119	55	95	61	100		385	565			715
19	150	149	118	54		566					1,390
20	13		60			456	1,313	509	850		2,856
21	16	19	91	56							582
22	5	12	28								101
23	62	73	27	252	181	1,081					162
24	77	142	298	106		293	2,540		919		5,080
25	145	232	267								1,962
26	26	26									52
27	37	83					664			4,207	4,991

130

28	1,254	2,158	2,791	1,623	522	3,146	1,906	505			13,905
29	71	24	72								167
30	184	82	139	70		146	262			1,226	2,109
31	395	324	254	60	88	236	428				1,785
32	936	1,834	827	708		243					4,548
33	40	21	46								107
34	396	304	192	181	78	301	592				2,044
35	330	465	215	184		697					1,891
36	15		108	57	171	242					593
37	432	452	196	182	351	442	535				2,590
38	193	299	292	239		363	668				2,054
39	3,091	1,115	452	275		139					5,072
40	73	336	455	201	256	2,458	1,597	673	850	1,060	7,959
41	214	406	563	981	429	1,843	757	700			5,893
42	108	271	507	446	761	2,493	4,437	1,796		1,508	12,327
43	297	927	1,623	888	1,256	3,670	4,611	1,569	2,426	1,225	18,492
44	283	151	192	54	280	206	724				1,890
45	243	237	332	112	174	114					1,212
46	183	298	177	441	92	202	656				2,049
47	8		117			459	718		1,636	5,162	8,100
48	68	896	1,303	659	460	1,452	2,567	629	1,660	4,661	14,355
49						250	652	1,167	928	1,275	3,576
50	19	16	150	136	264	847	1,879	678			4,099
51					258	672					964
52	8	15	148	360	522	2,182	838	1,399			5,814
53	10	37	111	51	177	540	591				1,727
54	43	67	347	183	381	690	313				2,024
55	5	137	163	51	79	927	271				1,633
56		45	314	68							427
57	40	33	79	326	278	796	1,305	524			3,381
58	9	46	40		84	200	488				867
59	663	1,849	2,865	2,439	2,432	4,572	251				15,071
60	178	259	176	54	81	101					849
61	799	1,058	1,140	382	516	1,027	601	529		1,440	7,492

132

Table 2.32.—contd.

Sub-activity No.	\multicolumn{11}{c}{Size group – employment}
	1–10	11–25	26–50	51–75	76–100	101–250	251–500	561–750	751–1,000	1,001+	Total
62	901	1,890	1,764	1,421	1,432	2,680	691	628			11,407
63	116	116	28			158	399				817
64	669	1,607	1,595	415	287	1,937	256				6,766
65	829	916	1,082	490	265	541					4,123
66	1,438	3,135	2,034	419	425	1,086					8,537
67	160	101	157					512			930
68	269	431	451	367	98	633		670			2,919
69	455	516	554	201	425	396	336				2,883
70	626	581	800	170	171	1,148	1,241				4,737
71	116	111	62								289
72	220	95	45	74		169					603
73	46	99	224	54	184	346	360				1,313
74	1,246	1,658	847	724	625	743	297				6,140
75	189	150	182	179	89	230					1,019
76	81	152	268		92	155					748
77	108	408	224	203	525	1,600	270	567			3,905
78	154	226	333	58		179	400				1,350
79	66	75	31			122					294
80	225	268	28	106	170	360					1,157
81	253	252	230	260	91						1,086
82	53	71									124
83	387	100	27			126					640
84	25	12									37
85	110	152	46	53	186	139					686
86	147	213	67			323					750
Total	22,247	30,473	31,019	19,222	16,660	52,475	40,594	15,185	11,813	21,764	261,452

For identification of Sub-activity number see Appendix 2.1.

Table 2.33. Total Office Employment in the City by Size Group and Sub-district

Sub-district No.	Size Group – employment										Total
	1–10	11–25	26–50	51–75	76–100	101–250	251–500	501–750	751–1,000	1,001+	
1	284	298	555	316	368	1,503	285				3,609
2	99	221	365	318	98	1,032	286	670			3,089
3	531	681	910	533	618	1,216	1,112				5,601
4	513	655	729	668	382	802	360	508			4,617
5	168	330	159	74		752	618			1,440	3,541
6	307	244	436			340	1,230	1,041			3,598
7	142	200	227	59		691					1,319
8	62	145	175	114							496
9	699	1,874	962	755	80	318	907			1,226	6,821
10	479	422	183	261	100	511	370	700	820		3,846
11	506	481	123	54	176		309				1,649
12	930	827	653	451	188	519		505			4,073
13	260	449	235	70	100	542					1,656
14	128	225	278	125	84	678	1,349	527	850		4,244
15	75	56	35	65							231
16	545	579	527	306	78	354	304				2,693
17	126	346	501	660	328	2,047	394				4,882
18	61	148	245	188	360	642	461				2,105
19	316	337	499	192	81	751	900				3,076
20	113	196	29	105		463	259		803		1,968
21	110	217	123	141	99	397	1,554	628			3,269
22	704	551	302	454	89	121	760	565			3,546
23	291	395	835	112	362	364	687	524	850		4,420
24	251	479	706	418	184	1,684	1,528	530		1,060	6,840
25	579	992	1,151	912	1,062	3,466	922			1,400	10,484
26	255	566	388	176	723	1,318	583		762	1,257	6,028
27	396	613	579	173	190	1,426	971	678		1,508	6,534
28	388	296	507	426	279	339					2,235

Table 2.33.—contd.

Sub-district No.	1– 10	11– 25	26– 50	51– 75	76– 100	101– 250	251– 500	501– 750	751– 1,000	1,001 +	Total
29	848	961	890	233	184	768	935		815	1,015	6,649
30	192	540	472	536	614	1,696	1,110	1,183	1,564		7,907
31	350	293	167	69	87	148	1,264	569		2,522	5,469
32	638	1,620	1,677	1,377	1,671	1,953	611				9,547
33	883	1,235	1,620	955	607	1,893	454		921		8,568
34	1,091	1,298	913	296	523	502	567				5,190
35	401	521	565	657	630	2,560	2,250		893	2,246	10,723
36	124	323	359	381	366	1,655	1,348	629	874	1,383	7,442
37	158	156	463	71	445	1,765	2,430	587			6,075
38	905	875	372	182	269	1,228		1,174			5,005
39	504	553	408	346	100	446				1,275	3,632
40	920	911	740	294	333	1,098	872	1,277			6,445
41	321	671	1,189	298	622	1,237	2,476	567		4,207	11,588
42	838	890	1,108	375		1,338	1,172				5,721
43	511	954	1,136	634	335	1,387	1,255	673			6,885
44	729	919	1,051	528	824	2,243	1,020				7,314
45	355	1,004	1,215	1,644	708	2,883	2,450				10,259
46	342	321	349	271	100	396	1,317			1,225	4,321
47	461	697	823	428	431	727	280		1,847		5,694
48	556	550	569	423	263	1,425					3,786
49	390	435	675	215	370	569	257		814		3,725
50	279	240	121	54	264	486	1,228				2,672
51	411	600	703	415	165	264					2,558
52	136	289	148		79	308		624			1,584
53	417	715	672	342	280	950	280	517			4,173
54	169	79	117	72	161	274	669	509			2,050
Total	22,247	30,473	31,019	19,222	16,660	52,475	40,594	15,185	11,813	21,764	261,452

Size Group – employment

For identification of sub-districts see Fig. 2.1 of Report.

Table 2.34. Number of Office Establishments in the City by Size Group and Sub-activity

Sub-activity No.	Size group employment										Total
	1–10	11–25	26–50	51–75	76–100	101–250	251–500	501–750	751–1,000	1,000+	
1	1										1
2	5	4				2	1		1		13
3	11	6	4	1		6	2				30
4	26	10	3	1	1	2					43
5	17	2			2	3					24
6	58	18	8	4		2		1			91
7	15	4									19
8	1						1				2
9	16	2									18
10	74	12	4	2		1					93
11	9	1									10
12	29	3	4								36
13	12	2				1					15
14	12	3	2	3	1						21
15	56	7	4	1	1		2				71
16	52	18	19	8	7	8	1	3	1		117
17	92	42	19	11	3	8	2		1		178
18	40	4	3	1			1				49
19	36	8	8	2	1				1		56
20	3	1	2	1		3	4				14
21	4	1	2			2					9
22	1		2	1							4
23	17	4	1								22
24	17	8	8	4	2	7	7	1			54
25	25	15	7	2		2			1		52
26	5	2									7
27	5	5					2			1	13

135

Table 2.34.—contd.

Size group – Employment

Sub-activity No.	1–10	11–25	26–50	51–75	76–100	101–250	251–500	501–750	751–1,000	1,001+	Total
28	217	134	76	27	6	19	5	1			485
29	13	2	2								17
30	40	5	4	1		1	1			1	53
31	79	21	8	1	1	1	1				112
32	187	108	24	11		2					332
33	8	1	1								10
34	101	19	5	3	1	2	2				133
35	70	30	6	3		5					114
36	3		3	1	2	2					11
37	91	30	5	3	4	3	2				138
38	41	19	8	4		2	2				76
39	808	74	13	5		1					901
40	11	19	13	3	3	16	5	1	1	1	73
41	37	22	14	16	5	13	2	1			110
42	18	15	14	7	9	16	12	3		1	95
43	53	52	43	14	14	23	13	3	3	1	219
44	63	9	5	1	3	2	2				85
45	61	14	9	2	2	1					89
46	32	16	5	7	1	1	2				64
47	1		3			2	7				13
48	9	49	38	11	5	9	2		2	4	135
49						1	2	2		1	6
50			4	2	3	6	2		1		21
51	2	1			3	4					10
52	1	1	4	6	6	13	5	1			38
53	3	2	3	1	2	3	1				15
54	7	4	9	3	4	5	1				33
55	1	8	4	1	1	5	1				21
56		2	9	1							12

	4,801	1,832	853	312	188	335	116	26	14	14	8,500
57	8	2	2	5	3	5	4	1			30
58	2	3	1		1	1	1				9
59	133	103	76	40	27	31	1				411
60	33	15	5	1	1	1		1		1	56
61	176	64	32	6	6	7	2	1			295
62	152	112	48	22	16	17	2				370
63	41	8	1			1	1				52
64	130	98	44	7	3	14					297
65	162	54	30	8	3	3					260
66	245	188	58	7	5	7					510
67	41	6	4					1			52
68	59	29	13	6	1	4	1	1			113
69	109	32	15	3	5	3	3				168
70	150	36	21	3	2	8					223
71	25	7	2								34
72	46	6	1	1	2	1	1				55
73	12	6	6	1	7	2	1				30
74	267	92	24	12	1	6					409
75	38	11	5	3	1	1					59
76	18	10	7		6						37
77	19	24	7	3		9	1	1			70
78	38	13	8	1	1	1	1				62
79	14	4	1		2						20
80	44	17	1	2	2	2					68
81	54	17	6	4	1						82
82	14	5									19
83	119	6	1	1	2	1					127
84	5	1									6
85	21	10	1		1	1					36
86	39	14	2		2	2					57
Total	4,801	1,832	853	312	188	335	116	26	14	14	8,500

For an identification of sub-activity numbers see Appendix 1.

137

Table 2.35. Number of Office Establishments in the City by Size Group and Sub-district

Sub-district No.	Size group										Total
	1–10	11–25	26–50	51–75	76–100	101–250	251–500	501–750	751–1,000	1,000+	
1	64	18	15	5	4	9	1				116
2	19	13	10	5	1	6	1	1			56
3	120	45	25	9	7	7	3				216
4	109	42	20	11	4	6	1	1			194
5	35	21	4	1		5	2			1	69
6	59	16	11			2	3	2			93
7	32	13	7	1		4					57
8	13	9	6	2							30
9	135	110	27	12	1	2	3	1		1	291
10	96	25	5	4	1	3	1		1		137
11	98	31	4	1	2		1	1			137
12	229	51	17	7	2	4					311
13	65	27	7	2	1	4					105
14	37	15	8	2	1	4	4	1	1		73
15	16	3	1	1							21
16	141	34	14	5	1	3	1	1			199
17	31	20	16	11	6	13	2				99
18	14	9	6	3	4	4	1				41
19	88	22	13	3	1	5	2				134
20	21	10	1	2		3	1	1	1		89
21	20	13	3	2	1	3	4	1			47
22	147	32	10	7	1	1	2	1	1		201
23	63	22	22	2	4	3	2	1			120
24	52	30	19	7	2	11	5	1		1	128
25	122	57	31	15	12	20	2			1	260
26	54	33	11	3	8	9	2		1	1	122

Sub-district	4,810	1,1832	853	312	188	335	116	26	14	14	8,500
27	87	39	18	3	2	10	3			1	164
28	97	18	13	7	3	2					140
29	185	54	24	4	2	5	3	1			279
30	45	33	12	9	7	10	3		1	1	123
31	90	18	5	1	1	1	4	2	2		122
32	127	94	46	23	19		2	1			325
33	196	74	44	16	7	14	1			1	351
34	234	81	26	5	6	12	2		1		358
35	85	30	16	10	7	4	7	1			175
36	30	18	10	6	4	17	3	1	1	1	84
37	28	8	12	1	5	10	6	2	1		72
38	210	56	11	3	3	11					293
39	97	34	12	5	1	8	3				153
40	182	54	21	5	4	3	7	2		1	279
41	60	39	32	5	7	8	3	1			160
42	189	51	31	6		8	3				288
43	105	60	30	10	4	8	3	1			222
44	156	54	30	8	10	8	7				275
45	69	57	32	27	8	9	4				218
46	79	19	10	4	1	14	1			1	121
47	104	43	23	7	5	18 3					189
48	115	33	16	7	3	4			2		182
49	81	28	19	3	4	8	1				140
50	58	16	3	1	3	3	3		1		86
51	77	34	19	7	2	2					141
52	27	18	4		1	2	1	1			53
53	81	43	18	6	3	6	2	1			159
54	36	5	3	1	2	2	2				52
Total	4,810	1,1832	853	312	188	335	116	26	14	14	8,500

For an identification of sub-district numbers see Figure 2.1. in the report.

Table 2.36. Percentage of Office Establishments in Main Activities by District 1964-6

District \ Activity	Banking	Other finance	Insurance	Wholesale markets	Commodity markets	Shipping	Professional services	Printing and Publishing	Central offices	Transport	Income-absorbing	Other
Fleet St	5·69	3·89	2·86	11·99	5·4	1·69	22·99	62·84	15·31	7·27	17·01	13·57
Smithfield	1·98	0·78	0·41	26·89	2·85	1·35	3·14	3·55	11·15	10·91	4·39	12·14
Barbican	6·93	6·36	2·99	4·75	3·46	0·85	5·73	1·37	9·26	3·64	4·84	4·29
Thames St	4·21	4·67	4·35	10·26	17·92	4·57	11·18	10·93	13·61	7·27	8·03	13·57
The Bank	38·61	25·55	16·6	4·86	12·02	7·95	17·4	7·38	9·83	12·73	16·88	10·71
Finsbury Circus	17·82	40·08	4·76	2·27	6·31	2·2	13·63	4·37	8·32	3·64	10·25	4·29
Houndsditch, Billingsgate	6·93	6·74	9·39	25·38	17·41	22·34	12·65	4·64	14·18	29·09	20·0	24·29
Lloyd's	4·46	3·76	37·01	3·13	5·9	12·18	4·05	1·09	4·73	3·64	7·83	2·86
Baltic	8·17	4·41	14·01	4·86	11·1	36·21	5·31	2·73	7·94	18·18	6·43	10·0
Fenchurch St	5·2	3·76	7·62	5·62	17·62	10·66	3·91	1·09	5·67	3·64	4·33	4·29
Total	100	100	100	100	100	100	100	100	100	100	100	100

Table 2.37. Percentage of Office Establishments in Districts by Main Activity 1964–8

Districts \ Activity	Banking	Other finance	Insurance	Wholesale markets	Commodity markets	Shipping	Professional services	Printing and Publishing	Central offices	Transport	Income-absorbing	Others	Total
Fleet St	1·95	2·55	1·78	9·42	4·5	0·85	27·93	19·52	6·88	0·34	22·67	1·61	100
Smithfield	1·57	1·17	0·59	48·73	5·48	1·57	8·81	2·54	11·55	1·17	13·5	3·33	100
Barbican	6·97	12·19	5·47	10·95	8·46	1·24	20·4	1·24	12·19	0·5	18·91	1·49	100
Thames St	2·11	4·48	3·98	11·82	21·89	3·36	19·9	4·98	8·96	0·5	15·67	2·36	100
The Bank	12·0	15·15	9·38	3·46	9·08	3·62	19·15	2·08	4·0	0·54	20·38	1·15	100
Finsbury Circus	7·69	33·01	3·74	2·24	6·62	1·39	20·83	1·71	4·7	0·21	17·2	0·64	100
Houndsditch, Billingsgate	2·11	3·93	5·21	17·75	12·92	9·97	13·67	1·28	5·66	1·21	23·72	2·57	100
Lloyd's	2·59	4·18	39·19	4·18	8·36	10·37	8·36	0·58	3·6	0·29	17·72	0·58	100
Baltic	4·17	4·3	13·02	5·69	13·78	27·05	9·61	1·26	5·31	1·26	12·77	1·77	100
Fenchurch St	3·75	5·18	10·0	9·29	30·89	11·25	10·0	0·71	5·36	0·36	12·14	1·07	100

Appendix 3

THE CENSUS OF POPULATION, 1966

Subsequent to the completion of our study, the results of the *Census of Population* for 1966 was published. This was a 10 per cent sample Census and was subject to severe statistical limitations[1] – particularly at a local authority level. Nevertheless, we reproduce data from three of the tables of this Census which are particularly relevant to the economic structure of the City, and compare these with those of Central London and England and Wales as a whole.

Even allowing for the large margin of error the implications of these data are quite clear. We would highlight just three points compared with 1961.

1. The City has slightly increased its industrial specialization. For example, those employed in insurance, banking and finance have risen from 31·2 per cent to 34·8 per cent of the total labour force. This particular activity has, however, increased rather more markedly in other parts of England and Wales, as have most of the other services in which the City specializes.

2. Clerical workers dominate the City's occupational structure. The Square Mile also has more than its average share of other white-collar workers – particularly administrators and managers. Apart from paper and printing workers, those engaged in secondary industry account for only a very small proportion of the labour force in the City.

3. Junior non-manual workers account for 51·2 per cent of the total employment in the City, classified by socio-economic groups, compared with 21·5 per cent in England and Wales. All kinds of administrative and professional workers are also particularly well represented while, compared with a national average of 45·5 per cent, only 18·2 per cent of the City's workers are classified as manual workers.

[1] Further particulars are given in G.R.O., *Sample Census, 1966, England and Wales*, workplace and transport tables, Part 1, 1968.

142

Table 2.38. Employment by Industry in the City, Other Central London, and England and Wales 1966

Industry orders	Employment (thousands)			Percentage of total employment		
	City of London	Central London	England and Wales	City of London	Central London	England and Wales
1 Agriculture, forestry, fishing	0·0	0·7	645	0·0	0·0	2·9
2 Mining and quarrying	0·1	1·7	503	0·0	0·1	2·3
3 Food, drink and tobacco	3·7	30·6	652	1·0	1·8	3·0
4 Chemicals and allied industries	3·0	21·7	460	0·8	1·3	2·1
5 Metal manufacture	0·5	5·0	536	0·1	0·3	2·4
6 Engineering and electrical goods	4·7	60·1	2,013	1·3	3·6	9·2
7 Shipbuilding and marine engineering	0·2	0·6	130	0·0	0·0	0·6
8 Vehicles	0·1	5·0	768	0·0	0·3	3·5
9 Metal goods not elsewhere specified	1·3	18·6	535	0·4	1·1	2·4
10 Textiles	1·1	8·4	628	0·3	0·5	2·9
11 Leather, leather goods and fur	0·7	10·0	55	0·2	0·6	0·2
12 Clothing and footwear	3·0	58·5	485	0·8	3·5	2·2
13 Bricks, pottery, glass, cement, etc.	0·2	5·4	307	0·0	0·3	1·4
14 Timber, furniture, etc.	0·6	18·0	273	0·2	1·1	1·2
15 Paper, printing and publishing	41·1	100·2	557	11·4	6·0	2·5
16 Other manufacturing industries	0·7	16·7	310	0·2	1·0	1·4
17 Construction	6·3	84·0	1,678	1·7	5·0	7·6
18 Gas, electricity and water	2·9	20·0	377	0·8	1·2	1·7
19 Transport and communication	51·7	181·4	1,457	14·3	10·8	6·6
20 Distributive trades	40·6	253·1	2,934	11·2	15·2	13·4
21 Insurance, banking, finance	125·5	183·8	609	34·8	11·0	2·8
22 Professional and scientific services	32·6	175·4	2,239	9·0	10·5	10·2
23 Miscellaneous services	28·3	273·2	2,428	7·8	16·3	11·1
24 Public administration and defence	11·0	130·3	1,291	3·0	7·8	5·9
Industry inadequately described	1·2	10·0	64	0·3	0·6	0·3
All categories	360·7	1,670	21,931	100	100	100

Source: Sample Census of England and Wales, 1966.
(1) Workplace and Transport Tables, Vol. 1.
(2) Economic Activity Tables, Vols. 1 and 3.

Table 2.39. Employment by Occupation in the City, Other Central London, and England and Wales 1966

Occupation orders	Employment (thousands)			Percentage of total employment		
	City of London	Central London	England and Wales[1]	City of London	Central London	England and Wales
1 Farmers, foresters, fishermen	0·1	1·7	742	0·0	0·1	3·3
2 Miners and quarrymen	0·0	0	330	0·0	0·0	1·5
3 Gas, coke and chemical makers	0·0	1·7	133	0·0	0·1	0·6
4 Glass and ceramics makers	0·1	1·7	99	0·0	0·1	0·4
5 Furnace, forge, foundry, rolling mill workers	0·1	1·4	191	0·0	0·1	0·8
6 Electrical and electronic workers	5·2	30·0	556	1·4	1·8	2·5
7 Engineering and allied trade workers n.e.c.	4·8	61·8	2,533	1·3	3·7	11·2
8 Woodworkers	1·3	18·4	414	0·4	1·1	1·8
9 Leather workers	0·2	6·7	131	0·0	0·4	0·6
10 Textile workers	0·1	1·7	344	0·0	0·9	1·5
11 Clothing workers	2·5	49·9	429	0·7	3·0	1·9
12 Food, drink and tobacco workers	2·0	14·4	348	0·6	0·9	1·5
13 Paper and printing workers	13·1	38·6	301	3·6	2·3	1·3
14 Makers of other products	0·9	13·6	317	0·2	0·8	1·4
15 Construction workers	1·4	20·0	539	0·4	1·2	2·4
16 Painters and decorators	0·8	13·6	294	0·2	0·8	1·3
17 Drivers of stationary engines, cranes, etc.	0·4	5·0	287	0·0	0·3	1·3
18 Labourers n.e.c.	15·0	40·4	1,136	1·4	2·4	5·0
19 Transport and communications workers	27·6	123·4	1,348	7·7	7·4	6·0
20 Warehousemen, storekeepers, packers, bottlers	7·2	48·6	790	2·0	2·9	3·5

21	Clerical workers	167·3	495·9	3,126	46·4	29·7	13·9
22	Sales workers	33·4	150·3	2,151	9·3	9·0	9·6
23	Service, sport and recreation workers	24·0	208·7	2,702	6·6	12·5	12·0
24	Administrators and managers	23·5	103·5	717	6·5	6·2	3·2
25	Professional, technical workers, artists	38·5	202·1	2,166	10·7	12·1	9·6
26	Armed forces (British and foreign)	0·1	8·4	232	0·0	0·5	1·0
27	Inadequately described occupations	1·1	8·3	159	0·3	0·5	0·7
	All categories	360·7	1,670	22,513	100	100	100

[1] Number of economically active persons.
Source: *Sample Census of England and Wales, 1966*
(1) Workplace and Transport Tables, Vol. 1.
(2) Economic Activity Tables, Vols. 1 and 3.

145

Table 2.40. Employment by Socio-economic Group in the City, Other Central London, and England and Wales 1966

Socio-economic group	Employment (thousands) [1]			Percentage of total employment		
	City of London	Central London	England and Wales[1]	City of London	Central London	England and Wales
1 Employers and managers in central and local government, industry, commerce, etc. – large establishments	27·7	95·9	642	7·7	5·8	2·8
2 Employers and managers in industry, commerce, etc. – small establishments	24·1	112·3	1,131	6·7	6·7	5·0
3 Professional workers – self employed	3·8	13·4	109	1·0	0·8	0·5
4 Professional workers – employers	22·4	85·3	619	6·2	5·1	2·8
5 Intermediate non-manual workers	17·6	115·6	1,414	4·9	6·9	6·3
6 Junior non-manual workers	185·0	610·0	4,850	51·3	36·6	21·5
7 Personal service workers	9·0	86·8	1,224	2·5	5·2	5·4
8 Foremen and supervisors, manual	2·7	23·6	564	0·8	1·4	2·5
9 Skilled manual workers	30·6	229·0	5,121	8·5	13·7	22·8
10 Semi-skilled manual workers	15·5	141·0	3,346	4·3	8·4	14·9
11 Unskilled manual workers	19·5	106·2	1,774	5·4	6·4	7·9
12 Own account workers (other than professional)	1·5	33·6	722	0·4	2·0	3·2
13 Farmers – employers and managers	0·0	0·2	116	0·0	0·0	0·5
14 Farmers, own account	0·0	0·3	152	—	0·0	0·7
15 Agricultural workers	0·0	0·6	339	0·0	0·0	1·5
16 Members of armed forces	0·0	7·7	232	0·0	0·5	1·0
17 Indefinite	1·1	7·8	159	0·3	0·5	0·7
All categories	360·7	1,670	22,513	100	100	100

[1] Numbers of economically active persons.
Source: Sample Census of England and Wales, 1966.
(1) Workplace and Transport Tables, Vol. 1.
(2) Economic Activity Tables, Vols. 1 and 3.

Chapter 3

THE CITY AS AN ECONOMIC UNIT

INTRODUCTION

The previous chapter described the distribution of manpower between different activities and different parts of the City, and gave some statistical measures of the association in space between various activities. The present chapter considers some of the economic forces underlying these statistical observations. We examine the special position of the City in the domestic economy and in international trade and finance; we discuss some of the reasons why firms in certain activities seek proximity to other firms engaged in the same activity and also to firms in related activities; we present the results of an inquiry we have undertaken into the actual contacts between people in and outside the City by meetings and messages; and finally, we discuss various centralizing and decentralizing forces affecting firms and activities in the City.

THE CITY IN THE DOMESTIC ECONOMY

We have already drawn attention to the high proportion of office work in the City and to its significant and rising degree of specialization. This arises partly because there are certain activities which are concentrated very largely, if not entirely, within the City, and partly because the City houses the headquarters of organizations whose activities have a nation-wide, or international, spread.

Among the most perfect examples of the former are some of the financial markets including the discount market, the money market, the inter-bank call loan market, the foreign exchange market and the bullion market; nowhere else in Britain is there any organized market for the transaction of these types of business. The same can be said of the shipping market of the Baltic and, to a very large extent, of the commodity markets of Mincing Lane and the Baltic, the Metal Exchange, Lloyd's Register of Shipping, and many of the specialized types of insurance transacted by Lloyd's underwriters.

147

The market for local authority loans is very highly concentrated in the City, and the London Stock Exchange does a business far transcending that of any provincial centre. All the merchant banks which are members of the Accepting Houses Committee have their main offices located in the City. A few operate one or two provincial branches, and there are a few small merchant banks in the provinces, but the issue of new securities, the financial advice and the other functions of the merchant banks described in Chapter 8 take place almost wholly in the City.

The City and the district immediately adjacent to it on the west contain the editorial and administrative offices, and the main printing works, of most of our national daily newspapers, though some of them also print provincial editions. Finally the Square Mile has very much more than an average share of legal accounting and actuarial services; of import and export merchanting and of wholesale trade.

Among the second group of activities – where the City houses the central administrative organs of activities carried on elsewhere – the most important is banking. Here the Bank of England occupies a unique position as the central bank, besides being concerned in a great many other activities; the Clearing House provides a channel through which there passes a great majority of the nation's payments; and the head offices of the 'Big Five' commercial banks, who do over 90 per cent of all ordinary banking business in England and Wales, are in the City.[1] Life, fire and motor insurance, and shipping, though rather more widely spread, are other important activities where the City contains the head offices of companies accounting for a high proportion of business. The head offices of other commercial and industrial companies are much more widely dispersed, but nevertheless more than fifty of the largest 300 such companies have their headquarters in or just outside the City, though their main operational centres are elsewhere.

This unusual structure of activities has a number of important implications for the economy of the City. As pointed out in Chapter 2, the final output of the City is sold almost wholly outside its boundaries, either to other parts of the U.K. or abroad. The inputs are very largely personal services and the services of land and property. Other forms of capital (e.g. plant and machinery) and raw materials are of comparatively little importance. There is little manual work in the City and, of course, a great deal of clerical and administrative work, including a much more than average share of 'top jobs'.

[1] This was written before the formation of the National Westminster Group and the absorption of Martins Bank by Barclays. See Chapter 8.

This, again, is reflected in the high average income per head earned in the City. The City is not a large generator of heavy traffic; the food markets, the printing industry, brewing and warehousing, all use heavy transport, but otherwise the flow of goods (so far as it touches the City at all) is through it, rather than to or from it. On the other hand, the movement of people, both to and from work and during work, and the transmission of messages, are outstandingly important; and some aspects of these are discussed in more detail later in this chapter.

THE CITY IN THE INTERNATIONAL ECONOMY

Previous chapters have shown that the City of London contains – as it has done for well over a century – a unique concentration of international commercial and financial activity. About 20 per cent of world trade is invoiced and settled in sterling, almost wholly through the City; British banks with their headquarters in the City provide banking services over wide areas of Africa, South-East Asia, Australia and New Zealand, the Caribbean and South America; there are more foreign banks with branches in the City than in any other financial centre. The London foreign exchange market is one of the most active in the world, especially for forward dealings; and in the rapidly expanding 'Euro-currency' market London has more than three times the business of its nearest rival.

The London gold market is the channel through which most of the new production of the non-Communist world, together with Russian sales, is distributed. There are organized international markets in copper, tin, lead, zinc, tea, coffee, cocoa, sugar, oilseeds and other commodities. Many of these markets also have 'terminal' or future markets associated with them. Besides the trade of these organized markets, there are also many merchanting firms who handle between them a great volume of general export and import business.

The London Stock Exchange quotes a larger number of securities – many of them international – than any other in the world; the City undertakes a large part of the country's overseas insurance business, partly through Lloyd's underwriters and partly through the offices of insurance companies; the Baltic Exchange provides the world's major market in shipping and air freights and in second-hand ships and aircraft; while Lloyd's Register of Shipping runs a world-wide service from its headquarters in Fenchurch Street, maintaining universally accepted standards of construction and seaworthiness. Finally, the City contains the head offices of shipping lines and a number of other companies doing an international business, and also the offices of accountants, lawyers, actuaries and consultants who are often involved in work for overseas clients.

These activities make a very important contribution to the U.K. balance of payments. Official sources estimated a figure of £125 million in 1956, rising to £160 million in 1960. A detailed study for 1965 was made by the Committee on Invisible Exports and the conclusions were published in their report, *Britain's Invisible Earnings*. The Economists Advisory Group acted as consultants to the Committee and we are grateful to them for permission to use information gathered in the course of that study, on which the following paragraphs are based. This study did not relate to the City as a geographical area, but to a group of activities, by far the greater part of which are carried on in the City, and which account for a large part of the economic activity of the City. These activities comprise four main groups: insurance, merchanting, brokerage and banking. The Invisible Exports Committee compiled estimates of the overseas earnings of each of these activities. These estimates include earnings – especially in insurance and merchanting – of firms outside the City, but they exclude some overseas earnings originating in the City, e.g. tourism, and the earnings of solicitors, accountants and consultants. In spite of these defects, however, we believe that the estimates give a fair impression of the order of magnitude of the overseas earnings of the City in 1965.

(a) *Insurance*

The overseas earnings of the insurance industry fluctuate considerably from year to year, as heavy claims arising from a bad hurricane or some other natural disaster can make a considerable difference. On the basis of information provided by the British Assurance Association, and by Lloyd's, the Committee estimated overseas earnings in 1965 as follows:

Companies	£ million
Overseas branches, subsidiaries and agencies	19
'Home foreign' business*	2
Income from head office overseas investments	25
Lloyd's, underwriting and interest	13
Brokers	22
Total	81

* Overseas business undertaken by U.K. companies operating in the U.K.

Head office portfolio investments in overseas securities (as distinct from those held by overseas subsidiaries) are not related primarily to overseas business, but form part of the general funds of the companies. They are thus closely analogous to similar securities in the portfolios of other financial institutions, e.g. investment trusts and pension funds. We believe that it is better not to count earnings from these investments for our present purpose, and so we put the earnings of insurance in 1965 at approximately £56 million.

(b) *Merchanting*

The earnings of British merchant firms arise from four sources: U.K. retained imports, U.K. exports, and re-exports, and trade between foreign countries where the goods never touch British shores at all. Only the last two categories were included in the estimates of the earnings of the City made in *Britain's Invisible Earnings*. In the 1956 estimate – the only one in which a breakdown of the total was given – these were put at £30 million.

The Invisible Exports Committee received information from a number of commodity market associations, derived from questionnaires addressed to their members. This information suggests that the earnings of the London commodity markets in 1965 were probably about £20–25 million, though they could have been higher. These earnings were derived mainly, though by no means wholly, from 'third country' trade. Earnings in other third country trade, and from re-exports were estimated at £15–20 million.

Merchanting earnings in respect of U.K. imports are included in the official estimates of the balance of payments. Total earnings from this source in 1965 were estimated at £82 million, but a very large part of this must have accrued to firms outside the City, and there is no reliable way of determining precisely what proportion should be attributed to the City for our present purpose. One possibility is to assume that the City's share of this £82 million was proportionate to the share of the Port of London in U.K. imports. In view of the close links between the Port and the City which we found in other sectors of our study, we think this assumption is not implausible, though we fully recognize that City merchants handle cargoes discharged at other ports, and that some cargoes discharged in London are handled by merchants outside the City. About 30 per cent of retained imports pass through the Port of London so on this assumption, the earnings of the City from this source would be approximately £25 million.

In the official estimates of the balance of payments it is assumed that merchanting earnings on British exports are included in the prices at which goods are declared and no separate estimate is made. The authorities concerned recognize that this assumption is not universally valid and, in so far as merchanting earnings are not included in declared values, the official figures understate the total overseas earnings of the country. Whether they get into the official figures or not, the earnings of export merchants are clearly a part of total overseas earnings, and the City's share of them should be counted for our present purpose. The Export Houses Association provided estimates for the Invisible Exports Committee which showed earnings (excluding re-exports and third country trade, which have already been discussed) of about £20 million. Some of these earnings would accrue to firms outside London but, on the other hand, the basis of estimation was very conservative; we believe, therefore, that the figure may be a fairly close approximation to the earnings of firms in the City.

We may summarize our estimates of merchanting earnings as follows:

	£ million
Commodity markets	20–25
Re-exports and third country trade	15–20
Imports	25
Exports	20
Total	80–90

(c) *Banking*

Information was supplied to the Invisible Exports Committee by about three-quarters of all British and overseas banks in London, accounting for nearly 90 per cent of deposits. This showed earnings of about £17·5 million from foreign exchange dealing and from the many and varied services performed for overseas clients; and £34 million from the profits of overseas branches and subsidiaries and from charges for services provided for them.

On interest account, however, the banks paid out substantially more to overseas residents than they received from them. This does not, of course, mean that the banks made a loss on their borrowing and lending operations; rather, it reflects London's position as an international financial centre. Overseas holders keep a great volume of short-term funds (the so-called sterling balances) in London, and a large part of this is deposited with banks. The banks, in turn, re-lend some of the deposits to overseas borrowers, but most of them are employed in the home market. Some are lent to the Government when the banks buy Treasury bills or government stock, or make advances to the discount houses against government obligations; some are lent in the local authority loans market; and some are employed in advances to domestic industry and trade. In these transactions the banks simply act as intermediaries between the original overseas lender and the ultimate British borrower, and it would be unreasonable to hold the banks responsible for the overseas payment.

The way out of this difficulty which was followed by the Invisible Exports Committee is to distinguish between 'working balances'–i.e. balances held by overseas holders with London banks for day-to-day business – and the rest of the sterling balances which are regarded as a form of overseas investment in Britain. Interest on working balances only is then subtracted from interest received by the banks from overseas in order to get their net position on interest account. The difficulty with this method is that the distinction is an arbitrary one, and there is no way of saying precisely how much should be included in working balances. This matter was considered in some detail by the Invisible Exports Committee (see pp. 191–2 of their report) who came to the conclusion that the best estimate of the banks' interest earnings for 1965 was about £25·5 million. Using this figure and 'grossing-up' the banks' other earnings to allow for those who did not supply information provides the following estimate of total earnings:

	£ million
Services and Foreign Exchange dealing	19·5
Overseas branches and subsidiaries	37·5
Interest	25·5
Total	82·5

(d) Brokerage

Again, on the basis of information given to the Invisible Exports Committee, we estimate the overseas earnings of the Baltic Exchange (excluding its commodities section which has been counted with the commodity markets) at around £25 million. Similar earnings of stockbrokers and jobbers were probably over £3 million, while a group of miscellaneous services, including underwriting, security management and the activities of Lloyd's Register of Shipping produced about £5 million. The total earnings of brokerage and closely related services can thus be put at between £30 million and £35 million.

Bringing all these estimates together, we may summarize the receipts of the four main earners of foreign currency in the City in 1965 as follows:

	£ million
Insurance	56
Merchanting	85
Banking	82
Brokerage	33
	256

The figures are not, of course, accurate to anything like the nearest million pounds; an error of £10 million in either direction is quite possible but we can say with fair confidence that the overseas earnings of this group of activities in 1965 were between £245 million and £265 million. This figure is higher than any previous estimate, mainly because of the inclusion of merchanting earnings in import and export trades.

More Recent Estimates of Invisible Earnings

Other estimates of invisible earnings are presented in Table 3.1. These are somewhat below ours for 1965 mainly because of differences in definition. For example, the official data include all the investment income of insurance companies; exclude merchanting earnings in import and export trade; include investment income of investment trusts, unit trusts and pension funds; and debit the banks with the whole of their interest payments overseas. If allowance is made for these differences, the two estimates for 1965 are not far apart.

We believe that our definitions are appropriate for considering the total earnings of the City. In order to compare them with the labour force employed, we should deduct profits of overseas subsidiaries. This would reduce the total to approximately £200 million in 1965, or rather more than £1,000 per head of those employed in banking, insurance, merchanting and brokerage in the City. A corresponding figure of overseas earnings per head in manufacturing industry for that year was about £450. If we take into account the import content of exports the performance of City activities is even more impressive. The import content of manufactures averages about 20 per cent, that of services is less than 10 per cent. Thus, in 1965, the net balance of payments contribution was over £900 per head in banking, insurance, merchanting and brokerage, against only about £360 per head in manufacturing industry.

Table 3.1. The Overseas Earnings of the City of London 1946–68
(£ million)

	1946*	1956*	1963*	1965†	1966†	1967†	1968†
Insurance	20–25	70	85	80	108	147	177
Banking	5–10	25–30	45–50	32	16	19	40
Merchanting	5–10	25–30	20–25	30–35	30–35	30–35	30–35
Investment trusts, etc.	—	—	—	35	37	37	48
Brokerages, etc.	10	15–20	20–25	28	27	31	42
Total		40–55 135–150 170–185		205–210	218–223	264–269	337–342

* Source: W. M. Clarke, *The City in the World Economy*, Penguin, 1967.
† Source: *U.K. Balance of Payments*, H.M.S.O., 1969.

Since 1965, the contribution of the invisible earnings of the City to the U.K. balance of payments has grown very considerably. In 1969 they accounted for 6 per cent of total visible U.K. exports, compared with 4 per cent four years previously. Special mention should be made of the earnings of the insurance industry which have quadrupled since 1965. Close on £150 million was earned by the insurance companies, Lloyd's and the brokers operating in the City. About 70 per cent of the total premiums received by the non-life sector of the British insurance industry was earned outside the U.K. On the definitions used in this study, the total earnings of the City in 1969 were close on £450 million and are likely to exceed £500 million by the early 1970s.

THE INTERDEPENDENCE OF CITY ACTIVITIES

Chapter 2 presented some statistical measures of the concentration of certain kinds of activities in different parts of the City, and the linkages between them. The following paragraphs outline some of the economic characteristics which are associated with, and help to explain, this pattern of location.

Some students of urban organization have described cities in terms of a 'central core' of activities closely related to one another with concentric circles of other activities clustering more or less closely around the core. This is too simple an idea to be of much help in understanding the City of London. No formal scheme can accommodate all its complex detail, but it may help to think of two central nuclei, one financial and one commercial. Firms in each nucleus are linked together, among other ways, by participation in one or more of a series of organized markets.

The two are closely related to one another and they have around them (and closely intermingled with them) a variety of firms enjoying close business contacts with each other, e.g. insurance companies, shipping agents and merchants. A further group consists of trades and professions providing services for firms in, and close to, the nuclei and to their employees – lawyers, accountants, actuaries and consultants, caterers, retail shopkeepers, cleaners and maintenance workers. Finally, there is a very heterogeneous group of activities including the Inns of Court, a large part of the national press, some small-scale manufacturing, brewing, education, hospitals, administration, and the head offices of national and international companies, which have no specially close connection with the central nuclei, but nevertheless have perfectly good reasons for desiring a location in the City.

The Financial Nucleus

The financial nucleus consists of the Bank of England, the clearing banks, the City offices of the Scottish and Northern Irish banks, merchant banks, British overseas banks, other overseas banks with offices in London, and the discount houses. Among the ties binding them together are the need for frequent contacts with the Bank of England; use of the facilities of the Town Clearing; the need for frequent and speedy transmission of documents; and the participation in one or more of a group of financial markets. The most important of these markets are: the money market; the bill market; the stock market, the local authority loans market, the inter-bank call loan market, the foreign exchange market, the Euro-dollar market, and the bullion market. The role various institutions play in these markets is discussed more fully in Chapter 8. The connections between them are illustrated in Figure 3.1.

The connections may be summarized as follows. The *money* market is a market for loans of very short duration – some overnight, some for up to seven days. The lenders are the banks, domestic and overseas; the borrowers are mainly the discount houses but also members of the Stock Exchange. The Bank of England does not take part directly but it influences the flow of funds to the money market by its operations elsewhere, especially in the bill market and, in fact, conditions in the money market are a matter to which the Bank gives constant attention.

FINANCIAL INSTITUTIONS AND ORGANIZED MARKETS

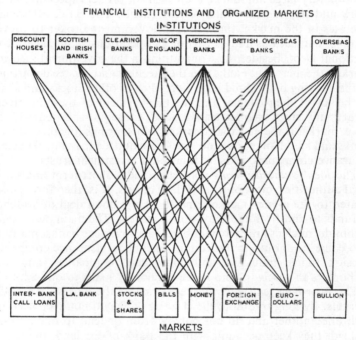

FIG. 3.1 Financial institutions and organized markets

The *bill* market, or *discount* market, is a market both in Treasury bills and commercial bills. The discount houses and all types of bank, including the Bank of England, take part. The Bank of England uses its operations in this market as the principal means of influencing the supply of money to the money market. Business in the bill market is transacted almost wholly by telephone. Bills change hands in very large amounts so that the small changes in rates which are constantly occurring may be very important and, again, 'knowledge in a hurry' is a strong motive for concentration. The discount houses also find it necessary to maintain close contact with one another in order to determine the bid at which they will 'cover' the week's Treasury bill tender.

The *stock* market, the *discount* market and the *clearing banks* are all very large holders of short-term government bonds, and most of the other banks have substantial holdings. Transactions are frequent and for very large amounts. A few firms of brokers specialize in this work and pay regular visits to their clients. The Bank of England operates in the market through the Government Broker to prevent extreme fluctuations and as part of its operations as manager of the National Debt. Besides these operations in the government securities market, the merchant banks and the executor and trustee department of the clearing banks hold large portfolios of other stocks and shares on behalf of their clients, and the management of these involves a great many stock market transactions. Closely associated with the stock market is the new issue market, which brings together brokers, banks and merchant banks and also (from outside the central nucleus) insurance companies, pension funds and investment trusts.

The *local authority loans* market provides short-term finance for local authorities, most of it for 7 days or less. It is, therefore, closely related to the money market, and there is a good deal of switching of funds to and from the Euro-dollar market. The main participants within the nucleus are merchant banks and overseas banks, but funds also come from outside institutions, including insurance companies, pension funds, industrial and commercial companies, and local authorities themselves, who make temporary loans to one another.

The *inter-bank call loan* market is one of the newest of London markets. By long tradition, the clearing banks do not keep accounts with one another and do not borrow from or lend to one another. Instead, they keep accounts with the Bank of England, make payments to one another through these accounts, and replenish them when necessary by calling in loans from the discount houses. The merchant banks and overseas banks are under no such constraint. The volume of their business has grown very rapidly in recent years, and with it has grown the volume of deposits which they keep with one another and with the clearing banks. These deposits are the 'raw material' which the banks concerned borrow and lend, though little is known about the exact mechanism or the volume of transactions.

The same reasons for proximity apply here as to the money market.

The *foreign exchange* market comprises the foreign exchange departments of the clearing banks, the merchant banks and the overseas banks; together with the Bank of England, which operates as agent for the Exchange Equalization Account. Besides the business arising directly from international trade, there is a large volume of arbitrage and of forward transactions.

The dealers in the *bullion* market are only four merchant banks, though they handle orders from many overseas sources. Until recently, the Bank of England operated on its own account and on behalf of foreign central banks, as agent for the sale of South African gold, and as manager of the Anglo-American gold pool. In March 1968, however, the gold pool arrangement was suspended and, since then, central banks have not dealt in the gold market.

The *Euro-dollar* market has grown up almost entirely in the last ten years. Dealers are the same group of banks, home and overseas, and merchant banks as in the foreign exchange market. Deposits are accepted and loans made in foreign currencies, usually, though not always, dollars. Longer-term loans, generally known as 'Euro-bonds', are also raised in foreign currencies and a market has begun to arise in certificates of deposits denominated in dollars.

The Trading Nucleus

The trading nucleus is less formally organized and much less well documented than is the financial one. Its main activities, described in Chapter 10, include the administrative headquarters of the Port of London Authority; the wharves and warehouses along the river; the shipping companies; forwarding agents; and a great variety of brokers, merchants and dealers. There is not the same closely-knit system of markets as in the financial sector, but organized markets still play a big part. The most important are the produce markets of Smithfield, Billingsgate and Spitalfields; the commodity markets of Mincing Lane, the Metal Exchange and the Baltic; and the markets in shipping and air freights and in second-hand ships and aircraft on the Baltic Exchange.

Besides the organized markets, there are other forces which cause firms in these activities to cluster together. There is a close, though by no means rigid, link with the Port of London; goods may pass through the Port without providing business to the City, and goods may be despatched by City firms through other ports. But a high proportion of goods passing through the Port gives rise also to transactions in the City. The Port handles the physical movement of goods, the City deals with the transfer of title, and with arrangements for transport, insurance and finance.

A number of City firms are often involved with the same consignment of goods: e.g. export merchant or forwarding agent, shipper, insurer and confirming house or factor. Many of these transactions involve the exchange of documents, and this has to be done quickly if some of the parties are not to lose interest or incur expense. For example, documents of title to imported goods may be handed to an importer or his agent by the agent of an overseas seller against the acceptance of a bill of exchange; the importer wants to get his goods off the ship and out of the dock as quickly as possible, while the exporter wants his money. Both would lose by any delay. The exchange of documents within the trading nucleus is one of the many things which is normally done in the City by messenger.

There are also advantages in close contact with banks (including the foreign exchange departments of the clearing banks and the merchant banks) who not only provide credit and handle foreign exchange transactions but also perform a number of other services including the handling of documents, the collection of maturing bills and drafts, and the provision of information and advice. The very important insurance business of the City, which is the subject of Chapter 9, clearly has close links both with the financial and the trading sectors.

Connected with these central activities are others which make use of one or more organized markets from time to time, or which have dealings with some of the firms in the centre. Proximity to related activities will be a convenience for them, but it may not be a decisive factor in their location, and it is not surprising to find some in the City and some elsewhere. A few examples are: life assurance companies, pension funds, investment trusts and unit trusts in relation to the Stock Exchange; some large companies in relation to the bill market, the foreign exchange market and the local authority loans market; and wholesale merchants in relation to commodity markets and importers.

Transport and communications, discussed in Chapter 10, affect all the activities above in several different ways. They perform a vital service for them; they influence the directions from which both people and business are drawn; and, as shown in Chapter 6, the existing pattern of communications, radiating as it does from London, is itself a centralizing influence. There are many other activities whose main function is to perform services of one kind or another, either for firms in the types of business described above, or for people working in the City. These include lawyers, accountants, actuaries and business consultants; caterers and retailers; public relations consultants and advertising agents; estate agents and employment agents; contract cleaners and repairers of office machinery; and computer service companies. These very diverse activities have one thing in common; their main reason for being in the City is that those who buy their services are in the City. The more important of them are discussed in Chapter 13.

Finally there are a few activities which have no very obvious links with either of the central nuclei, though they may have other good reasons for being in the City. By far the most important of these in terms of employment is the newspaper industry, discussed in Chapter 11. The only other of major significance is the head offices of industrial and commercial companies (Chapter 13). A location in the central area may be very important to them, but there may be little to choose between the City and the West End.

CONTACTS BETWEEN PEOPLE IN THE CITY

In order to find out more about the actual pattern of contacts resulting from the economic relationships described in the previous section, we conducted an enquiry in which respondents to a questionnaire were asked to keep a record of their business contacts with other people by meetings, telephone conversations and various forms of message, during a single day. Forms were sent to a random sample of firms in the City in May 1967, and, because of its special position, the Bank of England was asked to undertake a special survey among its staff, using the same questionnaire. In the random sample, respondents were allocated different days so as to get an even coverage of a whole week; in the case of the Bank of England, where there is believed to be no significant weekly cycle of activity, all the forms were completed on a single day. The results for the sample and for the Bank cannot, of course, be added together and they are summarized separately in the following paragraphs.

In the random sample, 1,500 forms were sent out, and 526 replies received, about a quarter of these were from partners or directors and a further 40 per cent from managerial or executive staff. Since respondents were asked to record both incoming and outgoing messages, there is the possibility of double-counting, but in view of the smallness of the sample we believe this to be negligible.

A striking feature of the result is the very large number of contacts recorded. These 526 people, in one day, took part in an aggregate of no less than 28,292 contacts, made up as follows:

Telephone calls	11,600
Letters by G.P.O.	10,393
Letters by messenger	1,482
Other messages	840
Meetings	3,977

Nearly 45 per cent of the telephone calls were between members of the same firm, and rather more than half of these were within the same building. A more detailed breakdown was:

	To or from members of own firm	To or from others	Total
In same building	2,870	159	3,029
Elsewhere in City	990	3,374	4,364
Elsewhere in London	947	1,794	2,741
Elsewhere in U.K.	484	745	1,229
Overseas	15	222	237
	5,306	6,294	11,600

The importance of calls between members of the same firm is itself an indicator of one of the difficulties which arises when departments are decentralized, or even housed in different buildings. Calls between members of a firm within its own building normally go through an internal system; those to other buildings must go either through a telephone exchange or over a direct Post Office line. Excluding internal calls (i.e. between members of the same firm within the same building, 8,730 calls were recorded of which 4,523 (52 per cent) were to other City numbers and a further 2,741 (31 per cent) to other parts of London.

As might be expected, the geographical spread of letters was rather different. Letters sent or received through the G.P.O. were distributed as follows:

	To or from members of own firm	To or from others	Total
In the City	363	1,790	2,153
Elsewhere in London	565	1,893	2,458
Elsewhere in U.K.	1,142	3,075	4,217
Overseas	390	1,175	1,565
	2,460	7,933	10,393

Corresponding figures for letters sent by special messenger were:

	To or from members of own firm	To or from others	Total
In the City	568	616	1,184
Elsewhere in London	162	69	231
Elsewhere in U.K.	60	7	67
	790	692	1,482

Respondents were asked to exclude circulars and similar routine communications from their definition of letters As might be expected, letters to or from places outside London precominate among those sent through the G.P.O., but even here there were nearly as many letters passing between different firms within the City as there were between the City and other parts of London. Letters sent by private messenger were nearly three per respondent per day, and over 80 per cent were within the City. It is interesting to note that letters between members of the same firm within the City were more likely to go by messenger than through the Post Office. Of 840 messages transmitted by other means, 612 were by telex and 220 were by telegram or cable. No less than 642 were to or from people overseas.

Respondents recorded 3,997 meetings, of which just over 90 per cent (3,589) were held in their own building; three-quarters of these lasted less than ten minutes. The breakdown by duration was as follows:

Duration in minutes

Under 10	10–29	30–59	60–119	120+
2,716	658	153	43	19

Of these internal meetings a great majority were attended only by members of the respondent's own firm, but over 700 were attended by outsiders. The large number of meetings attended by two or more members of the same firm is further evidence, along with the large volume of internal communication by telephone and messenger, of the obstacles to decentralization, or even to operating in different buildings within the City.

The composition, by activity and category of person attending is shown in Table 3.2.

Respondents to the questionnaire also attended 388 meetings outside their own building. It is interesting that visits paid outside the building were little more than half the visits received. Clearly a great number of people come into the City in order to make business

Table 3.2. Contacts in the City: Meetings Within Respondents' Own Building
May 1967

	Category of person attending meeting						
Activity of respondents' firm	Customers	Suppliers	Professional advisors	Fellow members of an Organized market	Representatives of official bodies	Others	Other members of own firm
Accountants	7	0	0	0	0	1	62
Solicitors	11	0	1	0	0	1	44
Stockbrokers	0	4	0	2	1	0	65
Insurance brokers	13	3	2	8	0	0	88
Insurance companies	62	0	2	1	2	4	325
Clearing banks	52	1	3	0	2	8	627
Other banks	67	16	5	16	2	6	319
Other finance	9	2	0	14	0	1	43
Printing, publishing, newspapers, etc.	9	9	2	0	1	3	144
Import/export merchants	18	6	2	0	0	5	91
Other merchants and agents	43	38	5	8	1	12	524
Professional services	58	7	0	0	1	7	91
Manufacturers	8	2	1	0	0	4	39
Others	61	39	12	5	8	11	212
Total	418	127	35	54	18	63	2,674

Table 3.3. Contacts in the City: Place of Meeting by Meeting Time
May 1967

Meeting time (minutes)	City	Central area	G.L.C. area	Home Counties	U.K.	Abroad	N/A	Total
0–9	51	2	5	—	—	—	4	62
10–29	111	13	10	4	1	1	7	147
30–59	47	18	5	4	2	—	3	79
60–119	41	10	5	2	1	—	3	62
120+	17	6	—	3	2	1	—	29
Not available	7	1	—	—	—	—	1	9
Total	274	50	25	13	6	2	18	388

calls. The breakdown of these meetings by place and duration is shown in Table 3.3. Over 70 per cent took place within the City and a further 19 per cent within the greater London area. Over three-quarters of the visits paid within the City were made on foot and the average travelling time was about ten minutes compared with thirty-four minutes in other parts of London.

Comparison of the distribution of visits and telephone calls gives some support to the case, often put to us in interviews, for the value of face-to-face contacts. Respondents attended roughly three meetings in the City for every one in the rest of London, and made or received two telephone calls in the City to one in the rest of London. Since there is no difference between the cost of telephone calls within the City and to other parts of London, we may argue that about two-thirds of the business requiring conversation (as distinct from written messages) was between people in the City. The average duration of meetings in the City was about thirty-eight minutes. A telephone call of that length cost only 1s 2d, at the time of this survey; considerably less than the value even of the short time spent travelling to and from meetings. Thus meetings are more expensive than telephone calls; yet, in relation to its share of the business assumed to require conversation, the City has a high proportion of meetings. Presumably these can only be made because the people concerned feel that there is something they can get from a meeting that they could not get from a telephone conversation.

A classification of visits according to activity of visitor and category of person visited is shown in Table 3.4. Comparison with Table 3.2 shows some interesting points. Customers or clients are the most important group both visiting and visited, while suppliers and fellow members of organized markets both show prominently in each category.

Some types of firms, however, are much more given to paying visits, and others to receiving them. This is shown in Table 3.5. Here we have considered only visits paid to, or received from, members of other firms. As might be expected banks contribute far more heavily to visits received than to visits paid. Stockbrokers, insurance brokers and the printing and publishing trades pay a large number of visits in relation to those which they receive.

Any attempt to gross-up these figures in order to provide an estimate of the total volume of communications in the City presents several problems. It is necessary to have figures for total population and here we have been able to use only the O.S.R.P. data. Since these cover by no means the whole working population the resulting

Table 3.4. Contacts in the City: Meetings Outside Respondents' own Building May 1967

Activity of respondents' firm	Category of person being met						
	Customers	Suppliers	Professional advisors	Fellow members of an organized market	Representatives of official bodies	Others	Other members of own firm
Accountants	4	0	0	0	1	0	1
Solicitors	2	0	3	0	0	1	0
Stockbrokers	43	0	0	0	0	0	0
Insurance brokers	3	0	0	19	1	1	0
Insurance companies	14	1	0	11	1	3	13
Clearing banks	2	0	0	0	2	3	8
Other banks	3	1	1	1	0	0	5
Other finance	2	1	1	9	0	1	1
Printing, publishing, newspapers, etc.	18	3	1	0	0	4	5
Import/export merchants	2	2	3	0	0	4	1
Other merchants and agents	23	9	3	9	5	6	18
Professional services	16	10	2	1	0	1	0
Manufacturers	5	3	0	0	0	0	1
Others	10	13	7	4	0	2	7
Total	147	43	21	54	10	26	60

estimates will be very conservative. Because not all activities were equally well represented in the sample, it is necessary to weight each activity group and we have done this by using for each activity a weight given by dividing the total number employed in that activity by the number in the sample. Finally, there is the question of double-counting. In order to avoid this, we took only outgoing messages within the City, and both incoming and outgoing ones to and from other places.

By these methods we arrived at the estimates of messages sent by various means of communication. See next page.

Disregarding telephone calls between members of a firm in the same building, it appears that over three million calls a day must go over the Post Office system. Letters sent through the post (excluding routine communications such as circulars and dividend warrants) numbered nearly four and a half million, while over 450,000 messages were sent by private messenger.

*Thousands
per working day*

TELEPHONE CALLS
Within the same building
To members of own firm	665
To others	38

Elsewhere in the City
To or from members of own firm	282
To or from others	768

Elsewhere
To or from members of own firm	655
To or from others	1,293

LETTERS BY G.P.O.
Within the City
To members of own firm	73
To others	383

Elsewhere
To or from members of own firm	1,050
To or from others	3,052

LETTERS BY MESSENGER
Within the City	325
Elsewhere	142

Table 3.5. Visits Paid and Received in the City by Activity of Respondents' Firm May 1967

Activity of respondents' firm	Visits paid		Visits received	
	No.	Percentage of total	No.	Percentage of total
Accountants	5	1.6	8	1·1
Solicitors	6	1·9	13	1·8
Stockbrokers	43	13·5	7	1·0
Insurance brokers	24	7·5	26	3·6
Insurance companies	30	9·4	71	10·0
Clearing banks	7	2·2	66	9·3
Other banks	6	1·9	112	15·7
Other finance	26	8·2	26	3·6
Printing and publishing	31	9·7	24	3·4
Import and export	11	3·5	31	4·3
Other merchants and agents	55	17·3	107	15·0
Other services	30	9·4	73	10·2
Manufacturers	8	2·5	15	1·8
Others	36	11·3	136	19·1
	318		715	

167

The number of meetings in some activities was not large enough to allow them to be grossed up by the methods used above, but the 526 respondents went out to more than 300 meetings with members of other firms and received visits from more than 700. Allowing for double-counting, the total number of meetings between members of different firms cannot be less than 300,000 a day.

To have combined the returns received from the Bank of England with those discussed above would have involved adding a single large selected unit to an otherwise random sample, and would have been inadmissible from a statistical point of view. On the other hand, a detailed analysis of the Bank, on its own, could not be given without disclosing confidential information. It can be said, however, that the general pattern of communications is broadly similar to that revealed in the random sample, though certain departments show special features related to their own particular activities.

As in the random sample, there is a high rate of internal exchange of messages, particularly by telephone and messenger; in contacts with other firms, those within the City predominate for telephone and messenger, while letters sent by the G.P.O. tend to go further afield because the Bank not only operates in the markets of the City but also fulfils a national, and international, role.

Private messengers are more important, relatively to telephone calls and letters through the Post Office, in delivering messages to and from the Bank than in the random sample. This reflects the very close proximity of most financial institutions to the Bank and the need for transmitting a large volume of documents. 'Over the counter' transfers of government securities, transactions with the money market and exchange control all give rise to a large number of messages.

It will be apparent from the description of the Bank's functions in Chapter 8 that many aspects of its business are closely interrelated, and a large number of internal meetings are essential. With few exceptions, it is the practice for members of outside institutions to visit the Bank for meetings, rather than the other way round. Again such meetings are very numerous, particularly with the banks and the money market, and in connection with the administration of exchange control.

The results of the inquiry do not reveal anything startlingly unexpected but they do give factual confirmation of a number of widespread beliefs about the nature of City life. Internal contacts between members of the same firm are very important, both in the form of meetings and telephone conversations. A representative

168

member of our sample had five face-to-face meetings and seven telephone conversations with other members of his own firm in the course of a working day. There are thus considerable diseconomies in dispersing the staff of a firm, even if only among nearby buildings. Some contacts will not then be made at all, with a consequent loss of efficiency, and others will have to be made by more expensive means or with more delay.

A very large proportion of contacts between members of different firms also took place within the City. Although less than 1·5 per cent of the working population works in the City, 62 per cent of telephone calls between members of different firms were within the City boundaries as were 25 per cent of letters carried by the G.P.O., 81 per cent of messages sent by private messenger, and 70 per cent of personal visits paid by respondents to the questionnaire. The City has a high proportion of meetings in relation to other methods of communication. By far the most common way of travelling to a meeting or carrying a message is on foot.

The results of the questionnaire thus confirm the view, put to us constantly in interviews, of the City as a place where firms are closely knit and where business depends upon very frequent and quick personal contacts. They also show the importance of London as the centre of a radial system of communications. This appears in the large volume of postal and telephonic communication between the City and the provinces, and also in the pattern of visits. Although City people pay a relatively small proportion of their visits outside the City, a high proportion of those who visit them come from outside. Such visits can usually be made more easily between the provinces and London than between provincial centres; because of the concentration of certain types of activity in the City, it is often possible for a visitor from the provinces to combine several business visits in a single trip.

CENTRALIZING AND DECENTRALIZING FORCES

The degree of concentration of economic activity in the City reflects the interaction of a number of forces. Changes in the degree of concentration may arise from at least three different causes:

(a) A relatively rapid rate of growth of an activity located and remaining in the City would add to concentration; conversely, if City activities grew more slowly than others concentration would be reduced.

169

(b) A change in the City's share in a particular activity. An increase (decrease) in this share can come about either through an increase (decrease) in the number of firms, or because firms in the City grow more or less fast than those elsewhere.

(c) Changes in the share of particular firms' activities carried on in the City. Such changes may take place, either because of a conscious decision to decentralize (or centralize) particular departments, or simply because work done at branches grows faster or slower than work done in London.

The factors determining the first category of changes are discussed in Chapter 6. Here we are concerned mainly with the second and third groups. We concentrate on factors affecting decisions taken by individual firms in response to ordinary commercial motives, ignoring, for the present, considerations of public policy, which are also dealt with in Chapter 6.

An inquiry undertaken for the Location of Offices Bureau by the Economist Intelligence Unit in 1964 asked respondents to name the four most important reasons for having their office in Central London (not the City) from the following list:[2]

Reason	Percentage of first choices	Weighted average support
Contact with *external* organizations	54·1	304
Contact with *internal* departments	5·1	84
Contact with parent/subsidiary companies	3·1	43
Communications, rest of U.K.	6·7	117
Communications, international	5·1	87
Supply of staff	2·8	76
Tradition	9·8	104
Prestige	5·9	128
Other reasons	7·4	57

The first column of figures shows the percentage of first choices; the second column is the result of weighting these percentages by four for a first choice, three for a second, two for a third, and one for a fourth. Measured by either method, contact with external organizations is far the most important. In terms of first choice, it scored 54·1

[2] *A Survey of Factors Governing the Location of Offices in the London Area*, by the Economist Intelligence Unit for the Location of Offices Bureau, 1964. The weighted figures are ours.

per cent, while if contacts with other departments or companies in the same organization are added the figure rises to 62·3 per cent. Good communications, which facilitate cortacts, claimed another 11·8 per cent so that almost three-quarters of respondents named ease of contact, in one form or another, as their most important reason for being in London. Tradition scored nearly 10 per cent of first choices, but declined in importance somewhat when second, third and fourth choices were taken into account. Prestige was given as a primary reason by only 5·9 per cent of respondents, but was mentioned rather more often as a subsidiary reason.

This analysis is of limited use for our purposes, as it gives little indication of the kinds of contact which are important, or the reasons why they are valued so highly. The following classification is suggested by the literature on the subject and by our discussions with people in the City.

(a) *'Knowledge in a Hurry'*. This is the phrase coined by Robbins and Terleckyj in their study of New York to describe the advantages of close contact between dealers in markets subject to rapid price fluctuations. Contact may be achieved by presence in a market place, as on the 'floor' of the Stock Exchange, or by very frequent telephone calls supplemented by personal meetings, as ir the money market or the foreign exchange market. In either case the constant exchange of information and opinion 'reduces the cost of transactions in the sense that it enables the participants to avoid being "off the market" – doing business on terms unnecessarily unfavourable'.[3]

(b) *The Building of Confidence*. In most of the financial and commercial markets of London contracts are made by word of mouth – either face to face or on the telephone. This obviously lends itself to speed and economy in transactions, but it depends on mutual confidence, and it has been put to us very often that close personal contact is important in establishing and maintaining confidence. In markets where dealers are individuals or partnerships this is obvious enough; it is less clear where the principals to a bargain are large firms, e.g. banks dealing in the Euro-dollar market; but even here it is felt to be important by many of those most closely concerned.

(c) *The Role of Top Management*. Directors of City firms seldom sit on only one board, and are often members of a considerable number. It is an obvious economy of their time to have their various activities close together, and their time is the most valuable commodity in the

[3] S. M. Robbins and N. J. Terleckyj, *Money Metropolis*, p. 35.

City. In themselves they are few in number, but to be fully effective they must be able to call quickly on a much larger number of executives and technical experts in their various organizations.

(d) *Links with Customers.* In some cases, e.g. the produce markets, these are still a matter of physical transportation. In the major financial and commercial markets, they are more a matter of being familiar with a set of complex and changing needs.

(e) *Links with Other Firms in Related Activities.* E.g. the merchant banker and the broker in relation to new issues, or the merchant, the confirming house, the insurer and the shipping firm in the export of goods. Closely related to these are the advantages of quick access to professional advisers such as lawyers, accountants, actuaries, and business consultants. A very special case is the importance of close contact between the financial community and the Bank of England.

(f) *The Use of Joint Services.* These may be either services set up by the firms concerned, e.g. the Bankers' Clearing House or the Stock Exchange Settlement Department, or services provided by specialist firms, e.g. computer services.

(g) *The Transmission of Documents.* Although most contracts are by word of mouth the activities of the City involve the movement of a great deal of paper – the clearing of cheques, the exchange of contract notes, the lodging of bills with banks as security for a loan, the collection and presentation of shipping documents, etc. In most cases, payment is made only against the delivery of a document, and the sums involved are large so that 'time is money' in a very real sense.

(h) *The Avoidance of Misunderstanding.* In so large a number of transactions, mistakes are bound to arise – a cheque wrongly delivered, an error in a contract note, a telephone message misinterpreted – and it is important that they should be remedied quickly and without friction. Close contact at a quite junior level often enables this to be done without wasting the time of more senior people (and possibly without getting those responsible into too much trouble).

These advantages all depend on contacts that can arise only from very close proximity. Another aspect of communications is the radial network from London. In general, it is easier and quicker to travel or send a message from London to some other place, either at home or abroad, than between two places on a 'cross-country' route. This is relevant to the need to maintain contacts with people and firms outside London and also to the journey to work.

As an illustration of the latter, we made a geographical arrangement of the private addresses of members of the Stock Exchange as shown in the current Year Book. Where more than one address is given we used the one nearest to London. The result was as follows:

London postal area		Outside London	
South-west	418	Kent	328
West	295	Sussex	333
North-west	142	Surrey	700
North	81	Hampshire	72
North-east	None	Berkshire	79
East	18	Buckinghamshire	75
South-east	49	Middlesex	98
		Hertfordshire	165
		Essex	344
		Other U.K.	104
		Overseas	5

This distribution is probably fairly typical of City workers in the higher income groups, though a movement down the scale would bring in a higher proportion from the east and north-east. The existence of this scattered residential pattern clearly does not dictate any exact location of work-place. It does, however, mean that any place of work far removed from the centre of the radial communications system would force a great many people either to move house or to spend a lot more time travelling.

These different types of advantage from contacts and communications will affect different activities to different degrees; few will be affected by all; all will probably be affected by some. Their importance for different activities will be considered in the relevant later chapters.

The main decentralizing forces are clearly the high cost of land and labour in the City, combined with official policy.[4] The shortage of land finds expression in rising rents for new property and property for which the lease falls in. There is, of course, a similar tendency for rents to rise in suburban and provincial centres where office develop-

[4] For an interesting analysis of the types of *manufacturing* industries most likely to be suitable for dispersal from the *Greater* London area, see A. H. Tulpule 'Dispersion of industrial employment in the Greater London area' *Regional Studies*, Vol. 3, 1969, pp. 25–40.

ment is taking place. A good example is Croydon, where rents of up to £4 a year per square foot were being obtained in 1970 for the kind of accommodation that would have been let for £1 or less, ten years ago. Nevertheless, accommodation in the suburbs and the provinces is still relatively very cheap; while rents for new accommodation in the most expensive areas of the City are over £10 a square foot, there are many suburban areas where it can be obtained for £2 or less, while in the provinces, rents of around £1·50 per square foot are still not uncommon.[5] Expanding firms, moreover, often find difficulty in getting suitable accommodation situated conveniently to their existing premises, and in a number of instances this has been a factor in a decision to move all or part of a firm's activities out of London. The present position with regard to land values and rents is described in Chapter 4. Future prospects are considered in Chapter 14.

Within limits, the City worker has a choice between living in a poor environment (in the East End), paying high housing costs (in the more desirable inner suburbs), or spending time and money on commuting. In either case these disadvantages must be compensated partly by higher wages and partly by 'fringe benefits'. Some firms pay 'London allowances', which may be up to 10 per cent of salaries; others make no special allowances, but simply pay the market rate. However, firms which decentralize do not always make the full saving in costs which they might do, since they feel an obligation to pay staff whom they have required to move at their old rates, and this may also influence the rates they pay new recruits. The Economist Intelligence Unit found that a majority of firms which had decentralized reported lower rates for clerical and secretarial labour, but a substantial minority said they were still paying their former rates.

City firms also provide a number of fringe benefits. For example, the Economist Intelligence Unit found that 96 per cent of respondents in London subsidize midday meals, either by providing a canteen or luncheon vouchers. Fifty-four per cent provided help for house purchase and 52 per cent for removal expenses, while help with transport was also common in the form of cash grants, loans to buy season tickets, company transport or free parking.[6] Many of these fringe benefits are, of course, not uncommon in the provinces, but there is little doubt that they are both more general and more expensive to provide in London. In spite of these inducements,

[5] Economists Advisory Group, *Office rents in the City of London*, Committee on Invisible Exports, London, 1971.

[6] E.I.U., op. cit., pp. 31 and 64.

however, firms tend to have a high rate of turnover among their clerical and secretarial staffs.

The recruitment of labour as well as its remuneration may be significant. The general view put to us is that recruitment of clerical and secretarial labour is easier in the provinces, but that the position is reversed for posts needing special skills and carrying a high degree of responsibility. In particular, the ambitious young executive feels, probably rightly, that he has a better chance of 'getting on' in London than elsewhere, either by obtaining rapid promotion in his own firm or by moving to another.

The present distribution of the City's labour force, and the prospective population growth in the areas from which people come to work in the City, were discussed in Chapter 2. The evidence given there indicated that there is likely to be a progressive 'labour shortage' in these areas, so that the differential advantages which City firms will have to offer in order to maintain their labour force are likely to increase rather than diminish.

Official policy is, of course, encouraging decentralization by restriction of new office building and by an extensive publicity campaign through the Location of Offices Bureau. The implications of this policy are discussed in Chapter 6.

Besides these major decentralizing forces, there are a number of minor ones, including the physical discomfort of travelling in congested conditions; the difficulties of parking in the City both for private cars and delivery vehicles; the high level of noise and fumes; the counter-attractions of rural amenities; and the comparative ease and cheapness of providing sports facilities outside London. All these are given full value in L.O.B. publicity, but they are unlikely to be of more than marginal significance in the taking of decisions.

SUMMARY

The city has a unique position in the national economy, both because many important financial and commercial activities are wholly or almost wholly concentrated within it, and also because it provides the administrative centre for firms and activities operating elsewhere.

The City is responsible for almost all the country's overseas earnings from banking and brokerage, and a large part of those from merchanting and insurance. Overseas earnings per head of the population directly employed in these activities are more than twice those of manufacturing industry.

175

The organization of City activities can be thought of in terms of a nucleus of banking and financial activities and a nucleus of trading activities. Firms within each nucleus have particularly close linkages with other firms in the nucleus, but there are also close linkages between commercial and banking activities and with firms related to them either as customers or as suppliers of services.

The results of a sample survey of methods of contact between people in the City provide further evidence of the closeness of linkages between firms, and of the importance both of face-to-face meetings and of the quick exchange of messages by telephone and messenger. The survey also provides evidence of the importance of London's position at the centre of a radial communications network.

Evidence, derived mainly from our interviews, leads us to believe that the main forces causing firms to desire a City location are: the need to be in constant touch with markets; the importance of personal contacts in building mutual confidence; the involvement of 'top management' in a number of different firms; links with customers; links with firms in related activities including specialist advisers; the use of joint services; the speedy transmission of documents; and the quick and easy correction of mistakes. Both prestige and tradition play their part, but we do not believe them to be of major importance.

The main decentralizing forces are the high and rising cost of accommodation and labour, though subordinate ones are discomforts of travelling and difficulties of parking; noise and fumes in the City; and the counter-attraction of rural amenities.

Chapter 4

LAND AND BUILDINGS

INTRODUCTION

The previous two chapters were concerned with the level and distribution of economic activity in the City, in terms of its labour force. This chapter complements this analysis by a study of land use and values in the City.

LAND USE IN THE CITY

Our data for the current structure of land use are based entirely on the Corporation of London's own Land Use Survey in 1966. This embraced the whole of the City; and, for each parcel of land, information was obtained on land use by broad types of activity (offices, industry, warehouses, etc.). In this chapter, we shall be concerned only with the more important conclusions of the survey.

Figure 4.1 shows the distribution of land use in the City in 1966. The greatest density of use is in the three quadrants bordered by St Paul's on the west and Houndsditch on the east. This is also where office activities are most concentrated; as Table 4.1 shows, more than two-fifths of the floor-space occupied by offices are to be found in this, the centre of the financial area, where such activities account for more than three-quarters of land use. There are also important office clusters in the eastern quadrants south of Cornhill and to the west of St Paul's through to Fleet Street and High Holborn. Commercial activities are most noticeable in the mid-eastern, north-western and central-southern parts of the City. Manufacturing industry is fairly widely dispersed outside the financial core. The most noticeable feature of the present allocation of land in the City, compared with past years, is the spread of office activities beyond the financial core, and the gradual squeezing out of the less intensive space using activities altogether. But, as shown in Chapter 2, within broad categories of activity, some tightly knit clusters still remain, and in some cases new ones have evolved.

178

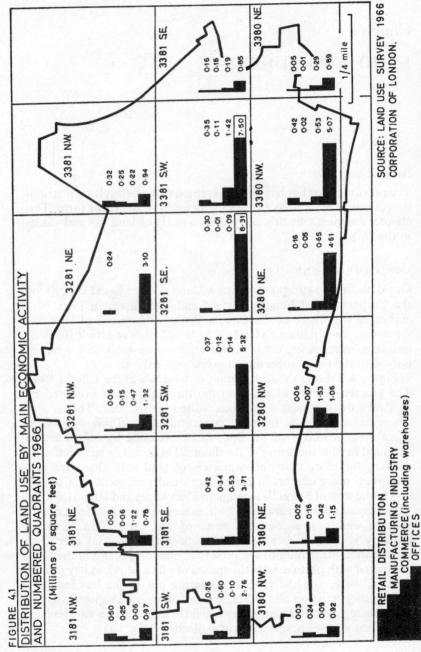

Fig. 4.1 Distribution of land use in the City, by main economic activity and numbered quadrants, 1966

Table 4.1. Distribution of Office Floor-space in the City by Map
Quadrants 1966
(millions of sq. ft)

Map Ref.*	OG	OP	OC & OL	Net total†	Percentage
3180NW	0·68		0·14	0·81	1·8
3180NE	0·99	0·06	0·02	1·04	2·3
3181NW	0·97	0·00	0·00	0·96	2·1
3181SW	2·50	0·10	0·06	2·59	5·6
3181NE	0·52	0·02	0·23	0·72	1·6
3181SE	2·86	0·74	0·30	3·29	7·1
3280NW	0·67	0·31	0·07	1·02	2·2
3280NE	4·27	0·13	0·12	4·46	9·7
3280SE			RIVER ONLY		
3281NW	1·12	0·06	0·11	1·23	2·7
3281SW	3·88	0·36	1·06	5·12	11·1
3281NE	2·62	0·09	0·13	2·80	6·2
3281SE	7·43	0·58	0·12	7·81	16·9
3282SW		RESIDENTIAL AND CHURCH ONLY			
3380NW	4·29	0·44	0·39	4·85	10·4
3380SW			RIVER ONLY		
3380NE	0·76	0·05	0·03	0·84	1·8
3381NW	0·88	0·02	0·00	0·88	1·9
3381SW	6·46	0·47	0·00	6·89	14·9
3381NE		FIGURES ON 3381NW			
3381SE	0.81			0·79	1·7
Totals	41·71	3·41	2·79	46·11	100·0

* See Figure 4.1.
† Total of office floor-space less car parking space.

Office Code Definition
  (i) OG – Banks, insurance companies, estate agents, friendly societies,
       offices of firms engaged in trade, transport, distribution,
       manufacturing, servicing, publishing, advertising, building
       and civil engineering, agriculture, entertainment, sport
       (other than betting shops), professional offices (e.g. solicitors,
       accountants, architects, etc.).
 (ii) OL – Offices of statutory boards, corporations, societies, institu-
       tions, unions, political parties, livery companies, research
       institutes.
(iii) OL – Local government offices.
 (iv) OC – Central government offices, including local Ministr offices
       but excluding post offices.

Buildings which were under construction or vacant at the time of the
survey but have been subsequently occupied are not included in the
figures contained in the undermentioned Schedule.
  N.B. All floor-space figures are in units of 100 sq. ft.
  Source: 'Land Use Survey', Corporation of London, 1966.

179

The Corporation's Land Use Survey also uncovered some interesting details about the ratio of vacant to occupied floor-space in the City. These are reproduced in Table 4.2, and reveal a very mixed picture, both between activity and quadrant. The greatest excess capacity of floor-space is seen to be in buildings scheduled for commercial uses – in some quadrants the vacant/occupied ratio is as high as 40 per cent. Space for both industrial and office accommodation is used more fully; indeed, allowing for the normal movement of occupiers, there is little spare capacity, except in two or three quarters, in either activity. These differential rates of land utilization reflect, on the one hand the demand conditions; on the other, the incidence of use zoning and the application of 'change of use' controls.

Additional to this empty floor-space there were, at the time of the Land Use Survey, vacant and derelict sites covering 675,000 sq. ft. There were also some 2·1 million sq. ft of floor-space under construction. A broad summary of land use is given in Table 4.2.

With rising standards of living and the growing importance of 'elite' type office activities in the City, the need for car parking space has increased. The Land Use Survey shows that there is some 1·80 million sq. ft of car parking space attached to offices. In addition some 0·99 million sq. ft of space is allocated to public and private car parks.

LAND VALUES

Both the extent and the form of land use influence, and are influenced by the price of land, which in turn is reflected in rents and the price of freehold and leasehold property. Such costs are often an important component in the total costs of operating a business in the City. They also account for a rising proportion of costs except where firms are leasing property on a fixed-price lease, in which case the relative cost of accommodation tends to fall over time.

While something can be said about site values in different parts of the City, it is difficult to generalize on rent and property prices due to the enormous variations in the age, condition of, and facilities provided by buildings in any particular part of the City. Two buildings could exist side by side but command very different rents, simply because one is an antiquated structure totally unsuitable to modern needs, and the other is a new property offering every service and amenity. In comparing rents or property values in different

Table 4.2. Ratio of Vacant to Total Floor-space in the City by Uses and Map Quadrants 1966 (millions of sq. ft.)

Map Ref.	Offices Occupied	Offices Vacant	Offices Ratio percentage	Commerce Occupied	Commerce Vacant	Commerce Ratio percentage	Industry Occupied	Industry Vacant	Industry Ratio percentage
3180NW	0.81	0.11	13.5	0.09		0.0	0.24		0.0
3180NE	1.04	0.11	11.0	0.23	0.19	45.2	0.16		0.0
3181NW	0.96	0.01	1.6	0.02	0.04	61.2	0.25		0.0
3181SW	2.59	0.17	6.7	0.10		0.0	0.49	0.11	18.9
3181NE	0.72	0.06	1.3	0.91	0.31	25.7	0.06	0.00	3.2
3181SE	3.29	0.42	11.3	0.43	0.10	18.4	0.33	0.01	0.9
3280NW	1.02	0.04	3.3	1.25	0.28	28.0	0.07		0.0
3280NE	4.46	0.15	3.2	0.46	0.19	29.4	0.04	0.01	15.8
3280SE				RIVER ONLY					
3281NW	1.23	0.09	6.5	0.36	0.11	23.7	0.13	0.02	11.7
3281SW	5.12	0.20	3.7	0.13	0.01	2.7	0.12	0.0	0.3
3281NE	2.80	0.30	9.7				0.01		0.0
3281SE	7.81	0.50	6.8	0.09		0.0	0.01		0.0
3282SW				RIVER ONLY					
3380NW	4.87	0.20	3.9	0.53		0.0	0.02		0.0
3380SW									
3380NE	0.84	0.05	5.3	0.28	0.01	4.7	0.01		0.0
3381NW	0.88	0.06	6.8	0.13	0.09	40.2	0.24	0.01	2.0
3381SW	6.89	0.61	8.2	1.40	0.02	1.4	0.11	0.00	0.3
3381NE				FIGURES ON 3381NW					
3381SE	0.79	0.06	0.6	0.12	0.07	34.5	0.15		0.0
Total	46.11	3.03	6.2	6.38	1.41	18.1	2.4	0.15	5.4

* See figure 4.1.

N.B. Percentage figures have been calculated from original data which were expressed in hundreds of square feet. This accounts for the fact that not all columns add up precisely.

Source: 'Land Use Survey', Corporation of London.

parts of the City, it is important, as far as possible, to compare like with like – including the conditions of land tenure.

In considering site values, one starts from the fact that the total quantity of land available, both in particular parts of the City and in the City as a whole, is fixed. Its value, at any given moment of time, will therefore depend upon the conditions of demand prevailing. These, in turn, will be influenced by:

(a) the demand for the products and services which the land is helping to produce;

(b) the nature of the production processes involved, e.g. the extent to which they are land intensive;

(c) the amount of accommodation which the land can support or is allowed to support;

(d) the availability and price of other inputs, e.g. labour, transport and buildings, used jointly with land;

(e) the external economies or diseconomies associated with a particular location.

Land values in the City, *vis-à-vis* other parts of the country, reflect all these things, but when seeking to explain the values of alternative sites, only (c) and (e) are likely to be important. In the last twenty years, land values in the City have risen more than in the rest of the country, principally because the demand for the type of services produced by institutions in the City has been growing so much faster. Because, too, the value of any site is influenced by the use made of adjacent sites, those areas of the City in which both activities are highly land productive and strongly dependent on the presence of related activities for their prosperity, can command higher prices than others.

One method of illustrating patterns of land values in urban areas is the value contour map on which bands or zones of different values are delineated by 'isoval' lines. The primary purpose of such a map is to locate the broad pattern of land values and pinpoint the variations which exist even within a closely knit geographical area.

In Figures 4.2 and 4.3 value contours have been plotted covering the greater part of the City for two years, 1950 and 1967. The first map shows the distribution of contours in 1950, or thereabouts, for an area of the City extending roughly from Barbican, Beech Street, Chiswell Street on the north side to Cannon Street on the south, and from Aldersgate, St Martin's-le-Grand, St Paul's on the west side, to near Bishopsgate on the east. The map is based on detailed work undertaken by Brian Anstey on the Ward of Cheap in 1949, and on the Barbican area in 1953.[1] The data are based mainly on the average selling price of freehold land in these areas at this time. For the purposes of this exercise, those isovals, which are indicated by a continuous line on Figure 4.2, have now been extended to indicate

CITY OF LONDON

FIG. 4.2 Isoval contours 1950

the approximate pattern in the remainder of the area. These extrapolated contours are shown by a broken line. Because they are based on less firm evidence than the earlier surveys they present only an approximate picture.

[1] See B. Anstey, 'Changes in Land Values 1950–64', in P. Hall, ed., *Land Values*, Sweet & Maxwell, 1965.

The principal feature of Figure 4.2 is the high plateau of values surrounding the Bank of England, the Stock Exchange and the Royal Exchange. This not only dominates the scene but also determines the general pattern of value contours throughout the City. It will be noticed that, in most areas apart from the Barbican, the

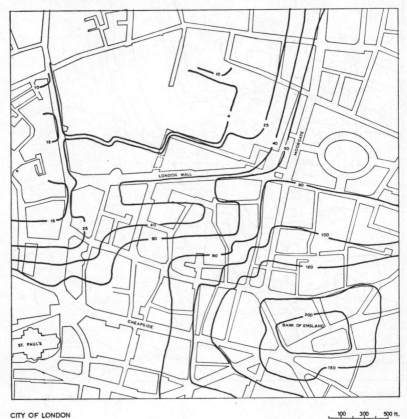

FIG. 4.3 Isoval contours 1967

contours are shown at intervals of ten units – a unit in this instance being £1 per square foot of land. The contours represent *average* prices. In certain areas, they may overlap; for example, the value of land in the network of small alleys and streets to the south of London Wall is seen to be less than that with a frontage to Gresham Street or Cheapside.

The map shows that the principal ridge of values lies along the main east–west highway – Cornhill, Poultry, Cheapside and to the north. There is quite a steep falling-off towards Queen Victoria Street and Cannon Street. A ridge of values extends out along Gresham Street towards the Guildhall, but this too peters out and falls away beyond Aldermanbury. Another ridge extends northwards from Princes Street, but values drop sharply at the approaches to the Barbican area; this, before the last war, was an area of narrow streets, warehouses, small shops, old converted residences, and railway goods sidings. It will also be noted that the south-west corner of the map is still within the plateau of high values. These would gradually fall towards the river, but probably not below ten units. If the study were extended eastwards to include the Baltic and Lloyd's, substantial peaks within a ridge of high values would be centred on these areas, after which values would decline sharply.

The second map (Figure 4.3) looks at the situation in 1967. It is derived from a detailed survey made of the Barbican area in 1964 by Brian Anstey, and on a less intensive review of the rest of the City. The pattern of value contours is based on information obtained from professional land valuers and on current market prices. Again, the contours represent average values in 1967. It is quite possible that, within any given isoval, zone prices might fluctuate considerably. In the Barbican area, there has been a strong simplification of the contours due to the compulsory purchase of the whole of the area and its comprehensive re-planning.

The general impression gained from this map – when compared to the previous one – is the tremendous surge in land values throughout the City since 1950. This reflects various forces, but perhaps most of all the pressure of demand for new office space. This pressure is mainly focused on the financial nucleus around the Bank of England (where values have risen four- or five-fold since 1950), from where it spreads out to St Paul's, northwards to London Wall and south to Cannon Street (off the map). Although land values decline as the distance from the Bank of England increases, the rate of decline is not as sharp as it was, and the large block of Bank buildings on the south side of Cheapside at the St Paul's end, together with Paternoster Development, have produced a steeper rise in values in this area than at the centre.[2] In fact, land values in the City are still extremely widely distributed, and the Square Mile cannot be thought of as homogeneous in this respect.

[2] Since 1967 this trend has been reversed: see p. 186.

185

RENTS IN THE CITY

We next discuss the level and structure of rents in the City. These are influenced by the forces determining site values, but also by building costs, government policy towards office development, local planning controls, facilities provided (central heating, air conditioning, lifts, etc.), elevation and entrance.

Buildings may be even more heterogeneous than sites. Within a particular street, where site values may be uniformly high, rents may vary considerably. This is because buildings often differ not only in the respects mentioned above, but in their conditions of letting: adjacent to a building, let on a long lease at a rent well below the current market price, may be another identical in all respects, whose lease, recently renewed, could be four times as expensive.

Our information on rents in the City mainly relates to office buildings. In our investigations we obtained two sets of data; first the trend in rents in particular areas of the City over time; and second the spatial pattern of rents throughout the City today.

First, some general observations. Taking as our starting point the early 1920s, it would seem that rents in the City were fairly stable until about 1929, after which they fell – following the pattern of prices generally – until 1933 or 1934. Partially recovering in the later 1930s they slumped to their lowest point in the early war years. Since 1944, they have been rising continuously. The large number of cases we have studied show that rents in 1967 were, on average, about twice those in 1957, three times those in 1950, and between six and eight times those of pre-war. But the most spectacular increase has taken place since 1967, when, in many areas, rents have doubled.

There are slight differences in the trend of rents in different parts of the City. Up to 1967, the gap between rents in the Bank of England area and in the rest of the City gradually narrowed, as the 'core' of the City gradually spread outwards embracing Lloyd's and much of the Baltic and London Wall districts. Since 1967, the most rapid increases in rents have occurred in these areas, due mainly to the almost complete inelasticity of supply of buildings. At the same time, there has been a reduction in the rent differential according to the floor of the building occupied.

Table 4.3 presents details of rent movements in different parts of the City between 1960 and 1970. This table largely speaks for itself, but we would emphasize two points. First, the rise since 1967 has been most marked for new and modern buildings; prestige accommodation has been particularly at a premium, due *inter alia* to the

186

Table 4.3. Office Rents in the City, 1960–70

(Rents exclusive of rates and services per sq. ft. per year)

	New	Modern	Modernized Old	Old
Banking area				
1960	£2·00	£1·50–£1·75	£1·25	£1·00
1965	£3·00	£2·50	£2·00	£1·00–£2·00
1967	£3·75	£3·50	£3·50	£2·00
1968	£5·00	£4·50	£4·00–£4·50	£3·00–£3·50
1969	£10·00	£9·00	£7·00	£4·10
1970	£13·00–£14·00	£10·00–£11·00	£9·00	£5·00
Insurance area				
1960	£2·00	£1·50	£1·25	£1·00
1965	£3·00	£2·25	£2·00	£1·25
1967	£3·50	£3·00	£2·50	£2·00
1968	£5·00	£4·50	£3·50	£3·00
1969	£7·00–£8·00	£7·00	£6·00	£4·00
1970	£10·00–£12·00	£10·00	£9·00	£4·50
Shipping and commodity markets				
1960	£2·00	£1·75	£1·25	£0·75–£1·00
1965	£3·00	£2·50	£2·00	£1·25
1967	£3·50	£3·00	£2·50	£2·00
1968	£4·50	£4·00	£3·50	£3·00
1969	£6·00–£7·00	£6·50	£6·00	£4·00
1970	£10·00–£12·00	£10·00	£9·00	£4·50
Smithfield				
1960		£0·75		£0·50
1965		£1·52		£0·80
1967	not known	£1·75		£0·85
1968		£2·00		£1·00
1969		£2·50		£1·00
1970		£3·50		£1·25
Fleet St. and Western areas				
1960	£1·75	£1·25	£0·75	£0·50
1965	£2·25	£2·00	£1·50	£0·75
1967	£2·75	£2·50	£2·50	£1·00
1968	£3·50	£3·00	£2·75	£1·25
1969	£4·50	£4·00	£3·00	£1·50
1970	£6·50	£5·00	£4·00	£2·00

Source: Economists Advisory Group, *Office Rents in the City of London and their effect on invisible earnings*, Committee on Invisible Exports, 1971.

187

influx of foreign banks. Second, even within these broad functional areas, rents and trends in rents, may differ quite markedly. For example, in parts of the insurance area (e.g. sub-district 48) rents, in 1970, were still substantially below the average quoted in the Table.

FACTORS INFLUENCING RENTS

Table 4.3 also gives an insight into the pattern of rents in different districts of the City in 1967. Here it is much more difficult to make meaningful comparisons. Beyond obvious statements, such as 'rents tend to fall as one moves further away from the Bank of England', or 'a new property in a given area can fetch two to three times that of an old property', or again 'central heating and air conditioning can add "X" new pence or more a sq. ft to the rent of a building', it is only by proceeding on a case by case basis that one can make much further headway.

This we obviously cannot hope to do in a study of this sort. Instead, we propose to examine a number of the main factors which influence rents in different parts of the City, illustrating these as far as possible from practical examples. We discuss five of these factors very briefly:

(a) Central Government policy and local planning controls.
(b) Planning 'blight' and rebuilding clauses.
(c) Characteristics of buildings.
(d) External economies and diseconomies.
(e) Conditions of letting.

Central Government policy towards office decentralization – particularly the operation of Office Development Permits (O.D.P.s) – affects office rents in the City by restricting the supply of new office space. We deal with the wider implications of this policy in Chapter 6. Here, we would observe that by keeping supply at a lower level than would exist in a free market, it tends to force up rents of both existing and new properties; this, in turn, encourages firms to remain in older and often less suitably equipped offices and hinders modernization of the City. It cannot be coincidence that where policy towards O.D.P.s has been most rigidly applied, e.g. in the City and West End, rents have risen the fastest.[3] The spatial effects of this restriction policy will vary according to the pressure of demand.

[3] This in spite of the fact that the *number* of O.D.P.s granted in the City rose from 16 in 1966/7 to 27 in 1968 and 80 in 1970. See Table 6.6, p. 226.

Local authority planning controls are mainly of three kinds: plot ratio controls, 'daylight' controls and use-zoning. The history of plot ratio controls in the City has been reviewed in Chapter 1: the 5 to 1 ratio still applies today throughout the City (with the exception of the Central Area around the Bank of England, where it is 5·5 to 1; around St Paul's, where it is 4 to 1; and in the area peripheral to Stepney, Poplar and Islington, where it is 3·5 to 1). Since these ratios are the same for all areas, they do not explain the spatial distribution of rents, though they are a factor influencing their level. Much the same applies to 'daylight' controls, save that areas of new development which previously would not have satisfied the 'daylighting code' of the G.L.C., have – in theory at least – had their potential area of accommodation reduced. Those parts of the City particularly affected by this measure include the areas north of Cheapside, south-east of St Paul's and the Aldersgate/Barbican/Moorgate complex.

Use-zoning controls have been a much more important factor in influencing City rents since the war. The Holden/Holford proposals were largely accepted by the Corporation and G.L.C., and these have affected the pattern of rents, first by redistributing the supply of sites in particular districts between different uses, and second, as a result of this and other factors, by altering the balance of the *intensity* of land use between districts. As a result, not only are some districts now engaged in office activities rather than industry and warehousing; their intensity of land use (measured by the plot ratio of the new activities) is considerably higher.

The effect of these use-zoning controls has generally been to reduce the dispersion of both land prices and rents in the City. Probably without exception, the average rents of properties in those declaratory areas developed by the Corporation since the war are higher *relative* to peak areas of the Bank, Lloyd's, etc., than before the war. Without use-zoning, we think it likely that rents in these latter areas would have risen even higher.

Planning blight normally results from *proposed* action by public authorities – e.g. a substantial road-widening scheme – which has the effect of depressing property values and rentals. Usually, a considerable advance warning is given, but values are often immediately affected. Occasionally, plans are unscheduled and speculation made extremely difficult. At present, planning blight is influencing values in various parts of the City, e.g. Wormwood Street, Upper Thames Street, Long Lane and the area south-west of St Paul's.

Rebuilding clauses have had a similar depressing effect on rents

189

since they undermine security of tenure and avoid some of the landlord's problems under the Landlord and Tenant Act, 1954. In the areas east of lower Moorgate and south of Cannon Street and Eastcheap these clauses have frequently been invoked and rents lowered as a result.

What of the *characteristics of particular buildings*? As might be expected, a very modern building commands the highest rent, followed by a modernized building, with an old building fetching the lowest. The 23-storey Commercial Union building at St Helens Place, completed in 1969, fetches rents of up to £14 a sq. ft and, equally impressive, the Kleinwort Benson building in Fenchurch Street not much less. In this latter case rents have nearly doubled over the last eighteen months or so.

In the Lloyd's insurance area new buildings were being let in 1969 for up to £10 a sq. ft (compared with £4.50 a sq. ft in 1966) while good older space could be had for only £3.25 a sq. ft. Another modern office building in Crutched Friars is currently being let for £6.50 a sq. ft although older space can be bought for about £3 a sq. ft. The same holds true for the Moorgate area and near the Bank, while further north older property is let for about £2.50 a sq. ft. In the Billingsgate and Smithfield area where there is a lot of older smaller property in very variable decorative condition, rents are usually below £2.50 a sq. ft. Modernized property in the central area fetches rather more; for example in Throgmorton Street the going rent is upwards of £5 a sq. ft and in the Leadenhall and Cornhill between £4 and £4.50 a sq. ft.

The *size of the floor* area is important. There is a big demand for accommodation under 10,000 sq. ft in the City, but the supply of modern space in these smaller parcels is severely limited. On the whole, it would seem that landlords prefer tenants to rent a whole building, or a substantial part of it – presumably to minimize management problems and expenses.

Though less pronounced than pre-war, rents still tend to fall as one moves back and up through a building. If lifts are provided the reduction on upper floors will be less. Where the building fronts on to a 'prestige' street or a vista of charm (e.g. Finsbury Circus) rentals are higher and the front/back differentials wider. An imposing façade or attractive entrance will also encourage higher rents. If the ground floor provides a suitable banking hall rentals could be upwards of £10 a sq. ft.

Central heating is now a fairly basic requirement of tenants and is usually (but not always) available in modernized buildings. Air conditioning is essential for computer users and most international (especially American) companies.

We have seen that rents around the financial nucleus of the City tend to be higher than in the peripheral areas but that the differentials are narrowing. These differentials are largely due to the forces mentioned in Chapter 3. In general, peak rents can only be afforded by those who need to be in close proximity to other firms and specialized knowledge, but there are sometimes external diseconomies which tend to depress rents. Office buildings around Billingsgate and Smithfield can command a rent of only £2 a sq. ft due to the smell and unpleasant outlook of the markets.

The prestige value of a good postal address is also important. It is noticeable that rents just outside the City boundaries to the northeast fall away quite quickly. Some firms will pay highly for a 'good' address on their notepaper. In September 1968, buildings in Farringdon Road, E.C.1, again outside the City's boundaries, fetched little more than £1.50 a sq. ft, yet in the same district, where it is inside the City boundaries, the average rent was considerably higher. Finwell House, on the north side of Finsbury Square, was built about 1958, but because it is outside the City – though in E.C.2 – nothing let in 1968 for anything over £2.50 per sq. ft. On the other side of the square, rents were higher by £0.50 or more a sq. ft.

Rents also reflect the *conditions of letting*, and, in particular, the length of time the lease has to run. Even within a particular building, it is unusual for all tenants' leases to come up for renewal at the same time. Besides buildings and districts there are many other reasons for rent differentials, such as the age and condition of property and the opportunities for sub-letting. In some parts of the City not affected by war damage, there are buildings still being let for office or general commercial purposes on late nineteenth-century leases of as little as 5p or 7·5p a sq. ft. In the post-war developed areas of the City, there is much less variation in rents, or indeed in the conditions of letting; mainly because most buildings are now let on shorter leases with rent review clauses in the contract.

It might be helpful to conclude this discussion on rents with a note on office rents outside the City, in particular in the West End and in a sample of towns outside London. In the West End, as in the City, rents are highly variable. At the end of 1969, accommodation in Park Lane was fetching between £4.75 and £7 per sq. ft. The Stag Development at Victoria varies from £5.50 to £7 per sq. ft and the St James's area commands about the same rents. Victoria is much the same as Mayfair and Westminster, with new offices leased for

191

up to £6 a sq. ft and old buildings for as little as £2 but averaging £3 to £4 a sq. ft.

Rents in the outer suburbs of London are now rising faster than in the City. In 1963–64 rents in Croydon were £0·875 to £1 per sq. ft; in 1968–69 they were between £1.50 and £2 with £2.50 being charged in a number of buildings. In Ealing an office block which fetched £1.125 to £1.25 in 1964, was sub-let in 1969 for £2. Near Romford, an office block let at £0.725 a sq. ft in 1964 was let at £1.50. Rents were £0.925 to £0.95 a sq. ft in a new office block in Bromley in 1965; in 1969 they fetched £1.75. An illustration of some other typical rents – the word 'typical' should be used with great caution – being charged for new office accommodation in various cities and towns in England and Wales in 1970 is given in Table 4.4. The average rise in such rents since 1968 has been 40–60 per cent, compared with 75 per cent to 100 per cent in the City of London and the West End.

SUMMARY

Though site values and rents are considerably higher in the financial core of the City than elsewhere – where the density of land use is also the greatest – the differential is narrowing and is considerably less than it was before the war.

The proportion of land used for office building has been expanding rapidly since the war as also has that set aside for car parking space.

The factors affecting rents are very varied. They include characteristics of buildings, central government policy and local planning controls, planning 'blight'. Even in the same building rents may differ according to the floor occupied, age of lease, central heating facilities and so on.

The trend in rents has been sharply upwards in recent years in all parts of the City; the operation of O.D.P. policy has almost certainly encouraged this rise – particularly since 1967.

Rents in the outer suburbs of London – which at one time were rising faster than in the City – are now rising less fast. In some of the larger provincial centres in southern England, e.g. Southampton, noticeable increases have occurred since 1967. In the north and Wales, rises have been limited from 25 per cent to 40 per cent.

Table 4.4. Some Examples of Rents of New Offices in
Different Parts of Great Britain 1970

Price per square foot
(£ and new pence)

SOUTH EAST REGION	
London (West End and City)	6·00 and upwards
London (Outer Area)	
Croydon	2·13 to 3·00
Ealing	2·00
Romford	1·50 to 1·75
Wembley	1·75
Rest of South East	
Aldershot	1·00 to 1·13
Andover	0·87
Ashford (Kent)	1·13 to 1·17
Brighton	0·85 to 1·25
Luton	1·00 to 1·25
Maidstone	1·25 to 1·50
Reading	1·63
Southampton	1·25 to 1·37
Tunbridge Wells	1·25 to 1·35
MIDLANDS AND EAST ANGLIA	
Birmingham	0·75 to 2·00
Corby	0·37
Ipswich	1·00 to 1·25
Leicester	1·00
Norwich	0·50 to 0·63
Nottingham	0·75 to 0·87
WALES AND SOUTH WEST	
Bristol	0·50 to 1·25
Cardiff	1·25 to 1·50
Cheltenham	0·87 to 1·00
Exeter	1·25
Gloucester	0·87
Plymouth	0·83
Salisbury	0·57
Torquay	0·93
SCOTLAND AND THE NORTH	
Darlington	0·85
Edinburgh	1·17
Gateshead	0·80
Glasgow	1·25 to 1·37
Harrogate	0·63 to 0·75
Leeds	0·83 to 1·50
Liverpool	1·03 to 1·35
Manchester	1·00 to 1·75
Newcastle	1·00 to 1·50

Source. *Location of Offices Bureau*

G

Appendix to Chapter 4

LAND TENURE IN THE CITY

In this Appendix, we begin by outlining the historical and practical aspects of land tenure in the City. We then briefly discuss leasehold interests in buildings and finally analyse some data on ownership and rents collected by the Offices, Shops and Railway Premises Act returns on ownership as this term is defined in the Act. Leasehold interests in buildings, and the O.S.R.P. data, are strictly not concerned with land tenure as such. In practice they are, of course, interrelated as are land values, rents and rates. The impact on location, in particular, of these variables differs greatly, however.

The casual observer, as he strolls through the City, will be struck by two physical features. First, the survival of buildings and open spaces which often have a public or institutional ownership and function, and are of historic and/or aesthetic interest. Second, the pattern and alignment of streets and blocks of buildings has evolved, and changed but little, from a medieval site plan.

While these two features add enormously to the attractiveness and atmosphere of the City, they also produce the gravest problems for working conditions and traffic circulation. A major factor in the post-war redevelopment of the City has been the large-scale planning of devastated areas under the provisions of the Town and Country Planning Act of 1944. This Act gave, to the Corporation of the City of London, powers to acquire the heavily war-damaged areas and additional adjacent properties, and to re-plan them as a single entity. In doing so, it was possible to alter the previous land-use pattern and to achieve some improvement in the layout of streets and pedestrian ways.

Land tenure plays a minor role in the functioning of the City, secondary to building values and rents, planning permissions and restrictions, and the multiplicity of other interests. The majority of land within the City's boundaries is owned freehold by the Corporation, in its various capacities, by Livery Companies, by Parochial Charities, and by a number of property companies. The area of land in which commercial establishments have a freehold interest is relatively small. Indeed, the majority of this area appears to be owned freehold by a few large institutions—joint stock banks, a few insurance companies, and one or two merchant banks. This pattern is particularly true of the Bank area; while the Fleet Street and Houndsditch areas are the only prominent exceptions. In the former a number of newspapers and press agencies own their own freeholds; in the latter an important residual area (especially within our sub-district 42) is composed of small, privately-owned, freehold parcels.

It is not surprising that the Livery Companies have tended to build up freehold interests in close proximity to their Halls. Thus Drapers and the Carpenters are important freeholders in the area between London Wall and Lothbury. West of Prince's Street and east of St Martin's-le-Grand the Goldsmiths, Mercers and Grocers still have important interests. Just off Bishopsgate, the Leathersellers have a fine development in St Helen's Place, compensation for their vandalism in 1799 when Nun's Hall was demolished. The Fishmongers own freehold interests west of their Hall by London Bridge, while further west still are six Livery Company Halls of which the Skinners is probably the most prominent in terms of freehold interests. To the north are the Salters with their interests in the Bow Lane area.

Generalizations are adequate as far as they go. But the Livery Companies also own between them land well removed from the Halls, and include Irish Estates. Let us illustrate from the property owned by three companies within the City.

The Merchant Taylors, whose early activities were centred on the clothing requirements of the army, met in the workshops of Cornhill and second-hand clothes sold in Birchin Lane, have their Hall on a site acquired in 1331 by John of Yakeslee, pavilion maker to the King. The freehold interests of this Company are far more widespread than this clustered history would suggest. They range from Bull Wharf in the south to Ropemaker Street in the north.

At the time of Edward I, the Ironmongers were situated in Ironmonger Lane, but early on they moved to Fenchurch Street where their forges would be less bothersome. During the First World War their Hall in Fenchurch Street was bombed, so the site was sold and they moved to Shaftesbury Place, Aldersgate Street, where they remain. But this was no strange choice of site. A former Master of the Company had reclaimed marshland on this spot in the early seventeenth century.

Our third example is the Founders, once centred by Lothbury

195

when this was on the outskirts of the developed area and close by the Walbrook. The site of the old Hall, by present-day Founders' Court, was let in 1844 on a building lease to the Electric Telegraph Company, who acquired a further site on a building lease from the Founders in 1853. With the proceeds, the Founders bought a site in St Swithin's Lane, where their present Hall stands.

The complexity of the freehold interests of Livery Companies is paralleled in the fragmentation of sites and the difficulty in buying fragments to make up a site. It is rare to find a block under one ownership, the main Bank of England building being the most prominent example. The Legal and General Assurance Company Ltd assembled more than one hundred freeholds and leaseholds over a decade in the preparatory stages of the development of Bucklersbury House and Temple Court. The National Provincial Bank took over 130 years to acquire the eighteen parcels in their attempt to rebuild their Bishopsgate headquarters – only to be stopped, for the time being at least, by development controls. Similarly, the process leading to the construction of the headquarters of Glyn, Mills & Co. in 1933 may be traced back to 1788, with the last freehold being acquired in 1905.

Such fragmentation continues, and freeholders range across a wide spectrum of individuals and institutions. They include elderly widows and Cambridge colleges. But increasingly, the economics of redevelopment and the impact of planning controls encourage the amassing of larger sites. Since the assembly of development blocks is a slow process, a long-term view must be taken and a willingness to tie up a large volume of working capital be accepted. Banks and insurance (particularly life) companies are well suited to this lengthy process, especially those who are prepared to establish an estates department to undertake such tasks. The larger property companies, too, are able to hold properties for considerable periods awaiting redevelopment. Thus the City of London Real Property Company Ltd took thirty years to consolidate the site, finally achieved in 1915, upon which Furness House now stands. The position can sometimes be speeded up, when large firms are involved, by the swopping of sites as mutually convenient. Thus one property company may relinquish a site in the City to help complete another company's development block, in return for a site in the West End.

The Second World War had a very important impact on land tenure. Charity trusts suffered along with other owners. One Livery Company with four property-owning charity trusts in 1939, holding seven properties in all, were left in 1963 with only two properties, one of which was a bare site used as a car park. The other five properties had been destroyed and later sold. The proceeds were not reinvested in City property.

The major change, however, was in the holdings of the City Corporation, as we indicated earlier. The Corporation's holdings are under the aegis of three bodies: the Town Planning and Improvements Committee; the City Lands Committee; and the Bridge House Estates trust. The first two are the most important in the present context, and it has been calculated that the freehold of rather more than one-tenth of the area of the City has been acquired by the Corporation in the course of the comprehensive redevelopment of war-damaged areas.

Of the various public bodies holding freehold land in the City, the British Railways Board and the G.P.O. (whose demand for office space continues unabated), are important. The British Railways Board hold both operational and non-operational lands, and since the Transport Act of 1962, they have been able to take an active part in the development of their properties where planning permission has been forthcoming.

In Figure 4.4 we have attempted to summarize, albeit in a rather incomplete way, the freehold ownership of land in the City held by certain selected bodies. In hatching are all the holdings of the City Corporation acting in its three capacities. In black are the holdings of such bodies as British Railways, G.P.O., and the Bank of England. In addition, an incomplete coverage of the holdings of a few of the larger property companies and some of the Livery Companies are shown, as well as Church properties excluding Parochial Charities. The blank spaces which are left are the areas owned by the remainder of the property companies and Livery Companies; by Parochial Charities, individual investors and charitable trusts; and by the banking, insurance, finance and shipping companies operating in the City.

It will be apparent that these blank areas are not very considerable in relation to the total area of the City. If we deduct the unknown holdings of those bodies and individuals which are investments not directly related to one of the specialized commercial functions carried on in the City, and also the known holdings of a few banks, insurance and shipping companies, we have accounted for almost all the land within the Square Mile.

Our conclusion follows, that with the possible exception of a very small number of commercial firms operating in the City, land tenure plays no significant part in location decisions. Building tenure is

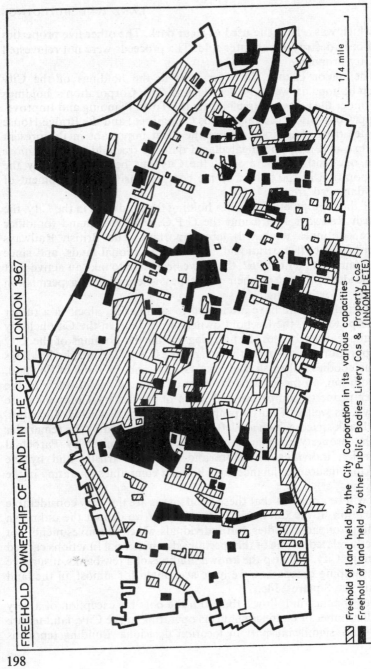

FREEHOLD OWNERSHIP OF LAND IN THE CITY OF LONDON 1967

Freehold of land held by the City Corporation in its various capacities

Freehold of land held by other Public Bodies Livery Cos & Property Cos
(INCOMPLETE)

1/4 mile

Fig. 4.4 Freehold ownership of land in the City of London 1967

much more important and we discuss leasehold interests briefly below. But essentially, firms are located in the City because they want to be there; because of the advantages of agglomeration: the ease of communication and functional linkages. When factors of property intrude it is not tenure in any legal sense but the actual level of rents, rates and service charges. Furthermore, the locations of the main functional areas are founded, in our view, primarily on historical factors which are not strongly correlated with the details of land tenure at the present time.

Leasehold interests are varied and complex. We have mentioned building leases earlier in this Appendix, while the tiers of head leases and the requirements of sub-letting make up the legal framework within which the majority of City establishments operate.

Rents and rates are the predominant factor influencing decisions on location after the situation and physical suitability of the premises. In the terms of the lease itself these further matters are of considerable importance and particular interest here. They are the term, or length, of the lease and the presence of rebuilding and rent review clauses. These are of relevance to, and can facilitate, redevelopment.

In general, the length of leases has been decreasing in the light of economic pressures and changes in the value of money. There is a complex tree-like structure of rights and responsibilities which have been effected. A building lease, where this has been granted by a freeholder, is the agreement from which other leases are derived. For a building, lease periods such as 99, 135 or 999 years may be encountered, while some owners prefer as little as 80 years and at one time might agree to 2,000 years. As a result of all these interests, various parts of the same building may be leased for different periods to different lessees at different rents per square foot. In one investigation we found some interesting examples of such rent differentials. In a number of cases tenants are still paying around 4p per square foot inclusive under a lease granted, say, in 1835 while other tenants in the same building are paying £2 per square foot exclusive. In another case a head-leaseholder is paying £.175 per square foot exclusive and sub-letting at up to £4–£4.50 per square foot.

Occupying lessees, as opposed to lessees holding for investment purposes, will in most cases hold for considerably shorter periods than those mentioned above. Periods of 7, 14, 21 or 35 year terms are commonly found and there is a growing practice to include rent revision clauses. This procedure may also be encountered with ground rents.

Although we do not propose to discuss the spatial distribution of

199

leasehold property in any detail, it may be of interest to conclude this section with some examples of the structure of leasehold interests.

One office property in the City, the freehold of which is held by a Livery Company, has a head lease owned by the Church Commissioners as an investment, and the 90,000 square feet of accommodation is leased to a number of banks and insurance companies.

In the case of another recent development of a multi-storey car park, the owners are Coal Industry (Nominees) Ltd, who hold the property investments of the National Coal Board Superannuation Schemes. The car park and service station are leased to the United Kingdom subsidiary of an overseas oil company, while an immediately adjacent development is let to an insurance company, a brewery company for a public house, and to a non-profit making organization as their headquarters.

A third example serves to illustrate both the possible variations in the terms of leases and the problems which may face a would-be developer even when he is the freeholder of an extensive area. In one part of the St Paul's Precinct redevelopment area, the Church Commissioners owned the greater part but the leases had revisions at various points of time to 2047. During the preparatory stages of an earlier development in the Precinct area one lease of 1,000 years had to be bought in. It will be appreciated that in such cases site assembly is not so much impossible as prohibitively expensive.

The usefulness of the returns to the Offices, Shops and Railway Premises Act 1963 on the question of ownership is severely circumscribed. There must be some doubt as to how accurately the original forms were completed but the major problem lies in the definition of the word 'owner' in the Act. The definition is:

'as respects England and Wales, means the person for the time being receiving the rackrent of the premises, building or part of a building in connection with which the word is used, whether on his own account or as agent or trustee for another person, or who would so receive the rackrent if the premises, building or part were let at a rackrent'.

It will be obvious that the returns give a great deal of information on who is entitled to receive rackrent, which is essential for the purpose of administering the Act. This information is not particularly useful for our purposes, however, since it tells us nothing specific about land tenure and is too general on the question of building tenure.

Finally, we present, in the accompanying tables and Figure 4.5, a

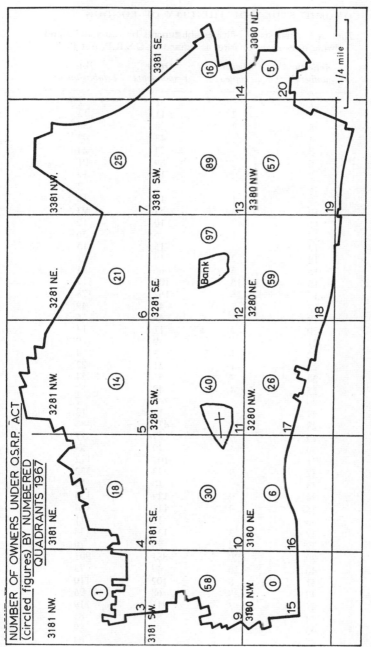

Fig. 4.5 Number of owners under O.S.R.P. Act by numbered quadrants 1967

Table 4.5. Analysis of office establishments by sub-activity and owner/non-owner division as defined by O.S.R.P. Act 1967

Activity number[1]	Owner occupied[2]	Other respondents	Total establishments
1		1	1
2	2	11	13
3	2	28	30
4		43	43
5		24	24
6	2	89	91
7		19	19
8		2	2
9	1	17	18
10	4	89	93
11		10	10
12	1	35	36
13		15	15
14	2	19	21
15	5	66	71
16	15	102	117
17	16	162	178
18	1	48	49
19	7	49	56
20	3	11	14
21		9	9
22	1	3	4
23	1	21	22
24	3	51	54
25	4	48	52
26		7	7
27	1	12	13
28	14	471	485
29		17	17
30	4	49	53
31	5	107	112
32	9	323	332
33		10	10
34	9	124	133
35	3	111	114
36		11	11
37	3	135	138
38	2	74	76
39	20	881	901
40	26	47	73
41	8	102	110
42	27	68	95
43	3	216	219
44		85	85
45	1	88	89
46	2	62	64

Table 4.5.—contd.

Activity number[1]	Owner-occupied[2]	Other respondents	Total establishments
47	11	2	13
48	30	105	135
49	4	2	6
50	3	18	21
51	6	4	10
52	9	29	38
53	3	12	15
54	2	31	33
55	4	17	21
56	2	10	12
57	8	22	30
58	2	7	9
59	2	409	411
60	3	53	56
61	137	158	295
62	1	369	370
63	8	44	52
64	5	292	297
65	5	255	260
66	32	478	510
67		52	52
68	1	112	113
69	35	133	168
70	5	218	223
71		34	34
72	7	48	55
73	3	27	30
74	9	400	409
75		59	59
76	1	36	37
77	11	59	70
78		62	62
79		20	20
80		68	68
81		82	82
82		19	19
83	4	123	127
84		6	6
85	1	35	36
86	1	56	57
Total	562	7,938	8,500

Notes:
1. For explanation of Activity Numbers see Appendix 1 to Chapter 2.
2. See text of the Appendix for definition of 'Owner' under this Act.

Source: Corporation of London.

summary analysis of the O.S.R.P. returns on ownership. The returns as analysed give 562 establishments as being owner-occupied. This compares with a total of just over 2,950 separate parcels of land owned in the City. In other words 6·6 per cent of the total number of establishments, in 19 per cent of the parcels in the City, considered they were owners within the meaning of the Act.

Chapter 5

FORECASTING THE FUTURE: METHODS AND ASSUMPTIONS

INTRODUCTION

The very nature of this study presupposes a view about the future economic structure of the City. For this purpose it may be useful to compare the City to a small country. Its various enterprises sell goods and services within its 'frontier' to households in the area and to private persons visiting it. They also sell goods and services to households 'abroad', both within the rest of the U.K. and overseas, as well as to central and local government inside and outside the City. They not only sell goods and services to households as 'final purchases', but also to other industries in the widest sense of that term, again within and beyond the 'frontier'.

The purchasing pattern is likewise complex. A large part of the purchases of City industrial and commercial concerns are labour services from individuals, most of whom not only live beyond the 'frontier' but also spend most of their income 'abroad'. Certainly, there are some direct purchases by industries and commercial concerns from one another within the City. But again, a considerable part of the input not represented by labour services is 'imported'. An obvious example is to be found in Smithfield which 'imports' meat as a raw material, re-exports it 'abroad', and employs personnel who cross the 'frontier' into the City in the early morning and again later in the day as they return home.

The complicated interlinking of the City, national and international economy can be represented in a matrix (see p. 206).

Such a matrix could be used as a method of recording the purchases and sales in money terms in a given period of time, which corresponds to the goods and services bought and sold as a result of the City's economic activities. Intra-city transactions are within the 'wall' round the sixteen boxes or elements in the left-hand corner of the matrix. The first number in the subscript to each x denotes the row in the matrix and the second the column. For example, x_{12} is

205

Purchases \ Sales	INTRA-CITY				EXTRA-CITY			
	Industry	Commerce	Other service	Consumer purchases	Consumer purchases	Government purchases	Exports to industry in U.K.	Exports to industry overseas
INTRA-CITY Industry		x_{12}	x_{13}	x_{14}	x_{15}	x_{16}	x_{17}	x_{18}
Commerce	x_{21}	—	x_{23}	x_{24}	x_{25}	x_{26}	x_{27}	x_{28}
Other service services	x_{31}	x_{32}	—	x_{34}	x_{35}	x_{36}	x_{37}	x_{38}
Factor services within City	x_{41}	x_{42}	x_{43}	—	x_{45}	x_{46}	x_{47}	x_{48}
EXTRA-CITY Factor services	x_{51}	x_{52}	x_{53}					
Imports from U.K.	x_{61}	x_{62}	x_{63}					
Imports from overseas	x_{71}	x_{72}	x_{73}					

both a record of the sale of manufactured goods, e.g. paper, and a purchase by commerce within the City. On the other hand, if the paper manufacturer 'exported' to other U.K. industrial or commercial sectors, this would be represented by x_{17}. Similarly, x_{52} would be the record of wages and salaries and other payments for personal effort paid out by commerce. And so on. Clearly this matrix is only designed to illustrate the principles of an input–output table, and as many sectors could be identified as were felt necessary for the economic study at hand. Such matrices have been constructed for regions but rarely for metropolitan areas. So far as we know none has been constructed for one segment of a metropolitan area.

FORECASTING PROBLEMS

The matrix can be used as a point of departure for the study of the forecasting problem. One might start by looking at some of the projections of the British economy which have been made for the division of the annual output of goods and services between each main economic activity according to the broad categories of the *Standard Industrial Classification* (S.I.C.). With information on the present proportion of each activity produced within the City (which would be very small for most kinds of manufacturing industry, and relatively large for banking, insurance and finance) we could hazard a guess at the total increase in extra-City demand for each sector, i.e. we could fill in the boxes to the right of the City 'wall' in our matrix for the relevant future year. Assuming that the expansion in sales to meet this demand would lead to a proportional expansion in purchases by each sector, we could then fill in the columns on the left-hand side of the matrix, both for intra-city and extra-city purchases.

One complication arising at this stage would be that produced by inter-firm 'linkages', to which we have referred already. An expansion in purchases, say, by commerce in response to an expansion of sales $(x_{25}-x_{28})$ would increase sales by intra-City industry, which in turn might increase the demand by intra-City sales industry for intra-City commercial services (x_{12}). Fortunately, with modern mathematical methods of computation this would present no problem in principle. A further complication might result from the 'feedback' of the increase in incomes generated by employment in the City in the form of increased consumer purchases. But these are likely to be very small relative to total consumer purchases and may be neglected. The final stage of the projection would be to match up the future

207

demand for the City's goods and services with a projection of the available supply of resources available to produce them.

So much for the global forecast, which would form the framework for further discussion on particular problems, such as the implications of changing economic structure on the demand for space, transport facilities, and so on. This method of projecting the future depends upon the possibility of fulfilling at least the following conditions:

(a) Adequate data of the existing inter-industry purchases and sales within the City compared with the rest of the economy and the rest of the world;

(b) A well-conceived projection of trends in the economy at large for the period in question, with sufficient detail for us to be able to detect the influence of national trends on the City's economy;

(c) Some reasonable hypothesis about the functional relationship between the demand for goods and services sold by the City and the demand for the various 'inputs' which have to be purchased to provide them;

(d) Adequate data on the existing supply of factors in the City and a well-conceived projection of the likely trends of future supply.

CHOICE OF PREDICTIVE METHODS

The conditions listed in the previous section are so exacting a requirement that we did not attempt to exploit this type of forecasting in any rigorous fashion. As regards data, we were constrained by the very broad classification of economic activities which is provided by the 1963 input–output table prepared on a national basis; this, for example, lumps all professional services together, and gives no separate information for banking, insurance and finance.

One might have begun at the other end, so to speak, and attempted a breakdown within the City; but, here again, any useful statistics would have taken many months to compile. As an example of the kind of difficulty involved, separate accounts are unlikely to be available on an establishment basis. A banking institution with a head office in the City, even if prepared to reveal unpublished information, may be unable to separate head office transactions from those of the whole organization scattered throughout the country.

The smaller the area – and statistically the City is a very small area for this kind of investigation – the more intractable the problem is likely to be. If anything, this problem may be even more acute in the study of the City than for other metropolitan regions, because of the business organization of the banking and insurance system and of transport services. Neither the single plant business – in which the firm and the plant are likely to be located in the same spot – nor the concentrated enterprise are likely to be the dominant forms of business organization. Consequently the accounting problem would appear to be insuperable.

An investigation of existing national projections soon reveals further problems of considerable magnitude. The *National Plan* projections are only available up to 1971, while the celebrated study by Wilfred Beckerman and others, published by the National Institute of Economic and Social Research,[1] only looks forward to 1975. The studies, while providing necessary background for this report, are not very helpful for our immediate purpose, as both employ very broad divisions of the nation's economic activities. Accordingly, a detailed projection on the demand side, required theoretically, is not practicable.

Even if we had a clear picture of the existing structure of inter-dependence in the City's economic activity, and of the possible effect of future national economic trends, computed in the manner described, a reasonable hypothesis which relates demand for City goods and services to the derived demand for labour and other inputs presents important difficulties. A common assumption, which has the advantage of mathematical convenience, is that any increase in the demand for any sector's output increases the demand for each of its inputs by the same percentage. One obvious trouble about this assumption is that our investigation covers a fairly long time-period for economic projections over which innovations of all kinds, e.g. in office production methods, may radically alter the 'input-mix'.

A general point about this whole approach to projecting into the future requires particular stress. It embodies a highly mechanistic view of the economic process. It visualizes a situation in which City activities are simply a response to demands originating elsewhere in the economy and in the world at large. This suggests an essentially passive role for City firms, which would merely expand in response to demands for their services; a picture which is at variance with the facts, as there is likely to be interse competition from other financial centres. In short, the City's future cannot be charted simply by hazarding a guess at global demand unless account is taken of the terms it can offer its customers and thus of its relative competitiveness.

We are forced to conclude that the conceptual and statistical

[1] *The British Economy in 1975* (Cambridge University Press, 1965).

problems are too formidable to permit an input–output approach with any degree of precision. This also applies to other techniques of forecasting the future of an urban economy. These are described in the Appendix to this chapter, but for one reason or another we found each unsuitable for the purposes of this exercise. In the end we decided to avoid making statistical projections, which are almost certain to be precisely wrong, and to offer instead some rather more general observations on future developments, which are likely to be at least approximately right.

We propose to do this in five ways. First, we shall look at the growth and future structure of the 'inputs' normally bought by firms in the City, paying particular attention to the prospects for availability of the kind of skills and buildings which City work requires. Second, we shall examine the implications of the more important developments in technology and government policy as they are likely to affect the locational decisions of firms. Third, we shall investigate the broad trends of national and international demand for the products and services at present supplied by industries located in the City. Fourth, we shall pay attention to some of the more important international institutional changes likely to impinge upon the City in the next decade or more. And lastly, we shall outline the prospects of each major activity in the City as it appears to those most intimately concerned.

Appendix to Chapter 5

REGIONAL MODELS AS A BASIS FOR FORECASTING

In Chapter 5, we discussed the theory and limitations of input–output models as a possible framework for an analysis of the economic structure of the City. During the earlier stages of our research we also examined other possible models, and two of the more important ones are discussed in this appendix. The first model is the *economic base* model which has had wide application by urban planners in the States. The second model employs a rather specialized input–output approach which is more applicable to regional analysis; this is called the *semi input–output* model.

Both of these approaches represent only a framework which can be used as a starting point for describing future developments. The actual forecasting of developments in growth sectors still has to be done in the wider context of the trends in the national economy. It is once these trends have been identified that their impact on individual activities can be calculated via the model.

ECONOMIC BASE MODEL

This model is conceptually a simple one. It relies upon the assumption that regional growth can only be induced by growth in the export sector of the local economy. The export sectors are the only income creators and can range from the export of goods produced by a manufacturer, based in the region, down to pensions paid from outside the region to individuals living within the region. The common feature of all these activities is that they create an inflow of income into the region.

All other activities are classed as non-basic activities. They rely upon the basic activities for their income, such that their growth or decline is clearly dictated by the economic fortunes of the basic sector.

The ratio between the basic and non-basic activities in any one

211

region is considered to be fixed, but this ratio can vary between regions. Therefore if the ratio in a particular region is 1:2; an increase in basic employment of 1,000 jobs will increase non-basic employment by 2,000.

Quite clearly, if the rather rigid assumptions of economic base theory are correct, then one has a very useful device for calculating the impact of external trends. The assumption of a fixed ratio between basic and non-basic activities means that one only has to forecast the developments of the basic sector to get an accurate picture of development throughout the regional economy.

We rejected the economic base theory as a model for analysis of the City on two grounds. Firstly, it rather oversimplifies the situation. Secondly, in an area as unique as the City the actual application of the model is difficult.

The first point is by far the more important. It is rather questionable whether a regional economy can grow only through growth in the basic sectors. Clearly the importing sectors have an influence too. Growth in imports will cause an outflow of income thus causing a contraction in non-basic activities. Similarly, a substitution of imports by a local producer will stop the outflow of income and divert it to people living within the region, thus promoting non-basic growth. In addition the qualitative nature of the basic activities is important. A physical expansion of exports by a local producer will have a very different impact on employment than an increase in welfare payments made by the central government, and yet both are basic activities.

The second point is more of a technical limitation. There is a problem in an area such as the City in identifying the basic sectors. One can take a broad definition and say that all activities which are not consumer services, i.e. not income absorbing, are basic; but if this is the case, then one discovers that over 80 per cent of City employment is in basic activities. Therefore one is concerned with forecasting the future developments in 80 per cent of the economic activity of the City in order to predict, via the model, the developments in the remaining 20 per cent. If one does not accept this definition, then the problem arises of identifying the direct exporters from those activities which are ancillary service to the exporters. Most definitely, situations will arise where one has to determine the proportion of the output of an accountancy firm which is exported from the City and that proportion which has been used by other City activities. The time and expense involved in such data collection made this model a non-runner from the start.

SEMI INPUT–OUTPUT MODELS

The second approach based on the use of the semi input–output model is rather limited in scope, in the sense that it attempts to measure the spatial linkages arising out of the limited mobility of goods. Goods can be classified according to the extent to which they can be transported. A local good is a good which for various reasons cannot be transported over local boundaries; a national good is one which cannot be transported over national boundaries and an international good is one enjoying complete mobility. The factors limiting mobility are numerous and include technical impossibility of movement, high transportation costs, etc. It is this limited mobility which often ties production to consumption.

To apply the model to a particular region the planner must have knowledge of the inter-industry linkages for the various industrial sectors and a classification of commodities by mobility according to the minimum amount of spatial linkages which originate in inter-industry linkages.

These linkages can be measured in two ways. The first is by using the ratio of the sum total of the transactions among the local and national sectors to the total value of the output of the national sectors. This ratio gives a measure of the direct effect upon the local sector from an increase in the production of the national sector. The second measure attempts to show the extent to which the demand for the local product is derived from its use in the production of national goods. This measure is given by the ratio of the sum total of transactions among local and national sectors to the total demand for the commodity of the local sector.

The model is very useful for regional planning purposes. It can be used to estimate the additional investment in local goods which is complementary to investment in national goods owing to the extents of inter-industry spatial linkages. In other words, the whole bunch of investments in one national sector and all complementary local sectors are evaluated together, instead of evaluating investment on one national sector only.

Unfortunately, the criticism levelled against input–output models in Chapter 5 also holds for the semi input–output model. First, it cannot take account of changes in inter-industry linkages arising from changes in technology. Secondly, the collection of the data for an input–output matrix of a regional economy would be very time-consuming. Finally, such a model would appear to have a greater applicability to regions specializing in the production of industrial goods, where some classification of mobility can be undertaken, than in an area, such as the City, where economic activity is service orientated.

BIBLIOGRAPHY

C. M. Tiebout: 'The Community Economic Base Study', Supplementary Paper, No. 16, Committee for Economic Development, December 1962.

R. W. Pfouts: 'An Empirical Testing of Economic Base Theory', *Journal of the American Institute of Planners*, Vol. 23, Spring 1957, pp. 64–69.

G. Rasul: *Input–Output Relations in Pakistan 1954*, Rotterdam University Press 1964, pp. 83–89.

J. G. Waardenburg: 'Space in Development Programming', paper presented at the Sixth European Regional Science Congress, Vienna 1966.

J. Tinbergen: 'Some Refinements of the Semi-Input–Output Method', Internal Paper, N.E.I/Div. B.I.G., Rotterdam 1966.

H. Blumenfeld: 'The Economic Base of the Metropolis', *Journal of the American Institute of Planners*, Vol. 21, Fall, 1955, pp. 114–32.

R. B. Andrews: 'Mechanics of the Urban Economic Base. The Problem of Base Measurement', *Land Economics*, Vol. 30, 1954, pp. 52–60.

C. M. Tiebout: 'Interregional Input–Output Models, An Appraisal', *Southern Economic Journal*, Vol. 24, Oct. 1957, pp. 140–7.

L. Moses: 'Interregional Input–Output Analysis', *American Economic Review*, December, 1955, XLV, pp. 803–32.

S. Czamanski: 'Industrial Location and Urban Growth', *Town Planning Review*, Vol. 36, 1965.

W. R. Thompson and J. M. Mattila: *An Econometric Model of Postwar State Industrial Development*, Wayne State University Press, 1959, pp. 28–34.

Chapter 6

FORCES LIKELY TO INFLUENCE THE FUTURE SHAPE OF THE CITY

INTRODUCTION

In this chapter we deal, at some length, with some of the important factors likely to affect the City's economic future in the next ten to fifteen years. Inevitably we have had to be selective in our choice of factors and, in each case, we shall be concerned with broad trends rather than detailed projections. Later, in Chapters 8 to 13, we shall consider the impact of some of the findings of this chapter on particular activities in the City.

The factors which we shall analyse in the following sections are:

(A) Labour supply.
(B) Office location and planning policies.
(C) Land and buildings.
(D) Technology.
(E) Trends in national and international spending.
(F) Transport developments.
(G) The international role of sterling.
(H) European integration.

(A) LABOUR SUPPLY

In 1966, no less than 99·2 per cent of the working population in the City lived outside it. Some 273,480 or 76·4 per cent lived in Greater London, 81,550 or 23·2 per cent in the rest of the South-East, and 2,990 or 0·8 per cent in other parts of England and Wales. Further particulars are given in Table 6.1.

The dependence on the City as a place of employment is shown in Figures 6.1 and 6.2. While these reveal the proportion of working population commuting to the City falling as travelling distance increases, there is no clear concentric pattern. The outer Home Counties to the south and north-east of the City still supply a larger share of their labour force to the City than do those to the west or

215

Table 6.1. Distribution of Working Population in the City by Place of Residence 1961 and 1966

	1961		1966	
	Numbers	*Per cent*	*Numbers*	*Per cent*
(a) *South East England*				
Berkshire	1,490	0·4	1,330	0·4
Buckinghamshire	2,690	0·7	2,340	0·7
London	133,480	34·4	273,480	76·4
Middlesex	47,510	12·3	*	
Essex	89,150	23·0	30,430†	8·4
Kent	38,320	9·9	12,240†	3·4
Hertfordshire	10,590	2·7	8,200†	2·3
Hampshire	1,400	0·4	1,490	0·4
Oxfordshire	220	0·1	190	0·1
Bedfordshire	340	0·1	350	0·1
Surrey	50,390	13·0	17,810†	5·0
Sussex	7,480	1·9	7,170	2·0
	383,060	98·8	355,030	99·2
(b) *Rest of England and Wales*	4,830	1·3	2,990	0·8
Total	387,890	100·0	358,020	100·0

* Included in London (= Greater London).
† Part included in London.
Source: *Censuses of Population 1961 and 1966.*

outer South-East (cf. Essex 8·25 per cent and Surrey 6·14 per cent with Berkshire 0·64 per cent).

The mean commuting distance travelled in 1961 (defined as the average of the distances from the centre of the local authority areas in the thirteen leading commuting counties to the Bank of England weighted by the number of commuters) was 10·8 miles. Table 6.2 also shows that 8·7 per cent of the working population travelled less than twenty miles. This distance is almost certainly increasing. Though we have no comparable data to those published in the 1961 Census, information on season tickets issued by British Rail to passengers travelling to Central London in the 1960s shows that the greatest rise occurred at stations in the outer Home Counties (particularly north-east and east Essex and north and central Kent).

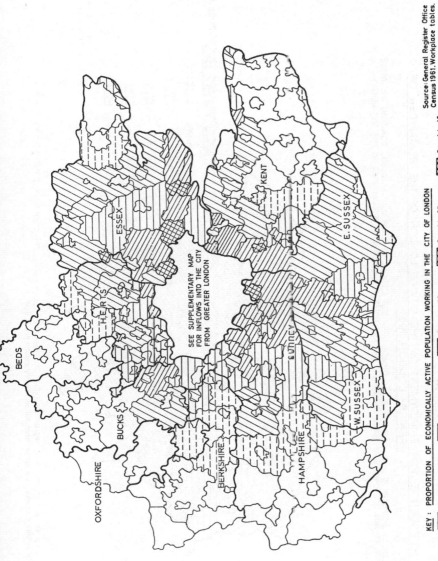

KEY : PROPORTION OF ECONOMICALLY ACTIVE POPULATION WORKING IN THE CITY OF LONDON

Over 1 in 200 Over 1 in 100 Over 1 in 50 Over 1 in 25 Over 1 in 10

Source: General Register Office Census 1961. Workplace tables.

FIG. 6.1 Dependance for employment on City of London of the Counties of South East England 1961

FIGURE 6.2 DEPENDENCE FOR EMPLOYMENT ON THE CITY OF LONDON OF THE REMAINDER OF GREATER LONDON. 1961

(THE GREATER LONDON BOUNDARY IS THAT ACCORDING TO THE LOCAL GOVERNMENT ACT 1963. THE COMPONENT MUNICIPAL BOROUGHS ARE THOSE IN EXISTENCE BEFORE THIS ACT CAME INTO FORCE, SINCE THESE ARE THE AREAS FOR WHICH DATA IS CLASSIFIED IN THE 1961 CENSUS WORKPLACE TABLES)

KEY: PROPORTION OF ECONOMICALLY ACTIVE POPULATION WORKING IN THE CITY OF LONDON

Over 1 in 200
Over 1 in 100
Over 1 in 50
Over 1 in 25
Over 1 in 10

Source: General Register Office Census 1961. Workplace tables.

N.B. FIGURES 6.1 and 6.2 ARE NOT STRICTLY INDICATIVE OF THE EXTENT OF COMMUTING (=daily travelling). THE COMPARISON IS BETWEEN WORKPLACE AND USUAL RESIDENCE (to which the person need not necessarily return every day).

Table 6.2. Distribution of Working Population in the City by Estimated
Miles Travelled to Work* 1961

Miles	Numbers working in the City	Typical locations
0–4	94,500†	Finbury, Chelsea, Deptford
5–9	140,200	Croydon, Hendon, East Ham
10–14	79,800	Romford, Orpington, Southall
15–19	20,700	Esher, Staines, Watford
20–24	13,900	Sevenoaks, Slough, Welwyn
25–29	12,100	Chelmsford, Guildford, Gravesend
30–34	5,600	Luton, Gillingham, Horsham
35–39	10,400	Southend, Aylesbury Farnham
40–44	1,500	Reading, Basingstoke, Burnham-on-Crouch
45–49	3,100	Bedford, Brighton, Ashford
50–54	2,200	Worthing, Hastings, Colchester
55–59	500	Clacton, Newbury, Chichester
60 and over	1,200	Southampton, Margate, Bournemouth
Total	385,700	

* Classified by distance from the centre of each local authority area to the centre of the City as the crow flies.

† Including residents in the City working there.

N.B. These data refer only to workplace movements from the following counties: London, Middlesex, Essex, Hertfordshire, Surrey, Kent, Sussex, Hampshire, Berkshire, Oxfordshire, Bedfordshire, Buckinghamshire.

It should be noted that the upper ranges of the distribution are understated because parts of other counties fall within the mileage limits.

Source: Census of Population 1961 – Workplace Tables.

This evidence, and that of the 1966 Social Survey of the City Corporation[1] suggests that the city is recruiting an increasing proportion of its labour force from further afield.

In estimating the future labour supply of the City, we look at the picture broadly. The size of the commuting population depends upon three things; first, the size of the economically active population in the areas from which the City draws its employment; second, the specific activity rates within each age-group of that population; and third, the proportion of the working population who choose to work in the City.

We have no means of precisely estimating trends in the economically active age-groups at local authority or even country areas: this is because of the unpredictability of migration in population change. The Registrar-General has, however, published projections of the

[1] 1966 Social Survey, Corporation of London.

'potential' labour force (defined as men aged from fifteen to sixty-four and women from fifteen to fifty-nine) for three regions in south-east England – viz. Greater London, the Outer Metropolitan Area and the rest of south-east England – up to 1981.[2]

These figures are set out in Table 6.3. They reveal that over the period 1966–81, the size of the economically active population in Greater London is expected to fall by 11·7 per cent, while that in the rest of the South-East is expected to rise by 19·2 per cent. These projections partly reflect the expected trends in the total population, and partly changes in the age structure of the population – both of which elements are influenced by the policy of the Government to disperse one million Londoners from Greater London by 1981.

Table 6.3. Economically Active Population in the South-East Region 1966–81

| | 1966 | | 1981 | | Change 1966–81 |
	Persons (000s)	Percentage of population	Persons (000s)	Percentage of population	Persons (000s)
Greater London Area	4,160	53	3,675	50	485
Outer Metropolitan Area	2,374	47	2,848	46	474
Outer South-East Area	1,828	44	2,163	42	335
Total	8,362	49	8,686	46	324

Source: *Strategic Plan for the South East H.M.S.O.* 1970.

Data on recent trends in *activity rates*, e.g. the proportion of those people aged fifteen or over either in work or involuntarily unemployed,[3] reveal that in Greater London there was a fall in the male activity rates between 1961 and 1966 from 87·3 per cent to 85·8 per cent; in the rest of the South-East region, the fall was from 84·0 per cent to 83·2 per cent. By contrast, over the same period, there was an increase in female activity rates from 45·5 per cent to 49·6 per cent in Greater London and from 33·2 per cent to 39·6 per cent in the rest of the South-East.[4] If these trends continue in the 1970s, this

[2] South-East Economic Planning Council, *A Strategy for the South-East*, 1967, Annex C, Table 3.
[3] See 1961 *Census of Population*, Occupation Tables pages XXIV ff.
[4] Greater London Council, *Development Plan: Report of Studies*, 1970, Table A3.6, p. 84.

would reduce the pool of labour in the Greater London and the Outer Metropolitan region still further – probably up to 100,000 less in the mid-1970s.[5]

Even assuming no change in the total population or the age structure in the main divisions of south-east England, the spatial distribution of the change in the ratio of females of working age to males of working age would lead one to expect some decrease in commuting from all areas. This is because:

(a) the proportion of female workers who commute to the City is lower than that of male workers, and declines rapidly as the travelling distance increases;

(b) the ratio of females of working age to males of working age is expected to decline in all parts of the South-East (see Table 6.4); and

(c) this decline is most pronounced in the Outer Metropolitan Area and least pronounced in the outer South-East.

Table 6.4. Estimated Percentage of Females of Working Age to Males of Working Age in the South-East Region 1961–81

	1961	1981	Per cent change 1961–81
Greater London Area	96·6	92·8	−4
Outer Metropolitan Area	95·1	89·3	−6
Rest of South East	95·1	93·8	−2

Source: *Registrar General*.

On the other hand, our reading of the occupational structure of the likely future labour supply suggests that the type of labour which the City is likely to want more of in the 1970s, viz. administrative and professional office workers, is likely to *increase* in supply; and that most of the decline in the working population will be concentrated in the operative and clerical office worker categories. To this extent, at least, the City is likely to fare rather better than other parts of the G.L.C. Moreover, such evidence we have suggests the commuting habits of professional and managerial labour are rather different from those of other socio-economic groups. In 1961 26·3 per cent of the professional and managerial workers in Central London lived outside

[5] In another (unpublished) paper the G.L.C. estimate that the total working population in the Greater London Area will fall from 4·2 million in 1966 to 3·7 in 1976.

221

the conurbation compared with only 15·3 per cent of the junior and intermediate non-manual workers. Since that date, the numbers working in Central London but living outside the G.L.C. Area have continued to increase but those working in Central London but living within the G.L.C. Area has hardly risen at all.

The overall effects of these expected changes in the size and structure of the population in the South-East, allowing for the differential impact between the three divisions of the South-East, are then twofold. First, assuming that the ratio of persons in each local authority area working in the City remains broadly the same as in 1961, there is likely to be a decline in numbers commuting to the City from 390,570 in 1961 to around 270,000 in the late 1970s. Second, as Table 6.5 sets out, the commuting pattern will change. The evidence

Table 6.5. Estimated Source of Employees in the City of London by Place of Residence 1961–81

	1961	1971	1981
Greater London Area	78·9	75·3	73·1
Outer Metropolitan Area	17·5	20·7	22·4
Outer South-East Area	2·4	2·7	3·1
Rest of England and Wales	1·2	1·3	1·3
Total	100·0	100·0	100·0

Source: Estimates by authors.

strongly suggests that the share of long-distance commuting (i.e. from outside the G.L.C. area) will increase and that of short-distance commuting (i.e. from the main London boroughs) will decline.[6]

Up to this point, we have assumed that the City's attraction as a workplace, relative to that of other areas, remains unchanged. The probability of this bold assumption is examined in later sections, as it involves wider issues than those considered here. Suffice it to mention at this point that there are several new road and rail developments planned which will make commuting to the City both speedier and more congenial.[7] In theory, it is always possible for the City to increase its share of the labour force from supplying areas by offering high enough wages or other inducements. Whether it can, in fact, do so depends upon its own economic position relative to that of the competing areas.

[6] This would suggest we expect a net *increase* in commuting from 1966.
[7] See Section F and Chapter 12 for more detail.

It can be shown that, purely on the basis of national and international expenditure trends, the demand for the type of goods and services supplied by the City is likely to increase in the next decade or so. But it is a big jump in the argument to assume that this will lead to more people working in the City. The City's share in this increased output may fall; while any additional production of goods and services might be made possible by further mechanization or the increased efficiency of existing resources. A detailed analysis of these other factors is made later in this chapter.

We can, however, point to various implications of the population trends described in this section. First, unless there is a reduced demand for labour by City employers, or further decentralization of activities from the centre, wages and salaries in the City will rise relative to other recruiting areas. Second, the type of activities which are most likely to be affected by these trends are those in which labour costs are an important component of total costs, particularly those employing routine and semi-skilled labour.

The changing structure of activities in the City may be an additional factor making for more long-distance commuting. It is also apparent that as older commuters retire they are not being replaced by younger commuters. This is most noticeable around areas of substantial new office development, e.g. Croydon and Heathrow.

It is, of course, possible that the official forecasts of population changes in the South-East might turn out to be wrong: already they have been revised downwards several times. The assumed rate of net emigration from London to the new and expanded towns on which these estimates are based may be exaggerated, or the estimated national excess of births over deaths miscalculated; these are basic assumptions in the Registrar-General's estimates. Neither have we allowed for the fact that some workers may either retire early or work beyond retirement age. In the case of the City, however, we suspect that these two forces may balance themselves out.

Nevertheless, the City (in common with the rest of Central London) may well be faced with a falling supply of labour, at least, until 1981, and particularly in the early 1970s. This being so, it is all the more important that the closest examination be given to the structure of economic activity in the City, so that those institutions and functions which are vital to its well-being and that of the national economy should be able to expand, and those which are less essential encouraged to decentralize. In most cases, we believe that the market mechanism is the most effective way of achieving this. The exception is, perhaps, where premises are being occupied at well below economic rents because of the leasing conditions entered into many years ago.

One possibility which comes to mind is for the local authority, aided by finance from other quarters if necessary, to purchase industrial premises which, from the community's viewpoint, could be better used for other purposes. Another, which is really outside the scope of our analysis to discuss, is the redevelopment of the 'twilight areas' around Central London, which could house the essential basic labour force of the City (junior executives, clerks, typists and service workers, etc.) in reasonable proximity to its work and without the incentive to work elsewhere. In this connection, it is unlikely that housing programmes planned within the City, e.g. in the Barbican area, will be much help, because rents are likely to be far higher than this type of labour can afford.

(B) OFFICE LOCATION AND PLANNING POLICIES

We have seen that the City's economic future is very largely bound up with office development. Of the increase in floor-space for the ten years 1961–70 in the Square Mile, offices accounted for 91 per cent; and about four-fifths of the workers in the City are currently employed in offices. Official attitudes towards office building and employment are therefore of crucial importance, and worthy of close examination.

Central Government Policy

Since November 1964, any new office development in the Metropolitan region of London of more than 3,000 sq. ft. has had to obtain, from the Central Government, an Office Development Permit (O.D.P.): this provision was extended to the rest of the South-East region in July 1966.

One of the aims behind the Government's regional office policy – like that of its industrial policy – has been to try and limit the congestion of population and employment in Greater London, and to try and divert new development into other parts of the country. This policy has achieved a certain measure of success. Between 1964 and 1967, only 28 per cent of the net addition to office floor-space in south-east England occurred in Central London, even though in this latter year it accounted for 51 per cent of the *stock* of office floor-space. The corresponding figures for the rest of Greater London were 39 per cent and 24 per cent; for the Outer Metropolitan Area 22 per cent and 15 per cent and for the rest of the South-East 11 per cent and 10 per cent. Since the mid-1960s, the increase in office workers in Central London has levelled off and, currently, only those engaged in administrative and professional activities are increasing in number.

The criteria for granting O.D.P.s differ according to whether the proposed offices are for a specified occupier or for unknown occupiers, i.e. a speculative development. Where there is a named occupier attached to an application for an O.D.P., then the criteria relate mainly to the claims of the particular company to remain in the area. Evidence must be provided that the activity could not be carried out elsewhere, particularly where all the activities, including routine, are concerned. Secondly, it must be shown that no other suitable space is available in the area. In the early days of O.D.P.s, e.g. between 1965 and 1968, applications for development in the City were sometimes refused because of the availability of empty offices at that time. Thirdly, the application is viewed in the light of 'the public interest'. Again, in the mid-1960s the need to avoid greater congestion or exacerbate labour shortages was given as a reason for refusal of a permit.

More recently, however, the public interest criteria for O.D.P.s appears to have been rather different. Nowadays, applications are more likely to be favoured if it can be shown that a London location will add to the efficiency of the enterprise, particularly in exporting, compared with that which would be achieved in another location. Also, with floor-space-per-employee needs rising at the rate of about 3 per cent every five years – mainly the result of improved standards and office automation, there is a tendency for new offices to create less demand for labour. The concept of the public interest may also be invoked where there is a new development which provides benefits of a better environment, more shops or easier access.

The criteria for the granting of O.D.P.s for speculative office development include the public interest clause mentioned above, and also the amount of empty offices available in the area. Initially, the O.D.P. policy was operated on the basis that there should be no prohibition of replacement and rebuilding. New space was to be allowed at 20 per cent less than the old space being replaced. With rising floor-space-per-employee, the policy was changed to a strict one-for-one replacement. A caveat is generally included that there must be no increase in employment on the site.

The position concerning the applications for O.D.P.s to increase floor-space in the City of London is shown in Table 6.6. These data

H

reveal that the last two years has seen a substantial rise in the number of permits allowed, both absolutely, and in relation to those applied for. Between January 1969 and December 1970, there were more than double the permits granted than in the previous three and a half years, while for the period January 1968 to December 1970, permits for over 5 million sq. ft were granted, compared with refusals of a quarter of this space. Indeed, permits allowed have shown a steady rate of increase throughout the period. Refusals, on the other hand, have averaged between one-third and one-quarter of approvals. The number of refusals, however, can be misleading as a first refusal

Table 6.6. Applications for Office Development Permits in the City 1965–70

| | | PERMITS | | | | REFUSALS | | |
| | | Thousands of sq. ft of floor-space | | | | Thousands of sq. ft of floor-space | | |
Date	Number	Gross	Relin-quished	Net	Number	Gross	Relin-quished	Net
1965 (Aug.–Dec.)	8	514	204	310	13	1,199	909	290
1966	9	296	207	89	4	22	4	18
1967	12	947	635	312	6	168	59	109
1968	28	3,366	2,065	1,301	6	305	164	141
1969	49	3,466	1,553	1,913	17	612	188	424
1970	80	5,156	3,182	1,976	18	1,249	430	819
Total	186	13,745	7,846	5,899	64	3,555	1,754	1,801

Source: Ministry of Housing and Local Government.

can be re-submitted as a new scheme and accepted. It will also be observed that over the last two years permits totalling a net addition of 5·2 million sq. ft of floor-space have been granted. This will presumably result in a sharp increase in the supply of office space in 1971 and 1972 – just as, during 1970, building completions largely reflect the O.D.P.s granted in 1968.

When the Board of Trade was responsible for O.D.P.s, it took six weeks, on average, for investigation. Large schemes would take a little longer and small schemes a shorter time. In October 1969, responsibility for O.D.P.s was switched to the Ministry of Housing and Local Government. Under the Board of Trade, the same department was responsible for both O.D.P.s and I.D.C.s. However, in October 1969, the majority of the department moved to the Ministry of Technology to continue dealing with I.D.C.s, which meant a shortage of staff at the Ministry of Housing and Local Government. The changeover, and the new Government and related uncertainties, has meant that the time taken to consider an application is now between eight and ten weeks. Applications for large schemes can take up to four months because many more departments and people are affected and must be consulted.

It is not possible to assess the precise extent to which the operation of O.D.P. policy has contributed towards this imbalance between supply and demand. But we think it has had quite a marked effect in at least three ways. First, policy initially took too much account of the *stock* of vacant floor-space at the time, and too little of rate of increase in demand. Moreover, insufficient allowance was probably made for the 'time lags' between the granting of an O.D.P. and the completion of the office building. The consequence was that by the time a more liberal policy towards O.D.P.s was being implemented (e.g. around 1968) the demand for new office floor-space had overtaken this supply and this was reflected in a sharp increase in rents. Second, we believe that O.D.P. policy might well have been psychologically damaging, to the extent that some (very worthy) firms have not applied for O.D.P.s simply because they believe (possibly quite wrongly) they would not get them. Instead, they have spent a lot of money in expensively modernizing and re-equipping existing premises. Third, even accepting the good intentions of the planners, there is no evidence that they know more than the market about the best distribution of land use in the City. Indeed we would strongly suspect that O.D.P.s have introduced an element of rigidity into the market, in that supply has not been allowed to adjust itself to demand in the way that would best utilize scarce resources.

Complementary to O.D.P. policy has been the operation of the Location of Offices Bureau (L.O.B.). This institution was set up in 1963 to encourage the decentralization of office employment from Central London. The Bureau, which is essentially an advisory body, assembles data on the costs and benefits of dispersion, and initiates research into this and related topics. Since its inception, the L.O.B. has consistently demonstrated the desirability of moving certain types of employment out of Central London, especially expanding firms and routine and semi-independent departments.

What is particularly noticeable, however, is the comparative lack of interest shown in the Bureau's work by City firms. Some of the reasons for this indifference will emerge from our studies of the main activities operating in the City. But it would seem that, at least for the majority of City firms, the advantages of the City outweigh the extra labour costs and rents.

The final aspect of official location policy which deserves brief mention is that of the proposed development of new office centres outside London. It seems likely that over the next decade or so every encouragement will be given to creating a number of large new towns or cities in south-east England to act as counter-magnets to London. The proposals for the new town at Milton Keynes, which will house up to 250,000 people, have already been approved, and those for the development of an even larger conurbation in south Hampshire based upon Southampton and Portsmouth are under consideration. Similarly sizeable schemes are already under way or are being contemplated at Swindon, Ipswich, Peterborough and Ashford.[8]

Local Government Policy

An enterprise sponsoring a new office development of 3,000 sq. ft or more in the City of London must not only obtain an O.D.P., but planning permission from the local authority – the Greater London Council (G.L.C.). In its attempts to relate the level and distribution of office accommodation in Greater London to estimated trends in the demand for, and supply of, office labour, the G.L.C. is currently thinking in terms of a 'target' net addition to office floor-space in Central London between 1972 and 1976 of 8 million sq. ft,[9] compared with a target for the preceding five years of 7 million sq. ft. For the G.L.C. area as a whole the proposed office floor-space target in the 1972–6 period is 20·5 million sq. ft, compared with 16·0 million sq. ft for the previous five years. It is thus planned that 60 per cent of new office development will take place outside Central London in the early and mid-1970s. This is a considerable increase on the share of this area of the *stock* of office floor-space in 1966, viz. 40 per cent.[10]

The G.L.C. bases these targets on the projected demand/supply relationship for labour in Greater London in the foreseeable future. Essentially, it considers that both the demand for, and the supply of, labour will fall in most G.L.C. boroughs in the 1970s. This, in turn,

[8] *Strategic Plan for the South East*, H.M.S.O. 1970.

[9] *Greater London Development Plan*, Supplementary Paper 390, October 1970.

[10] See also D. R. Denman, 'Why office control failed', *The Times*, July 24, 1970.

is related to the estimated decline in the population of Greater London from 8·0 million in 1961 to 7·3 million in 1981.[11]

In its evidence given to the Greater London Development Plan inquiry in October 1970[12] E.A.G. criticized these estimates and particularly the (high) labour availability estimate for the City in 1981 of 361,000. We think that a more reasonable estimate of the size of the labour force in the Square Mile in 1981 would be 380,000 to 390,000; the City Corporation would like to think a figure of 400,000 would be achieved. But the fact remains that, if the City's share of the increased floor-space *available* in Central London between 1966 and 1971 remained the same for the period 1972–6, it would be granted only 2·4 million sq. ft.

From what has been written, this figure would seem to be very inadequate. Between 1966 and 1971 it is estimated that the increase in floor-space *used* in the City was 4·6 million sq. ft (2·1 million of net addition to floor-space and 2·5 million of floor-space available in 1966 but not used then). Between 1968 and 1970, O.D.P.s to approve an additional 3 million sq. ft were granted. Most of this building is now in the pipeline and is unlikely to be completed by 1971. The G.L.C. assumes that the rate of demand for office accommodation in the first half of the 1970s will be considerably less, and probably not more than one-half, of that in the second half of the 1960s.

All indications are that this is an implausible assumption and that unless the G.L.C. raise their 'target' office floor-space for the Central Area (or allow the City a larger share of this target) the rate of increase in the demand for office floor-space in the City will exceed that of supply, and, as a consequence, there will be a further sharp rise in rents. Indeed, on occasions, there will just not be certain kinds of office accommodation available (just as in rapid wage inflation, the supply of certain types of labour becomes completely inelastic), and this will drive potential office users (particularly foreign operators) from London to the Continent.

(C) LAND AND BUILDINGS

Chapter 4 has described the pattern of land use in the City. Among other things it indicated that, at the time of the Land Use Survey in 1966, there were vacant and derelict sites of some 675,000 sq. ft

[11] Report of Studies (G.L.D.P.), G.L.C., 1970.
[12] See the written evidence presented on behalf of the Corporation of London, October 1970.

which, if developed on a 5:1 plot ratio basis, would provide further accommodation of 3·35 million sq. ft.

Table 6.7 presents details by quadrant of the vacant floor-space and sites in the City in 1966 and the amount of new building then taking place. Between that date and mid-1970 some 2·1 million sq. ft were added to the office floor-space and 2·5 million of the 3·0 million sq. ft of the floor-space unoccupied in 1966 was taken up. If this

Table 6.7. Development Plan Zoning of Vacant and Derelict Land in the City 1966 (Hundreds of square feet)

Map reference	Offices	Com-merce	River-side	Open space	High-way	Public buildings	Mixed	Total
3180NW*								
3180NE		104		554				658
3181NW								
3181SW	439							439
3181NE		51				13		64
3181SE	119			128	235			482
3280NW		102	74	88				264
3280NE	79	226		161				466
3280SE			RIVER ONLY					
3281NW	174	231		65	16	46	1,508	2,040
3281SW	174			79	166	65		484
3281NE		5						5
3281SE	122					13		135
3282SW								
3380NW	291			106				397
3380SW			RIVER ONLY					
3380NE	79	148		139		64		430
3381NW							17	17
3381SW	39			4				43
3381NE			FIGURES ON 3381NW					
3381SE	144	17			275	39	347	822
Total	1,660	780	178	389	1,392	475	1,872	6,746

* See Figure 6.5.
Source (and of Table 6.8): Corporation of London.

additional office accommodation was occupied at the average density of 175 sq. ft per worker in the City this would mean the City was housing up to 26,000 more office workers in 1970 than in 1966.

It is not, however, as simple as this. Some – perhaps the majority – of new buildings completed in the City in recent years have been occupied by firms already operating in the City. Sometimes they continue to occupy their existing premises but, in most cases, they relinquish them. Where the vacated premises are in an area scheduled for redevelopment they may be left empty or demolished; more often than not, they are bought or rented by other firms. What net difference this makes to the labour force in the City will depend on the circumstances involved. We have seen, in Chapter 4, that most new office buildings operate at a lower population density than old ones: they also make possible more efficient and labour-saving methods of production. Quite often, in our experience, additional premises are required, not to accommodate more labour, but to house existing labour more comfortably and efficiently. If, as a result of each move – and the occupation of a new building (like a new house) often sets in motion a whole chain of moves – the population density is reduced, the net effect on employment might be quite small.

Looking ahead, there is currently very little vacant office accommodation in the City. On the other hand we have seen that, in the eighteen months between January 1969 and December 1970, O.D.P.s for a net addition to office floor-space of 3·9 million sq. ft were approved. The early 1970s should then see more sites, or redevelopment of existing sites being used for office development in the Square Mile.

Crucial to the whole problem, is the land-use zoning policy of the Corporation. There is no doubt that additional land in the City could be made available for office development should the need arise for it. For instance, due to the movement downstream of an increasing proportion of London's trade, and the trend for goods to be dispatched directly to (and from) internal wholesalers or manufacturers, many wharves and warehouses in Upper Thames Street are being closed down. Much of this could be given over to offices. Even accepting the present plot ratios and daylight controls, and assuming no restrictions on office development, we see no *physical* reasons why a daytime population of 472,000, as envisaged by the Holden/Holford report, should not be reached or, indeed, exceeded.

But issues other than the physical and the economic are involved in land-use zoning. One of the stated aims of the Corporation of London is to strengthen the educational, cultural and recreational environment of the Square Mile. The desire to ensure an adequate supply of certain types of labour within the City was only one of the reasons for launching the Barbican residential scheme. Included in the scheme are a multi-million-pound concert hall, a theatre for the Royal Shakespeare Company, and a new London Museum, possibly to be sited on the corner of Aldersgate and London Wall. The educational facilities include the City University. There are also proposals for the expansion of hotel accommodation.

231

Similarly, the building of precincts around the Tower of London and St Paul's are not only intended to aid the tourist trade but to preserve the historical heritage of the City. There is considerably more open space in the City than before the war.

Table 6.8. Schedule of Vacant Land and Accommodation in the City 1966
(Hundreds of square feet)

Map reference	Vacant Floor-Space				Sites		Construction at Survey	
	Offices	Commerce	Industry	Other	Vacant	Derelict	Now complete	Construction
3180NW*	1,087							
3180NE	1,137	1,890		116	580	78		
3181NW	149	358						
3181SW	1,743		1,142	42	439		458	
3181NE	61	3,149	20	16	64			
3181SE	4,202	979	30	419	273	209	1,533	
3280NW	353	2,831		8	210	54		1,596
3280NE	1,494	1,914	80		322	144		
3280SE				RIVER ONLY				
3281NW	861	1,132	170	55	2,033	8		485†
3281SW	1,968	36	3	510	380	104	1,111	309
3281NE	3,015			108	5			5,270
3281SE	4,981			90	13	122		2,650
3282SW								
3380NW	1,982			127	223	174		149
3380SW				RIVER ONLY				
3380NE	472	140			391	41		
3381NW	648	906	50	75	17			
3381SW	6,122	204	3	45	43			7,398
3381NE				FIGURES ON 3381NW				
3381SE	48	650		90	630	192	1,588	
Total	30,323	14,147	1,497	1,701	5,623	1,126	4,690	17,847

* See Figure 6.5.
† Barbican residential area must be added to this figure.

All these developments compete with the use of scarce resources and involve a 'cost' of opportunities forgone. But, in the last resort, the choice of this kind of space usage must be taken on non-economic grounds. Such guidance as we can give, and hope to give in later sections of this study, is concerned solely with providing some of the facts on which an appropriate decision can be made, and the implications of alternative lines of action.

(D) TECHNOLOGY

There are a great variety of technological changes which may have some effect on some firms in the City. The chief areas, however, in which such effects seem likely to be widespread and important are office automation – which is mainly centred around the installation of automatic data processing (A.D.P.), and closely related to this, telecommunications between firms, or within a firm.

Automatic Data Processing

Among the firms in the City who have already installed A.D.P. are the Bank of England, the clearing banks, a number of merchant and overseas banks; stockbrokers and insurance brokers; insurance companies; the Stock Exchange; the London Produce Clearing House; Lloyd's policy signing office; Lloyd's Register of Shipping; and the Port of London Authority. There are also several computer service firms which specialize in providing services for the City.

Almost all A.D.P. owners in the City use their equipment for handling their accounts and payroll, and a large number of specialized uses have also been developed. Examples include; the keeping of stock and share registers and the payment of dividends by the Bank of England and the registrars' departments of clearing banks and merchant banks; clearing operations by the banks, the Stock Exchange and the London Produce Clearing House; contract notes by stockbrokers; investment analyses by stockbrokers and institutional investors; premium renewals, life valuations and bonuses by insurance companies.

The development of A.D.P. seems to be going on in two different but not necessarily inconsistent directions. One is the production of larger and faster central processing units with multiple access and 'on-line' data transmission equipment, so that a large number of users can be connected to a single control computer installation. The banks are already beginning to do this for their branches, and it may not be too long before similar facilities may be available, on a rental or subscription basis, to anyone who requires them.

In the opposite direction is the development of more compact equipment, leading towards the production of cheap 'desk top' machines which are nevertheless capable of carrying out quite sophisticated programmes.

Both developments will increase the availability of computer services to small firms and to decentralized branches or departments of large ones. The big installation is bound to be the more flexible but it will still have disadvantages, including the cost of data transmission, the risk of widespread disruption in case of a breakdown, and the difficulty of ensuring complete secrecy for confidential information.

Other developments which are taking place and which will no doubt continue are: the improvement and cheapening of data transmission; improved multiple and random access systems; greater standardization both of equipment and programming; the simplification of programming with a consequent simplification of training; and a relative (if not absolute) cheapening of equipment.

These developments will obviously lead to the extension of existing uses within the City and to the development of new ones. There is still a lot of room for both. For example, the banks are only just beginning their 'on-line' branch link-up; few discount houses are yet using a computer, though others are installing them; and only a relatively small number of stock exchange firms are yet big enough to make it worth their while to have their own equipment. Developments affecting particular activities are discussed in Chapters 8–12.

There seem to be three questions of general interest:

(a) How much labour will computers directly use in the City?
(b) Will they be a centralizing or a decentralizing influence?
(c) What differences will they make to the demand for different types of work (e.g. clerical, technical and managerial)?

It is very difficult to get any firm quantitative measure of the amount of labour saved by the introduction of office automation; and the picture portrayed by most investigators who tried to find one is very confused. This is so for various reasons: the volume of work in the activities concerned has generally been growing rapidly; the expansion of a firm's business, especially if it is accompanied by difficulty in recruiting labour, is an important motive for installing a computer; and once it is installed there is a tendency to find secondary uses for it in the keeping of more detailed records and the presentation of more frequent and more elaborate statistical returns all of which may be very useful to management but which would not in themselves have been strong enough motives to lead to the purchase of a computer. A.D.P. also creates jobs for its own technical operation.

Perhaps the most comprehensive analysis of the problem made in this country was that of the Manpower Research Unit (M.R.U.) of the Ministry of Labour in a report published in 1965.[13] This showed that, up to that time, automatic data processing (A.D.P.) had affected less than 1 per cent of the total working population in Great Britain; when expressed in relation to office employment the percentage is higher, but it is still less than 10 per cent. More interestingly, M.R.U. attempted to estimate the *reduction* in the total demand for office workers due to the introduction of A.D.P. They concluded, with many qualifications, that the net reduction had been very small, probably around 0·75 per cent of the total number of office workers in the U.K.

The main reasons given by those firms approached by M.R.U. for installing A.D.P. were the need to economize on data processing costs, and the wish to provide better services for management. This is confirmed by our own investigations, which suggest that if the City is faced with a labour shortage in the next few years this itself, through its effect on rising labour costs, is likely to stimulate A.D.P. installation.

At the same time, the M.R.U. report concludes that A.D.P. is not likely to produce any dramatic changes in the national level of office employment in the immediate future. It suggests that the total effect over the seven years 1964–70 may be a reduction of about one-fifth in the demand for *additional* office manpower. When applied to the City's situation, this could bring a slight decrease in the demand for office workers, but even this prediction could easily be proved wrong. It has been the general experience, both in this country and in the United States, that actual reductions in labour, resulting from automation have been less than was originally expected, and our interviews with computer users have confirmed this impression. Statements such as, 'we get more (or quicker or better) work with the same amount of labour' were much more common than evidence of an actual reduction in the payroll.

There are, however, some notable exceptions. The Bank of England has achieved substantial economies on its maintenance of the register of government securities, and so have other registrars' departments. The banks have made big savings on their clearing operations, but these have been offset by the very rapid increase in the number of items going through the clearing. Stockbrokers have achieved big savings on extract notes and valuation though these have tended to be offset not only by a rising volume of business but also by the expansion of other work, mainly investment analysis.

[13] Ministry of Labour, Manpower Studies: No. 4, *Computers in Offices*, H.M.S.O. 1965.

Besides its direct effect on employment, A.D.P. technology will also affect the demand for labour in the City in so far as it affects the attitude of firms toward decentralization. Here the evidence is conflicting. Several insurance companies have decentralized part of their activities, including their computer facilities, while keeping some in the City, and the same is true of several big firms of insurance brokers. Others, however, have preferred to remain wholly in the City. Stockbrokers have generally installed their computers in their own building if they had room and, if not, as near to hand as they could find suitable accommodation. At least one merchant bank, which has a registrar's department in the provinces, nevertheless decided to install its computer in the City, and uses the Securicor service to bring data in and send out processed work each day.

Finally, one of the clearing banks which had previously decentralized part of the clearing work, brought it back to the City as it extended its computer centre, though they also had other reasons for being disillusioned with decentralization. In general, the banks regard its influence as on the side of centralization.

Up to now, it seems that the computer has not been a decisive influence either way, though it may reinforce other reasons. If, however, there is a big fall in the cost of data transmission, its influence may operate more on the side of decentralization.

So far as the overall level of employment in the City is concerned, we expect that there will be an increase in the banking sector as a result of greater use of computers, but a decrease elsewhere. The 'Big Four' banks are committed for a long time ahead to operating their main computer installations in London and to putting an increasing number of branches 'on line' to these installations. This will thus bring into the City a substantial amount of work formerly done at the branches, and we expect that the increase in employment resulting from this will outweigh any further savings of labour at City branches. The big clearing banks are, however, unique in this respect, and we do not expect that other firms will bring large amounts of new work into the City, as a consequence of installing computers.

When computers are used to do work already being done in the City by other means, there is normally a saving of labour, though not always as much as was initially expected. Finally, the development of data transmission equipment gives firms the opportunity to decentralize some of their operations. By no means all firms will find this practicable, but we have shown examples of firms which have already done so and we expect there will be more.

On balance, therefore, we believe that the net effect of office mechanization will probably be a slight reduction in the demand for labour, but we do not expect the computer to exert a major influence on the overall level of employment.

Some students of automation have argued that it leads to a standardization of decision-taking processes, which reduces the status and responsibility of 'middle' management. If this were so in the City, it would run counter to recent trends which have shown a marked increase in the numbers engaged on this type of work. We have, however, found very little evidence that this is likely to be so. The processes that are being computerized, or which seem likely to be in the foreseeable future, involve repetitive work with little, if any, decision-taking, while the types of decision that have to be taken even by fairly junior management in the City do not lend themselves to automation.

On the contrary, we believe that the opposite tendency is at work, particularly with regard to research and investment analysis, among merchant banks, stockbroking firms and the Bank of England. Access to a computer enables analysts to take account of more variables, but this only increases the knowledge and judgment required in order to decide what is worth putting in and to interpret correctly what comes out.

Telecommunications

Technological developments in the field of telecommunications may affect the life and work of the City both in their own right and as an adjunct to computers.

At present, the telephone is by far the most important means of communication in the City. In 1967, there were 44,600 G.P.O. telephone connections in the City, which served more than 200,000 instruments. There were also nearly 2,500 telex connections. Figures provided by the G.P.O. showed that in 1966 the system carried nearly 370 million calls, 320 million of them local. There were over 46 million trunk calls (42 million of them on S.T.D.) and 635,000 calls overseas. These figures include data transmission calls as well as conversations, but the proportions between them are unknown.

Besides the G.P.O. facilities, there are 64,500 private telephone circuits in the City, Closed-circuit television is used by the Bank of England, the discount houses, a number of banks and commodity dealers. The Stock Exchange started a service to members' offices in 1969.

Developments in transmission enabling as many as 2,000 messages to be sent simultaneously along a single pair of wires have reduced the cost of direct telephone lines, but this is still expensive for long distances. A line of 200 yards costs only £9 a year, whereas one from London to Liverpool would cost about £3,000 a year. The development of central computer stations offering 'on-line' service to large numbers of customers over a wide area clearly depends on a substantial further reduction in these costs which, we are informed, is probable.

The use of closed-circuit television over anything but very short distances again depends on a reduction of transmission costs. Given such a reduction television could be used not only for transmitting news and prices, as it is now, but also for document transmission. Two other developments which would greatly help in this are electronic filing systems and equipment capable of reading information from a television screen straight into digital form. These may well be available at a price which many business users could afford within the next fifteen years.

One application of closed-circuit television is the television phone. There are sharp differences of opinion as to whether this is an instrument with great potential, which may largely avoid the need for face-to-face meetings, or whether it is an expensive gimmick.

Another development, which may, or may not, emerge from the gimmick class, is the pocket radiophone, which would enable its carriers to conduct conversations from wherever they might be; it is only a logical development of the radio telephones already used by police and taxi drivers, but a widespread extension of its use would cause formidable congestion of wavebands.

In the course of interviews, several examples were cited to us of planned future developments in the field of telecommunications. One of the more ambitious is the Central Closed-Circuit Television (C.C.T.V.) network which the Stock Exchange introduced in 1969. This is, at present, serving only addresses within the City, but it is also technically feasible to serve offices further afield, as telephone cables are used for this system. The service enables brokers to get all recorded Stock Exchange prices on screens in their offices; it also provides them with an instantaneous reference back service. However, supplementary equipment at high extra cost would be necessary should a broker require to translate the data on his screen into digital form for recording purposes. The Stock Exchange has estimated that this television service will reduce members' telephone calls by 80 per cent.

238

In February 1970, the Stock Exchange also introduced a personal paging system with a capacity of 4,000 connections. This will enable a dealer on the market floor to receive a signal informing him that he is required to receive a call in his box or hood.

Some of these advances – if they come about – will have a profound effect on the workings of the City. Television telephone, for example, could fundamentally affect the movement of people within and into the City. Many meetings as we know them today would be unnecessary and road traffic would be reduced. The pocket telephone would have much the same effect. The extension of technical advances in telephony will almost certainly reduce the demand for telephone operators in the City; the new system being installed by the Stock Exchange is likely to require only three operators compared with the sixty-two now being employed.

The greater use of C.C.T.V. for document transmission will tend to lessen the need for messengers in the City. Electronic filing and record systems will revolutionize office procedure and design, but will probably result in a net saving of space. Better access to shared computer services by firms of varying sizes will make it easier (but not necessarily more economical) for them to move their recording and statistical service out of the City. On the other hand, the advantages of being close enough to the centre of the most up-to-date telecommunication methods could attract firms to establish offices in or near the City. The following fascinating glimpse into the life of a City executive of the future was written for us by one of the contributors to this report.

'He arrives at his office in the morning and reads his mail, which has arrived electronically, on his desk data screen. By pressing a button he "destroys" some letters; by pressing another button those letters that require a reply or need to be kept are transferred to the memory stores of a fully electronic filing system. His television telephone is available for "meetings"with this colleagues. He discusses his clients' problems with them (perhaps even European ones) on his video screen, and can during such discussions "call" any data required, e.g. prices, stock positions, shipping dates etc., onto his data screen. His secretary types his letters directly onto a facsimile screen. One button signs them, another files copies, yet another dispatches them to their destinations, where they are stored until their recipients are ready to read them. Should he leave his office he is easily contacted on his pocket radiophone.'

Such a picture of business communications is no longer a science

239

fiction fantasy. It is already technically possible, and much of it will become economically feasible over the next twenty years. The pace at which we can expect such systems to be commercially applied will certainly depend to a large extent on further cost-reducing technical innovations, but the considerable investment at present taking place in more conventional telecommunication systems will probably act as a barrier to change.

(E) TRENDS IN NATIONAL AND INTERNATIONAL SPENDING

We divide this section into two parts. The first is a general review of the main factors likely to influence the future level and structure of demand, for the type of products and services which the City provides. The second part is a little more ambitious and tries to project forward the numbers employed in the main activities of the City, on certain clearly defined assumptions about the future of the national economy.

Part I

Changes in the general pattern of spending, both national and international, clearly affect the demand for the services provided by the City. Unfortunately, the sectors most important to the economy of the City are those about which we have almost no statistical data and which have been generally the most neglected in forecasts of economic growth.

Banking, insurance and finance are classified as a single category both in the National Income statistics and in the Ministry of Labour's employment figures. There is no doubt, however, that the group as a whole is a 'growth industry'. In terms of output at constant factor cost it grew by 129 per cent between 1948 and 1969 whereas Gross Domestic Product (G.D.P.) grew by only 75 per cent. Moreover, the rate of growth has been increasing; the increase between 1958 and 1969 was 71 per cent, a figure exceeded only by chemicals and public utilities among the sectors distinguished in the National Income Blue Book. Employment has also been rising from 538,000 in June 1960 to 691,000 in June 1969. The rapid growth of these activities is a feature which the British economy has in common with those of the United States and Western Europe and we believe that it will continue.

Legal and accountancy services are linked in the National Income Blue Book with a variety of others under general heading of 'Professional and Scientific Services'. The output of this group rose by rather more than gross domestic product (98 per cent) over the whole period 1948–58.

From 1958 to 1969 it grew by 43 per cent against 40 per cent for G.D.P. Some idea of the growth of legal and accounting services since 1959 can be gained from employment figures though these, of course, refer only to employees, not partners. The figures for Great Britain are:

	1959	1962	1964	1966	1967	1968	1969
				Mid-year thousand			
Legal services	85	95	96	103	103	110	108
Accounting services	78	86	89	91	91	92	92

The rate of growth was 19·2 per cent for accountancy and 22·4 per cent for legal services for the seven years 1959–66. Again, with the growing complexity of the financial and legal system it would be very surprising if this trend were reversed.

Wholesaling and merchanting are linked with other distributive trades in the Blue Book. This group expanded at almost the same pace as G.D.P. over the whole period 1948–69, but slightly more slowly since 1955. Employment figures, available separately for wholesaling, show a rise from 538,000 to 577,000 (7·2 per cent) between 1959 and 1966. However, the trend in consumer spending (e.g. towards services and large items of durable goods) and the growth of the chain store and the supermarket dealing direct with the manufacturer, may be slowing down the growth of wholesaling.

Of the leading City activities, printing and publishing is the one which appears to have the least growth prospects. The book trade, which is the one rapidly expanding section of the industry, has largely moved out of the City. For newspapers and magazines, figures of consumers' expenditure (at constant 1958 prices) are available since 1955. Expenditure on newspapers fell from a peak of £145 million in 1956 to only £131 million in 1967, while magazines, which were earning about £50 million a year up to 1958, dropped to £45 million in 1967. Employment grew up to the early sixties but has remained nearly constant since then. For other printing and publishing, only employment figures are available and these have moved very erratically. They rose sharply from 232,000 to 254,000 between 1959 and 1962, then fell slightly, but rose again to 262,000 in 1966.

So far as the domestic economy is concerned, then, the City has more than its share of 'growth industries'. However, the fact that demand in the economy as a whole is growing strongly does not necessarily mean that it will grow equally strongly in the City. The relationship between the two may be expected to vary widely from one activity to another, and is discussed for each in Chapters 8 to 12.

Turning to the international side, we give details in Chapter 8 of the rapid growth of the City's financial activities and our reasons for expecting this to continue. Demand for the commercial, as distinct from the financial, services of the City will be influenced largely by the nature and direction of trade, and the extent to which it goes through the Port of London. The link between the City and the Port is not, of course, rigid, City merchants use other ports and traders from outside the City use London. Nevertheless, as shown in Chapter 10, the links are close and a given expansion of trade through the Port of London is likely to bring much more commercial business to the City than is a similar expansion elsewhere.

Altogether, London handles about a third of Britain's imports and exports, but the proportions vary considerably between different categories. Figures for the main sections of the Standard International Trade Classification are given in Table 6.9. For imports, London's share of trade in food is notably high and that in mineral oils and miscellaneous manufactures is rather above average, while its share of trade in the main categories of manufactures is relatively small. Manufactured imports are, of course, growing much more rapidly than food so, in this respect, the pattern of specialization of the Port may be rather unfavourable to the City. On the export side, London handles a large share of the rapidly growing exports of machinery and transport equipment as well as miscellaneous manufactures. This, however, may be of only limited advantage from the point of view of the City, as engineering firms, especially those making large items, tend to deal directly with overseas customers rather than using the services of merchants. London has a very small share in exports of manufactures classified by materials, (e.g. leather, rubber, wood, paper, textiles, metals) but this is an advantage rather than otherwise, as the group as a whole is not growing fast.

Re-exports are also of considerable importance to the City, and here again there are some unfavourable features. The total amount of re-exports has risen quite sharply in recent years after a period of stagnation, but the growth has been in manufactures. Re-exports of food and crude materials are both well below what they were ten years ago and (with a growing tendency for importing countries to buy direct, and increasing competition from Rotterdam in the entrepôt trade) this trend does not seem likely to change. Unfortunately London's trade is heavily concentrated on food and raw materials.

Table 6.9. London's Share in U.K. Trade 1964 and 1968

	IMPORTS				EXPORTS			
	1964		1968		1964		1968	
Section	U.K. total (£ million)	London's share (per cent)	U.K. total (£ million)	London's share (per cent)	U.K. total (£ million)	London's share (per cent)	U.K. total (£ million)	London's share (per cent)
0. Food and live animals	1,622	40·1	1,711	33·2	159	44·8	172	27·9
1. Beverages and tobacco	149	19·3	193	16·1	124	26·6	227	22·9
2. Crude material	1,065	22·3	1,142	20·5	152	15·1	172	15·1
3. Mineral fuels	584	34·8	905	33·1	139	42·1	166	44·0
4. Animal and vegetable oils	54	25·4	68	22·0	6	19·0	7	21·4
5. Chemicals	252	28·3	416	19·2	412	33·1	599	28·0
6. Manufactures classified by materials	1,072	25·0	1·705	31·3	1·137	19·2	1,571	31·8
7. Machinery and transport equipment	545	26·5	1,187	11·2	1,830	41·7	2,588	30·1
8. Miscellaneous manufactures	292	34·7	464	27·6	316	42·8	520	36·5
9. Others	62	11·6	107	34·6	137	34·5	154	32·5
Total	5,696	30·3	7·899	26·0	4,412	33·7	6,175	30·5

Source: *Annual Statement of Trade of U.K. for years 1964 and 1968*

243

The port handles two-thirds of re-exported food and 37 per cent of raw materials, but only 23 per cent of manufactures. On the other hand, the City has, for a long time, been developing into a centre where titles to goods rather than the physical possession of them are exchanged. City markets and City merchants deal in many goods which never touch the shores of Britain and this aspect of their trade is likely to become relatively more important.

Part II

In this part, we shall examine the prospects of the future labour force of the main activities in the City under three different sets of assumptions. We cannot stress too strongly that the figures which we shall be presenting are not our predictions of what *will* happen (we have already outlined, in the previous chapter, the extreme difficulties involved in making such predictions) but what *would* happen under certain assumptions about (a) the trend in national employment and (b) the City's share of that employment.

We make projections based on three sets of assumptions these are probably the best that can be made, given the very severe limitations of the data available:

(i) that the growth of employment in the main activities of the City between 1966 and 1981 will be at the projected national rate of growth;

(ii) that the growth of employment in the City will be at the same rate of growth as it was (in the City) between 1951 and 1961;

(iii) that the growth of employment in the City will be at the rate, predicted by (i) but adjusted to allow the differences in the national and City rate of growth between 1951 and 1961.

We examine five activities in detail: (1) insurance, banking and finance; (2) printing and publicity; (3) wholesaling; (4) professional services; and (5) postal and telecommunication. These, according to our data, employed 227,341 people, about 70 per cent of the employment in the City[14] in 1964–6. The remaining 95,367 workers we classified as 'all other'. The projections are based upon actual date returns and not any 'grossed up' estimate, and for this reason are on the low side.

Data on the national employment of these industries were obtained from the *Annual Abstract of Statistics 1966* and the *Censuses of Population 1951 and 1961*. We were not always able to achieve an

---

[14] Unadjusted for errors and omissions.

identical match of activities with our classificat on, but in all instances it was close or very close.

The results of our exercises are given separately for three years in Table 6.10. The way in which they were achieved is as follows. For Projection 1, we extrapolated the trend of national employment for each activity in the years 1952 to 1965[15] through to 1971, 1976 and 1981. We then applied the percentage increase between 1966 and the later years to the numbers employed in the City in 1966, to arrive at an estimated labour force in 1971, 1976 and 1981.

Projection 2 is completely straightforward: we have just assumed that employment in the five main and 'all other' activities in the City will increase (or decline) in the period 1966 to 1981 at the same rate per annum as it did in the ten years 1951 to 1961.

Projection 3 takes as its starting point Projection 1. It then adjusts the results to allow for the fact that there are differences between national and City employment trends. It does this by multiplying each prediction by the percentage City rate of growth 1951–61 and dividing it by the percentage national rate of growth 1951–61. Thus, if the extrapolated trend for a particular activity predicted an increase of 1,000 people, but the rate of increase in employment in that activity in the City over the period 1951–61 was one-half of that of England and Wales, the final predicted increase would be 500.

What do the tables show? In each case the total numbers employed in the City are likely to increase quite considerably between now and 1981, but the distribution of the increase varies according to the form of the projection. The fastest growth centre is insurance, banking and finance. This sector is expected to expand by approximately 60 per cent in the period 1966–81. In all three projections an expansion in all sectors is forecast, except for wholesaling in Projections 2 and 3, where a decline is predicted.

(F) TRANSPORT AND COMMUNICATIONS

Transport and communications, in general, form the subject of Chapter 12. Here, we are only concerned with the features of the present system, and of developments planned in the near future, which may have a special bearing on the development of the City.

The *railways* have always exerted a strongly centralizing influence and this has been increasing. It is hardly conceivable that new inter-city railways will be built, so that we shall be left with the existing pattern with its strong emphasis on lines radiating from London. A

[15] By way of 'least squares' regression analysis.

Table 6.10. Projected Employment in the City 1971–81 on the Basis of Three Different Assumptions

	(O.S.R.P. Data)	1971 Projections			1976 Projections			1981 Projections		
		(1)	(2)	(3)	(1)	(2)	(3)	(1)	(2)	(3)
1. Insurance, banking and finance	124,621	147,925	141,819	146,055	171,976	161,259	168,188	199,892	183,442	193,162
2. Printing and publishing	34,144	36,773	37,456	36,773	38,992	41,144	39,402	41,382	45,173	42,031
3. Wholesaling	18,098	20,106	17,492	16,824	21,663	16,851	15,890	23,202	16,259	14,856
4. Accountancy and law	18,173	20,663	19,299	19,590	23,516	20,480	21,117	26,659	21,753	22,952
5. Postal and tele-communications	16,233	17,678	16,963	18,160	19,009	17,710	19,930	20,340	18,506	21,735
6. All other	114,439	116,454	118,905	125,480	120,577	126,818	137,025	133,727	135,176	148,669
Totals	322,078	359,599	351,934	362,882	395,733	384,262	401,552	445,202	420,309	443,405

major part of British Rail's modernization effort has gone into the provision of faster and more comfortable services between London and the major provincial centres. There have been improvements in services between some provincial centres, but, in general, these have not been comparable with the improvements between those centres and London. Given the basic structure of the rail network, this seems inevitable. Freight services also tend to be better between London and the large provincial towns than between one provincial centre and another, though this is not of direct importance to the City.

Several new rail developments are also planned for the London and the South-East Region. These are described in the Greater London Development Plan[16] and include the proposed reconstruction of London Bridge Station; the electrification of the line from King's Cross to Welwyn and Hertford; and an addition to the underground system in the form of the Fleet Line from Baker Street, south-east to New Cross/New Cross Gate.

Airport and air transport policy, at present also seems likely to attract people and business to London. Unless helicopter or vertical take-off planes are developed to a point where they can operate between city centres, there will always be a high proportion of internal traffic – both passenger and goods – where aircraft cannot hope to compete with road or rail. For longer journeys where air travel is an effective competitor, services are again, much better between provincial centres and London than between one provincial centre and another. In international traffic, the dominance of London will be enhanced by the building of a third airport. The City of London may be particularly affected if King's Cross becomes the main passenger traffic terminal.

The rapid growth of air freight has reached the point where – in terms of value for trade – Heathrow ranks as the country's third most important port. As indicated in Chapter 10, the physical handling of goods within the City is likely to be increasingly concentrated on high value, low bulk articles, which are precisely those most suited to air freight.

The radial nature of the telephone system may affect location in a rather complex way. For firms which need to keep in close touch with a large number of branches or customers scattered over the whole country, the structure of the telephone system provides a strong motive for having a headquarters in London The banks are an outstanding example, and the relative ease of getting direct lines from the City to branches was put to us as one of the factors in the

[16] See Chapter 6 of *Report of Studies* (G.L.C.), 1970.

247

banks' decisions to site their main computer installations in the City.

On the other hand, where the flow of communication is mainly between departments of a single office, good telephone communications between London and the provinces may be an aid to decentralization. One example of this is a firm of consulting actuaries whose partners and professional staff are in London, but which has its computer and most of its clerical staff in Southend. At present, however, there is an acute shortage of telephone lines, and we have found cases in which the inability to get a sufficient number of direct lines has been a serious obstacle to decentralization.

Looking at the pattern of the transport and communications system as a whole, there is no doubt that it is a strongly centralizing influence. Because of the durability of capital and the very large investment required to make a major change, this influence is likely to persist for a long time. The only major changes in the structure that seem likely over the next twenty years are in roads and, possibly, in the telephone system.

At present, the road network is still predominantly radial, both in the immediate vicinity of Central London and further afield, but this is likely to change considerably within the next ten to twenty years. Even the present motorway plan, scheduled for completion by 'the early 1970s' will give Birmingham motorway connections with Bristol, Bath, Wales, Lancashire, Yorkshire and Leicester – as well as London; likely extensions would complete the link between the Midlands and Scotland and provide new routes from the Midlands to Southampton and East Anglia. The result will be to make many provincial centres more easily accessible by road from the Midlands than from London, as well as providing much better direct access between other provincial areas, e.g. Yorkshire – Lancashire or East Anglia – Scotland.

Nearer to the centre, detailed G.L.C. road plans are still being worked out, but it seems certain that the major effort over the next twenty years will be put into a series of orbital roads, eventually providing two or three concentric rings at varying distances from the central area. In this connection, work has already started, or is planned, on the eastern parts of Ringways 1 and 2, and on the M11, M12, A12 and A20. These will both facilitate lateral communication between suburbs, and also divert through-traffic from the central area, including the City.

The influence of this on the demand for City locations may operate in two conflicting ways. Good inter-suburban communications lessen the relative advantages of being in the centre. On the other hand a reduction of heavy traffic through the streets of the City would not only make it a more pleasant place to work, but would also facilitate the internal journeys, discussed in Chapter 3, which form an important part of the business life of the City.

The system of communications, as well as transport, is at present largely centred on London. Long-distance mail goes by train, and so reflects the features of the railway network already discussed. The postal service has been a matter of very widespread complaint to us in interviews, and its defects act as a centralizing influence in two ways. Firms which have to transmit large numbers of documents, and for which speed and reliability are essential, have a motive for being near enough to the centre to use their own messengers. On the other hand, it is generally believed that the service is better in London than in the provinces, and this is supported by the views of firms who have moved out. Firms who do not make extensive use of messengers therefore still have a motive for being in London.

(G) THE INTERNATIONAL ROLE OF STERLING

Sterling at present fulfils two distinct functions in international payments: it is one of the two currencies which are widely held as a reserve by the central banks of other countries; and it is a currency in which about 20 per cent of world trade is invoiced and settled.

A rough idea of the amount of sterling held for the two purposes by non-residents can be gained from the division between 'official' and 'non-official' holdings in the figures published by the Bank of England. Recent changes in these amounts are given in Table 6.11.

The Bank of England figures were changed substantially at the end of 1962, and they have been distorted at various times by large sums borrowed by the Bank to meet balance of payments crises, shown as 'official' holdings. Apart from these special holdings, there has been a tendency for official sterling to decline in amount, partly because some sterling area central banks have reduced the proportion of their reserves held in London. Non-official holdings (mainly for trading purposes) rose sharply in the early sixties, following the restoration of non-resident convertibility at the end of 1958 but have since levelled off. The rise has been divided fairly evenly between sterling area countries and others.

Some of the plans put forward for the reform of the international monetary system would involve the conversion of at least part of the official sterling balances into either gold, balances with the International Monetary Fund, or some newly created international unit.

249

Table 6.11. Non-resident Sterling Holdings
1951–69

End of year	Official*	Non-official
1951	2,811	666
1955	2,704	936
1960	2,528	1,355
1961	2,537	1,009
1962	2,431	1,070
1963	2,223	1,788
1964	2,335	1,897
1965	2,470	1,948
1966	2,540	1,995
1967	2,793	1,953
1968	3,247	1,902
1969	3,821	1,768

* Official holdings are taken as 'central bank and other official' up to December 1962 and, 'central monetary institutions' thereafter. For the changes in the series, see Bank of England, *Quarterly Bulletin*, June 1963.

Source: *Bank of England Statistical Abstract* No. 1. Tables 21 and 22 (2)!

In 1968, the Government arranged a line of credit with the Bank for international settlements, and a number of overseas central banks for the express purpose of enabling it to offset withdrawals of sterling balances. However, neither this arrangement nor any other that has been suggested would prevent central banks which so desired from holding working balances in sterling, and none would interfere with non-official sterling deposits.

It has been argued that the withdrawal of overseas balances ag gravates balance of payments crises and causes 'stop–go' policies, and that their partial removal would be a benefit to the British economy. We find little truth in this contention. When embarrassing withdrawals have occurred they have usually been more in unofficial than official balances, and in any case they have usually occurred only after confidence has been shaken by a large and persistent deficit in the balance of payments.

On the other hand, we can find no close connection between the holding of central bank reserves in sterling and the use of sterling in international trade and finance, and no strong reason to suppose that a reduction in the use of sterling as a reserve currency would seriously affect its use in trade. We therefore believe that the adoption of any likely arrangement regarding international reserves would have little direct effect, for good or ill, on the City. But it might have important effects in other directions.

It is estimated that the 20 per cent of world trade invoiced and settled in sterling is made up of 90 per cent of intra-sterling area trade, 55 per cent of trade between the sterling area and the rest of the world, and 5 per cent of trade between non-sterling area countries. This trade is sometimes described as also 'financed' in sterling; not all of it, however, is financed in the sense that sterling credits are involved, though much of it undoubtedly is. The proportion of world trade settled in sterling has declined somewhat in recent years – largely because of the relatively slow growth of sterling area trade. Its absolute value has, however, increased from about £12,000 million in 1960 to about £20,000 million in 1968.

This trade is a direct source of income to banks in the City and is the main reason why commercial banks and other private institutions hold deposits in London. In turn it gives rise to other business connections, and indirectly to incomes for agents, brokers and insurance firms.

Anything which undermines foreign confidence in the pound and makes foreigners less willing to hold sterling deposits is likely to damage this complex set of relationships. There are, of course, ways of avoiding currency risks and we have seen examples of two of them in the growth of business in forward exchange and the growth of the Euro-dollar market.

Moreover, we believe that the use of sterling in actual payments has important indirect effects. Two examples have been mentioned to us. When a foreign shipowner arranges fixtures on the Baltic, with payment being made to his London broker in sterling, the broker must keep an account for his foreign client. This not only brings an immediate income but also forms the basis of a continuing relationship which brings business in the future, and which may also create business for other people, e.g. insurance firms. If sterling ceased to be used as an international means of payment and were replaced, for example, by the dollar, these connections would gradually be loosened, and it is very probable that a good deal of the business would eventually be lost.

The second example concerns the commodity markets. When a market in London establishes a sterling price which is accepted as a standard and used as a basis for contracts in other parts of the world, these contracts tend to be invoiced in sterling and settled in London. This, again, brings business directly to London banks and, less directly, to brokers, agents and insurers. If sterling were not acceptable internationally the functioning of the commodity markets would be impaired, and the other types of firm mentioned above would also find their earning opportunities reduced.

These are only examples of the kind of effect that must be common in the complex interplay of City activities. We believe, therefore, that the continued role of sterling as an international trading currency is important to the City, and that if foreign confidence in sterling were permanently destroyed neither the forward exchange market nor the use of other currencies could fully repair the damage.

Fortunately, confidence has shown itself fairly resilient, and balances which have been withdrawn in a crisis have very quickly returned. It will be assumed in subsequent chapters that this state of affairs continues. If so, we can expect a continued increase in the value of trade settled in sterling, even if there is a continued decline in the proportion of world trade handled in this way. Closer integration with Europe, discussed in the next section, might accelerate the decline of the Sterling Area's share in world trade, but it might also bring an increased use of sterling in third country trade.

(H) EUROPEAN INTEGRATION

Whatever the outcome of negotiations with the European Economic Community, it is probable that over the period covered by this study Britain will develop closer economic links with Europe. This could affect the City both by changing the pattern of international trade and by enabling British financial institutions to participate in a European capital market.

Major changes in the direction of British trade have been going on since 1945; they were greatly speeded up after the removal of import restrictions in the late nineteen-fifties. The figures in Table 6.12 summarize the main changes since 1959. These changes show the combined effect of many different influences.

World trade in manufactures has been growing faster than trade in primary products. Between 1959 and 1965 world imports of manufactures rose by 74 per cent against only 52 per cent for primary products: an increase which has been much more marked in British trade than in world trade. Percentage increases in the main categories of British imports (by value) between 1959 and 1969 were:

Food, drink and tobacco	27
Basic materials	27
Fuels	111
Semi-manufactures	92
Finished manufactures	388

Britain has for a long time imported more food and raw materials and fewer manufactures than other industrial countries, so that these changes bring Britain nearer to their pattern of trade.

Table 6.12. The Geographical Structure of U.K. Trade 1959–69

	U.K. Exports		U.K. Imports	
	1959	1969	1959	1969
	£ million			
Industrial countries	1,531	3,748	1,769	4,595
Non-industrial countries	1,892	3,291	2,318	3,720
Total	3,423	7,039	4,087	8,315
	percentages			
E.F.T.A.	14·9	14·8	13·8	15·0
E.E.C.	11·3	20·0	11·5	19·4
Other industrial countries*	18·5	18·4	18·0	20·9
Total industrial	44·7	53·2	43·3	55·3
Overseas sterling area	39·5	28·2	37·0	28·9
Rest of world	15·8	18·6	19·7	15·8
Total	100·0	100·0	100·0	100·0

* U.S.A., Canada and Japan.

There have also been changes in the U.K. share of overseas markets. Between 1959 and 1969 Britain's share in exports of manufactures to industrial countries fell from 13·9 per cent to 9·3 per cent, while for non-industrial countries there was a fall from 23·1 per cent to 15·0 per cent. However, there were considerable differences between different regions, partly due to tariff changes. E.F.T.A. countries have taken a larger share of British exports and their share in our market has likewise increased with the reduction of duties. Our share of the E.E.C. market rose in the early 1960s but fell back after the breakdown of negotiations for entry in 1963. The share of 'the Six' in the British market has, however, continued to rise. Both the British share in the overseas sterling area market and their share in ours have diminished. This has been associated with a decline in the importance of Commonwealth Preference, and has been brought about by (among other things) the removal by Britain of small preferences on tea and butter; steps by developing countries to foster infant industries; the formation of the Australia–New Zealand free trade area; and the growth of trade between Overseas Sterling Area countries and other industrial countries, e.g. Australia and Japan.

These trends may be expected to continue, though probably not at the same rate, and they will be reinforced by the effects of the 'Kennedy Round'. The major tariff cuts therein agreed are in industrial products, so that the growth of trade between the industrial countries will be further stimulated.

Entry to the Common Market would lead to a further rise in the share of the E.E.C. countries in the British Market, and should also produce a renewed expansion of the British share in their market. The growth of trade with other industrial countries would be slowed down. There would be a cut-back in imports of temperate foodstuffs from the Commonwealth, principally from Australia and New Zealand; and this would presumably entail some further reduction in their imports from Britain. On the other hand, the tropical and sub-tropical members of the sterling area might not be greatly affected, especially if the developing countries in general succeed in their efforts to get industrial countries to abolish duties on tropical products.

But if we do not join E.E.C., we can expect trade with them to decline somewhat in importance as the full effect of tariff discrimination is felt, and this would be accentuated if Britain and other E.F.T.A. countries were to join North America, and possibly Australia, New Zealand and Japan, in a new free trade area.

Whether or not we join the Common Market, the trends outlined above are likely to produce a continuing rise in the relative importance of trade in industrial products between one industrial country and another; a relative decline in the importance of trade in primary products; and a relative decline in the proportion of British trade which is done with the sterling area. This does not mean that this trade need decline absolutely either in volume or value.

The City has been particularly closely associated with the conduct and finance of sterling area trade, including that in primary commodities. The growth patterns indicated above would, therefore, limit the scope for expansion of some City firms in their traditional types of business.

On the other hand London is geographically very well placed to take part in an expanding trade with Europe, and this advantage will be increased when the Channel Tunnel is bui t. This should provide opportunities for new firms to expand and for existing ones to diversify. As will be seen in Chapters 8 and 10, the C ty is already beginning to meet this challenge.

Article 67 of the Treaty of Rome requires that members shall, 'in the course of the transitional period and to the extent necessary for the proper functioning of the Common Market, progressively abolish as between themselves restrictions on the movement of capital belonging to persons resident in member States, and also any discriminating treatment based on the nationality or place of residence of the parties or on the place in which such capital is invested'. Subsequent articles of Chapter 4 of the treaty empower the E.E.C. Council to issue directives for the implementation of this article, but also to impose qualifications where members are in balance of payments difficulties, or where movements of capital lead to disorganization of domestic markets. Exchange restrictions on important classes of capital transactions were removed by two directives of the Council in 1960 and 1962, and a panel of experts set up by the Commission and reporting in November 1966 made a number of recommendations for further integration of capital markets within the Community.

The London capital market is, in many ways, broader and more highly organized than those of the main European centres, and in conditions which allowed freedom of movement of capital London would be in a powerful competitive position. It already has the biggest concentration of international banking in the world; in 1964 there were 98 branches or representative offices of foreign banks, compared with 63 in New York, 48 in Paris, 25 in Frankfurt, 16 in Brussels, 9 in Milan and 6 in Amsterdam.[17] By October 1969 overseas banks in London had increased to 135; there were also increases in other centres, but London has retained its relative advantage.

The London money market is also unique in the opportunity that it gives for the profitable use of short-term banking funds. London has already achieved a predominant position in the 'Euro-dollar' market. London banks (including the London offices of overseas

[17] W. M. Clarke, *The City in the World Economy* Institute of Economic Affairs, 1965, p. 12.

banks) hold more than three times as much in 'Euro-currency' deposits as those of any other financial centre, and approximately as much as all the other centres in Europe combined. The London discount market also provides a highly economical way of obtaining credit by means of bills of exchange, which are still widely used in the finance of European trade.

At the longer end of the capital market, the London Stock Exchange has a much larger number of securities, and a much larger turnover, than any European exchange. The estimated market value of securities quoted on the principal European exchanges at the end of 1965 was as follows:

U.S. $ (*thousand million*)

	Equities	Fixed Interest Securities
U.K.	76	53
Germany	20	22
France	19	15
Italy	10	17
Netherlands	10	5
Belgium	5	7

Dealing in London tends to be rather more expensive than in some continental centres, but this is often far more than compensated by the breadth of the market and the resulting ease and speed with which large transactions can be handled.

The relative strength of London is greatest in the equity market. The total volume of new equity issues in France, Germany and Italy from 1960 to 1965 was similar to that in Britain, but the starting point was very different. Continental countries had, and still have, a smaller proportion of quoted companies and those which are quoted tend to have a higher ratio of fixed charge capital. Both these features can be sources of instability, and the risks involved in them have been the subject of comment by the expert committees both of E.E.C. and O.E.C.D.

This strength of the equity market in London is due very largely to the influence of the big financial institutions – insurance companies, pensions funds, investment trusts and unit trusts. The following figures illustrate the position with regard to life assurance companies:[18]

[18] *The Development of a European Capital Market* (Report of an E.E.C. Group of Experts, 1966), p. 375.

	Germany	France	Italy	Netherlands	Belgium	U.K.
Total assets (end 1964), U.S. $ million	6,394	2,792	1,351	2,518	1,292	22,212
Percentage in ordinary shares	4·5	14·9	—	3·0	6·0	22·5

Continental pension funds and investment trusts are also much smaller in scale and less interested in ordinary shares than those of the U.K. These institutions are of great value in a number of ways. They provide a continuous source of funds which is not unduly influenced by short-term market fluctuations; they bring to the selection of investment a high standard of expertise; the size of their holdings facilitates the making of large bargains; and they play an important part in the sale or placing of new issues.

London's combination of merchant banks, brokers, financial institutions and a broad 'secondary' market in existing securities has created an efficient mechanism for handling new equity issues. The E.E.C. group refers to 'the efficiency of the United Kingdom for putting on the market the shares of even relatively small companies'.[19] Large firms can raise equity capital in London more cheaply than in continental centres, while smaller ones can borrow in London whereas they would find difficulty in doing so at all on the Continent.

The one significant counter-weight to these advantages of London is the more direct participation of some continental banks in the provision of medium and long-term finance for industry, though the value of this is controversial.

Many changes would be necessary both here and in Europe before there could develop a fully integrated market with Britain participating in it. There are big differences between national systems in regard to company law, taxation, accounting practice, disclosure of information, and regulations governing the investment powers of financial institutions, which would have to be removed. The exchange risk would tend to diminish as national economic policies become more closely aligned, and in any case it can be partly met by issues in more than one currency or in 'units of account'.

Perhaps the biggest difficulty from the British point of view would be in removing the restrictions on overseas portfolio investment by British residents. The present effect of these restrictions is that the London capital market can take part in an 'entrepôt' trade in international loans but cannot actually supply capital for them. The scope for expansion of the one without the other must be limited.

[19] *Ibid.*, p. 60.

I

The effects of further integration with Europe on the U.K. insurance industry are difficult to judge. At present, U.K. insurance companies enjoy only 4 per cent of the European market. But with the doors closing to the industry in many parts of the world and with the recent serious losses experienced in the U.S. market, British insurers, if they are to maintain their international role, need to venture elsewhere and the E.E.C., still with its tremendous growth prospects, would seem to offer real rewards. On the other hand, the present somewhat inhibited trading attitude of the industry towards international insurance – even within the E.E.C. – leaves some room for concern to U.K. insurers, should they become subject to the same legislation. It is hoped, however, that present negotiations within the industry (in which Britain is playing a part) might result in a more liberal atmosphere being created.

Assuming that these obstacles are gradually overcome, we believe that closer integration with Europe would be likely to result in a number of developments affecting the City, including the following:

(a) A further increase in the number of foreign banks with offices in London, and a greater participation by these banks in the London money market.

(b) A greater use of the London discount market in the finance of European trade.

(c) An accentuation of the present tendency for British banks, especially merchant banks, to open offices in Europe, to acquire European subsidiaries, or to form associations with banks in European centres.

(d) Increased scope for the financial advice of merchant banks in connection with mergers and working arrangements between European companies and between companies in Britain and in Europe.

(e) An increase in the number of European securities quoted on British Stock Exchanges and in the number of British securities quoted in Europe.

(f) An increased use of the London capital market by European countries, especially for raising new equity capital, though this would need considerable changes in accounting practices and disclosure by European companies.

(g) A greater participation by British institutions, both as holders of securities and as underwriters, in the supply of capital to Europe.

(h) Possibly a greater use by British firms of European banks for the supply of medium- and longer-term bank credit.

Chapter 7

COSTS AND BENEFITS OF ECONOMIC ACTIVITY

THE MARKET ECONOMY AND ECONOMIC WELFARE

The object of this chapter is to discuss some of the general principles involved in measuring the values of the contribution made by activities in a particular region to the national economy, and in estimating the costs and benefits associated with a change in these activities. The economic case for acts of State intervention, such as the restriction of office development or the selective employment tax, which are designed to change the allocation of resources, rests upon the assumption that market prices do not adequately measure values to the community, and that decisions made by ordinary commercial responses to market prices bring about an allocation of resources which is not in the best interests of the public. We feel, therefore, that it is important to examine how far, and in what circumstances, these assumptions may be valid. We should emphasize that, as economists, we are concerned with economic issues. There may be circumstances in which social or political considerations may be held to outweigh economic ones, but, if so, this should be clearly understood.

In a market economy, the value of an activity is normally measured by the price paid for its end-products. In the national income accounts, for example, the contribution of different sectors to the national income is measured by the sum of the individual incomes received, or by the value of total net sales. In so far as the market establishes a set of prices that are a satisfactory reflection of social values, it will also tend to bring about a 'right' allocation of resources. Subject to certain assumptions about the distribution of incomes, those who can afford to bid the highest prices for land, labour or capital will be those who can get the most valuable end-product from them. In going to the highest bidder, therefore, resources will also be going to the point at which they make the greatest contribution to the national economy.

Applying this argument to the City, we find that rents, wages and

259

salaries are, as shown in Chapters 3 and 4, higher there than in most other places. It can be asserted, therefore, that firms will only come to (or stay in) the City if (a) they reap advantages, by comparison with other locations, which are at least enough to cover their higher costs; and (b) they produce goods and services that are so valuable that users are willing to pay prices that will cover these costs. This is the logic behind statements like, 'We wouldn't be paying these high costs if we did not find it necessary to be here', which have often been made to us in interviews.

We should state at the outset that we believe this argument to be broadly true. The function of market prices is to allocate resources, and in very large areas of activity the market performs this more efficiently than any other means. A number of examples of the way in which this process has worked and is working in the City have been given in Chapter 1. Activities which are lavish users of space and/or labour in relation to the value of the product they produce have been progressively squeezed out over the years. The first to go was residential accommodation and this has been more recently followed by a large part of warehousing and manufacturing activities, and by much of the trade involving the physical handling of goods. The activities which have continued to expand and now dominate the economic life of the City are financial and commercial transactions and professional services, whose end-product is very valuable in relation to the space and labour used.

Nevertheless, economists have formulated some important qualifications to the general principle that market forces produce an optimum allocation of resources, and those concerned with physical planning have sought to modify the distribution of resources brought about by the market. The following paragraphs first discuss the approaches of the economist and the planner in general terms, and then apply the ideas so developed to two matters of importance in the study: the case for decentralization, and the contribution of the City to the balance of payments.

THE ECONOMIC CASE FOR INTERVENTION

The circumstances in which economists would hold that a price system will not produce a wholly satisfactory allocation of resources can be summarized in three categories:

(a) Where prices are other than those which would prevail in a competitive market. Four sub-divisions of this category may have some significance in relation to the City:

(i) Where prices are restricted by agreement, e.g. certain rates charged by the banks, some insurance premiums, and commissions on the Stock Exchange.

(ii) Where the conditions of demand or supply are affected by other than market forces, e.g. Government policy, with respect to Office Development Permits, on the supply of office accommodation.

(iii) Where public enterprises are run at a loss, e.g. some services of British Rail.

(iv) In the short run, where prices fixed under previous contracts have become out of line with those currently quoted. This arises under the leasehold system where firms, which enjoyed a low rent under a long lease, may be encouraged to stay on in property which they would otherwise have relinquished rather than pay the current market rent.

(b) Where those taking decisions do not act 'rationally', i.e. do not evaluate carefully their prospective gains from a purchase, and compare them with the price. Such conduct may be due to lack of knowledge, to prejudice or to inertia. It is often said that firms are prepared to pay unreasonably high rents for 'prestige' addresses, but we have found little evidence of this. On the contrary, most of the firms interviewed appear to have given careful consideration to alternative possibilities before making a decision about a site.

(c) Where decisions impose costs or confer benefits on others which are not reflected in any monetary payments made by, or receipts accruing to, the decision-taker (generally called 'externalities'). Some of the most important examples for the City occur in transport. The firm which increases its employment in the City has to pay its workers enough to compensate them for the costs and discomfort which they suffer in travelling, but it does not pay for the extra discomfort which their travelling creates for others. Similarly, the motorist who brings his car into the City does not pay for the additional costs which he imposes on other road users by adding to congestion.

Whenever situations can be shown to exist which fall into any of these categories, it is possible, on strictly economic grounds, to make a *prima facie* case for modifying the operation of market forces. In order to establish the case fully, it would also be necessary to show that the proposed intervention would bring about an improvement big enough to justify its cost. If, however, such a situation cannot be

261

shown to exist, it should be assumed that the allocation of resources produced by market forces is that which is in the public interest.

PHYSICAL PLANNING AND MARKET FORCES

The case for modifying the operation of market forces put forward by those concerned with physical planning is usually couched in a different language, and is not always easy to reconcile with the economic approach. For example, a document circulated by the Department of Economic Affairs in 1967[1] lists five objections to the continued growth of office accommodation in Central London:

(a) It reduces 'variety of life in the centre'.
(b) It leads to 'the most intensive possible occupation' of land.
(c) It increases the peak load on the transport system while, at the same time, depriving it of profitable 'off peak' traffic.
(d) It increases the pressure of demand for housing in commuter areas.
(e) It may have 'regional implications' in encouraging further migration from the less prosperous areas to the south-east.

Of these objections only (c) and possibly (d) can be readily translated into the economic terms used above. The rest can be justified, if at all, only in much more general and less rigorous terms, and in any case, are heavily loaded with value judgments. An economist might well argue that variety is not necessarily a good thing if purchased at the price of the efficiency which comes from specialization; that where land is particularly scarce it is desirable that it should be used intensively; and that migration from less prosperous to more prosperous areas may have real advantages. To some extent, differences between economists and planners may result from the use of different jargon and may be more apparent than real, but we believe it is important that they should be clarified.

There is another sense in which it may be said that market prices do not reflect the full value of an activity to the national economy. To illustrate this by a fanciful example, if all the banks in the City were forcibly closed, the damage to the economy would obviously be far greater than the loss of the wages, salaries and rents which they pay, and the profits which they earn. In order to make this point, we need not suppose that an entire activity disappeared; the same

[1] K. Barnaby Williams, *The Factual Basis of Office Policy in South East England*, 1967.

principle would apply to any substantial reduction in scale or in efficiency.

The reasons behind it are twofold: First, market prices indicate the value of a product or service at the margin, i.e. in its least valuable use. Any significant reduction in supply, however, must affect, not only the least valuable use, but others for which purchasers would be prepared, if necessary, to pay more

Secondly, many activities confer benefits or others, benefits which are not included in the prices charged. To quote one example, when a commodity market establishes a 'world' price in sterling, dealings between foreign countries in that commodity tend to be invoiced in sterling, which encourages settlement through London, and brings business to London banks. This is a case of the 'externalities' referred to above, and further examples will be given later in this chapter.

A less formal way of putting the matter is to say that all economic activities are interdependent, so that anything which benefits one will benefit others, and anything which damages one will damage others. This applies to any activity in any part of the country and not merely to the City. It could be argued, however, that because a number of activities are so highly concentrated in the City, it applies with particular force there. Where the output of a product or service is widely scattered, a substantial fall in the supply from one source will have only a small effect on the total supply in the country as a whole. But this cannot be so when output is highly concentrated, as is the case with the financial and commercial activities of the City.

THE CASE FOR DECENTRALIZATION

The case for decentralization can be approached from two directions. The first is by an application of the economic argument about externalities outlined above; the second by an attempt to assess the costs and benefits of alternative locations.

Following the first approach, the case for decentralization rests primarily on the contention that the operations of the City involve 'external diseconomies': i.e. the actions of some firms impose costs on others which they do not themselves pay, so that market forces cause some firms to choose locations in the City which they would not choose if they had to bear the full social costs of their decisions. The two examples usually quoted are transport and housing, but both need careful examination.

As already noted, the market rate of wages or salaries may be assumed to include compensation for the cost and discomfort of workers' own travel. But this rate does not include any allowance for the additional discomfort the workers impose on *other* travellers, or for the cross-subsidization of these workers. Similarly, the employer who moves from the City to some other location may gain by paying lower wages to workers who have lower travelling costs, but he does not get anything for his part in reducing congestion.

This argument applies not only to the City and central London area; it also applies to any communications system which is used to the point at which anyone suffers delay or overcrowding. Whenever such conditions exist (or are on the point of arising), additional use of the system either imposes delays and/or discomforts on other users or else makes necessary capital expenditure to increase capacity.

Virtually all centres where organized economic activity takes place on a significant scale have some congestion problems, and new development will add to existing congestion or create congestion where it did not exist before. An example of this can be very clearly seen in Croydon. In considering, therefore, whether the market creates a distorted pattern of location as between realistic alternatives, it is only *differential* rates of increase of congestion between different places that are relevant.

The pressure of demand for housing in suburban areas, due to growing employment at the centre, may be expected to push up suburban property values but, again, this need not necessarily entail an economic loss to the community as a whole. It is a disadvantage to the buyer but it is equally an advantage to the seller. It is only if we are prepared to make the judgment that it is, in some sense, a good thing for people to live in one part of the country rather than another, or for one person to be 'better-off' rather than another, that we can claim a real social disadvantage for this type of movement.

The external diseconomies to the nation as a whole of concentrating economic activities in a particular centre are thus much less than might be inferred from considering that centre alone, and there are also external economies to be considered. Chapter 3 has shown that there are strong linkages between various City activities: firms in one line of business gain in efficiency from being close both to other firms in the same line and to firms in different but related lines of business. Further examples will appear in Chapters 8–12.[2]

[2] For a general discussion of externalities see T. Scitovsky, 'Two concepts of external economies', *Journal of Political Economy*, Vol. LXII, April 1954, pp. 143–51; and P. W. Towroe, 'Industrial linkage, agglomeration and external economies', *Journal of the Town Planning Institute*, January 1970, pp. 18–20.

These advantages are the main reason why firms are able and willing to pay high rents for central sites. The newcomer would have to pay a rent which would represent the market value of the advantages he gets, just as (on the other side of the picture) he must pay his workers wages which include compensation for their costs and inconvenience in transport. But just as he does not pay for the additional transport costs which his employee imposes on others, neither does he gain any benefit from the fact that his activities may, apart from the direct services which he performs, enable others to function more efficiently.

One example of these external economies has already been quoted. Many others could be given from the financial and commercial activities of the City. Consider, for example, the Stock Exchange. The fact that brokers and jobbers are all so close together enables the Council to provide clearing facilities, a very advanced telecommunications system, and many other special services for members. Private firms also offer specialist services. At least one such firm is using a computer to provide almost instantaneous information about price–earnings ratios and ratios used in investment analysis over direct telephone lines; if brokers had been scattered, the cost of telephone lines would have been prohibitive and no one could have gathered enough customers to make such a service worth while.

Again, the presence in the City of so many people interested in investment analysis has not only promoted discussion between them, but has led to the formation of the Society of Investment Analysts, and the publication of a technical journal. This has helped to make possible the great increase in expertise that has taken place in recent years. All brokers reap a benefit from these advantages, but none of them gains a benefit from the fact that his presence in the City helps to make these advantages available to others.

Other examples could be found from the banking system and the foreign exchange market. As shown in Chapter 8, the managers and staff of particular branches specialize in meeting the needs of particular activities, e.g. the Stock Exchange, Lloyd's, the Baltic or Mincing Lane, because these activities are highly localized. Every new bank which establishes itself in London helps to broaden the foreign exchange market and this, in turn, encourages the keeping of deposits in London and the financing of trade through London. Frequent contacts between members of the market also lead to the diffusion of new ideas and the development of new techniques; it is inconceivable that the markets in Euro-currencies, Euro-bonds and dollar

265

certificates of deposit could have developed as they have if international banking had been widely scattered.

These are only a few instances. Many more could be produced by applying the same reasoning to the various examples of interdependence given in Chapters 8–12. These external economies have been well known since the work of Marshall and Pigou, but they are so complex that it is virtually impossible to measure them. The external diseconomies of concentration are more easily seen than the economies; it is only necessary to drive on a crowded road to see evidence of the diseconomies. By contrast, it is necessary to have an intimate knowledge of particular industries and trades in order fully to appreciate the economies. When, however, the two are examined carefully and compared as far as they can be with one another, it is by no means obvious that the market mechanism produces a bias towards 'too much' concentration.

Looking at the problems from the other point of view, it is generally assumed that decentralization will confer a social benefit by reducing the amount of travel and cutting down congestion on transport systems. This is not necessarily so. If we assume that all workers keep their existing jobs and their existing homes, then the movement of work from the centre towards the perimeter of an area will almost certainly increase the amount of travel. If workers are drawn at random from all parts, the journeys of some will be reduced as the place of work is moved nearer to their homes, but the journeys of others will be lengthened, and the total mileage travelled will normally be increased. Total travelling time will be increased still further, as the shortest distance will normally lie not on a main radial route, but on a 'cross town' route which is relatively ill-provided with transport services.

An obvious corollary to this is that when a firm moves out of a central area, a large proportion of its workers change either their homes or their jobs. With a sufficient rearrangement of jobs or homes or both, it would be possible to reduce the total both of travelling distance and travelling time. However, the changing of jobs or homes imposes a cost which has to be offset against the advantage of reduced travel. For a change of job, the costs include the period of unemployment which may ensue between leaving one job and taking another; the subjective value of the anxiety, loss of contact with friends, etc., that may be involved; and the cost to the employer of training a new worker. In the case of moving house the costs are the waste of capital in leaving a house 'unemployed' between the departure of one occupant and the arrival of another; the time spent in house-hunting; legal and other charges and actual removal expenses.

Two further points must be made about these costs. First, they do not necessarily stop at stage one, as described above. For example, firm A which is moving out of the centre and losing some of its employees may replace them by attracting workers from firm B, who may replace them from firm C, and so on. Secondly, costs of movement must be incurred 'once and for all' whereas the benefits are incurred over time in the future. The relationship between the two is essentially that of a return on capital investment, and the two sets of values can only be compared by reference to a rate of interest or discount. The higher the relevant rate, the greater must be the relevant saving in order to make it worthwhile to 'invest' in moving.

Besides the non-recurrent costs of moving (which will of course include those of the firm itself as well as its employees) we must also consider the recurrent costs which a firm will have to bear in its new location. On some items it will probably save, but on others it will have either to pay more or else make do with inferior service. The composition of these costs will vary with the nature of the business. For a manufacturing firm they will include the transport of materials and finished products. There will probably be increased costs of other forms of communication: firms which have decentralized have generally found that their telephone bills have increased, and frequently complain that letters take longer in the post. Since it will be necessary to retain some contacts with the centre, decentralization will cause some journeys to be made that would not have been necessary before, and sometimes these have to be made by senior people whose time is valuable. Finally, the decentralized firm loses these advantages of proximity to others which has already been discussed.

It is obvious from this brief discussion that it would be impossible to evaluate the costs and benefits to society of decentralization in general. The most one could hope to do would be to measure them in relation to the movement of a particular firm to a particular place. But even this would be a formidable task, and it would not be possible to trace and evaluate all the indirect effects. It is clear that the balance of costs and benefits is by no means necessarily in any one direction. Neither the cost–benefit approach, nor the argument based on externalities, create a general presumption that market forces make for too much concentration. Neither, therefore, can provide a logical basis for a policy of decentralization.

THE CITY AND THE BALANCE OF PAYMENTS

Estimates of the contribution of the City to the balance of payments were given in Chapter 3. In spite of the difficulties of estimation discussed there, three things are clear: the City generates very large overseas earnings; the 'import content' of these earnings is low; and the net contribution to the balance of payments per head of population employed in the City is very high. The considerations set out at the beginning of this chapter prompt three questions:

(a) Is the money figure an adequate measure of the value of this contribution to the national economy?
(b) Are there also indirect effects on the balance of payments arising from the activities of the City which are not included in the estimate?
(c) How far does contribution, both direct and indirect, of the activities carried on in the City depend upon their concentration there?

To answer the last of these questions first, the strength of the City, both direct and indirect, depends on the efficiency of its various institutions and markets. It was shown in Chapter 3 that proximity to one another is an important factor in the efficient working of many of the City's activities, and further examples of this will be found in Chapters 8–12. Any measures which deprived firms of these advantages would, therefore, impede the growth of export earnings as well as creating an inefficient use of national resources.

An important point here is that in a variety of ways the various activities of the City help to sell one another. Goods handled by London merchants are likely also to be financed and insured in London; the organized commodity markets attract third country trade; and the existence of this unique concentration of trade and finance attracts foreign banks, which help further to build up the volume and variety of business.

As shown in Chapter 3, the estimated earnings of the City do not take account of a number of its direct exports, though the value of these is probably not large in relation to the four big categories of banking, insurance, merchanting and brokerage. In addition, the City renders important indirect services to exporters. Its various banking services provide credit facilities which, as shown in Chapter 8, compare very favourably both in costs and flexibility with those of other centres, and the network of overseas offices and correspondents maintained by the banks provides a valuable source of information for exporters.

Finally, there is the question of whether the money measure of overseas earnings is a true indication of the value of these earnings to the economy, or whether, in view of our chronic balance of payments difficulties, they may not be worth even more. It can be argued that there is no fundamental difference between selling something to a resident in another country and selling it to someone at home, and hence that a pound earned abroad is worth neither more nor less than a pound earned at home. In a free market economy without extensive government intervention, or in one in which intervention pursued only consistent sets of objectives, we believe this to be so. In recent years, however, governments have often pursued mutually inconsistent sets of objectives, and one of the ways in which this inconsistency has shown up is in a chronic tendency to balance of payments deficits.

This weakness in the balance of payments has led to a number of special measures, which have discriminated in favour of exports (or import savings) and against production for home consumption. At various times in recent years, industries exporting goods have been given priority in the allocation of scarce materials, in building licences, and for bank loans during periods of 'credit-squeeze'. The Government provides insurance against default for export credits and, together with the Bank of England, has arranged with the commercial banks for the extension of credit at special rates. One of the arguments in favour of the bonus given to manufacturing by the selective employment tax is the contribution which manufacturers make to exports; and exporters get a rebate to compensate them for the addition to their cost brought about by certain forms of taxation. All these concessions apply to 'visible' exports but not to the 'invisible' items earned in the City.

Concern for the balance of payments has also led to restrictions on both direct and portfolio investment overseas which, if long continued, could have a serious effect on the City.

All these policies, as already noted, are based on the assumption that there is some special value about activities which either create overseas earnings or reduce overseas payments. We are far from convinced that this assumption is generally valid, but so long as it is applied to a wide range of other activities, it should be applied to the invisible earnings of the City, and the activities generating such earnings should receive support commensurate to that given to other exporters. Any other policy would not only place the City at an unfair disadvantage, but would also help to promote an inefficient allocation of national resources.

SUMMARY

The economic case for government intervention to modify the allocation of resources depends on the assumption that market forces do not bring about the allocation which is in the best interests of the nation as a whole. Examination of this assumption in relation to the City does not suggest that it is likely to be generally valid. On the contrary, market forces are bringing about a continuing process of reallocation, which is attracting to the City activities which derive the most valuable end-products from their use of scarce land and labour, and causing other activities to move out.

The market value of the City's output is not, however, an adequate measure of the damage to the national economy which might be done by policies which seriously interrupted or undermined the efficiency of the City's activities. Because of the interdependence of economic activities, this damage would be very much greater than the loss of output (or earnings) in the City itself.

Neither the external economies and diseconomies of concentration, nor the costs and benefits of decentralization, can easily be measured quantitatively, but a qualitative examination suggests that neither approach gives any clear-cut evidence in support of a *general policy* of decentralization as applied to the activities of the City. This is not to deny that in certain instances decentralization may confer a net advantage, both privately and socially.

The invisible exports of the City depend to a large extent on the advantages which its firms and markets enjoy from proximity to one another.

Government policy in relation to visible exports is based on the assumption that a pound earned abroad is of more value to the economy than a pound earned at home. So long as this assumption is applied to visible trade, it should also be applied to the invisible earnings of the City. Any policies which treat the suppliers of invisible exports less favourably than the suppliers of visible exports tend to produce a mis-allocation of resources and to damage the national economy.

Chapter 8
BANKING AND FINANCE

INTRODUCTION

Banking and other financial activities employ over 74,000 people in the City. Data supplied by the Corporation of London show that in 1964–66 there were 50,005 persons employed in various forms of banking, 15,071 in stockbroking, jobbing ard in the Stock Exchange itself, and 9,208 in 'other finance'.

In our work on the banking sector, we have followed the main categories used by the Bank of England. These are:

Description	No. employed O.S.R.P. returns (1964–66)
Bank of England ⎱ Clearing Banks ⎰	30,130[1]
Scottish and N. Irish banks	964
British Overseas and Commonwealth banks	5,814
American banks	1,727
Foreign banks and affiliates	2,024
Members of the Accepting Houses Committee	3,381
Other banks	5,538
Discount houses	427
	50,005

The way in which these institutions are knit together in a series of organized markets has been mentioned in Chapter 3. This chapter presents more details of some of these linkages, together with information relevant to assessing their future growth prospects.

THE BANK OF ENGLAND

Besides its main building in Threadneedle Street, the Bank of England

[1] It appears that certain departments of the Bank of England were not included in the summaries of the O.S.R.P. returns prepared for us. It has not been possible to make a precise check owing to the confidential nature of the information but we believe that between 1,500 and 2,000 people have been omitted.

271

has office buildings in Princes Street, and in New Change (near St Paul's) and a branch near the Law Courts. It also has a printing works at Debden in Essex; a records office at Roehampton; branches at Southampton, Bristol, Birmingham, Manchester, Liverpool, Leeds and Newcastle-on-Tyne; and an office in Glasgow. Total employment in the City is over 4,500.

The Bank has a very wide range of functions which bring it into contact with the Government; the clearing banks, discount houses and all the other important financial institutions of the City; overseas central banks; and representatives of industry and trade. The following paragraphs indicate these functions in very summary form with the main emphasis on linkages with other institutions which they involve.

The Bank keeps the accounts of the Exchequer and other government departments and performs ordinary banking services for them. It acts as registrar for all quoted British government securities and for some others including those of the G.L.C. and certain Commonwealth governments. Other activities in relation to these securities include the preparations for new issues, the receipt of subscriptions, and the payment of dividend warrants.

Of the various functions of the Bank, their work as registrar is that which employs most labour in the City. (The note issue employs more in total but most of it is done at Debden.) The Accountant's Department, which maintains the register, has a staff of just over 1,300 and handles about 2·5 million accounts. Besides the register, kept by stocks, there is also a general card index giving, for each stockholder, all holdings of securities registered at the Bank. Transfers vary between 10,000 and 20,000 a week without any significant trend. One of the major developments of the past few years has been the transfer to computers firstly of the work of preparing dividend payments and more recently of the registers themselves. This work is less closely linked to other institutions than are most of the Bank's activities. However, the provision of 'over the counter' transfer facilities for jobbers and (in securities maturing within five years) discount houses, requires proximity to the Stock Exchange and the discount houses. Moreover a large proportion of other transfers originate in or near London, so that any other location would increase the average distance over which letters had to travel, with more work for the Post Office transportation services and more risk of delays.

The weekly Treasury Bill tender is supervised from Threadneedle Street, while bills are issued and paid at the Loans Office in Princes

Street. These offices clearly need to be close to the discount houses and other financial institutions which tender for, and hold the majority of, the Treasury Bill issue. The issue and surrender of Tax Revenue Certificates are also handled by the Loans Office.

The Bank manages the Exchange Equalization Account (which constitutes the gold and foreign exchange reserves) and the exchange control as agent for the Treasury. Management of the Exchange Equalization Account involves transactions in bullion, foreign exchange and foreign securities. Links with the gold market, and the foreign exchange markets in London and overseas, are obvious. The administration of exchange control is operated through about 180 'authorized banks' (banks, merchant banks and overseas banks). Points of interpretation of the regulations require very frequent communication between 'authorized banks' and the Bank and often such consultations also involve stockbrokers and representatives of firms engaged in overseas transactions. The commodity markets need more flexibility than the normal regulations allow, so special schemes have been devised for them. Again, these involve frequent contact between members of the markets concerned and the Bank.

The Management of the note issue includes printing, checking and destruction of notes (the operations which involve most of the work), which are carried out at Debden. The issue of notes to the banks is handled by the Issue Office (in London), which also performs ancillary functions connected with the note issue. Notes are also issued to the banks (and returned by them) through the Bank's branches.

The Bank still performs a small amount of ordinary banking business for private customers and staff, but this has little economic significance. Apart from its services to the Government, the crucially important banking function performed by the Bank of England is that of banker to the rest of the banking system. It holds accounts for the clearing banks, the discount houses, other U.K. banks and overseas central banks, and it is through their accounts at the Bank of England that the clearing banks settle balances due to one another as a result of their clearing operations. These operations are closely linked with those of the Clearing House, described in the next section.

The Bank's management of the money market is described in detail in an article 'The Management of Money day by day' (Bank of England *Quarterly Bulletin*, March 1963). Transactions are mainly in Treasury bills; they are both numerous and large; they have to be compressed into a very short period of time; and they are based on information derived from a constant exchange of news and views

273

with the discount houses and the banks. A high proportion of the operations are of a technical nature, designed to smooth out shortages and surpluses of money that would otherwise occur as a result of irregular large transactions (especially on Government account). They are also used, however, to create conditions suitable for the implementation of the Bank's monetary policies.

Operations in the stock market include:

(a) Purchase or sales to meet particular requirements in relation to the Bank's own portfolio or those of its customers, who include the National Debt Commissioners, and a number of sinking funds and charitable trusts.

(b) Transactions in relation to the management of the National Debt. When a new stock is issued a large part of it is normally taken up by the Bank on behalf of the official funds which it manages. This is subsequently sold on tap by the Government broker on the Stock Exchange. The Government broker, on behalf of the Bank, also buys in stock nearing its redemption date, thus achieving a continuous process of refinancing and avoiding the inconvenience of very large cash subscriptions and redemption.

(c) Transactions designed to prevent violent fluctuations in gilt-edged prices. These technical operations can of course be used, like those in the discount market, to create conditions favourable to the Bank's more general policies. These operations are on a very large scale and require continuous consultation between the Bank, the Treasury, the Comptroller of the National Debt Office and the Government broker.

The Bank operates in the bullion market, as in the bill market and the stock market, through a broker (in this case, N. M. Rothschild & Sons). Until March 1968 the Bank dealt on behalf of the Exchange Equalization Account and as agent for the South African Reserve Bank, which is responsible for the disposal of newly mined South African gold, and a number of other central banks. The Bank also intervened, 'in order to avoid violent and unnecessary movements in the price', for which purpose it operated the so-called 'gold-pool' under an arrangement with the Federal Reserve Bank of New York and certain European central banks (*Quarterly Bulletin*, March 1964). However, this arrangement was discontinued in March 1968, and at present central banks are not operating in the gold market.

The Bank assists the Treasury and other government departments in the formulation of monetary policies which the Bank itself will implement. It also advises the government on economic and financial conditions overseas. Responsibility for such matters lies with the Governor and Court of Directors, but senior officials in almost all departments are bound to be involved. The Governor had a record kept of contacts with Whitehall during the last three months of 1958, and submitted the following figures to the Radcliffe Committee. Meetings and personal discussions with Ministers or officials:

Involving Governor and/or Deputy	'over 60'
Involving executive directors or Bank officials	'over 300'
Letters, telephone calls other than routine	'over 400'
Routine communications	'several thousands'

(Radcliffe Committee, Minutes, Q12,814).

As a background both for its operations and its advice to Government, the Bank must have an intimate knowledge and understanding of economic and financial developments both at home and overseas. This involves not only economic and statistical analysis, but a reference library, an extensive filing service and a great number of personal contacts both here and overseas. The Bank have also accepted responsibility for producing many of the U.K.'s basic financial statistics which are published in their own *Quarterly Bulletin* and in the Central Statistical Office's *Financial Statistics*.

From time to time policy requires a major and publicly announced decision such as a change in Bank rate, a call for 'special deposits' or the imposition of a 'ceiling' on lending by banks and other institutions. Such dramatic moves, however, are only occasional and, in between them, the Bank is continually pursuing its policy aims in a number of less conspicuous ways. As already noted, routing technical operations in the bill market, the stock market, the foreign exchange market or the bullion market may be used to create conditions in keeping with the Bank's general policies. The Bank operates a 'queue' for local authorities and governments of overseas sterling area countries wishing to issue securities in London and gives approval to the timing and terms of such issues; industrial and commercial companies wishing to raise £1 million or more in fresh capital require the Bank's consent to the timing of such issues. Finally, there are a great variety of contacts, formal and informal, between the Bank and other institutions at which the Bank can make its views known.

Apart from its advice to Government the Bank is very frequently asked by banks and others for advice on a variety of matters. It also

275

keeps a watchful eye on the activities of the City with a view to preventing the development of unsound trading or financial practices. For example, the Bank regularly buys samples of commercial bills in the market and analyses them to show the nature of the transactions financed in this way.

In earlier chapters we have presented the manifold activities of the City as clustering around a financial nucleus and a trading nucleus. This account of the operations of the Bank of England, brief as it is, should demonstrate that the Bank is the core of the financial nucleus and has very strong links with the trading nucleus. It is inconceivable that the main operations of the Bank should be conducted anywhere but in the City, and its presence there has an important (and in some cases, decisive) influence on the location of other financial institutions.

The Bank, like other City institutions, is actively pursuing the economies offered by computers and other technological developments but it does not seem likely that there will be major changes in its needs either for space or manpower in the City. The two areas in which fairly large changes have occurred in the recent past are the management of the public debt, and exchange control.

The introduction of a computer to handle stock transfers and the preparation of dividend warrants has brought substantial savings, and there has been a gradual fall in the number of accounts, reflecting a reduction in the number of small private holdings and a growing concentration of the debt in the hands of financial institutions. The number of stock accounts has fallen from 3·25 million in the early 1950s to 2·5 million at present. Apart from a once-for-all increase due to Steel Nationalization the slow downward trend will probably continue. The decline in personal holdings is partly offset by the fact that institutions deal more actively than individuals and, as already noted, there is no apparent trend in the number of transfers.

In the early 1950s exchange control employed over 1,300 people; this fell to about 250 in the mid-1960s, but subsequent tightening of the controls has led to an increase to about 500. The nature and extent of control is the main determinant of employment; the volume of trade and payments has comparatively little influence as the routine work is nearly all done by the other banks who are authorized banks. Changes in other departments are unlikely to be large. The greater use of computers will enable quicker and more elaborate studies to be done especially in the research and information field, while the development of 'random access' systems may enable information to be stored on tape, with a saving of filing space and clerical labour. On balance it seems likely that there will be a slight decline in the Bank's total employment in the City over the next few years, especially if there is some relaxation of exchange control. The decline is likely to be in the more routine forms of work but it will probably be very gradual and it is unlikely to be large enough either to create internal problems or to have any significant effect on total employment in the City.

(B) THE LONDON BANKERS' CLEARING HOUSE

The Clearing House, which occupies a comparatively small space in the City of London, is the central point to which the majority of cheques from all over the country are sent for payment. Each day between two and three million orders for payment of one kind or another pass through the banking system. The main methods of dealing with them are as follows:

(a) Where a transfer is between two accounts at the same branch, only an internal book-keeping adjustment is needed.
(b) Transfers between different branches of the same bank are cleared through the bank's own regional offices or head office.
(c) All items drawn on branches of the clearing banks other than those in (a) and (b) above pass through the Clearing House.
(d) Cheques on branches of banks in Scotland and Ireland are sent direct for payment.
(e) Cheques, drafts, etc., on the London merchant banks, on the London offices of overseas banks and of Scottish or Irish banks, and on certain government departments are presented (and payment collected) by clerks or messengers on daily 'walks'.

It is estimated that the Clearing House handles between 70 per cent and 80 per cent of all transfers passing through the system. The volume and number of clearings are shown in Tables 8.1 and 8.2. The precise amount of payments settled outside is not known.

The work of the Clearing House is organized in three sections: The Town Clearing; the General Clearing; and the Credit Clearing. The first two are known as 'debit clearings' because the articles handled are debit items for the banks to which they are presented, e.g. a cheque drawn by a customer of bank A in favour of a customer of bank B will be presented by B at the clearing and will be a debit item for A. By contrast, a credit transfer voucher is a credit item for the bank to whom it is delivered.

The Town Clearing is much the most important from the point of view of the City. With a few exceptions, the Town Clearing deals

277

Table 8.1. London Bankers' Clearing House: Value of Clearings 1955–68

Year	Town (1)	Town (2)	General (1)	General (2)	Credit (1)	Credit (2)	Total (1)	Total (2)
1955	118·6	—	34·0	—	—	—	152·6	—
1956	125·8	6·1	35·1	3·2	—	—	160·9	5·4
1957	135·4	7·6	37·3	6·3	—	—	172·7	7·3
1958	142·3	5·1	38·6	3·5	—	—	180·9	4·7
1959	156·8	10·2	42·4	9·8	—	—	199·2	10·1
1960	179·3	14·3	46·1	8·7	2·3*	—	227·7	14·3
1961	195·7	9·1	46·7	1·3	5·3	130·4	247·7	8·3
1962	224·2	14·6	48·6	4·1	6·0	13·2	278·8	12·6
1963	250·2	11·6	52·1	7·2	6·9	15·0	309·2	10·9
1964	297·2	18·8	58·6	12·3	7·9	14·5	363·6	17·6
1965	346·5	16·6	62·1	6·2	8·7	10·1	417·3	14·8
1966	384·5	11·0	67·8	9·2	9·5	9·2	461·8	10·7
1967	486·0	26·4	72·7	7·2	10·2	7·4	568·9	23·2
1968	515·7	6·1	83·8	15·3	11·6	13·7	611·1	7·4

Col. (1) £000 million.
Col. (2) Percentage increase over previous year.
* Credit clearing started on May 1, 1960.
Source: Committee of London Clearing Bankers.

Table 8.2. London Bankers' Clearing House: Number of Articles Cleared 1955–68

Year	Town (1)	Town (2)	General (1)	General (2)	Credit (1)	Credit (2)	Total (1)	Total (2)
1955	—	—	—	—	—*	—	366*	—
1956	—	—	—	—	—	—	376	2·7
1957	—	—	—	—	—	—	387	2·9
1958	17	—	380	—	—	—	397	2·6
1959	20	17·6	398	4·7	—	—	418	5·3
1960	20	0	418	5·0	29	—	467	11·7
1961	20	0	428	2·4	64	120·7	492	5·4
1962	20	0	438	2·3	77	20·3	535	8·7
1963	20	0	468	6·8	89	15·6	577	7·9
1964	20	0	505	7·9	103	15·7	628	8·8
1965	20	0	525	4·0	116	12·6	661	5·3
1966	14	− 30·0	560	6·3	131	12·9	705	6·7
1967	7		602		154		753	
1968	7		671		176		854	

Col. (1) millions.
Col. (2) Percentage increase over previous year.
* Affected by rail strike.
Source: Committee of London Clearing Bankers.

with articles over £2,000 in value drawn on and paid in to one of a
group of branches all within easy walking distance of one another,
and all in the E.C.2, 3 and 4 postal districts. All Town Clearing
branches are in the City, but not all City branches are in the Town
Clearing. The branches included have been changed from time to
time. They at present number ninety-eight, including three offices of
the Bank of England. The banks involved, with the number of their
Town Clearing offices are:

Bank of England	3
Barclays	19
Coutts	2
District	1
Glyn Mills	1
Lloyd's	15
Martins	5
Midland	20
National	2
National Provincial	12
Westminster	16
Williams Deacon's	2
	98

The Town Clearing handles almost all the transfers arising from
the purely financial business of the City – the money and bill
markets, the Stock Exchange and the foreign exchange market, and a
great number of payments arising from insurance, shipping, commodity dealing and merchanting.

The number of articles cleared is relatively small. From 1959 to
1965 it remained constant at 20 million a year, while the numbers
passing through the General Clearing rose from 389 million to 525
million. Over the same period, however, the value of Town Clearings
more than doubled from £156·8 thousand million to £346·5 thousand
million whereas the value of General Clearings rose barely 50 per
cent from £42·4 thousand million to £62·1 thousand million.
In 1965 the Town Clearing accounted for less than 2 per cent by
numbers of all debit clearings but for more than 85 per cent by value.
The average value of articles passing through the Town Clearing in
1965 was over £17,000, compared with under £130 for the General
Clearing.

In July 1966 the morning sessions of the Town Clearing were discontinued, with the result that a large number of (relatively) small transactions were switched to the General Clearing. The number of articles cleared fell sharply but the growth in value terms continued at a pace not much less than in the recent past, and the average value per item rose to over £27,000. During 1967 and 1968 the number of articles cleared was steady at about 7 million, but the average value per item during 1968 had risen to over £73,000.

With these very large sums, the loss of interest even overnight is a significant matter, and the essence of the Town Clearing is simplicity and speed. Each Town branch sorts cheques drawn on the Town branches of each other member bank as they come in and makes them into bundles, keeping a running total for each bundle. These bundles (known as 'out-work' are then taken to the Clearing House between 2.30 p.m. and 3.45 p.m. on Mondays to Fridays, and presented to the banks on which they are drawn (whereupon they become 'in-work' to the bank receiving them). A clerk of the receiving bank immediately checks the total on one of the adding machines in the Clearing House and agrees it with the clerk of the presenting bank. By this means each bank can keep a running total of the payments it is due to make to each of the others, and an over-all balance can be struck and settled within minutes of the end of deliveries.

These facilities for speedy settlement are, of course, passed on by the banks to their customers, and a cheque on a Town branch paid into another Town branch by 3 p.m. is cleared the same day. This is vital to the money market, and very important to other financial institutions that have to make and receive large payments. So long as the cheque remains the normal means of making large payments, the Town Clearing will retain its importance.

The procedure of the General Clearing is rather different. As already noted, it handles a far larger number of articles of much smaller average value and drawn from a much wider area. Branches throughout the country send cheques on other banks to their clearing departments in London, which pass them through the Clearing. Deliveries are made each morning between 9 a.m. and 10.15 a.m. The Clearing is settled on the next business day after delivery.

Since the beginning of 1968 the ground floor of the Clearing House has provided drive-in facilities for the delivery, by electric vans and trolleys, of cheques for the General Clearing. At peak periods over three million cheques are exchanged here in a day, being transported to clearing departments of the respective member banks in special trays to avoid damage which would prevent their being processed by automated methods.

The Credit Clearing was established in 1960 to facilitate the exchange and settlement of Credit Transfers, including 'traders' credits' which had long been used for settlement of debts and payment of salaries direct to employees' banking accounts. This facility is widely used and the number of vouchers exchanged has risen very rapidly from 64 million in 1961, the first full year, to 176 million in 1968. The latter figure includes vouchers passed through the Inter-Bank Computer Bureau, which commenced operations in April 1968. The Bureau supplies details of credits on magnetic tapes to the banks whose customers are to be credited.

(c) THE CLEARING BANKS

At the time when this study was undertaken there were eleven Clearing Banks, but the 'Big Five' (Barclays, Lloyd's, Midland, National Provincial and Westminster) did over 85 per cent of the business. They also control three of the other clearing banks. All the 'Big Five' have head offices in London, and nation-wide branch networks ranging in numbers from 1,400 to 2,500; Coutts and Glyn Mills operate in London only. The District, Martins and Williams Deacon's have offices in London but most of their business is in the north and their head offices are in Liverpool and Manchester. Subsequently, Barclays has absorbed Martins and National Provincial (which already controlled the District Bank) and has combined with Westminster to form the National Westminster Group. The four big groups thus have about 97 per cent of all clearing bank deposits. The questionnaires and interviews that form the basis of this chapter were all completed before these changes, and we have, therefore, retained the old names. The absorption of Martins and the integration of the District into the National Westminster Group cannot have more than marginal effects on the City, as their business was almost wholly in the north, and, as shown in section B, they had only six clearing branches between them. The reasons, given later in this chapter, that have prevented any significant reduction in the number of City branches in the past, will not be affected by the merger. National Westminster is planning a new office in the City to house the headquarters of the Group.

In the course of our investigations, a questionnaire was sent to each of the clearing banks and was completed by ten of them including all of the 'Big Five'. The following paragraphs draw heavily on the replies received, though conclusions have often to be expressed in rather general terms to avoid disclosing confidential information.

The main lines of the banks' business are well known – the provision of means of payment and the making of loans both to the public and private sectors. They also perform numerous ancillary services for their customers, of which the most important from the present point of view are executor and trustee business, overseas business and company registration. Most of the banks have interests, in some cases controlling, in hire-purchase finance companies, and some have subsidiaries operating overseas and providing export finance. The number and variety of these subsidiaries has been increasing and some of the clearing banks have entered into joint operations with merchant banks and with overseas commercial banks.

The banks provide a means of payment mainly through the cheque systems though, as shown in the previous section, the use of credit transfer has grown rapidly since 1960. The number of items handled in an average working day is between two and three million. Each of these transactions involves the handling of a document – the cheque or credit transfer slip – and (in most cases) the crediting of one account and the debiting of another. All transactions except those between customers of the same branch also involve a clearing operation, and between 70 per cent and 80 per cent of them go through the Clearing House.

All the 'Big Five' have their main clearing departments in the City, though two of them have decentralized their branch clearings (i.e. those between different branches of the same bank, which do not go through the Clearing House). A third, which experimented with decentralizing branch clearings, has brought them back to the City in order to put them on its central computer

An important subsidiary part of the banks' activity as providers of means of payment is the distribution of coin and notes – receiving them over the counter when paid in by customers or by people without a bank account who want to make a credit transfer; paying them out to customers cashing cheques; returning worn notes to the Bank of England for cancellation; and drawing new ones from the Bank.

Most of the work in relation to advances to customers, and some of that in connection with the discount of commercial bills, is done in the branches, though the sanction of regional or head offices is required for large loans. All the other lending transactions of the banks, however, require centralized operation as well as control, and have strong linkages with financial markets – the call-money business is linked with the London money market and with the Stock Exchange; the bill business with the Discount Market; and the management of the banks' portfolios of government securities with the Stock Exchange. Each of these is the responsibility of a department or head office.

The banks conduct their overseas business, much of which originates in the branches, through overseas departments or subsidiary companies. Dealings in foreign exchange are on a very large scale, but they involve only a small proportion of the staff. The departments also maintain contact with correspondent banks overseas which number many hundreds; handle documentary credits and other documents arising from the finance of international trade; issue travellers' cheques; pay foreign banks for their own travellers' cheques presented by them, and collect payment for foreign travellers' cheques cashed by their own bank; handle customers' transactions in foreign securities; and do much of the day-to-day work of Exchange Control as dealers authorized by the Bank of England. Proximity to the Bank of England and to the foreign exchange market is essential, as is membership of the Town Clearing.

Executor and Trustee Departments have to handle the legal business of obtaining probate and administering an estate, but in their capacity as Trustees they also have to manage a considerable volume of investments. There is an obvious link with the Stock Exchange here as well as with solicitors and accountants; some executor and trustee offices are also members of the Town Clearing.

The new issues and registrars' departments of the banks receive subscriptions for new issues of company securities and (for some companies) maintain share registers, record transfers and pay dividends. There is no very obvious reason why registers should be kept in London, and Lloyd's in fact has its registrars' department in Worthing and is very happy with this arrangement. The new issue business, however, involves close links with merchant banks and stockbrokers.

Besides the departments related to the specific activities discussed above, the head offices of banks – like those of any large business organization – have a wide range of general administrative work – secretarial, accounting, costing, organization and methods, economic intelligence, legal, premises, establishment, welfare, public relations, etc. Some of these have their own reasons for being in London, e.g. economic intelligence departments; but in general their links are more with one another, with the operating departments for which they provide services or over which they exercise a measure of

283

control, and with their own top management. The common use of a computer is also becoming a force linking a number of departments together.

There are some differences between banks in their attitude towards the decentralization of these activities, but our inquiries showed that these were not very great. Some banks have more regional or district offices than others, and allow more local discretion in matters such as the sanctioning of loans. At least one of the 'Big Five' operates all or part of the following departments outside London: branch clearings; registrars'; executor and trustee; income tax; stock office; premises; and stationery. In most cases, however, only part of the department has been moved, and none of the banks has decentralized the main administrative and decision-taking complex of its head office. The figures supplied to us show a striking degree of similarity in the proportion of head office staff in the City to total employment in the bank among those banks with a national branch network. Information given to us indicates that head office activities of the 'Big Five' – the only ones for which the distinction between the head office and other activities in the City is really valid – employed about 12,000 people in 1965.

Besides their head offices and specialized departments the larger clearing banks all have a substantial number of branches in the City. Altogether the eleven banks have 121 offices in the City in which ordinary banking business is carried on, of which 108 belong to the 'Big Five'. The average employment per branch is rather over sixty-five, though many branches are much smaller than the average. Total employment is around 8,000.

The number and distribution of branches is much influenced by past history; the present structure of banking was achieved very largely by a series of amalgamations and absorptions between 1880 and 1920. When an old-established bank was taken over, its principal offices were usually maintained. There is a reluctance to close branches, as it is believed that customers have a loyalty to a particular branch, so that its closure is likely to lose business. Some branches destroyed by bombing between 1939 and 1945 have not been re-opened, but there have been very few closures since the war. The 'Big Five' reported the closing of only seventeen branches since 1950, and the opening of twenty-eight. More than half of the seventeen were transfers to very nearby premises, usually as part of a rebuilding scheme, while the remainder were closed because of the termination of a lease. In only one case was lack of business mentioned as a cause, and this was in very special circumstances. Those of the new branches which were not merely transfers were mostly in areas of extensive rebuilding.

The maintenance of so many branches so close together might seem an uneconomic use of space and manpower, and this was discussed at some length at interviews. One manager of a fairly large branch said that he could take over the work of two smaller nearby branches and effect economies by so doing, but this was unusual. In general the banks seemed satisfied with their existing branch networks and did not anticipate any major change. Among the points made were:

1. Most branches are small, both in terms of space and manpower.
2. In larger branches both space and manpower are generally fully occupied, so that no great savings could be made by consolidation.
3. Small branches give more personal service, which is valued by customers.
4. Some branches cater for specialized business, e.g. the Stock Exchange, Lloyd's, the commodity markets, etc. Thus customers gain not only the advantage of having a bank very near to their place of business but also that of dealing with a manager and staff who are familiar with their particular type of business.
5. The established City branches are all very profitable in spite of high costs. The banks stress that they pay close attention to the profitability of branches and even the Prices and Incomes Board acknowledge their efficiency in this respect.

It does not seem likely, therefore, that there will be many changes in the branch system in the foreseeable future, especially as the determinaton of leases will not exert any strong pressure. Of 111 branch offices (including some housed in head office buildings) about which information was given to us, twenty-two were freehold, another forty-nine had leases of more than twenty-five years, while only ten had five years or less to run. One possible qualification is that access to central computers may reduce staff in a few big offices and so free space which could be used for absorbing nearby smaller branches, but this is not likely to happen often, if at all

No single indicator gives an accurate impression of the growth of the banks' activities. Among those which give partial indications are: amount of deposits; amount of advances; number of branches; number of accounts; volume of clearings. Between 1965 and 1969 deposits of all clearing banks rose by 66 per cent; the highest rate of growth among the 'Big Five' was 88 per cent and the lowest 50 per cent. Advances rose much more steeply owing to the relaxation of official restrictions in the late fifties. The average rise was 200 per cent and one of the 'Big Five' achieved an increase of more than 250 per cent. Advances involve more work than other forms of bank lending: so that a rise in their proportion increases the demands on the banks' staff. However, most of this is in the branches rather than the City.

There are approximately 13,000 clearing bank branches in England and Wales and the number has recently been growing at about 2 per cent a year. There are about 20 million separate bank accounts. There is no precise information about the rate of growth of the number of accounts, but it has been considerably greater than that of deposits. The resulting tendency to a fall in the average size of account is another factor tending to increase the banks' work load though, again, mostly in the branches.

The figures for bank clearings are given in Table 8.1. Town Clearings have remained stable in number (apart from the big reduction associated with the abandonment of the morning session) but have increased rapidly in value. The number of items and value of General Clearings have been growing considerably faster than deposits and the introduction of credit clearing has added a large number of relatively small items. This, of course, has added to the workload both of branches and of central clearing departments in the City.

The report of the Prices and Incomes Board[2] gives numbers employed in the clearing banks (excluding about 3,000 woman part-time workers) as follows:

	1960	1965	Percentage increase
Appointed			
Men	17,922	21,527	
Women	379	687	
	18,301	22,214	20·4
Clerical			
Men	42,044	46,825	
Women	46,789	66,460	
	88,833	113,285	27·5
Other			
Men	5,110	6,265	
Women	246	302	
	5,356	6,567	22·6
Total	112,490	142,066	26·2

[2] National Board for Prices and Incomes, Report No. 34, *Bank Charges*. CMND. 3292, p. 76.

During the same period, the volume of deposits rose by 25·7 per cent. Employment would have been expected to rise more rapidly than deposits, because of the increasing proportion of advances, the growing number of small accounts, and the increase in the volume of clearings. These influences were, however, almost completely offset by mechanization and other improvements in efficiency.

In our questionnaire we asked for figures of employment in the City and by the banks as a whole for the years 1950, 1958 and 1966. The figures for the total of the 'Big Five' (in index number form) are as follows:

Index numbers: 1950 = 100

	1958			1966		
	Male	Female	Total	Male	Female	Total
In the City	104	139	117	140	201	163
In the banks as a whole	101	150	116	125	281	172

Both in the City and in the country as a whole, employment was growing more rapidly in the second half of the period than in the first; but in the second half the growth of employment in the City was rather less than in the country. However, these figures conceal a big difference between head offices and branches.

Employment in the City branches was growing at a rate well below the national average. The total increase for the five banks was only 25 per cent. Several influences have contributed to this slow rate of growth. The number of branches in the City, as indicated above, has not been rising nearly as fast as the national average. The business of the City has been becoming more financial and less commercial, so that the number of small transactions has declined. A reflection of this is the contraction in number, and the rapid rise in value, of items passing through the Town Clearing, which was shown in Table 8.1. Finally, City branches were among the first to be put on computer, so that the 1966 figures already reflect savings due to automation. On the other hand, employment in head offices has risen by no less than 125 per cent.

(D) OTHER BANKS

Although the 'other banks' are so much more numerous (there are approximately 160 of them operating some 250 offices) they employ only about 20,000 people in the City compared with about 27,000 employed by the clearing banks.

287

The seventeen firms who are members of the Accepting Houses Committee are generally known as merchant banks, and the name is also used for a number of smaller firms included in the official statistics as 'other banks'. They vary greatly in size and in the relative importance of different activities, but all take part in domestic and overseas banking, corporate finance and investment, while some have miscellaneous domestic activities including bullion dealing and trading in commodities, and many of them have affiliated or associated companies abroad.

In their domestic banking business they take deposits, make loans and provide facilities for payment much as the clearing banks do, though they are not members of the Clearing House. Their customers are fewer, but tend to be larger, and overseas customers are relatively much more important. A high proportion of their deposits are in 'deposit accounts' and their cheque-paying facilities are much less widely used than those of the clearing banks. The acceptance credit business, which fell markedly during and immediately after the war, recovered with the revival of the commercial bill of exchange. At the end of 1952 the acceptances of members of the Accepting Houses Committee were £55 million for U.K. residents and £18 million for foreigners; at the end of 1968 they had outstandingly £251 million and £68 million respectively. They are, of course, large operators in the foreign exchange and Euro-currency markets, and some of them are active in the international syndicates that issue Euro-bonds.

The merchant banks have these activities in common with most other banks in London; their operations in corporate finance and investment are much more peculiar to themselves. Banks which used to specialize in new issues for overseas clients turned, during the 1930s and still more since 1945, to issues for British companies. From this, in turn, there has developed a much more permanent relationship between the merchant banks and many of their company clients, in which the merchant bank gives regular advice, especially in relation to take-overs and amalgamations. This side of the merchant banks' work is expanding very rapidly. It is not a large employer of labour, but those engaged upon it are highly expert and highly paid.

The investment side of merchant banking has also grown very rapidly. Originally this consisted mainly of managing the affairs of wealthy private clients but now the institutional business – pension funds, investment trusts, unit trusts and charities – has become much more important. Only a few firms give the value of the portfolios they manage; the biggest is believed to be over £500 million. The total for all members of the Accepting House: Committee is probably at least £3,000 million and may well be higher. One large firm disclosed an increase in its portfolio of 66 per cent between 1962 and 1966, and this could probably be matched by others.

As shown in Chapter 3, the merchant banks have close links with almost every other financial activity, and many of the commercial ones in the City. Some of them have decentralized certain activities – notably company registration – and some have opened small provincial branches, but it is impossible to conceive of their main centres of operation being anywhere but in the City.

Employment shown by City Corporation sources was just under 3,400, but this seems implausibly low since the bigger firms employ 500 or more each. It was not possible to get figures for changes in employment, except for a few firms, and these showed wide differences of experience. One large firm had a steady increase and its labour force grew by nearly 80 per cent between 1950 and 1965. Two others showed a rapid growth up to the early sixties, followed by a levelling off of the labour force (though not the volume of business) when they introduced a computer. The volume of employment is not related in any simple way to the volume of business because (apart from automation and other influence on productivity) some types of business are much more labour-intensive than others. Company registration and the documentary work connected with acceptance credits, for example, use a lot of labour in relation to the value of output, corporate finance work uses relatively little. The use of computers is still in its early stages and will certainly bring more savings of labour, but the merchant banks' business is growing so fast that they are unlikely to be able to avoid a further substantial rise in employment.

The overseas banks are, of course, largely concerned with financial transactions between Britain and their respective countries, and with managing the balances which they and their clients hold in London. This necessarily involves them in dealings in the foreign exchange market, the money market, the bill market and the securities market. In addition, a number of them participate, in competition with British banks, in accepting and re-lending sterling deposits; in the local authority loans market; in the markets for Euro-dollars and dollar certificates of deposit; and in the syndicates which issue Euro-bonds. The American banks have been particularly active in most of these ways during recent years.

A few of the overseas banks are the head offices of British firms operating a substantial branch network overseas, e.g. Barclays

K

D.C.O., and Bank of London and South America. These have administrative activities similar to those of the head offices of any other big international company, besides their banking business, and employ large staffs. The remainder are branch or representative offices of firms with headquarters overseas, and are often quite small. Ninety-five of the 189 establishments in the O.S.R.P. returns employed fifty people or less.

Some of the main features of the growth of business are shown in Tables 8.3 to 8.6. Statistics prior to 1962 are much less satisfactory than afterwards, but Table 8.3 shows clearly the rapid rise of over-

Table 8.3. Deposits of Main Categories of Banks 1955–61
(£ million)

End of year	London clearing Banks	British overseas banks		American banks		Foreign banks and affiliates		Accepting houses	
		(1)	(2)	(1)	(2)	(1)	(2)	(1)	(2)
1955	6,612	545	99	122	27	140	11	152	71
1956	6,856	515	98	107	24	95	15	159	75
1957	6,929	497	98	114	60	106	16	151	71
1958	7,199	573	113	129	58	171	22	212	100
1959	7,667	659	175	206	77	203	40	259	114
1960	7,831	767	212	389	99	311	60	423	174
1961	7,928	820	244	406	81	293	66	494	209

Col. (1) Total.
Col. (2) U.K. business included in total.
Source: Bank of England, *Quarterly Bulletin.*
Figures refer to gross deposits of Clearing Banks and 'current and deposit accounts' of others.

seas business and the way in which banks outside the Clearing House were increasing their sterling business. Between 1955 and 1961 deposits by non-residents with overseas banks and merchant banks rose from £751 million to £1,413 million (88 per cent). At the same time, resident deposits rose from £208 million to £598 million (87 per cent). Meanwhile, the gross deposits of the clearing banks were rising by only 20 per cent.

Table 8.4 shows the recent statistics in rather more detail. The previous figures included a certain amount of double counting as sums deposited with one bank are often re-lent to another. These are largely excluded from Table 8.4 by omitting deposits by one bank with another. In the six years 1962–8 deposits by residents rose from

Table 8.4. Deposits of Main Categories of Banks 1962–68
(£ million)

End of year	London clearing banks	British overseas banks (1)	(2)	American banks (1)	(2)	Foreign banks and affiliates (1)	(2)	Other banks (1)	(2)	Accepting houses (1)	(2)
1962	7,903	155	806	78	363	23	253	34	278	215	346
1963	8,337	193	925	138	487	37	251	41	327	329	384
1964	8,996	200	977	140	712	316	334	133	577	385	436
1965	9,454	262	1,089	197	1,010	41	358	194	543	442	398
1966	9,501	297	1,141	233	1,609	67	343	210	595	474	434
1967	10,262	315	1,398	327	2,300	93	362	281	832	592	551
1968	10,736	427	1,742	408	3,896	103	606	694	1,200	749	760

Col. (1) U.K. residents.
Col. (2) Overseas residents.
Source: Bank of England, Quarterly Bulletin.
There have been some changes in coverage explained in detail in the Bulletin, and the sterling value of foreign currency items is affected by devaluation. Figures for overseas banks and accepting houses exclude deposits with other U.K. banks.

£507 million to £2,381 million (370 per cent) and deposits by non-residents from £2,056 million to £8,204 million (300 per cent). The rise in clearing bank deposits was only 36 per cent. Table 8.5 shows the division of deposits between sterling and overseas currencies. As might be expected, deposits by U.K. residents are mainly in sterling;

Table 8.5. Overseas Banks and Accepting Houses: Distribution of Deposits (Excluding those by Other U.K. Banks) between Sterling and Overseas Currencies 1962–68
(£ million)

End of Year	Total	U.K. Residents Sterling	Other currencies	Overseas Residents Sterling	Other currencies
1962	2,562	431	76	1,096	960
1963	3,102	655	83	1,207	1,166
1964	3,928	815	78	1,283	1,752
1965	4,534	1,046	90	1,356	2,042
1966	5,404	1,159	122	1,250	2,793
1967	7,055	1,399	211	1,167	4,030
1968	10,585	1,939	277	1,084	6,523

Source: Bank of England, Quarterly Bulletin.
The totals in this table are not identical with those of Table 8.4, as Table 8.5 excludes negotiable certificates of deposit. See also notes to Table 8.6.

non-residents hold considerable quantities of sterling but the big increase has been in overseas currencies. The total increase in sterling deposits was 98 per cent while deposits in foreign currencies rose by 556 per cent. Finally, Table 8.6 shows the growth of advances, which is even more striking than that of deposits; advances to U.K. residents rose by over two and a half times while those to non-residents increased more than fivefold.

Table 8.6. Advances by Overseas Banks and Accepting Houses 1962–8
(£ million)

End of year	Total	U.K. residents other than banks			Overseas residents		
		Total	Sterling	Other	Total	Sterling	Other
1962	1,608	454	439	15	1,155	248	907
1963	2,016	595	568	27	1,421	327	1,094
1964	2,734	870	804	66	1,864	397	1,467
1965	3,210	1,047	912	136	2,163	377	1,785
1966	4,134	1,086	933	153	3,048	278	2,771
1967	5,548	1,257	982	275	4,290	249	4,041
1968	8,619	1,640	1,164	476	6,979	241	6,738

Source: Bank of England, *Quarterly Bulletin.*
See note to Table 8.4.

Whether this growth will continue depends on many influences. Business with overseas clients will be affected by our success in maintaining confidence in sterling, by the extent to which the balance of payments permits a relaxation of controls over capital movements, by developments in the Euro-dollar market, and by the progress of negotiations with the E.E.C. Reasons have been given in Chapter 6 for taking an optimistic view. In their domestic business, merchant banks and overseas banks have been helped by the fact that they have not been as strictly controlled as have the clearing banks; in particular, they have not been required to conform to minimum cash or liquidity ratios, or to make special deposits with the Bank of England, though they have been subject to the 'ceiling' on credit imposed from time to time by the Bank of England.

In his 1967 Budget speech the Chancellor of the Exchequer announced that the Bank of England would hold discussions with non-clearing banks and other financial institutions with a view to devising some control analogous to that which the Bank exercises over the clearing banks, and in February 1968 the Bank of England announced the 'cash deposits' scheme. This was to come into operation when the 'ceiling' restrictions imposed in November 1967 are abandoned. It does not seem likely, however, that it will impose more than a very slight check on the growth of the non-clearing banks which will probably remain one of the most rapidly expanding types of business in the City

(E) THE DISCOUNT AND MONEY MARKETS

The London Discount Market is made up of eleven firms who are members of the London Discount Market Association and who enjoy the privilege of access to the Bank of England as 'lender of last resort'. There are also a few small firms outside the Association who act as brokers, as distinct from dealers.

The main functions of the market are well known and will not be described in detail here. It began in the nineteenth century as a market in commercial bills; the Treasury bill became important during World War I and practically supplanted the commercial bill in discount houses' portfolios during and immediately after World War II. The business in short-dated government bonds began on a small scale in the 1930s and developed during the war, but it was greatly expanded during the period of cheap money policy immediately after 1945.

The main assets of the discount houses are shown in Table 8.7.

Table 8.7. London Discount Market: Main Assets 1955–68
(£ million)

End of year	Total assets	Treasury bills	Other bills	Government securities
1955	1,068	652	45	307
1956	954	523	85	294
1957	956	585	84	223
1958	1,053	594	70	321
1959	1,135	635	118	322
1960	1,197	574	117	440
1961	1,216	533	185	449
1962	1,250	502	189	488
1963	1,305	529	249	442
1964	1,283	453	302	438
1965	1,455	484	339	500
1966	1,565	424	404	542
1967	1,747	548	437	544
1968	1,663	471	560	306

Source: Bank of England, *Quarterly Bulletin.*

293

Total assets underwent a period of stagnation in the mid-fifties, grew steadily if fairly slowly from 1957 to 1964, and increased much more sharply from 1964 to 1967. Treasury bill portfolios have shown a downward trend with the decline in the total volume of 'tender' bills over the past ten years. Government securities on the other hand have shown a fairly strong upward trend, while commercial bills rose by more than twelve times during the period covered by the table. There has also been a sharp rise in assets outside the three main categories (largely local authorities' yearling bonds and sterling and dollar certificates of deposit) in recent years, and those amounted to £326 million at the end of 1968.

Besides their own capital and reserves, discount houses obtain funds by accepting deposits from the public, by borrowing from the clearing banks and other banks with offices in London, and in the last resort from the Bank of England. Borrowed funds at the end of 1968 were:

	£ million
Bank of England	–
Clearing banks	1,132
Other banks	319
Other sources	121

There has been a tendency for the proportion of loans supplied by the clearing banks to rise, but funds from other banks are still very important, as they may enable houses to avoid borrowing at penal rates from the Bank of England. These loans are, of course, raised in the money market. The clearing banks lend part of their funds, known as 'fixtures', at an agreed rate of 1⅝ per cent below bank rate. The rest of clearing bank money, and all of that from other banks, is lent at market rates which fluctuate continually with changes in supply and demand. Here is another case where being able to get 'the feel of the market' is very important.

Although the volume of business is so large, and not in general highly mechanized, much of it is routine and requires little labour. City Corporation sources show two firms employing twenty-five or less, nine employing between twenty-six and fifty, and only one over fifty. Total employment was only 427, of whom all but seventy-two were male. The importance of the market, for our present purpose, is not in the work it provides directly but for the link which it forges between other institutions.

All the firms in the market have offices very near to the Bank of England, and regard proximity to the Bank, and other financial institutions, as essential. The senior partner (or manager) of each house pays a visit to the Discount Office of the Bank each morning. Although these visits are normally very brief, the Bank regards them as important in helping it to get the 'feel' of the market, as well as giving an opportunity to discuss any unusual development. At these meetings, discount houses tell the Bank the amount of 'calls' which they will have to meet; this, together with information from the clearing banks and other sources, gives the Bank a preliminary impression of the amount of assistance it may have to give and forms the basis for planning its own market operations. The Bank regularly buys and analyses samples of commercial bills on the market, and any unusual feature of these may be discussed. In addition to these morning calls, houses which want to borrow from the Bank pay a further call in the afternoon. The practice of sending messengers to the Bank to bring news of the Thursday announcement of Bank rate is still maintained but, like the traditional top hat, is little more than a gesture. Firms admit (a little shamefacedly) that they get the news quicker by closed circuit television.

The banks – both clearing and non-clearing – are the main participants with the discount houses in the markets both for bills and for call and short loans. Both money market and bill market are very active, individual transactions are large, rates are constantly changing, and margins are very fine. By contrast with the foreign exchange market, banks and discount houses deal directly as principals and not through brokers, both in the money market and the bill market. Though a great deal of business is done on the telephone, personal contacts are regarded as highly important. The managers of a large firm pay daily calls on about a hundred banks. When a loan is made, bills or bonds are always lodged as security, and the delivery and collection of these is another reason why discount houses need to be within easy walking distance of the banks from which they borrow.

The Bank of England provides the discount houses with 'over the counter' facilities for transfers of bonds within five years of maturity, and the very active market in these requires a location close both to the Stock Exchange and the Bank. The discount houses are not members of the Clearing House, but cheques to and from them have to go through the Clearing and they must, therefore, be within the 'Town Clearing' area.

The growth of the markets' business in Treasury bills and bonds is determined largely by the Government's debt management policy. The influences affecting commercial bills are more complex, involving not only monetary policy but also the volume of trade, the relative cost of finance by bills and overdrafts, and changing customs in various sections of trade and industry. Besides their use in overseas trade, commercial bills have been found convenient by large firms in domestic industry, including oil and tobacco firms. Some of these firms would like to borrow more in this way, and others may well be attracted to it.

The London market, both for money and bills, is wider and more highly organized than those of Continental centres, and those whom we interviewed believed that entry into the Common Market would lead to an increase in Continental business. This might include increased participation by overseas banks in the money market and the development of a market in bills denominated in Continental currencies.

It is possible to envisage certain changes in procedure which might bring limited economies in manpower and somewhat reduce the tightness of linkages with other institutions, though all have disadvantages. Among the possibilities are:

(a) The abandonment of daily personal calls. There is strong opposition to this. Though it is admitted that a large part of the markets' business is now done by telephone, personal knowledge of one another is regarded as important, and it is argued that there are many things that can be discussed face to face between people who know one another well that could not be dealt with over the telephone.

(b) A central depository for bills. Instead of passing bills from hand to hand when they are bought, sold or pledged as security, they could be left in a central place and transferred from one account to another – possibly by computer – in response to instructions over telephone or teleprinter. This might be applied to Treasury bills, though there would be considerable difficulties in applying it to commercial bills.

(c) The Bank of England's putting of the bond register on computer tape could lead to a development similar to (b), above, for short bonds.

(d) The development of unsecured loans. These are general practice in the Euro-dollar market, though banks put limits on the amounts of their lending to each other member of the market and this sometimes gives rise to difficulties.

None of these developments is, however, likely in the near future. Several firms have installed or are installing computers; the labour-saving possibilities are clearly limited, but computers are expected to enable firms to handle a larger volume of routine business without an increase in staff. The handling of commercial bills, however, requires more judgement and entails more work than do Treasury bills, and continued growth in this field may bring some increase in employment.

(F) THE FOREIGN EXCHANGE, EURO-CURRENCY AND BULLION MARKETS

The foreign exchange market is one of the most specialized in London. Besides transactions in currencies, both spot and forward, the market also deals in 'Euro-dollars', i.e. inter-bank loans in foreign currencies.

As shown in Chapter 6, a very considerable volume of foreign trade is invoiced and settled in sterling. Other trade, of course, requires a foreign exchange transaction, as does the transfer of funds on capital account. However, the volume of transactions is very much greater than the volume of ultimate payments because of a large arbitrage business and very large forward dealings. London's spot business is said to be smaller than that of some Continental cities, but the London market is the principal centre in the world for forward dealings. As an example of the volume of such transactions Lloyd's Bank states in its balance sheet that it has forward contracts outstanding to a value of more than £1,200 million.

'Spot' contracts are normally for delivery two business days afterwards though delivery on the same day can be arranged. The most common periods for forward deals are either one month or three months, but contracts can be arranged for any time up to a year, and occasionally longer. Payment is due on delivery, and all payments must be made by a cheque on a bank in the 'Town Clearing'.

Dealing in foreign exchange is confined under the Exchange Control Regulations to firms authorized by the Bank of England. The present list of authorized dealers numbers about 180 and includes the clearing banks, the members of the Accepting Houses Committee, members of the British Overseas Banks and Affiliates Association, the American and Japanese banks in London, and a few others both British and foreign. All these banks put the whole of their London business through brokers, of whom there are only nine. Business is almost entirely by telephone, and nearly all by direct line. The desk of a single dealer may have sixty to eighty such lines.

Employment in broker firms is very small, about thirty for an average firm and between 250 and 300 for all the nine firms in the market. The foreign departments of the clearing banks employ much greater numbers (see section (C)), but only a very small proportion of them are engaged in dealing.

The Euro-currencies market is essentially a market in bank deposits in currencies other than that of the centre where dealing takes place. Some 80 per cent of all dealings are believed to be in dollars, and the term 'Euro-dollar' market is widely used to cover all such transactions. The ultimate lenders are non-banking institutions who deposit dollars in banks, and the ultimate borrowers are non-banking customers who raise loans from banks. However, individual banks' deposits and loans are not normally in exact balance and so there is a large volume of borrowing and lending among banks both in and between the main financial centres.

The market has grown up almost entirely in the last ten years, and has been helped at various times by a number of special influences including the restriction of the use of sterling acceptance credits in foreign trade; restrictions on the rate of interest which American banks could pay on dollar deposits in their own country; and the United States balance of payments deficit.

However, the market has shown itself to be much more than the product of special circumstances. The rapid growth of business is shown in the figures for deposits in overseas currencies in Table 8.5 on p. 291. The market has become an extremely useful instrument for financing short-term capital movements without exposing either the borrower or lender to an exchange risk, and without strain on the reserves of the countries through which transactions take place. These advantages are likely to ensure its continued growth. Transactions in Euro-currency balances held in London are all done through the foreign exchange brokers, but London and overseas banks deal directly with one another in balances held in foreign centres.

The principal contacts are between dealers and brokers and between both and the Bank of England. Proximity between dealer and customer does not seem particularly important, as foreign exchange business usually arises out of other banking business. In the case of the clearing banks, business comes in to the foreign exchange department from branches all over the country, and the personal contact of the customer is with his branch manager. The following reasons for concentration in the City were given (not in order of importance) by members of the market whom we interviewed:

The large number of direct telephone lines required.
The Town Clearing.

Contact with the Bank of England.
Quick transmission of documents.
Personal contact with broker and dealer.

Foreign exchange brokers expect that the volume of business will continue to grow, but point out that the average size of bargain is also increasing. They do not, therefore, expect any large changes in employment. Any changes big enough to be significant from the point of view of the City as a whole would result, not from exchange dealing itself, but from the related banking activities that have already been discussed in section (D).

Banks which are authorized to deal in foreign exchange are also authorized to deal in bullion. In fact, however, only five firms attend the daily 'fixing' at the offices of N. M. Rothschild & Sons. Though a large volume of business takes place outside the fixing, most of it goes through one of these firms. The market was closed at the outbreak of war in 1939 and was not reopened until 1954. It is remarkable that it so quickly attracted a major part of world gold-dealing and became, in the words of the Bank of England, 'the largest and most important gold market in the world'.[3]

It is not possible to separate employment in bullion dealing from that in the many other activities of the banks concerned, but the numbers involved must be very small. The significance of the market, in the present context, is that it forms one of the many links which bind members of the banking community to one another and to the Bank of England.

(G) THE STOCK EXCHANGE AND THE NEW ISSUE MARKET

There has been a Stock Exchange on part of the present site since 1802, and the site is now being redeveloped to provide a completely new building by 1972. The members' offices tend to cluster around the Exchange though, as shown in Chapter 1, some firms have recently moved westwards along Cheapside, northwards to London Wall and southward towards the Monument

A distinctive feature of the Exchange is the division of functions between jobbers, dealing as principals, and brokers acting for clients. In the 1969–70 members' list there were nearly 3,000 brokers operating in 194 firms, and about 500 jobbers in 31 firms. There has been a strong tendency in recent years to move to a smaller number of larger partnerships. This is shown in Tables 8.8 and 8.9. Both

[3] Bank of England, *Quarterly Bulletin*, March 1964.

brokers and jobbers have been affected, but the tendency has been most marked in the case of the jobbers. The large firms now employ between 200 and 300 people, though the smaller ones still have only a minimal clerical staff. The Stock Exchange itself has a staff of about 600, and total employment shown in City Corporation sources was just over 15,000.

Table 8.8. London Stock Exchange: Number of Firms and Members at Selected Dates 1939–69

Date (31 March)	Brokers			Jobbers			Non-active members	Total member-ship
	Firms	Part-ners	Associ-ates	Firms	Part-ners	Associ-ates		
1939	434	1,767	704	324	1,123	275	238	4,107
1950	364	1,743	913	187	791	217	228	3,892
1955	329	1,791	823	135	632	177	166	3,589
1960	305	1,886	783	100	545	174	120	3,507
1966	239	1,908	826	49	365	201	100	3,400
1969	195	1,772	1,010	33	295	203	63	3,571

Source: Information supplied by the Stock Exchange.

Table 8.9. London Stock Exchange: Number and Size of Firms 1950–69

Number of partners	1950		1958		1969	
	Broker	Jobber	Broker	Jobber	Broker	Jobber
1	21	21	13	8	—	—
2	74	36	47	29	16	3
3	64	38	53	16	22	4
4	50	26	38	14	12	7
5–9	128	59	121	38	77	8
10–14	23	10	32	10	20	2
15+	7	1	11	5	47	7
Total	367	191	315	120	194	31

Source: Stock Exchange, Members Lists.
Associate members not included.

Outside the Stock Exchange there are twenty-one American firms in London (sixteen of them in the City) who belong to the Association of New York Stock Exchange Members, and eleven Canadian firms belonging to the Association of Canadian Investment Dealers (all in the City). These Associations both work very closely with the Stock Exchange. There are also a few firms which are not members of any association of which the largest is the New York firm, Merrill Lynch.

In the provinces, the Midland and Western Exchange has 224 members (43 firms) in Birmingham, Bristol, Cardiff, Nottingham and Swansea; the Northern Stock Exchange has 354 members (72 firms) in Bradford, Halifax, Huddersfield, Leeds, Liverpool, Manchester, Newcastle, Oldham and Sheffield; and the Scottish Stock Exchange has 195 members (39 firms) in Aberdeen, Dundee, Edinburgh and Glasgow. There are about 190 members of the Provincial Brokers Stock Exchange scattered very widely over medium-sized provincial towns. Provincial firms usually have a close contact with one or more London firms, and a great deal of business originating with the provincial brokers is eventually transacted in London. In 1965 the London and Provincial Exchanges formed the Federation of Stock Exchanges in Great Britain and Ireland, and in 1969 the Federation set up a committee to prepare plans for bringing its members into a single organization. Only the Scottish Stock Exchange gives turnover figures. These have been running at between £30 million and £40 million a month in about 25,000 bargains, only about 1 per cent in value of London's business.

At the end of March 1969 there were 9,356 securities quoted on the London Stock Exchange with a current market value of £132,000 million. By far the biggest volume of business is in British Government securities and in the shares of British commercial and industrial companies. Some other sections (e.g. oils, mines and plantations) provide active (sometimes very active) markets, but many quoted securities are comparatively rarely dealt in. These are handled only by a few jobbers, and an advantage of concentration is to allow this kind of specialization.

Besides the main lines of business there are a number of ancillary activities in which, again, a few firms tend to specialize. These include international arbitrage; option dealing; new issue business; acting as brokers for local authority loans; and 'money-broking', i.e. arranging short-term finance for the jobbers.

A very important influence on Stock Exchange business has been the rapid growth of financial institutions and the relative decline in importance of the personal investor. Official estimates show that individuals were net sellers of stock exchange securities between 1962 to 1968 as follows:

Net Sales in Individual Holdings of Securities (£ million)

	1962	1963	1964	1965	1966	1967	1968
Government securities	32	229	92	90	13	236	251
Company and overseas securities	412	577	666	771	584	735	768

Source: *National Income and Expenditure 1968.*

The evidence of a decline in personal holdings of government securities is supported by the fall in the number of accounts on the registers of the Bank of England. The large sales of company securities are difficult to reconcile with the widespread impression that the number of personal holders is growing. Possibly there has been a decline in the number (and/or size) of very large holdings and a growth in the number of small or medium ones.

During the same period, 1962–8, the annual increase in the assets of life assurance and pension funds, and holdings of unit trust units was:

£ million

	1962	1963	1964	1965	1966	1967	1968
Life assurance and pension funds	941	1,073	1,164	1,187	1,287	1,474	1,603
Unit trusts	34	60	77	59	105	84	258

Financial institutions now hold far more government securities than do individuals. The Bank of England's estimate for March 1968 is:

Holders	£ million
Banks	2,106
Other financial institutions	5,801
Persons (March 1, 1967)	2,678

Personal holdings of ordinary shares are still relatively large. The most authoritative recent estimate is by J. R. S. Revell[4] for the end of 1963. His figures are shown on facing page.

Including executors and trustees, persons held just over half the total amount of ordinary shares, but the institutions were supplying all the new money and also buying substantial amounts from individuals every year.

The rise of the institutions has been the major factor in the move-

[4] J. R. S. Revell, *The Ownership of Ordinary Shares*, Chapman and Hall, 1966, p. 20.

Holder:	£ million
Persons	11,220
Executors and trustees	3,628
Insurance	2,750
Pension funds	1,761
Investment trusts	2,037
Unit trusts	344
Other financial	1,450
Other (including overseas)	4,308
	27,498

ments towards larger and fewer Stock Exchange firms. Bargains have become much bigger; the scale of commissions is such that big bargains are relatively much more profitable than small ones and there is intense competition for institutiona. business. This competition is largely in providing information and advice, and so it has led both to the development of specialized research departments and to a higher general level of expertise both among partners and staff. Finally, the increasing size of orders has led brokers to 'match' buying and selling orders and then 'put them through' the market, and so has contributed to the difficulties of the jobbing system.

Figures of total turnover on the London Stock Exchange are only available since September 1964. Quarterly summaries are given in Table 8.10. Prior to that date the only indication of turnover was the number of 'marks received', but this is of very little value as many bargains were not marked and a 'mark' simply represented a bargain, without any indication of size. The level of activity fluctuates considerably depending, among other things, on the cyclical changes in economic activity, the monetary and financial policy of the Government, changes in taxation, and the operations of the authorities in their management of the National Debt.

Table 8.10 shows, however. an important contrast between the markets in government securities and ordinary shares. Measured by number of bargains, the share of the gilt-edged market has varied over the last five years between 5·8 per cent and 13·6 per cent, but in turnover it ranged from 57·5 per cent to 85·6 per cent. Ordinary shares, on the other hand, have accounted for between 63·3 per cent and 84·3 per cent of bargains, and between 8·4 per cent and 35·0 per cent of turnover.

The gilt-edged market also differs from other sections in that dealing is for cash, not for the account. As already mentioned, the Bank provides 'over the counter' transfer facilities for jobbers and

Table 8.10. Turnover on the London Stock Exchange 1964-69

Quarter	All bargains		Government securities				Ordinary shares			
	Number (thousands)	Value (£ million)	Number (thousands)	Percentage of total	Value £ million	Percentage of total	Number (thousands)	Percentage of total	Value £ million	Percentage of total
1964 4	1,261	5,357	84	6·7	4,197	78·4	1,055	84·3	957	17·9
1965 1	1,261	4,736	102	7·3	3,497	74·8	1,031	81·8	981	20·7
2	1,015	4,158	82	8·0	3,111	74·8	816	80·4	841	20·3
3	953	5,815	96	10·1	4,875	83·8	698	73·3	705	12·1
4	1,131	5,777	91	9·1	4,513	78·1	871	77·0	951	16·4
1966 1	1,271	6,506	95	7·5	4,063	62·5	1,010	79·5	1,098	16·9
2	1,094	4,092	85	7·8	2,714	66·3	869	79·4	1,049	25·6
3	938	4,556	84	9·0	3,496	76·7	709	75·6	779	17·1
4	839	7,437	110	13·1	6,334	85·2	531	63·3	639	8·6
1967 1	1,008	10,213	137	13·6	8,735	85·6	703	69·7	856	8·4
2	1,214	9,497	108	8·9	7,585	79·9	938	77·3	1,309	10·8
3	1,246	7,269	101	8·1	5,121	70·4	986	79·1	1,659	22·8
4	1,537	8,978	105	6·8	6,532	72·8	1,264	82·2	1,980	22·1
1968 1	1,592	8,236	106	6·7	5,868	71·2	1,298	81·5	1,994	24·2
2	1,679	7,261	95	5·7	4,484	61·8	1,401	83·4	2,375	32·7
3	1,728	10,406	102	5·9	6,426	61·8	1,400	81·0	2,496	24·0
4	1,524	7,074	91	6·0	4,257	60·2	1,214	79·7	2,253	31·8
1969 1	1,805	7,595	105	5·8	4,368	57·5	1,435	79·5	2,658	35·0

Source: London Stock Exchange.

(for stocks with under five years to run) for discount houses. When a broker buys from a jobber, the jobber must deliver a blank transfer form on the next business day and the broker pays at once by a cheque on a bank in the Town Clearing. All this is normally done by messenger. The 'shorts' (stocks within five years of maturity) are dealt in actively by the banks and the discount market, while the Government broker is normally a buyer of issues most nearly due for redemption.

In March 1969, an active month in the gilt-edged market, the 'shorts' accounted for only 2·4 per cent of all bargains but for 37·4 per cent of total turnover of quoted securities. The average size of bargain was nearly £75,000 compared with £27,000 for other government securities, and less than £1,800 for ordinary shares. Brokers specializing in this section maintain constant contact with clients, both by telephone and personal visits.

The big operators in medium- and long-dated gilt-edged are largely insurance companies and pension funds. Brokers maintain regular telephone contact with clients – often by direct line. Personal discussions are also regarded as important, but they are less frequent than in the 'shorts'.

As already noted, the institutions have become increasingly important in the equity market in recent years, but private client business is still relatively large. Dealing is for the account, usually a fortnight but sometimes three weeks, and settlement takes place on the eleventh day after the end of each account. Speed does not, therefore, play the same part as in the gilt-edged market, and the main unifying force is the services provided by the Stock Exchange itself, especially the dealing floor and the clearing house. The 'floor', with its traditional arrangement of jobbers' 'pitches' according to the securities in which they specialize, makes for quick and easy dealing, and is equipped with an elaborate telecommunications system. There are several hundred thousand bargains a month; the same shares may change hands several times in the course of an account; a single sale may be split among several buyers or a single purchase built up from a number of sales. The clearing house provides an essential service in sorting out all these transactions. Part of these operations is already being handled by computer, and a new inter-firm accounting system, due to go into operation in the summer of 1970, will provide for computerized checking of bargains, calculation of 'differences' and issue of delivery instructions.

The main linkages which lead Stock Exchange firms to seek proximity to one another and to clients may be summarized as follows:

(a) *Internal*
    (i) The conduct of business on the 'floor' of the House.
    (ii) The clearing and other services provided by the Exchange.
    (iii) The ready exchange of information (the 'knowledge in a hurry' of Chapter 3).

(b) *External*
    (i) Jobbers with the Bank of England.
    (ii) Brokers with banks and discount houses.
    (iii) Jobbers with 'money brokers' and, through them, with banks.
    (iv) Brokers with merchant banks in relation to new issue business and also to funds managed by them.

The Exchange brings together a concentration of expertise, both about particular securities and about general economic and financial conditions. Brokers obtain information from the clients and from their own research departments, and in turn pass information and advice to clients; while jobbers are in constant communication with brokers, besides carrying out their own studies of the factors affecting markets in which they specialize. As a result, the ruling price for a security reflects not only the present state of supply and demand, but also (since buyers and sellers are both concerned with the future) a consensus of expert opinion about its future prospects.

A number of large clients, including some insurance companies and investment trusts and many pension funds, are located outside the City. Here the general pattern of communications is relevant. It is easier for brokers to visit clients from London, or clients to visit brokers in London than elsewhere. Finally, the pattern of dispersion of members' own homes, described in Chapter 3, is a centralizing force.

Looking to the future, it is possible to foresee a number of developments that will affect the Exchange, but owing to the lack of statistics it is impossible to quantify them.

Business, measured in value of turnover, will continue to grow with the increasing amount both of public and private securities in the market. The volume of company securities may well be increased by the effects of the 1967 Companies Act, which reduces the advantages enjoyed by the 'private company' and so may induce some of the larger private companies to become public. The financial institutions will continue to grow rapidly unless checked by drastic state action, e.g. in the field of pensions, and the relative importance of the personal investor will probably go on declining for some time.

These developments might be expected to increase the average size of bargain. In fact, however, the average size has fluctuated considerably but with a slight downward trend.

There are slight signs of increasing competition from the provincial stock exchanges and even closer links are being forged between London and the provinces. A recent example of this is the take-over by a big London firm of four provincial ones.

From time to time investment managers express dissatisfaction with the cost of dealing on the Stock Exchange and talk of direct bargains with one another. Although much talk has cropped up occasionally over a long time, there is no evidence of the development of any such outside market.

The number of small firms is likely to go on falling, while big ones will become bigger. Until recently, the size of partnerships has been restricted by law to twenty; some firms, however, have had associate members, and the removal of the legal limit is already leading to some firms taking more than twenty partners. The increase in the average size of firms is likely to be associated with a further increase both of mechanization and in the range and sophistication of investment analysis and advice which firms provide. A number of the larger firms already own computers, while others use computer services provided by specialist firms. The installation of more and bigger computers will both reduce the amount of routine work done manually and also provide facilities for more elaborate economic and financial studies.

Looking at these tendencies together, it seems unlikely that total employment in stockbroking in the City will change very much; a slight fall is probably more likely than a rise. Within the total, however, there will almost certainly be a fall in the number of clerical workers engaged on contract notes, clients' accounts, valuations and other routine jobs, and a rise in the number of more highly trained people, economists, statisticians, accountants, actuaries, financial analysts, etc.

New issues of securities for the British Government and a few other public authorities are handled by the Bank of England. A large part of a new government issue is normally taken into one or other of the official funds and then resold piecemeal by the Government Broker on the Stock Exchange. These sales are mixed up with a great many other operations so that it is not possible to compile meaningful figures of new issues of government securities.

Other issues are normally handled by one of the firms who are members of the Issuing Houses Association, which includes all the merchant banks who are members of the Accepting Houses Committee. The issuing house usually operates in conjunction with one of the larger firms of stockbrokers. The annual amount of net new issues (i.e. gross issues less redemptions) since 1954 has been as follows:

Year	Total net Issues (£ million)	Of which U.K. quoted companies (£ million)
1954	265	209
1955	275	270
1956	269	222
1957	341	307
1958	295	227
1959	425	386
1960	483	431
1961	629	583
1962	572	439
1963	547	438
1964	669	514
1965	668	437
1966	867	679
1967	805	456
1968	993	619

These figures include quoted securities issued by local authorities and overseas borrowers, but not the very large sums of money raised by local authorities in the temporary loans market. The series shows considerable fluctuations but a strong upward trend. The average value of new issues for 1966–8 was more than three times that of 1954–6.

New issues may be either 'placed' with financial institutions or offered for sale either to existing shareholders or to the general public. Issues offered for sale are normally underwritten by the financial institutions. An issue of this kind involves a great deal of routine work in sending out application forms, receiving subscriptions and dispatching allotment letters and share certificates. The shareholders of a large company may run into hundreds of thousands, and when a new issue is offered to existing holders each one must be sent particulars and an application form.

There is no compelling reason why this routine work should be done in the City, and a number of firms already handle it from registrars' departments which they have established elsewhere in London or in the provinces. However, the fixing of the terms and timing of an issue, and the arranging of underwriting or placing, involve very close contact with the market and delicate negotiations between issuing house, client, brokers and financial institutions. It is thus one of the many close links which the merchant banks have with other City institutions.

We expect that the volume of new issue business will continue to grow in the future and, as suggested in Chapter 6, it could receive further stimulus from closer integration with Europe. However, the number engaged on other than routine work is small, so that even a substantial growth of business would bring only a very modest increase in the total demand either for space or manpower in the City.

(H) OTHER FINANCIAL ACTIVITIES

Besides the main activities described in sections (A) to (G) there are a few large firms and a great many small ones engaged in financial work in the City. City Corporation sources showed 360 firms employing over 9,000 people. Average employment was only about twenty-five per firm, and 211 firms employed ten persons or less. Some of them are ancillary to the activities already discussed, e.g. brokers in the local authority loans market, bill brokers (as distinct from discount houses), and security dealers who are not members of the Stock Exchange.

Investment trusts and unit trusts are shown in City Corporation sources as employing some 900 people, but this is almost certainly an understatement as many people engaged in this work must have been shown as employees of the banks, accountants or stockbrokers who manage trusts. The English investment trusts are highly concentrated in the City, but there is also a very strong group in Scotland. A list of the fifty largest trusts compiled by *The Times* includes nineteen in Scotland and twenty-five in the City.

Unit trusts were usually formed initially either by merchant banks or by accountants, and most of them are still run by their promoters. Unit trusts are very heavily concentrated in the City, though there are a few small ones in other parts of London and in the provinces, and one large group in postal district E.7. Many of them are already associated with merchant banks and stockbrokers, though the clearing banks are also beginning to take an active interest in the movement.

There has been little new activity in investment trusts in recent years, but unit trusts have been growing very rapidly. They have many advantages for the small saver: he can put in money in modest amounts, and get it back quickly and easily when he wants it; and he can enjoy the benefits of a diversified portfolio and expert management. The participation of the banks is likely to bring the trusts to the notice of a larger number of people and stimulate still faster growth.

Hire-purchase finance companies are another group which, according to City Corporation sources, employs about 900 people. Unlike investment trusts and unit trusts, however, hire-purchase finance is not highly concentrated in the City. The largest company in the business has its head office there, as do three smaller members of the Finance Houses Association and a few small firms which are not members. All the other major firms are outside London. Although finance houses have dealings with the banks and the discount market (and the banks have a share-holding in a number of them), their main operations are not closely linked to the City but rather with the stores and garages throughout the country, from which their customers are mainly derived. Building societies and property companies are also to be found in the City, though only in small numbers and without any very strong linkages with other City activities. Pension funds, when not in the form of insurance, are usually managed either by merchant banks or by the head offices of the firms concerned. The pension business of insurance companies and merchant banks will bring an increasing amount of work to the City, but this has been taken into account in discussing the prospects of these institutions in section (D) of this chapter and in Chapter 7.

SUMMARY

The main financial activities of the City all have strong and numerous linkages one with another.

The Bank of England has very close contacts with all other financial institutions, and proximity to the Bank is a major factor in these institutions' choice of location.

The Bank of England is not likely to increase its employment in the City and there may be a slight fall in the number of clerical jobs with the extended use of computers.

The Clearing House also acts as a very strong cohesive force. This is particularly important in relation to the Town Clearing. But the banks find it economical to centralize all their clearing operations, and the proximity of their head offices to one another and to the Clearing House greatly facilitates the exchange of documents.

Employment in branch banking in the City has grown only slowly since 1950 and we do not expect much further increase. Employment in head offices and in overseas departments, however, has been increasing rapidly. We expect this trend to continue and to be reinforced by the increased use of computers.

The clearing banks have taken a carefully considered view of decentralization and we do not expect this to go much further than it has already.

The business of the merchant banks in the fields of corporate finance and investment has been growing very rapidly and we expect this growth to continue.

The foreign exchange and 'Euro-dollar' business of both merchant banks and overseas banks has also been growing very rapidly, and this could be further stimulated by closer integration with Europe and greater freedom of international capital movements.

The discount market and the foreign exchange market both employ so few people that changes in their labour force cannot be significant from the point of view of the City as a whole; but both are, and will remain, very strong cohesive forces in relation to other financial institutions.

We expect that the volume of Stock Exchange business will continue to grow, and that the concentration of brokers and jobbers into a smaller number of larger firms will also continue. This will provide further opportunities for automation and is likely to lead to a reduction in clerical labour, but an increase in the employment of specialized research workers and investment analysts.

In view of the great diversity of influences affecting the future growth of financial activities in the City, we have not found it possible to make worthwhile numerical forecasts. We feel confident, however, that employment will continue to increase at a rate well above the national average; that routine clerical work will become relatively less important; and that the proportion of responsible posts in management and research will increase.

Chapter 9
INSURANCE

INTRODUCTION

In terms of numbers employed, insurance is the second largest activity in the City. According to the data supplied by the City Corporation, there were 49,822 people employed in insurance offices in the City in 1965–6. This excludes the labour force of two very large insurance companies on the borders of the City. It is not known how many people are employed in the insurance industry in the U.K. as a whole. The British Insurance Association (B.I.A.) estimate that its member companies employed 184,000 in 1966.[1] To this figure must be added the pay roll of a large number of insurance brokers and agents, as well as Lloyd's underwriters. Since many of these brokers and agents are part-time workers and based outside London, it may be fair to assume that the majority of specialist firms are located in the City or the West End. Our very tentative estimate is that between 220,000 and 250,000 people were employed in the U.K. insurance industry in 1966.

The distribution of employment in the City between the various insurance activities, already given in Chapter 2, is repeated here.

Life assurance companies	7,959
Non-life insurance companies	5,893
Life and non-life companies	12,327
Lloyd's insurance brokers	18,492
Other insurance brokers	1,890
Underwriters and underwriters' (mainly Lloyd's) agents	1,212
Other insurance	2,049
	49,822

[1] Compared with 169,000 in 1960 and 161,000 in 1956. Since 1966, the total employment has remained around the 185,000 mark.

In this chapter we shall be particularly concerned with three sections of the insurance industry in the City:

(a) the insurance companies,
(b) Lloyd's,
(c) the insurance brokers.

We deal with each in turn.

THE INSURANCE COMPANIES

There are at present about 500 insurance companies operating in the United Kingdom, and it is known that at least 280 offices of these companies are located in the City. Seven of the twenty largest life insurance companies, which account for 36·5 per cent of the premium income of all life insurance companies, have their head offices in the City[2]; the others operate a branch in the City.

Insurance business is essentially of two kinds: life and non-life (or general), but most of the larger companies are involved in both classes of insurance. Life business falls into two main divisions: ordinary life and industrial life. General business is traditionally divided into three main branches: fire, accident and marine.[3] Some insurance companies also specialize in the products of services they underwrite, e.g. motor-car insurance.

The trend in premium income of the main classes of insurance in the last fifteen years is presented in Table 9.1. This shows that insurance is one of the growth industries in the U.K.: indeed the increase in premium income of both the insurance companies and Lloyd's between 1957 and 1966 averaged 8·5 per cent per annum, about a third higher than the corresponding growth of gross national product and only slightly below the rate of growth of world premium income at 10·0 per cent per annum. The total assets of British insurance companies at the end of 1969 were more than £12,000 million. The fastest sectors of growth are currently ordinary life business, which is now one of the chief outlets for personal savings, and motor and aviation insurance.

The second main activity of insurance companies is the investment of premium income. Next to the joint stock banks they are by far the largest financial intermediary in the U.K. economy, and for most of

---

[2] Notable exceptions are the Royal and Lancashire (Liverpool), the Norwich Union (Norwich) and the Pearl (High Holborn). The premises of the Prudential in High Holborn are bisected by the City boundary.
[3] Which now includes aviation.

313

Table 9.1. Total Net Premiums Underwritten by British Insurance Companies 1952–68 (£ thousands)

	General				Life			Total	G.N.P. (£ thousand million)
	Fire	Accident (non-motor)	Motor	(Non-motor)	Marine	Ordinary life	Industrial life		
1952	208,094			266,722	67,539	260,745	122,324	925,468	14·0
1953	210,421			288,448	60,743	279,086	127,073	965,771	15·1
1954	213,758			307,898	59,041	310,582	131,813	1,023,902	15·9
1955	224,287			338,524	61,450	335,681	138,394	1,098,336	17·0
1956	253,098			396,001	65,951	365,428	145,160	1,225,638	18·4
1957	265,126			444,935	74,109	407,253	150,932	1,342,355	19·5
1958	270,399			479,298	73,508	444,260	157,669	1,425,134	20·4
1959	283,825			510,467	76,124	484,913	164,715	1,520,044	21·4
1960	293,488			550,556	80,040	539,790	172,699	1,636,573	22·8
1961	308,633			588,329	85,673	599,249	202,214	1,784,098	24·4
1962	319,985	274,958	345,691		85,285	660,765	219,594	1,901,359	25·6
1963	321,732	288,923	391,034		89,521	763,867	214,675	2,074,721	27·2
1964	339,689	312,658	436,641		96,772	830,072	230,040	2,245,872	29·3
1965	369,125	339,372	463,724		108,059	833,905	240,083	2,359,268	31·3
1966	396,260	368,730	496,403		109,987	905,137	252,570	2,529,087	33·0
1967	425,018	403,954	542,999		124,775	1,016,723	262,923	2,776,392	34·8
1968	495,079	459,107	603,361		155,141	1,112,030	273,811	3,098,529	36·8
Percentage increase 1952–68	137·9				129·7	326·5	123·8	234·8	162·8

Source: British Insurance Association; National Income Blue Book 1966.

the 1960s life assurance or pension funds have attracted between 50 and 60 per cent of gross personal savings in the United Kingdom.[4]

As has been shown in Chapter 3, the insurance companies are large foreign exchange earners. This they accomplish mainly through the operation of their overseas branches and subsidiaries – the assets of which totalled £1,200 million in 1968. London is the largest international insurance market in the world. In 1967, probably one-tenth of the life assurance premiums and nearly two-thirds of general insurance premiums originated abroad. This business is more highly concentrated in the hands of the larger insurance companies than is domestic business. Probably not more than 50 of the 400 British incorporated companies[5] operate overseas on any scale.

LLOYD'S

Lloyd's is a society whose members (known as underwriters) accept insurance on their own account and risk with unlimited liability. At the same time, it is the name of a place where this business is transacted, and which is also the world centre of shipping intelligence. Lloyd's is one of the oldest institutions in the City of London, dating back to the late seventeenth century, when a group of individual merchants gathered together at a coffee house in Tower Street to 'underwrite' or insure the value of ships and cargoes entering or leaving the Port of London. This business – at first very much a sideline of the merchants – grew and prospered, and in 1774 independent premises were secured at the Royal Exchange. Lloyd's became a Corporation under Act of Parliament in 1871, with its affairs governed by a Committee elected from among its members. With expansion it moved in 1928 to a new suite of buildings in Leadenhall Street, and in 1958 additional accommodation was secured in Lime Street, which now houses the famous underwriting 'Room'.

There are two main markets at Lloyd's – the marine and aviation markets – which, in mid-1968, insured about one-half of the business underwritten in the U.K., and the non-marine market. This latter market covers many types of risk, e.g. fire, accident, third-party liability, etc. The main exception is life insurance and financial guarantees. The non-marine market has grown up particularly rapidly in this present century, and now accounts for more than one-

[4] For further details see G. Claytor, *Insurance Company Investment*, Allen and Unwin, 1965.

[5] In addition to these firms, fifty companies operating in the U.K. are incorporated in other Commonwealth countries and the remainder elsewhere abroad.

half of the annual premium income of Lloyd's. The trend in premium incomes of Lloyd's underwriters since 1948 is presented in Table 9.2. A feature worthy of comment here is the rapid growth of aviation and motor business; these two types of business now account for about one-eighth of insurance transacted at Lloyd's. Of the total U.K. general non-marine business underwritten in the U.K., Lloyd's accounts for about one-fifth.

About three-quarters of the premium income of Lloyd's is derived from its foreign clients. Much of this takes the form of reinsurance – Lloyd's is, indeed, the largest reinsurance market in the world.

There are approximately 6,000 underwriting members at Lloyd's. They are formed into groups called syndicates which vary in size from a handful to a hundred or more members; these syndicates are represented at Lloyd's by Underwriting Agents. It is these agents who negotiate with the many hundreds of brokers representing the clients wishing to be insured, and only these brokers or their substitutes have right of entry to the 'Room'. In the same way as Stock Exchange deals in stocks and shares, Lloyd's is an insurance market with the underwriters and insurance brokers corresponding to jobbers and brokers on the Stock Exchange.

Up to 4,000 people may be doing business at Lloyd's at any given moment of time – about 1,250 underwriters and 2,750 brokers or their substitutes. In all, there are nearly 250 firms of Lloyd's brokers. These are the largest single group of employers in the insurance industry; our data reveal that they employed 18,492 people in 1966. The number of underwriting syndicates has remained fairly constant between 1948 and 1966 – around the 290 mark. But the number of underwriting members, who may also engage in brokerage business, has risen by two and a half times. The Corporation of Lloyd's, which is responsible not only for the administration of the insurance market but also for shipping and aviation intelligence, and for the organization of a number of departments contributing to the functions of the insurance market, e.g. policy signing, claims settlement, audit, etc., at present employs 2,000 staff. This means that well over 20,000 people in the City are directly dependent on the existence of Lloyd's in its present form.

In most lines of business, Lloyd's and the insurance companies compete with each other. The exceptions are life business, which is not accepted at Lloyd's, except on a short-term basis, and marine and aviation business where Lloyd's and insurance companies often jointly accept risks. (A good recent example is the insurance of the jumbo-jets which carry a total liability of up to £50 million each.)

316

Table 9.2. Total Net Premiums of Lloyd's Underwriters 1948–66

(£ millions)

	Marine	Aviation	Motor	Other non-marine	Life	Total
1948	61,558,539	6,170,910	3,895,643	54,388,975	7,024	126,021,090
1949	73,777,873	8,261,549	4,626,082	77,508,646	7,538	164,181,688
1950	75,992,619	8,257,601	5,018,110	89,022,662	6,311	178,297,302
1951	88,161,600	7,579,734	5,772,823	94,110,435	5,903	195,630,494
1952	95,175,736	8,441,199	6,399,568	107,694,129	5,693	217,716,325
1953	95,158,974	8,570,331	6,831,043	115,696,840	11,087	226,268,274
1954	92,205,539	9,456,882	7,409,698	122,481,740	24,450	231,578,309
1955	93,354,340	9,970,130	8,165,859	118,695,421	44,915	232,430,866
1956	97,204,656	12,956,394	8,689,481	132,111,967	51,115	251,013,611
1957	105,270,571	13,623,569	9,762,658	147,725,821	69,370	276,449,988
1958	107,992,688	17,327,171	11,750,437	164,315,646	75,139	301,461,099
1959	111,987,709	20,743,031	13,159,587	173,932,809	99,476	319,922,612
1960	115,758,273	25,603,138	14,607,923	186,414,783	117,600	342,501,717
1961	121,473,809	23,139,913	16,790,477	184,504,534	119,638	346,008,266
1962	119,477,861	25,955,352	18,460,284	194,262,055	187,270	358,342,823
1963	122,988,452	24,679,007	20,521,157	200,674,676	251,111	369,114,403
1964	125,255,019	25,317,878	24,401,258	213,998,641	307,832	389,120,626
1965	145,491,667	30,646,047	27,189,794	257,675,851	393,068	461,396,427
1966	162,231,164	34,594,463	30,326,270	298,571,622	563,784	531,287,303

Source: Corporation of Lloyd's.

A number of insurance companies have their marine departments located in the Lloyd's buildings in Leadenhall Street and Lime Street. In this intensively competitive field it is necessary for firms to be located in close proximity to each other to aid easy shopping. More generally, Lloyd's provides not only a venue for the transaction of insurance, but a wide range of expertise necessary to the judicial underwriting of any risk. It is a market where specialists in all types of insurance gather together in one place, and as such represents a focal point in the whole of the insurance world.

THE INSURANCE BROKERS

Insurance brokers commonly obtain cover for their clients from both Lloyd's Underwriters and Insurance Companies. There are basically two types of insurance broker – those who are acceptable to Lloyd's and who are known as Lloyd's brokers and are freely allowed to negotiate their business in the Underwriting Room at Lloyd's, and those who are not permitted to enter the Underwriting Room at Lloyd's but who may have an arrangement through an accredited firm of Lloyd's brokers whereby it is possible for them to obtain for their clients an insurance or reinsurance with Lloyd's underwriters.

There are various sizes and types of brokers who, besides arranging insurance, negotiate claims, bill accounts and prepare policies on behalf of the insurers where practice requires that this be done.

There are approximately 250 Lloyd's brokers who comprise a number of large firms employing around 1,500 staff; probably there are about a dozen of this size. Some twenty firms employ up to 700 staff and perhaps another forty employ in the region of 200. The rest of the Lloyd's broking firms are small. Amongst non-Lloyd's brokers the vast majority are small broking houses whose staffs are not large.

Some brokers specialize in particular types of insurance or reinsurance and others are general insurance brokers. Lloyd's brokers have a vast foreign business which they bring to the United Kingdom; some of this business which by reason of size may not be totally placed in the United Kingdom might then be offered by the brokers to other national insurance markets in the world.

Lloyd's brokers are estimated to earn between £20 and £25 million foreign currency in commissions alone each year.

For obvious reasons, the offices of Lloyd's brokers must be within easy access to the Lloyd's Underwriting Room, although there has in recent years been a tendency to move administrative offices away from London.

318

Insurance brokers must have a constant knowledge of those insurance companies and Lloyd's underwriters most likely to give clients the best deal and this essentially means that they have to be close to the institutional centre of insurance in the City of London.

Data presented earlier reveal that Lloyd's insurance brokers (43) while particularly associated with general insurance and reinsurance business with Lloyd's underwriters and insurance companies also have considerable life business which they transact for their clients and are thus also active with life assurance companies (41). In addition, insurance brokers become closely linked with a variety of commodity markets, surveying, assessing and legal services which form part of the City of London. Non-Lloyd's brokers (44) do not necessarily have to be so close to the City of London because they employ Lloyd's brokers to obtain their Lloyd's insurances or reinsurances. They, therefore, may be found throughout the United Kingdom similarly to insurance agents (46). As shown in Chapter 2 the insurance, shipping and commodities complex is one of the tightest knit groups of activities in the City.

INSURANCE COMPANIES IN THE CITY

While the employment generated by Lloyd's is essentially concerned with its underwriting business, the greater proportion of those employed by the insurance companies in the City are engaged in other activities. Essentially these are of two kinds: first the head or central office activities of national and international concerns; and second, specialist activities undertaken on behalf of the rest of the company.

There are two main functions of an insurance company: (a) the initiation and underwriting of new business and the settlement of claims; and (b) the investment of premium income and pension funds. The locational requirements of these two activities and the departments which service them are not necessarily the same. As far as the former is concerned, only a small amount of home business is initiated by the insurance companies in the City; this is done in branch offices up and down the country, and sometimes in the field itself as typified by 'the man from the Pru'. In a special survey we made of the activities of insurance companies, to be described later in the chapter, we found that 15 per cent of full-time staff of insurance companies located outside the City were engaged in this kind of work in 1966. Rather more international business is handled in the City, but, for the most part, it is the second main function of insurance

319

companies, particularly life assurance companies, that are concentrated in the City.

Most of the larger and many of the medium-sized insurance companies have their investment and trustee departments in the City.[7] These departments are closely linked, via the security and money brokers, with the new issue market, the Stock Exchange and the money market. With the development of modern communication techniques, the necessity for close personal contact may be slightly less than once it was, so far as the *actual transactions* are concerned. In our opinion, the really important centralizing force is the need to be in immediate and speedy touch with news, gossip, contacts, favours and specialist advice about market trends and development. If there was perfect knowledge and no uncertainty in the security market, such clustering of activity would largely disappear as few external economies would exist. The future of this side of the insurance business depends not only on the introduction of new communication techniques (e.g. closed circuit television); but on the degree of risk and uncertainty in the U.K. economy (as reflected in the fluctuations of share prices). A sedate and predictable economy will minimize the need for clusters; a swiftly changing one, with all its uncertainties, will increase it. As Chapter 3 has shown, to avoid the loss of even a day's interest, cheques received at out-of-town insurance offices are sometimes brought up by special messenger and deposited before the banks close.

The investment and trustee departments of insurance offices probably account for about 3,000 of the total numbers employed in the City, and underwriting business another 2,000–3,000. The remainder are mainly engaged in head office activities which are extremely varied but include, *inter alia*, policy-making, general administration, settlement of claims, centralized accounting, actuarial and legal services, market intelligence.

It is some of these latter activities which have been the chief candidates for dispersal from the City in recent years, due chiefly to their intensive use of manpower and space. Mechanization, and particularly the introduction of automatic data processing (A.D.P.), has helped to keep any increase in employment down to the minimum; it has also standardized and regularized some operations and made it less necessary for them to be located in the centre. Increasing rents, and labour shortages (particularly of female labour) have encouraged firms to look outside London for new offices; perhaps

[7] Though some operate these departments jointly with similar departments outside London.

more than any other activity it has been the insurance industry which has most decentralized since the war.

In our investigations, we found that twenty-five of sixty-six insurance companies had decentralized part of their head office activities since the war; and that, at the end of 1966, these employed nearly 6,000 people. By the end of 1968 at least 8,000 were employed in dispersed offices. In 1958, the British Insurance Association (B.I.A.) made a similar inquiry of the extent to which the head office staff of its member companies had been dispersed from the G.L.C. area. Some 114 companies were asked to complete questionnaires; 99 did so. These firms employed 41,300 staff in their head offices, of whom 3,467 represented staff dispersed from the G.L.C. area. Of these 99 companies 74 had not dispersed any of their head office activities, nor did they contemplate doing so. Of the balance, 1,047 males and 2,420 females had been dispersed out of a total of 10,869 males and 10,751 females. A paper outlining the advantages and disadvantages of dispersal as seen by the B.I.A. is appended at the end of this chapter.

In 1964, the Economist Intelligence Unit (E.I.U.) was commissioned by the Location of Offices Bureau (L.O.B.) to undertake a survey of some of the causes and consequences of office dispersal from Central London. Its results included the experiences of a number of insurance companies; again, we give some of these later in the chapter: the report confirms that most of the advantages and disadvantages listed by the B.I.A. applied in practice but forecasts that some of the drawbacks of dispersal had been underestimated. However, the great majority of firms felt, *on balance*, they had been right to move part of their operations from Central London.

On the other hand, in the course of interviews we met some very varied attitudes to dispersal policy. Some companies appear to be decentralizing their activities as quickly as possible; others hold strongly to the view that the advantages of centralization outweigh those of dispersal. In the last ten years or more there have been very substantial changes in the operating conditions of insurance companies in the City. These are not only the outcome of mechanization and rising labour and space costs; the structure of the insurance industry has been changing and several important mergers have taken place.[8] These mergers have enabled better advantage to be

---

[8] Most of the important horizontal mergers in the industry occurred about ten years ago – e.g. Commercial Union/North British and Mercantile (1959), Sun/Alliance (1960) and Royal/London and Lancashire (1969) but in 1968 came one of the biggest mergers of all between the Royal Exchange and the Guardian.

taken of new technological developments. In other cases (and this trend is more noticeable in New York than in the City) insurance firms have pooled certain of their activities, e.g. by setting up common book-keeping and/or computing facilities. This has tended to favour a centralized location.

There is also a new awareness among insurance companies of the need to improve efficiency. A survey of thirty member companies, undertaken by the B.I.A. in 1964, showed that nine had organization and methods (O & M) departments and nineteen had arrangements for reviewing O & M periodically. In 1963 the B.I.A. set up a productivity sub-committee to assist member companies to improve their operating efficiency, and commissioned various studies including one on the ways in which computers might best be applied to insurance operations.

Productivity at Lloyd's has been raised considerably in the last decade as a result of four major developments:

(a) the introduction of modern computer systems, not only in Lloyd's Policy Signing Office, but also in the offices of many underwriting agents and/or the firms of accountants who keep their books;

(b) the simplification of documentation, particularly in relation to small premium business;

(c) the introduction of a Central Accounting System which has removed the necessity for individual accounting as between the many Lloyd's syndicates and Lloyd's brokers; and

(d) the introduction of a number of schemes in the market, e.g. for eliminating detailed work where only comparatively small sums are involved.

While most of these activities are, at present, undertaken in the City, it is hoped that it will be possible to decentralize some in the future. During the war, the policy writing and signing division of Lloyd's was dispersed to Pinewood. We understand that this worked quite successfully.[9]

The new group – the Guardian Royal Exchange Group – had assets of more than £900 million at the end of 1969 and is the third largest composite group in Britain. Other recent mergers, prompted mainly by the need to cut costs, include the Northern and Employers and Commercial Union, and the General Accident and Yorkshire Insurance Company.

[9] Since this chapter was written a working party set up under Lord Cromer has completed a study on the structure and efficiency of Lloyd's. See 'Summary of the Report of the Cromer Working Party to the Committee of Lloyd's', Lloyd's Information Dept, April 1970.

The implications of new office techniques in the insurance industry are not confined to the department in which they are introduced; they affect the functioning of the firm as a whole. It is true that the introduction of automatic data processing and the like is tending to separate the routine office functions from the 'elite' decision-taking activities. On the other hand, top management is becoming more and more mindful of the need for close relationships with the programming of computers and the speedy communication and interpretation of data once processed. It is for this reason that one large insurance company has brought back its computer facilities from outside London to the City. Another factor in this decision is that the space and linkage needs of third generation computers are not quite so demanding as those they replace.

In general, we foresee further centralization of top management activities in the insurance industry. This is because such decision taking needs to maintain three links in the chain of communication:

(a) an easy flow of facts and decisions from itself to lower management both at head office and branch offices;
(b) close contact between the different sectors of activity in different sectors of the same firm; and
(c) an easy interchange of ideas between staff and outside specialists, advisers and contacts.

On all three counts, the interpretation of facts and figures necessary for central policy-making tends to lead to more rather than less centralization. This contrasts with the automation of certain routine activities, e.g. policy signing, despatch of renewal notices, billing and accounting, etc. which are likely to be more and more dispersed in the future.

THE IMPACT OF CHANGES

The impact of the various factors described in this chapter on the future of the insurance industry in the City is essentially twofold. First, we expect further decentralization of routine and repetitive operations in all branches of the industry, but especially of the insurance companies and insurance brokers. We also think it likely that there will be further mergers in this industry, in order to take advantage of new developments in automatic data processing and communication techniques.[10]

[10] It will be recalled from Chapter 1 that the number of Lloyd's insurance brokers operating in the City declined from 209 in 1950 to 174 in 1967.

Second, we envisage that an even closer spatial relationship will emerge between those insurance activities which are likely to remain in the City (i.e. those which are strongly communication oriented and/or involve top decision taking) and the money and capital markets, commodity markets and shipping firms. Apart from Lloyd's itself, however, and a certain amount of international business, we anticipate a further decline in most kinds of underwriting, particularly life assurance, in the City.

Third, we expect that the City's share of employment in the U.K. insurance industry will decline in future years, and that it is quite likely, due to further rationalization, more intensive mechanization, improved productivity and continued dispersal, there will be an absolute fall in insurance employment in the City in the next decade.[11]

To try to quantify some of the impressions gained from our interviews with members of the insurance industry, we circulated, with the co-operation of the B.I.A., a questionnaire to a group of the member companies asking for particulars of their operations in the City and their plans for the future. The results are contained in the following paragraphs.

THE 1966 SURVEY

Questionnaires were sent to all member companies of the British Insurance Association (B.I.A.) in early June 1967. By mid-August we had received replies from sixty-six firms, which, in December 1966, employed 91,484 people – approximately one-half of the estimated total number of employees in B.I.A. companies at September 1966. The distribution of employment by sex was as follows:

	Male	Female	Total
(a) B.I.A. total (to nearest thousand)	116,000	68,000	184,000
(b) Our sample	47,699	43,771	911,484
Percentage of (b) to (a)	41·1	64·4	49·7

Our coverage of life and non-life insurance companies operating in the City (sub-industries 40, 41 and 42) would seem to be a very good one, although it is to be recalled that the City Corporation data cover not total employment but only the maximum working in insurance offices at any one point of time.

---

[11] For an examination of other changes now taking place in the insurance industry see J. H. Dunning, *Insurance and the Economy*, Institute of Economic Affairs, Occasional Paper No. 34, London, 1971.

	Male	Female	Total
(a) Employment in City	16,884	13,426	30,310
(b) Our sample	13,892	11,517	25,423
Percentage of (b) to (a)	82·2	85·8	83·9

Table 9.3 summarizes the total numbers employed in our sample companies in 1958 and 1966. Separate particulars are given for those employed in City offices and the rest of the country. The male and female employment for both years does not sum precisely, as three companies did not give us a breakdown of employment by sex in 1958 and one did not for 1966.

Table 9.3. Employment in 66 Insurance Companies 1958 and 1966

	Year	City	Rest of U.K.	Total
Male employment	1958	14,710	27,404	42,114
	1966	13,892	33,807	47,699
Percentage change 1958–66		−6%	+16%	+9%
Female Employment	1958	12,359	21,689	34,048
	1966	11,517	32,254	43,771
Percentage change 1958–66		−7%	+41%	+23%
Total Employment	1958	27,187	40,284	77,471
	1966	35,423	66,061	91,484
Percentage change 1958–66		−7%	+27%	+15%

Source (Tables 9.3–9.10): Survey undertaken by Economists Advisory Group, 1967.

This table reveals some very interesting facts, but perhaps the most striking is the fall in the numbers employed in the City since 1958, compared with an increase in the rest of the country of 27 per cent. In 1958, 34 per cent of those employed in the sample were employed in City offices: by 1966 this proportion had fallen to 28 per cent. This trend reflects the operation of various forces, notably decentralization, the rapid increase in branch office work of insurance companies, and the impact of mechanization and rationalization.

We also classified the growth in employment according to whether insurance companies were 'City-oriented' or not. We defined City-oriented companies as those which either had more than 250 employees or more than one-half of their total employment in the City in 1966. The results set out in Table 9.4 not only show that the non-City-oriented companies grew faster than City-oriented companies, but that they markedly shifted their activities from the City to the rest of the U.K. The data suggest that the main avenue for growth, in recent years, may well have been that of decentralization. They also indicate that it is not necessary for a company to operate a sizeable City office to ensure national growth (at least not when growth is measured in terms of employment). Indeed, rather to our surprise, the firms which had the smallest stake in the City (relative to their overall size) were the ones which grew the fastest between 1958 and 1966.

Table 9.4. Percentage Changes of Employment by City-oriented and Non-City-oriented Insurance Companies 1958–66

Where oriented	Class of employment	City (per cent)	Rest of U.K. (per cent)	Total (per cent)
City	Male	−5	+12	+6
	Female	−5	+37	+21
	Total	−5	+23	+13
Outside City	Male	−19	+51	+32
	Female	−31	+62	+39
	Total	−25	+54	+35

Some twenty-seven of the sixty-six firms indicated that they had already undertaken some decentralization from the City, and seventeen that they were considering decentralization. None of the firms had moved the whole of its staff: at least a small City office is always retained. In assessing the significance of these figures, it should be remembered that twenty-two are non-City-oriented on our definition. Of the sixteen firms which indicated they have not decentralized and do not intend to decentralize their activities, eleven employed less than eleven people in the City and only one over 500; of the firms that have already decentralized only five employed less than 100 and seven employed over 1,000.

There were forty-two decentralized insurance offices at the end of 1966: these employed 5,993 people or 23·6 per cent of the labour force in the City and 6·6 per cent of that in the U.K. as a whole. Twelve new offices were set up in the period 1951–8; these now employed 3,271 people in 1966. Twenty-eight offices were established between 1959 and 1966 – twenty since the beginning of 1963; these employed 2,691 people at the end of 1966. As one would expect, the *present* average size of offices earlier established is generally higher than those more recently set up. The potential employment of all dispersed offices is probably between 8,500 and 10,000.

A regional distribution of dispersed offices is given in Table 9.5. It shows that two-thirds of employment is in the G.L.C. or Outer Metropolitan Area; this confirms the data given to us by the Location of Offices Bureau (L.O.B.) on which we commented in Chapter 6.

We did not ask firms to give reasons for decentralizing from central London; the question has been adequately covered by the survey of the Economist Intelligence Unit (E.I.U.) for L.O.B. and, earlier in 1958, by some work of the B I.A. We did, however, examine the forms completed by the sample of insurance companies covered by the E.I.U. survey. Lack of space for expansion in the City, high labour costs, difficulty of staff recruitment (particularly female labour), high rents and expected improvements in labour efficiency,

Table 9.5. Regional Distribution of Insurance Offices
Dispersed from London 1966

Region	Number of firms	Number employed
South-East		
Greater London Council	14	916
Outer Metropolitan Area	13	3,780
Other	3	113
South-West	4	659
West Midland	3	101
North-West	3	275
Yorkshire and Humberside	1	140
East Midland	1	9
	42	5,993

were the reasons most commonly cited for dispersal. Our own survey reveals that the departments which are most likely to be decentralized include accounts, statistics, policy preparation, printing and stationery, pensions and premium renewals. These are all more or less routine and self-contained departments; they do not usually deal directly with the public or with other business interests.

Departments such as those just mentioned are also the ones which tend to be the most mechanized. In answer to the question 'Which departments have you most mechanized since 1961', 'accounts' was mentioned thirty times, 'premium renewals' eight, 'statistics and actuarial' six, and 'policy preparation' four. In addition seven firms said that they had applied automatic data processing (A.D.P.) to most departments. This is particularly interesting as it may well mean that dispersal and mechanization go hand in hand and that, at the

327

time of dispersal, the reduction in employment in central London is greater than the addition to the labour force in areas of decentralization.

Some twenty-six of the sixty-six firms (39 per cent in our sample) spent money on computers in the three-year period 1964–6, compared with only twelve (18 per cent) in the period 1961–3. A number of the larger companies own their A.D.P. equipment; the great majority of the medium and smaller companies prefer to rent theirs. Thirty-seven of the sixty-six firms (56 per cent) bought (or rented) mechanical calculating machines in 1964–6 – about the same proportion as in 1961–3. But, since only twenty-two of the twenty-six firms which had computers in 1964–6 also had mechanical systems, it can be inferred that mechanization of both types has increased substantially in recent years.

Table 9.6. Percentage Change of Employment in Insurance Companies by Computer Users and Others 1958–66

	Class of employee	City (per cent)	Rest of U.K. (per cent)	Total (per cent)
Computer	Male	−9	+12	+5
users	Female	−10	+40	+18
	Total	−9	+23	+11
Others	Male	0	+27	+18
	Female	+2	+52	+36
	Total	0	+88	+26

A classification of firms by size reveals that fourteen of the eighteen enterprises (78 per cent) employing more than 1,000 people, and five of the eleven (45 per cent) employing between 501 and 1,000 people used computers in 1964–6. On the other hand, only 19 per cent of the companies with a labour force of 500 or under, and 6 per cent of those with an employment of 100 or less, spent money in this direction.

Though it is extremely difficult to separate the effects of computerization from other factors influencing employment trends, the data in Table 9.6 are very revealing. It shows not only that there is a marked difference in the growth of firms according to their use of computers, but that the decline in employment in City offices is entirely concentrated in this group of firms. It was not possible to relate this data to changes in premium income of insurance companies, which is obviously a more realistic measure of a firm's rate of expansion. But a spot check on the share of the total premium income accounted for by the twenty largest life insurance companies reveals that this was practically stable during the period 1958–63.

The total expenditure on computers by firms in our sample increased from £955,000 in 1961–3 to £4,939,000 in 1964–6: expenditure on accounting machines dropped very slightly from £1,538,000 in 1961–3 to £1,464,000 in 1964–6. Expenditure varied very considerably between firms: one company spent more than £1 million a year on computers in 1964–5, another under £3,000.

We have already expressed our scepticism at making precise forecasts of employment or space requirements in the City. But in our questionnaire we asked firms to give very approximate indications of their likely labour needs in 1970 and 1975. The results are reproduced in Tables 9.3 to 9.10. We would make the following comments:

(a) About one-half of the firms in the sample did not anticipate any increase in their City offices by 1970 or 1975, and one in five thought that their labour force would fall by more than 10 per cent. Only one firm foresaw a substantial increase in its City labour force by 1970, but nine firms expected such an increase by 1975.

(b) Only one firm thought its labour force outside the City would fall by more than 10 per cent by 1970, nine foresaw a rise of 25 per cent or more. A third of firms expected their provincial labour force to increase by more than 25 per cent and two-thirds by more than 10 per cent.

(c) On balance the larger insurance companies expect a slightly higher rate of increase in employment than the average, but our sample is too small to say anything really definite about this. By taking the mid-points of the range it is possible to make very crude estimates of employment in 1970 and 1975. These are presented below:

	City (64 firms)	Per cent change compared with 1966	Rest of U.K. (62 firms)	Per cent change compared with 1966
1966	23,347	−1	60,920	
1970	23,180	−1	63,389	+4
1975	22,876	+1	65,535	+8

These figures suggest there will be a slowing down in the rate of growth of insurance employment throughout the country in the next decade or so, but that the fall in employment in the City which has

Table 9.7. Expected Percentage Change in Employment in Insurance Companies in the City 1970/71

Expected change in employment	SIZE OF LABOUR FORCE									
	Under 100		100–499		500–999		1,000 and over		Total	
	Number of firms	Per-centage	Number of firms	Per-centage	Number of firms	Per-centage	Number of firms	Per-centage	Number of firms	Per-centage
Down more than 10%	5	29	2	18	4	19	3	20	14	22
About the same	9	53	6	55	7	33	7	47	29	45
Up 10%–24%	3	18	3	27	9	43	5	33	20	31
25%–49%	0	0	0	0	1	5	0	0	1	2
50%–99%	0	0	0	0	0	0	0	0	0	0
100% and more	0	0	0	0	0	0	0	0	0	0
Total	17	100	11	100	21	100	15	100	64	100

330

Table 9.8. Expected Percentage Change in Employment in Insurance Companies in the Rest of the Country 1970/71

SIZE OF LABOUR FORCE

Expected change in employment	Under 100		100–499		500–999		1,000 and over		Total	
	Number of firms	Per-centage	Number of firms	Per-centage	Number of firms	Per-centage	Number of firms	Per-centage	Number of firms	Per-centage
Down more than 10%	1	6	0	0	0	0	0	0	1	2
About the same	10	58	3	27	9	43	13	86	35	55
Up 10%–24%	6	36	5	46	8	37	0	0	19	30
25%–49%	0	0	2	18	3	15	1	7	6	9
50%–99%	0	0	1	9	1	5	1	7	3	5
100% and more	0	0	0	0	0	0	0	0	0	0
Total	17	100	11	100	21	100	15	100	64	100

Table 9.9. Expected Percentage Change in Employment in Insurance Companies in the City by 1975

SIZE OF LABOUR FORCE

Expected change in employment	Under 100		100-499		500-999		1,000 and over		Total	
	Number of firms	Per-centage	Number of firms	Per-centage	Number of firms	Per-centage	Number of firms	Per-centage	Number of firms	Per-centage
Down more than 10%	3	18	1	10	4	19	3	21	11	18
About the same	7	41	4	40	5	24	4	29	20	32
Up 10%-24%	6	35	3	30	7	33	6	43	22	36
25%-49%	1	6	2	20	4	19	0	0	7	11
50%-99%	0	0	0	0	1	5	1	7	2	3
100% and more	0	0	0	0	0	0	0	0	0	0
Total	17	100	10	100	21	100	14	100	62	100

Table 9.10. Expected Percentage Change in Employment in Insurance Companies in the Rest of the Country by 1975

SIZE OF LABOUR FORCE

Expected change in employment	Under 100		100–499		500–999		1,000 and over		Total	
	Number of firms	Percentage	Number of firms	Percentage	Number of firms	Percentage	Number of firms	Percentage	Number of firms	Percentage
Down more than 10%	0	0	0	0	0	0	0	0	0	0
About the same	6	35	1	10	5	24	11	79	23	37
Up 10%–24%	10	59	3	30	7	33	1	7	21	34
25%–49%	1	6	4	40	4	19	0	0	9	14
50%–99%	0	0	0	0	4	19	2	14	6	10
100% and more	0	0	2	20	1	5	0	0	3	5
Total	17	100	10	100	21	100	14	100	62	100

occurred in recent years will be halted in the early 1970s and there-after will slightly increase. The implication of this is that the dispersal and mechanization and rationalization plans of insurance companies will keep the numbers employed in the City below their present level, but that their impact will gradually lessen and eventually be out-weighed by the general increase in business as it affects City activities.

The total floor-space occupied by sixty-six insurance firms in the City was 3,060,776 sq. ft in 1966, or 120 sq. ft per person. Sixteen of these firms, using 308,850 sq. ft estimated that they would be needing more space in the City by 1970 and twenty-seven firms with 810,050 sq. ft forecast they would need more by 1975. Thirty-three firms using 1,991,657 sq. ft in 1966 thought their space needs would remain unchanged until 1970, and twenty-seven firms with 1,545,457 that there would be no change by 1975. Seventeen firms with 760,269 sq. ft considered their space requirements would be reduced by 1970, and fifteen firms with 705,259 sq. ft that they would fall by 1975.

CONCLUSIONS

Insurance companies do not, as a whole, anticipate an expansion of their City activities in the period up to 1975; if anything there will be a very slight decrease in both numbers employed and space needs.

Dispersal is likely to continue for the next few years at least, but will probably become less important by the early 1970s. Similarly, expenditure on all forms of mechanization, but particularly automatic date processing equipment, will increase.

Together with expected increases in productivity, arising both from structural improvements within the insurance industry and the adoption of better production methods by particular firms, the industry should be able to cope with a substantial expansion in the quantity of business in the City, without drawing further on the scarce resources of the Square Mile.

Appendix to Chapter 9

BRITISH INSURANCE ASSOCIATION SURVEY ON DISPERSAL OF OFFICE STAFF, 1958

1. *Area considered*

   Dispersal from the Greater London Council area.

2. *Special Aspects*

   (a) There are a few companies who have dispersed virtually all their administrative staff from the above area to the Home Counties. The totals of staffs of such offices are, of course, included under Item 5.

   (b) Mechanization when first introduced before the war gave initial encouragement to the dispersal of relative staff – mainly on grounds of rental economy – and this movement has been further stimulated by the advent of the computer.

3. *Advantages and Disadvantages of Dispersal*

   (a) *Advantages*

   (i) Economy on rents, rates and to a very limited extent, salaries.

   (ii) Administration facilitated by adequate space for employment of up-to-date methods and improvement in the flow of work and for expansion.

   (iii) As there are few commuting problems, time-keeping by staff tends to be better.

   (iv) Staff enjoy the benefits of working in light and airy offices and are able to participate in weekday evening sport during the summer months. (In some cases playing fields are provided adjacent to the dispersed offices.)

   (v) Concentration of employees in the area generally produces local contacts which make staff recruitment of school leavers much easier.

(b) *Disadvantages*

    (i) Difficulty in overcoming the reluctance of senior employees to co-operate in dispersal plans.

    (ii) The acquisition of new housing in already congested areas for dispersed employees.

    (iii) Difficulties involved in change of schools.

    (iv) Although recruiting of junior and unskilled staff locally is easy, the converse applies to specialized staff – for example, actuarial students. Moreover certain types of junior employees consider their ambitions are more likely to be realized by working in the City.

    (v) Time spent in staff travelling to the dispersed offices.

    (vi) Difficulty in general communication with the dispersed offices, but some offices have overcome this in time, for instance, by use of direct G.P.O. lines and operating own transport.

On balance, though, offices regard dispersal as a distinct advantage.

The Insurance Companies

4. *Sickness*

There is no evidence to support a view which has been advanced that absences due to sickness are cut down by virtue of a healthier environment.

5. *Statistics*

The following statistics have been collected from B.I.A. member companies.

(a) Total staff at present employed in Greater London Council area:

Male	23,861
Female	21,196
	45,057

(b) Total staff dispersed (to places listed under (d))

Male	2,505
Female	2,284
	4,789

(c) Anticipated dispersal (to places listed under (d))

Male	677
Female	553
	1,230

(d) Areas to which staff have been dispersed:

Ascot	Guildford	Reigate
Aylesbury	High Wycombe	Rickmansworth
Birmingham	Hitchin	Rochester
Brighton	Horsham	Southampton
Bristol	Kingswood	Stevenage
Cambridge	Leatherhead	Tonbridge
Cheltenham	Liverpool	Tunbridge Wells
Derby	Lytham St Anne's	Watford
Dorking	Manchester	Weston-super-Mare
Exeter	Newcastle	Welwyn
Glasgow	Reading	

Chapter 10

TRADE, COMMERCE AND THE PORT

INTRODUCTION

This chapter deals with the City's trading function – the handling of goods, the transfer of rights and their physical environment.

COMMODITY AND PRODUCE MARKETS

The distinction between the commodity and produce markets discussed in this chapter is in some degree arbitrary. We use the term 'commodity markets' to designate all those markets in food or raw materials which are internationally traded. This incorporates both markets which still handle actual produce and those which are wholly or primarily markets in 'rights'.

The term 'produce market', by contrast, is used to designate the great wholesale markets – Billingsgate, Smithfield and Spitalfields – and the associated retail/wholesale markets such as Leadenhall and the London Fruit Exchange.

In so far as these latter markets have a distinguishing characteristic, it is that they are essentially regional and local wholesale/retail markets, though with some relevance to national and even international trade in the commodities concerned, and that they are, in one way or another, under the control of the local authority.

The future of these markets depends, of course, on the future trends in the volume and character of trade in the relevant commodities. This is a matter of especial difficulty in regard to the wholesale markets. Even at the national level, forecasts of trends in food consumption are hazardous. They require predictions of population, of changes in the tastes and preferences of consumers, and of the growth of Gross Domestic Product. In addition to these general considerations, U.K. food consumption may be affected by a variety of other influences. These include, *inter alia*, government policies (agricultural support policy, regional policies, etc.), and labour market problems

338

which affect consumption patterns, for example by stimulating the demand for convenience foods by employed married women: also the possibility – and precise terms – of the U.K.'s entry into the E.E.C., developments in overseas-supplying countries, and technical innovation by way of the creation of new products and new processing or marketing techniques.

Prediction is made no easier by the fact that our concern is not with general changes in demand, etc. *per se*, but with the consequences of these changes for the throughput and activities of the City wholesale markets. This requires forecasts of local demand factors (such as population growth), and an assessment of the impact of, for example, the qualitative and technological changes upon the future demand for the services now performed by these markets.

Given these difficulties, it is clear that the results of the forecasts must be subject to wide margins of error and are best treated as no more than 'guesstimates' about future trends of the size and character of the throughput of the markets. In view of this, and of the place of the produce markets in the totality of City activities, it would not have been reasonable to attempt an original forecasting study. The relevant section (which follows our discussion of commodity markets) consequently brings together a variety of existing information, and derives some very general conclusions from it

COMMODITY MARKETS

Nature and Location of the Activity

The economic activities grouped under the general title of commodity markets and merchanting, comprise industrial sub-groups 75, 76, and 79–86 of the classification of City Employment Statistics. In 1966, the group provided employment for 7,891 people, of which the organized produce exchanges and terminal markets, with which this chapter will essentially be concerned, accounted for perhaps 3,500. The remainder of employment in this group is accounted for by the timber trade (85), a miscellaneous group (85), and a variety of merchanting activities, probably mostly concerned with domestic (U.K.) markets that lie outside the organized commodity markets.

The activities of the commodity markets themselves are diverse. They comprehend transactions in goods and services ranging from the organizing of international trade in cashew nuts to air chartering, and an even more varied traffic in 'rights'. Thus, we are concerned with transactions in goods: with trade in goods on the basis of samples with the actual commodities being handled elsewhere

339

(increasingly, outside the City); with transactions in contracts in 'unseen' commodities sold by description, in relation to which City firms enter as brokers and may or may not establish temporary rights in the commodity; and with transactions in prices. These last are futures contracts entered into in order to assume, or to hedge against, risks of changes in commodity prices, it being intended that the contract should normally be completed by the payment of a cash 'difference' when the price of the commodity changes, rather than by actual delivery of the produce.

Typically, these activities centre upon an organized Market, often controlled by an Association of interested brokers, traders and others. The organization and administrative control of these associations has become an increasingly specialized and technical activity: there are now individuals who act as secretary to more than one association and who may themselves be active in bringing market associations into being in new commodities as the need for them is recognized.

The location of the markets in particular commodities is the outcome of long-term historical and geographical influences, of the cost of land, and of a complex process of adaptation to change. Plantation House illustrates this complexity. The present site is still in the Mincing Lane area in which colonial (mostly tropical) produce was landed. The building was originally leased by the London Rubber Exchange, but was taken over in 1954 by a new company, The London Commodity Exchange, to fulfil the trading functions of the London Commercial Salesrooms, destroyed during the Second World War. The seven floors of Plantation House occupy the major portion of the rectangle bounded by Mincing Lane, Fenchurch Street, Road Lane, and Great Tower Street. They contain a number of Exchanges and a tea auction room, but most of the space is occupied by the offices of the association's brokers, dealers and merchants in the produce traded. This comprehends almost all the tropical 'groceries' – tea, coffee, cocoa, sugar, spices, drugs, dyes, rubbers, essential oils, vegetable oils and oil seeds, shellac, jute, copra, gums, waxes, and a heterogeneous group lumped together as 'general produce'.

Nearby in St Mary Axe and Mark Lane are the markets historically associated with international traffic in cereals. These are the Baltic Exchange, historically concerned with 'Baltic' commodities, but now given over much more to transactions in shipping space and ships, and more recently to air chartering and trade in aircraft, and the Corn Exchange. There is still a close link between the Baltic's freight market activities and the international grain trade (in

340

'marrying up' cargoes, etc.), although a considerable proportion of grain transactions no longer takes place on the floor. Trading in metals is centred at the London Metal Exchange in Whittington Avenue, south of Leadenhall Market. Transactions in furs, which are dominated by the Hudson's Bay Company, are located around Beaver House, Garlick Hill, in Upper Thames Street. Diamonds are traded around Hatton Garden, and the London Fruit Exchange is located adjacent to Spitalfields Market. This Exchange should perhaps be treated as a wholesale market, but it requires mention here since the same premises house the London Wool Auctions although wool future trading is centred at Plantation House.

The importance of the City in the actual handling of products derives from the heyday of Britain's colonial empire. However, changing world trading relationships, the development of markets in producing countries; technological change (particularly in the handling and processing of commodities and in the creation of synthetics), have all combined to reduce the importance of this type of trade, and this trend we would expect to continue. Some direct physical trade persists; for example, furs are still stored above the Fur Exchange at Beaver House, and a number of commodities, such as tea, wool, furs and a miscellany of other products are still auctioned, normally by sample.

There is a flourishing *tea* auction handling around three million 108 lb. packages annually; the value and volume of trade was somewhat larger in 1968 than in 1952. This is a considerable business, but one that is perhaps unlikely to grow very much, in the light of trends in domestic tea consumption. There is some re-export and 'third country' trade, but discriminatory measures are being adopted in countries of origin to protect and encourage domestic markets and the proportion of all tea produced which is sold in countries of origin has been growing.

Wool is auctioned by sample at the Fruit Exchange near Spitalfields; it is stored in part in Port of London Authority and other City warehouses. As can be seen from Table 10.1 the annual volume of trade has considerably declined in recent years. This has been due to the combined influences of overseas auctions, notably in Sydney; declining U.K. trade; and the growing importance of synthetics. The auction remains important, however, as a 'marginal' supplier of immediate requirements for European centres.

Auctions in some other commodities persist. But the general picture is one of steady decline; a decline exemplified by the failure to

341

re-establish a coffee auction, despite serious efforts to do so after the Second World War.

The change is also illustrated by the continued importance of c.i.f. trading (transactions in goods for shipment on 'cost, insurance and freight' terms). These products traded through London are increasingly being handled directly across the quays rather than through P.L.A. warehouses.

The changed character of commodity market activity is also illustrated by the use of space in Plantation House where the top floor auction room replaces the many auction rooms of the destroyed London Commercial Salesrooms, as well as the similar facilities commonly provided in the old brokers' offices. Another illustration is provided by the changes, already mentioned, in the character of the Baltic Exchange.

The different market associations vary in the categories of trader they will admit to membership. They give little direct employment, providing rather the environment within which other employers (brokers and others) operate. They also vary in the extent to which they provide – rather than allow members to provide – accommodation and communications facilities. These, however, tend to be ample and sophisticated. The sugar terminal market, for example, has closed-circuit television. At least one firm has plans to equip floor members with 'bleepers'.

Some trade is still carried on 'spot' (sale of goods in warehouses by grade or sample), and auctions have already been mentioned. The bulk of brokers' activity, however, is now concerned with 'c.i.f.' trade in the commodity, or with trading in terminal (futures) markets.

Very briefly, the broker interested in c.i.f. trading contacts sellers, and uses the market floor as well as more direct means to 'match-up' demand and supply. This activity involves bids and counter-bids within a short time-restriction, rapid communications all over the world, and easy contact with other City brokers and traders. While by no means all transactions are made by personal contact on the floor, brokers themselves clearly regard such contact as important to their efficiency.

The terminal markets are governed by elaborate rules designed to ensure the efficiency of the futures contracts as a hedge and to ensure their efficient fulfilment. They are linked with similar markets elsewhere, and are affected by – and so need to be in constant awareness of – the whole of the world trade in the relevant commodity. Recent developments in metals provide an illustration of this international character. The London Metal Exchange is actively establishing continental delivery points under its contracts; these are at present at Rotterdam, Hamburg and Antwerp. Additional cocoa contract delivery points have recently been established at Hull, Avonmouth, Amsterdam and Hamburg.

The importance of very close proximity to other market traders and ancillary facilities is outstandingly evident in futures trading. The rules require changes ('differences') in settlement of transactions to be handed over daily. Warrants recording transactions are often distributed by the Exchange and are used as security: they are effectively bearer bonds. Delay in communications, for example, overnight, would put brokers' books out and would greatly reduce the price-making efficiency of the market.

A practical example of the value of proximity was recently provided by the new member admitted to the L.M.E. although the firm had only a West End Office. The firm of its own accord very shortly found premises within easy walking distance of the Exchange.

A different illustration of the nature of the City 'tie' is provided by the fur auctions. The trade is international, the main consumers being American, German and Italian. South-East African persians have customarily been sent back to South Africa for processing after auction. The City contribution is a set of finance and credit arrangements of some sophistication and complexity, which traders still find it worth their while to use.

To complete this section, some reference must be made to the London Produce Clearing House (L.P.C.H.) This is a specialized organization located in Plantation House which registers, clears and guarantees commodity market contracts. It has been in existence since 1888 and at one time or another has dealt with most of the commodities under discussion. It has forty employees, and would employ more – possibly over 100 – but for the introduction of a computer in 1967; since then the volume of contracts dealt with has increased sevenfold. The computer has now been hived off to a subsidiary company, Assets Computer Services Ltd, with over 100 employees, some of whom work on L.P.C.H. business; the rest providing specialized services to brokers and others.

This development is interesting from the viewpoints of employment trends, specialization, and the evolving linkages between City institutions. The latter are also illustrated by the locational constraints upon L.P.C.H. itself. It is actively concerned in the initiation and administration of new markets, is responsible for call prices in the case of some commodities, and in any case must send represen-

343

tatives to all relevant markets since its calling of margins – e.g. the payment of differences – relates to the official quoted prices. The L.P.C.H. also keeps seven messengers occupied delivering forms of registration (some of which are the equivalent of contracts) to many of the 250 L.P.C.H. members who operate in the City. It will be apparent that these activities together determine the physical location of L.P.C.H. very closely. In November 1969 a branch office in Sydney, Australia commenced clearing and guaranteeing futures contracts for the Sydney Greasy Wool Futures Exchange Ltd.

Trends in Terminal Market Activity

It seems clear that the commodity market activities likely to be of continuing importance to the City are those concerned with rights (contracts) rather than with the handling of physical products. These 'rights' activities in turn may relate to commerce in actual commodities or to transactions in their prices (futures trading). It is not uncommon for the same firms to undertake both types of transaction, though the very nature of the markets makes for some specialization: for example, a specialist merchant might have reservations about using the services of a broker who was himself a merchant. But the relation between merchanting transactions on international markets, and hedging and speculative transactions concerned with future prices, is clearly an intimate one. Some assessment of the characteristics and future prospects of firms engaged in merchanting and/or brokerage is attempted in the next section. Here, as a necessary preliminary, we consider the recent history and possible future of trading in particular commodities.

Table 10.1 gives terminal market turnover statistics for particular

Table 10.1. Annual Turnover in Some Major Terminal Commodity
Markets

LONDON PRODUCE CLEARING HOUSE REGISTERED CONTRACTS
(*a*) *Before the Second World War*

	Sugar (tons)	Cocoa (tons)	Pepper (tons)	Shellac (cases)
1930	2,074,100	20,370	—	—
1933	2,605,300	21,950	—	—
1935	1,770,600	102,470	—	—
1937	3,930,000	352,250	145	—
1939	1,221,300	80,280	80	23,250
(8 months)				

Table 10.1.—contd.

(b) Since the Second World War

	(1)			(2)
	Sugar (tons) (Contract unit 50 tons)	Cocoa (tons) (Contract unit 5 tons)	Coffee (tons) (Contract unit 5 tons)	Wool (lb.) (Contract unit 5,000 lb.)
1952	—	121,850	—	—
1954	—	284,795	—	95,045,000
1956	—	211,920		108,755,000
1957	—	222,290	—	184,780,000
			(from 2/7/58)	
1958	—	365,110	13,935	202,885,000
	(from 2/10/59)			
1959	166,400	292,850	127,165	281,850,000
1960	1,119,150	257,890	115,180	269,540,000
1961	2,256,000	420,410	39,985	265,780,000
1962	3,967,000	459,395	26,650	149,090,000
1963	15,121,000	901 550	79,195	238,235,000
1964	13,092,900	712,210	315,555	233,550,000
1965	10,132,700	1,243,680	448,465	162,970,000
1966	8,602,300	1,946,155	324,180	121,700,000
1967	22,874,550	2,084,660	191,845	141,085,000
1968	19,777,850	3,539,465	187,835	94,625,000
1969	28,732,950	4,844,900	233,645	41,895,000

Notes:
1. Sugar No. 2 Contract. Business in the No. 1 Contract, which ran from January 3, 1957 to August 31, 1960, amounts to 1,905,400 tons. Of the total business transacted in sugar, 1,071,550 tons were in options.
2. The Crossbred Wool Tops Contract, which was current from November 2, 1956 to January 23, 1961, turned over 16,475,000 lb. of business. The Greasy Wool Contract, current from April 30, 1962 to December 31, 1964, registered a turnover of 7,686,000 lb. There were also two post-war Shellac contracts, namely the Shellac T.N. Contract, current from June 25, 1956 to December 31, 1959. Business in this amounted to 71,650 bags. The Standard 1 Contract ran from February 3, 1959 to December 31, 1965 but the total turnover amounted to only 8,400 bags. The Contract unit was 50 bags, calculated on the basis of 72 cwt. 2 lb.
3. Turnover in some recently-introduced contracts has been:
Soyabean (commenced July, 1967) – 1967; 101,600 tons; 1968: 109,320 tons; 1969: 68,340 tons.
Sun-oil (May 1968) – 1968: 78,700 tons; 1969: 36,540 tons.
Coconut (July, 1969) – 1969: 29,600 tons.
Cotton (May 1969) – 1969: 5,548,800 lb.

commodities for a number of years. In the nature of things, it is less easy to provide useful data about 'merchanting' transactions, which may, and often do, involve the intervention of a City firm in the movement of goods between other countries. Given the links already referred to, however, the terminal market data are not without interest – bearing in mind that the volume of transactions reflects uncertainties about future trading conditions as well as changes in the actual magnitude of world trade.

The Plantation House commodities provide a useful illustration of the diversity of conditions with which commodity market traders have to deal. Trading in sugar, coffee and cocoa futures is active and would appear to have been growing, although the volume of transactions in particular markets is related to the special risk-conditions affecting the commodity concerned. International agreements – such as those in sugar and coffee – can be important influences, as of course can international disturbances. For instance, the Cuban crisis was reflected in the volume and value of transactions on the sugar terminal market. Changes in the scale of production may also be of importance, though in the case of chocolate and cocoa products even the larger manufacturers continue to depend upon the London actuals market for a significant proportion of their requirements.

Wool provides a contrast. The market was set up in 1953 following violent price fluctuations related to the Korean War. Turnover was soon greater than that of Antwerp (established 1884) or New York. Recent experience, however, has been less favourable. The absolute volume of transactions has declined dramatically – more severely than in the other terminal market centres. In fact, futures trading in wool has declined in all centres taken together, perhaps because of the influence of synthetic substitutes upon the behaviour of international wool prices. The London Market, however, is constantly used by Bradford traders and manufacturers, and it seems likely that the decline is not unrelated to conditions in the domestic industry.

The Rubber Trade Association of London was formed in 1913, and the terminal market as now functioning is one of the oldest in London, having been instituted in 1923. Rubber is another commodity in which changes in world trading conditions have influenced the operations of the London terminal market. It is affected by the development of synthetics, by the establishment of terminal markets in producer countries, and by the fact that it is now possible to trade in physical rubber up to two or three years forward. The London turnover for 1966 was 134,000 tons; comparable figures for other years are not available. But while transactions in rubber occupy a diminishing proportion of the London Commodity Exchange floor – sharing with the new soya-oil and sun-oil markets as well as with coffee – the market is likely to be of some continuing importance, not least because of the demand for its arbitration facilities and the continuing domestic demand for rubber.

The soya-oil and fishmeal markets demonstrate the adaptability of the structure to changes in world trading conditions (a characteristic which is discussed further in the next section). Both were created in 1967 to meet an emergent need It is an interesting illustration of the nature of City specialization that for technical (shipping) reasons the London soya-oil terminal contract specifies Amsterdam delivery.

Shellac provides an interesting example of a terminal market destroyed by government. After being 'called over' without business for some time the market has now ceased to exist. But the underlying conditions for a terminal market remain and it could be revived by a change in Indian Government policy or new sources of supply.

Transactions on the London Metal Exchange (copper, tin, lead, zinc and silver) are unusual in that the same contract is used both for actual and for futures trading, and because it is much more common to use the contracts to obtain physical supplies than is the case elsewhere; around 20 per cent of all contracts are completed by delivery.

This high proportion of deliveries must of course make the terminal markets less satisfactory as a medium for futures (hedging) transactions. The reasons are complex, and in no way the responsibility of the London Metal Exchange, which clearly makes the markets in metals nearer perfect than they would otherwise be. An illustration of the problem is provided by copper. This metal, which has been in tight supply over the past few years, is priced on the London Metal Exchange. But the *large* producers will not allow their copper to be delivered or re-delivered into L.M.E. warehouses. In time of acute shortage, some copper users turn to L.M.E. as a delivery market. But suppliers who might be willing to deliver small surpluses to L.M.E. warehouses are precluded from doing so by the terms of their bulk supply contracts. This imperfect market in marginal supplies clearly encourages price instability.

Such uncertainties reinforce rather than diminish the importance of the exchange. Indeed, it is the *world* centre, e.g., for transactions in copper. Seventy per cent of the turnover of the Exchange originates overseas, and since there is little arbitrage in metals, delivery arrangements on the London contracts already include a large and increasing number of international centres.

As illustrated in Table 10.2, turnover in the metals traded has been growing impressively; the volatility of the markets, however, makes interpretation difficult for relatively short periods. A market in

347

silver has recently been added, and possibly others in nickel, aluminium and mercury will follow.

The Corn Exchange Company in Mark Lane was established in 1751, and has some 500 merchant and broker members dealing in all varieties of grain and animal feeds. Cargoes of wheat, barley, feeding stuffs, etc. may be sold in small lots, and may change hands several times within a short period. Since transactions are not necessarily made by recorded contracts, the Corn Exchange has no records of the relevant tonnages. But the market in grains serves to illustrate the

Table 10.2. Annual Turnover in Some Major Terminal Commodity Markets

LONDON METAL EXCHANGE

	Copper (tons)	Tin (tons)	Lead (tons)	Zinc (tons)	Silver (lbs)
1950		48,380			
1951		40,470			
1952		30,375			
1953		27,120	235,300	217,050	
1954	253,400	29,550	159,100	194,825	
1955	346,500	39,760	163,025	212,825	
1956	395,175	47,910	209,825	222,300	
1957	467,250	60,595	201,375	301,075	
1958	634,625	64,850	274,575	336,100	
1959	772,250	42,965	398,275	334,750	
1960	767,025	40,990	388,875	299,800	
1961	796,275	98,170	428,950	373,725	
1962	509,750	80,840	350,900	346,175	
1963	187,350	75,325	447,025	396,350	
1964	725,600	82,465	569,750	518,675	
1965	886,950	95,690	579,025	352,725	
1966	1,282,975	87,695	438,775	303,475	
1967	1,805,525	86,415	454,500	222,725	
1968	2,099,450	122,675	555,775	271,975	214,190,000
1969	2,298,800	120,585	688,850	385,450	379,830,000

process of change and the flexibility of market institutions in another way. Thus, after the return of the trade in the commodities to private hands in 1953, future markets were reintroduced in imported barley and maize, under the aegis of the London Grain Futures Association Ltd at the Baltic Exchange. A similar market in wheat would have been pointless in the face of international price-fixing arrangements, but a 'home-grown' contract was developed. Since then, the market in maize has disappeared, the imported barley contract has been replaced by a home-grown contract (under the influence of the government-encouraged growth in domestic production), and the home-grown wheat market continues to be active. These markets make minimal demands on space – only a few square yards in a corner of the Baltic Exchange floor.

In sum, apart from the decline in all physical trade in commodities, which is already well advanced, it seems likely that there will also be a decline in all types of transactions in some of the 'traditional' commodities handled in the City, for the kind of technical reasons we have iterated. On the other hand, there is evidence of new developments that make use of similar skills in relation to new commodities. The importance of these developments for the future of employment and space-use in the City will be assessed below.

Table 10.3. Annual Turnover in Some Major Terminal Commodity Markets

LONDON GRAIN FUTURES ASSOCIATION

	Imported barley (tons)	Home-grown barley (tons)	Home-grown wheat (tons)
1961–2	990,875		
1962–3	760,250		
1963–4	529,000		
1964–5	80,875		
1965–6	1,500	381,375	38,125
1966–7		321,625	66,500
1967–8		288,500	128,625
1968–9		504,625	205,875

Merchants and Brokers' Activities and Trends

Commodity market merchants and brokers employ perhaps 3,000 people in the City. The size of firms ranges from less than ten to, say, 170. The activities of the individual firms are diverse. Nevertheless, it may be useful to describe a typical, but hypothetical, large firm, to illustrate the nature of the trade and its dependence upon a City location.

The firm might deal in a number of products, but with metals broadly separated from other commodities in terms of specialization. Its geographical specialization will often have been historically determined by the earlier pattern of trade in commodities. Transactions in the relevant commodities will normally embrace buying and selling between countries outside Britain. The firm will probably be a ring member of a number of terminal markets, and might or might

349

not use this facility for purposes other than the hedging of its own 'actuals' transactions. Its staff will be fairly highly-skilled, making a restricted demand upon space, and requiring a considerable amount

Table 10.4. Activities of Commodity Brokers as Shown by Membership of Terminal Market Associations at Plantation House 1967

Number of firms who are floor members in:	Membership totals	Number of floor members in individual markets	
1 Market = 54	54	Rubber Trade Association of London	14
2 Markets = 16	32	London Wool Terminal Market Association	14
3 Markets = 16	48	London Cocoa Terminal Market Association	46
4 Markets = 5	20	London Coffee Terminal Market Association	35
5 Markets = 2	10	United Terminal Sugar Market Association	18
6 Markets = 1	6	London Fishmeal Terminal Market Association	15
7 Markets = 1	7	London Soyabean Oil Terminal Market Association	33
		Add 2 London Metal Exchange ring-members included in 'membership totals'	2
Totals 95	177		177

Notes:
1. Apart from the two firms included, no other ring-members of the London Metal Exchange are floor-members in other futures markets, i.e. of the 30 ring members of the L.M.E., 28 are specialist metal dealers and merchants. The use of the L.M.E. both as a delivery market for physical metal, and for trading in rights, has tended to exclude the international commission houses from this Exchange. The other futures markets excluded from the above list are those in home-grown barley and wheat, on the Baltic Exchange. These were still comparatively small in 1967, and so had not attracted the large broking firms.
2. The table takes no account of membership of overseas exchanges.
3. Many firms included above are subsidiaries of other commodity broking, banking, and other firms.
4. The activities of many of the larger broking firms range not only across the markets, but in some cases also embrace agency functions in the physical products. Some ring-traders, moreover, are also merchants, while others are manufacturers.

of capitalization (perhaps £2,000 per head in 1970), primarily in telex, telephone, television and other communications equipment.

Two characteristics are of major importance for the future. First, firms are skill- rather than product-oriented, and the ability to move between markets is very important. What, for example, would have happened otherwise to a 'specialist' firm in shellac? The extent of this specialization of skills – implying diversification between markets – is illustrated by Table 10.4. The second characteristic is brought out by Table 10.5. This shows the trend in membership of the London

Table 10.5. Membership of the London Commodity Exchange
1961–9

	1961	1964	1966	1969
Sponsor members	237	192	178	160
Trading members	372	319	286	258
Nominees	366	304	300	300

Note:
Sponsor members are firms which are shareholders in the Exchange Company, which runs the Exchange through a Board of Directors assisted by a Floor Committee. Sponsor members have the right of representation in the Exchange. These representatives are members of the Sponsoring firms, and are known as Trading members. They, in turn, may appoint Nominees who also enjoy trading rights. The only other persons allowed on the Exchange floor are clerks who are registered by name, but not authorized to trade.

Commodity Exchange – the Company administering Plantation House and concerned with the commodities traded there. The decline there shown illustrates not simply the reduced importance of trade in particular commodities, but also a tendency towards a reduction in the number of smaller and more specialist firms through amalgamation, and a general growth in the size of firms. These tendencies have not been so evident on the London Metal Exchange, where turnover generally has been buoyant; and where a number of large overseas companies are showing an interest in dealing membership through U.K. subsidiaries.

The trend towards larger units lies partly in the changing importance of different types of commodity market activity already referred to; partly in the growing complexity of communications and their implications for specialization and capitalization; and partly in the need for size to create and maintain the international links and other facilities necessary to cope with a shifting pattern of world trade, of which Britain is no longer the natural geographical 'focus'.

Conclusions

The use of City space for the storage and trading of physical commodities has already declined greatly, and there are good reasons to expect this decline to continue. Trading in rights is another matter. However world technology may develop, production must continue to depend upon raw materials, and international transactions in these commodities must be expected to continue and grow. But why should not these transactions be administered and financed by those already directly involved in them? And if there is a role for British intermediaries, why need these intermediaries be located in the City?

It is possible to envisage a situation in which poorer raw material producing countries, as they grow richer, try to develop their own brokerage facilities and terminal markets. It is hard to believe, however, they will seriously displace activities at present carried on in the City, at any rate within the next generation. Attempts to create such facilities in developing countries have not been particularly successful; and even countries like Australia and Japan, which can hardly be called underdeveloped, still find it mutually convenient to use a London broker as an intermediary for their trade in sugar.

A more serious problem might be that of deliberate attempts to substitute barter-type transactions for free markets, resulting in a particular pattern of development of world political relationships. The past history of such attempts suggests, however, that this possibility, while relevant, should not be exaggerated. Even Communist countries have shown interest in the role of futures markets in the case of some commodities of interest to them.

Finally, commodity market activities involve a high proportion of very skilled labour and are highly capitalized, and they are typically concerned with trade on a world-wide scale. These skills and services will be needed as long as traders in international markets are faced with unpredictable fluctuations in the supply of, or demand for, the products they buy and sell, but they do not require a location directly related to transactions in the actual commodity. We have argued that the essential skills developed by brokers are transferable between commodities, though there is some tendency to specialization by geographical regions. Thus the trade in particular commodities must be expected to decline with the development of synthetics or for other reasons. But it would be rash to conclude that brokerage activities as a whole will similarly decline.

This last point also bears upon the importance of a City location for the activities in question. The linkages upon which the City commodity markets and brokerage firms depend are complex, requiring, on the one hand, rapid communication with all parts of the world, and, on the other, access by brokers to a commodity (rights) market that is typically within walking distance. Around this concentration, within easy, that is walking, access, must be clustered legal, banking, and other ancillary facilities, such as the branch offices of overseas shipping enterprises. Essentially, the important advantages of specialization would be lost by an attempt to locate some of these activities elsewhere. An attempt to move all the closely-linked ones would come close to an attempt to move the whole of the City.

At the same time, the type of brokerage and terminal market activity that seems most likely to develop in the future is one characterized by a smaller number of firms of larger average size, high capitalization, skilled – but not numerically important – workers, and a relatively low demand for floor-space per worker. Thus, the demands for City space for the commodity markets and their related activities are more likely to decline than to increase, and will in any case not be considerable. But the continuing activities are quintessentially City activities.

THE PRODUCE MARKETS

Introduction

The activities to be dealt with in this section comprise 'wholesale distribution—other food' (32) and 'wholesale distribution – groceries, provisions, confectionery, drinks' (31). Between them they employed over 4,500 persons in 1966. To supplement the dearth of published data, we made a survey of the produce markets. This incorporated a set of three very detailed questionnaires sent to each of the three great wholesale markets. Thus, some data in the text refers to 1966 rather than later years: but the brief summary of the detailed questionnaire conclusions has of course been verified so far as possible against more recent information.

M

The future activities of the produce markets will clearly depend upon the development of food consumption generally, and upon any associated changes in the pattern of distribution that affect particular markets. It has already been pointed out that predictions of this type over the kind of period in which we are interested are inevitably hazardous and subject to large margins of error. We are at the mercy both of unpredictable changes in consumer tastes and of changes in technology and discovery. We have made a number of forecasts on the basis of different assumptions, both for food consumption generally and for produce handled in the particular markets. The tentative conclusions from the general forecast are presented in an introductory section. This provides an indication of the general developments that we would expect to affect all the relevant city markets. Thereafter, more specific problems will be discussed in sections dealing separately with the major wholesale markets.

These later sections will also comment upon the traffic implications of the markets, which might be considered relevant to the question of the social costs of City activities. It should be emphasized that no conclusions have been drawn concerning the possible future relocation of the markets. This is not a matter that falls within the scope of our study, nor would our information support firm conclusions. In the absence of any system of market pricing for roads, evidence of congestion caused by particular activities provides incomplete information as to their optimal location. Admittedly, the existence of the markets in the City may impose social costs on others by slowing the progress of non-market vehicles. But the obverse is also true: the market vehicles are also victims of congestion. This must be a disincentive to traders: if they continue to use the markets it must be an open question whether relocation would confer a net gain or loss on the community. (We might also draw attention to the fact that – on the experience of Les Halles – a redevelopment of this kind might take a decade to achieve, and the indications are that the volume of market traffic is in any case unlikely to grow in the foreseeable future.)

The Demand for Market Produce

Time-series analysis of trends in U.K. food consumption from 1954 to 1965 indicates that the annual consumption of fresh, frozen and cured fish per head of population has been declining. During the same period, the annual per capita consumption of fresh and frozen

Table 10.6. Estimated Food Supplies Per Head of Population 1954–65
(lb. per head per annum)

Produce	1954	1955	1956	1957	1958	1959	1960	1961	1962	1963	1964	1965
MEAT												
Fresh and frozen meat	83·8	89·0	93·2	93·5	92·3	88·9	91·6	94·0	97·5	98·5	94·0	92·6
Offal	7·9	8·0	8·3	8·8	8·7	8·6	9·1	9·7	10·0	10·1	10·3	10·1
Canned meats	7·5	8·5	7·9	9·1	8·7	8·9	8·6	8·8	8·3	7·5	7·7	6·7
Bacon and ham	25·0	24·8	22·7	23·6	24·2	24·2	25·0	25·3	26·0	25·2	25·3	25·7
Poultry	5·6	6·4	7·2	7·9	9·5	11·1	11·5	13·9	14·6	14·6	15·8	16·5
FISH												
Fresh, frozen, cured	18·3	19·0	19·3	18·9	18·8	17·8	18·2	17·5	17·7	16·7	17·6	17·8
Canned	1·8	1·6	2·4	2·2	3·2	3·6	2·6	2·1	3·2	2·6	3·2	3·0
FRUIT AND VEGETABLES												
Fresh citrus fruits	18·6	18·6	16·5	18·2	16·7	19·9	20·7	19·8	20·1	18·1	20·5	19·1
Other fresh fruit	47·4	47·9	49·2	49·6	47·3	51·1	53·1	49·9	52·0	33·4	53·2	54·2
Canned and bottled fruit	10·5	13·9	13·8	15·9	16·2	17·4	17·7	17·9	18·8	18·8	19·9	18·7
Dried fruit	8·4	6·4	5·7	6·7	6·4	6·3	6·1	5·7	6·9	6·3	5·8	5·8
Potatoes	242·3	234·2	224·5	223·8	212·0	214·8	223·7	227·1	213·6	229·0	226·4	223·2
Fresh tomatoes	13·7	15·7	14·3	15·8	14·4	15·8	15·0	15·0	13·9	13·1	14·2	13·1
Other fresh vegetables	93·3	94·2	93·0	97·6	94·2	91·6	98·3	93·0	95·4	92·9	102·2	102·1
Canned vegetables	9·4	9·6	10·0	10·2	10·7	10·5	10·8	11·6	12·8	13·6	13·1	13·5

Source: Annual Abstract of Statistics, 1966.

meat has risen, and there has been a rapid increase in the consumption of fresh fruit and vegetables. Table 10.6 gives the data, which fit a set of linear trend lines reasonably well.[1]

The Annual Report of the National Food Survey Committee provides evidence of recent developments in food consumption and expenditure of a kind which, if continued with the future, would be of significance for the activities of the City wholesale markets.

In regard to *fish*, the evidence shows a fall in the consumption of fresh filleted white fish (cod, halibut, plaice) with increased purchases of quick-frozen white fish and of flat processed fish (such as kippers).

Meat products show a demand for beef which appears to be highly elastic in terms of its own price (price elasticity of demand $= -1.5$)[2] so that a relatively small price change should result in substitution between the consumption of other products and of beef. In fact scarcity of beef and rising incomes appear to have been associated with a shift of demand towards poultry. This could have important implications for the future of the wholesale market in so far as the increased demand can be satisfied by frozen produce, whose distribution can by-pass the traditional wholesale markets.

Fruit and vegetables show an increasing demand for fresh produce, but also a rise in demand for 'convenience' packs, e.g. pre-packed as against loose potatoes, and canned and bottled products. The demand for quick-frozen vegetables and other prepared products appears to be generally elastic in respect of both prices and incomes (e.g. the available measures indicate a price-elasticity of demand of -1.4). Although the statistical measures cannot be more than a rough guide, it seems likely that sales of this kind of produce will expand more than proportionately to rising incomes.

Although the City wholesale markets are in some respects national markets (in that, for example, they perform the function of 'making a price' for markets generally) and so are influenced by national trends, they are also clearly affected by local (regional) developments, since their physical trade is significantly concentrated in the areas adjacent to the City. This is of interest *inter alia* because there is evidence of differences in household consumption patterns in London

---

[1] Fully comparable data are not available for more recent years; it is our impression that there has been no striking change in the pattern.

[2] The elasticity figure measures the percentage change in quantity demanded resulting from 1 per cent change in price or income, as the case may be.

and the South-Eastern Region on the one hand, and the rest of Britain on the other.

The available evidence[3] indicates that in 1964 London and the South-Eastern Region consumed a more than average amount of poultry, pork, mutton and lamb, and of fresh fruit and vegetables. This difference in consumption patterns is likely to be related to the higher incomes earned in the area, which is itself related to the high proportion of households owning a refrigerator. The evidence also indicates that the number of households possessing a refrigerator has been rising with the rise in incomes, and that the proportion of owners is greater in higher income groups; and is also higher in southern and eastern England than elsewhere. In general, households with refrigerators buy more canned fruits, fruit juices, fresh fruit and fresh green vegetables, poultry and carcase meat, and fresh and processed fish. They buy less cooked fish and chips, canned meats and vegetables. Quick-frozen fish, in contrast, appears to be bought for immediate consumption: possession of a refrigerator makes much less difference than for frozen goods as a whole. This is less surprising in that the demand for fish as a whole appears to be less buoyant than that for other foods in respect of either incomes or prices.

The general evidence about the recent past, then, shows the growth of demand for quick-frozen, pre-packed and canned produce as a significant development. Similarly, there is a growing emphasis with rising incomes upon 'convenience' foods (i.e. processed goods with advanced, labour-saving preparation by manufacturing firms).

These developments, if continued into the future, suggest a change in the magnitude and character of the throughput of the City's wholesale markets. This interpretation is consistent with recent projections of the future of the economy[4] (though we would not suggest that this consistency adds any particular weight: it arises materially from the fact that the authors of these recent projections interpret the recent history which they extrapolate into the future in much the same way as ourselves.) Thus, D. B. Rowe forecasts a growth in real expenditure on food of 17·4 per cent between 1960 and 1975, with the meat, bacon and fish, and fruit and fresh vegetables groups growing more quickly than the average.

The 1964 National Plan provides a related view of the *character* of future consumption. 'For some time, increases in *per capita* expenditure on food have taken the form almost entirely of improve-

---

[3] See, in particular, the *Annual Reports of the National Food Survey Committee*.
[4] W. Beckerman and associates, *The British Economy in 1975*, National Institute of Economic and Social Research, Cambridge 1965, Chapter 7.

ments in quality and attractiveness, including convenience in preparation, rather than increases in the quantity of basic foodstuffs consumed. Nevertheless, the rate of growth of expenditure has been getting steadily less as the scope for improvements in processing diminishes. Unless there is some new technical break-through comparable with quick-freezing, it seems likely that the majority of the increase in expenditure over the next few years will be devoted to improvements in the quality of fresh foods purchased, in particular meat, fruit and vegetables' (p. 166). And again: '. . . the trend towards increased demand for higher quality products and more expensive processing and packaging is expected to continue as consumers' incomes rise' (Part II, p. 7).

Ronald Brech in *Britain 1984: Unilever's Forecast* predicts (without describing the forecasting model and evidence in detail) that increased consumption of food will come primarily from increasing population, with a relative growth in demand for the more expensive, better-quality meats and particularly poultry. People are expected to consume more fruit and fruit juices, particularly out of season. Consumption of vegetables would be broadly unchanged, with a shift towards prepared and preserved products. The demand for fish is expected to grow less than in other food groups, though with some kind of shift in tastes.

In sum, the forecasts, and our interpretation of the evidence of the recent past, suggest that the growth in food consumption generated by rising population and incomes is likely to be associated with an increasing emphasis on convenience and on fresh, quality foods, and that the shift is likely to be of especial importance in the areas covered by the City wholesale markets. At the general level, this may have implications for the amount of present market trade which is replaced by direct movement or other bulk-breaking arrangements, and for the possible increased importance of the market as sampling markets and channels for speciality produce. But these possibilities are best considered in detail in relation to the individual markets.

Billingsgate Market

The Market is concerned with the buying and selling of fish. The main buildings occupy a ground-floor area of approximately 5,951 sq. yd (the associated Leadenhall Market occupies another 2,890 sq. yd). But the activities of the Market in fact occupy a much larger area, since the figure excludes parking and quayside space and the ground areas occupied by market-fringe traders. (Only about 10 per cent of produce delivered enters the market proper; it is essentially a 'sampling' market. Delivery vehicles act as temporary 'warehouses' for the rest.) In addition, there is 114,000 cu. ft of storage and 'chill' space under the market,[5] and tenants use similar storage elsewhere, for example in the City at Monument and Blackfriars.

The tonnage of fish passing through the market has been declining steadily over the last fourteen years, from 118,803 tons in 1957 to 60,798 tons in 1969. One of the causes of the decline has been a growth in filleting at the ports. If we adjust for this by increasing the tonnage figures by one-third, we still find a decline in the proportion of wet fish landed in the U.K. which passes through Billingsgate from one-seventh in 1955 to one-fourteenth in 1969. These figures are consistent with the argument of the earlier sections. They also suggest that the falling volume of trade may be reducing the importance of the market's role as an outlet for 'marginal' supplies, and hence as a price-setter for other markets.

Since 1955, the proportion of U.K. white fish to be quick-frozen has risen from one-twelfth to one-fifth, and of herrings from 34 per cent to around a quarter. Quick-freezing, and more recently freezing at sea, have greatly weakened the constraints upon marketing methods formally imposed by perishability. Through the improved possibilities of storage, they also reduce price instability. Also, and most important for the future, the involvement of manufacturing industry in processing, etc. and the erosion of specialist retailing outlets (fish, as well as meat, poultry and fruit and vegetables, can be sold in processed form through common outlets), may encourage the growth of contract or integrated trading, using bulk-breaking arrangements that by-pass traditional markets. The major changes in Billingsgate's tonnage since 1955 are given in Table 10.7.

We turn now to the market as a source of congestion. The questionnaire results, stated very summarily, indicated no problems in respect of delivery to the market; the bulk of fish is delivered before 6 a.m., when there is idle capacity in road-space. Congestion is a problem in the market area itself, with vehicles after arrival being used as stores. But congestion of this type is not necessarily uneconomic, in that its reduction might involve an unreasonably costly use of space.

Outward traffic must clearly add to congestion: the peak for vehicle departures is between 8 a.m. and 9 a.m. A range of particular points of congestion in and around the City were cited, most of them

[5] See *Billingsgate Market Redevelopment: Layout and Material Handling*, November 1966 (Lockyer Report).

well known. This spread accords with the distribution of outward traffic, which is appropriate to a market serving primarily the Greater London Area and surrounding regions (though, from limited evidence, the E., S.E. and S.W. postal districts are best served in terms of the number of deliveries per week). It is of interest that, despite the declining tonnages handled, the evidence suggests that the area served by the market has not changed greatly since 1960, and may actually have increased.

Table 10.7. Billingsgate Fish Trade: Volume and Market Shares 1955–69

Year	Billingsgate tonnage	Billingsgate adjusted tonnage[1]	U.K. total tonnage (wet fish)[2]	Billingsgate percentage total tonnage[3]
1955	111,803	149,071	1,039,635	14·3
1958	96,980	129,307	952,147	13·5
1959	90,083	120,111	949,743	12·6
1960	87,355	116,473	921,847	12·6
1961	77,140	102,853	874,932	11·7
1962	75,134	100,179	901,009	11·1
1963	73,223	98,631	919,006	10·6
1964	74,429	99,239	939,828	10·5
1965	71,151	94,868	1,001,775	9·4
1966	67,411	89,881	1,009,600	8·9
1967	64,675	86,233	1,058,000	8·1
1968	63,538	84,713	1,026,450	7·7
1969	60,798	81,064	1,108,100	7·3

Notes:

1. Adjusted tonnage is actual tonnage plus one-third to allow for filleting loss: it is an estimate of 'whole fish equivalent' and permits assessment of the market's share in total U.K. landed fish supplies.
2. U.K. total tonnage is an estimate of wet fish tonnage.
3. The Billingsgate share figure is only an approximation. To the extent that the U.K. figures exclude some categories of fish which are included in the Billingsgate tonnage, the share estimates are too high. The share estimates are based on adjusted Billingsgate tonnage.

Source: Market Superintendent, Billingsgate Market; White Fish Authority and Herring Industry Board.

In order to give body to our qualitative views, we have made a series of forecasts of the possible demand for the services of the market in 1981, based upon the White Fish Authority's projections of national fish consumption. These suggest a possible (perhaps optimistic) throughput of 45,000 tons. It has already been pointed out that such projections need to be treated with caution: the out come will be affected, for example, by the success with which the market adapts to the new environment and associated new special needs.

The figure does, however, provide a useful guide to possible space and labour requirements. However successful the adaptation, it will be to a situation in which other specialized activities grow relative to bulk handling. Thus, if our projection is reasonably accurate, it suggests that, at the least, there will be no increased pressure for City space, and that any redevelopment should be flexible enough to accommodate not only changed use of market space but also alternative-use possibilities. The argument is strengthened by the fact that the market has shown itself in the past to be capable of handling a wide range of variation in throughput within a given physical capacity.

Finally, there are some implications for the labour force. Our returns show some 1,120 persons (employers and employees) employed in the market and market fringe in 1966. Of these, 374 were licensed porters. If we assume that the number of licensed porters is a fair reflection of the number actually working, and that they continue to handle the same weight of fish, we can obtain some very general indication of the possible change in the labour force. With a throughput of 45,000 tons, this would amount to a fall of about one-third.

Spitalfields Market

This is a wholesale fruit, vegetable and flower market: the market complex embraces the London Fruit Exchange and covers an area of seven acres.

It is estimated that the market handles 220,000 packages a day. Tonnage figures are not available. Some information can be obtained from Covent Garden. On the basis of heroic assumptions about the comparability of the productivity of Covent Garden and Spitalfields porters, and of tonnage/space ratios in the two markets, we estimate the probable upper and lower limits of throughput of Spitalfields at 290,000–390,000 tons, with a mean estimate of 340,000 tons.

We have no time-series data for either packages or tonnages. Failing these, we have made use of information on the number of licensed porters over a series of years (Table 10.8) as a very tentative guide to changes in market throughput. On the basis of examination of a number of different assumptions about the continuation of the downward employment trend into the future, we would estimate the

1980–1 volume of trade at around 200,000 tons. We would emphasize that this is very much a best guess based upon data that we do not consider adequate. But the predicted decline in throughput is supported by some other general evidence.

Apart from the decline in licences issued over the last twelve years, trends in the national marketing of the produce suggest a decline. The general nature of these developments has already been indicated. Factors of special relevance may be the growth of bulk-buying by supermarkets and department stores, and the demand of self-service stores for pre-packed produce delivered directly to the retail outlet. The establishment of growers' co-operatives and an increase in the canning and freezing of produce may tend in the same direction.

Table 10.8. Spitalfields Market: Number of
Licensed Porters 1959–69

1956	513	1963	422
1957	474	1964	410
1958	455	1965	396
1959	451	1966	381
1960	446	1967	375
1961	435	1968	354
1962	423	1969	337

Entry into E.E.C. could also be important, for two kinds of reasons. On the one hand, it might well result in a fall in the U.K. production of some of the commodities handled (such as non-horticultural produce like flowers and bulbs), though the precise consequences will depend upon the conditions of entry. On the other hand: '. . . common standards of quality are progressively being made mandatory for fruit and vegetables . . .'.[6] This could be a matter of some importance for Spitalfields, for reasons now to be elaborated.

Within the predicted decline, we have earlier argued for a shift in demand towards fresh, quality produce and convenience foods. This, associated with developments in grading and standardization, might facilitate an increase in trading by sampling at such a market as Spitalfields. The idea is not new: the Runciman Report stated that: 'If home-grown produce were graded to common and reliable standards, it might be possible for a major market to act largely as a brokerage market or produce exchange at which sales would be made

[6] *Common Agricultural Policy of the E.E.C.* (Cmnd. 3274, H.M.S.O.).

on the basis of sample or description without any need for the produce to be inspected.[7] Given the general trend in City activities from goods towards rights, it is perhaps also to the point to draw attention to the fact that in the U.S.A. terminal (futures) markets have been established in produce such as lettuce, although no similar facilities exist in Europe. This is perhaps looking to the more distant future, but there seems no overwhelming reason why similar facilities should not grow up in London if produce markets remain reasonably free from government interference.

The future of Spitalfields will also be affected by the relocation of Covent Garden. This must clearly influence traditional buyer–seller relationships, and so affect the City market because the two are to some degree interdependent. We have treated a study of Covent Garden as outside our brief. In qualitative terms, one might expect some short-term advantage to accrue to Spitalfields from the dislocation at Covent Garden. Further ahead, however, much will depend upon the efficiency of the market in its new location: and that is a matter of uncertainty. All things considered, then, we would expect the decline in traditional functions, even with the addition of new activities (but of a kind that makes smaller demands on space), to produce a situation in which the market generates no new demands on space, and may in fact be able to incorporate new activities.

While the response rate to the Spitalfields traders' questionnaire was not high enough for confidence, it suggests a 1966–7 level of employment in the market of around 1,600. Our forecasts of throughput suggest a decline in this figure of fairly considerable magnitude, though probably associated with some increase in the relative importance of skilled activities.

The congestion problems associated with Spitalfields are essentially similar to those itemized in the case of Billingsgate: produce is delivered generally outside the hours of congestion (60 per cent of all *buyers* visit the market before 10 a.m.). The market area served (primarily the London region, concentrated 5–15 miles from the market) does not seem to have been changing greatly, and if our predictions are accurate congestion from outward journeys may decline rather than become worse. Firms appear to find strong advantages in the present location: few who provided information have considered setting up elsewhere, and there is no common view as to what kind of alternative location might produce comparable advantages (or least disadvantages).

[7] *Report of the Committee of Enquiry into Horticultural Marketing*, January 1957, pp. 55–6.

The Central Markets (Smithfield)

This is the City wholesale market for meat and poultry: there is an associated retail market (the Farringdon Market). It is the largest U.K. market concerned with the buying and selling of home and imported dead meat. Wholesaling activities occupy a total ground floor-space of 31,700 sq. yd. The area underneath the market contains cold storage facilities. The existence of the market has generated a set of 'fringe' activities (including transport facilities). Within the market fringe there are offices, warehouses, privately-owned cold stores, banks, meat equipment showrooms and even a bacon factory. This is the most complex set of linked activities of all the City markets.

In the mid 1960's, the market handled over 360,000 tons of meat per annum; by 1970 the figure had declined to less than 310,000 tons. There was some decline in the proportion of total U.K. trade passing through the market, from around 13 per cent in 1955 to slightly less than 10 per cent in 1970. Within this figure, however, Smithfield remains the major U.K. trading market in imported meat supplies. Around 1960, Smithfield's trade in imported meat accounted for some 19 per cent of total meat imports; the figure had fallen to 15·5 per cent by 1965 and about 12·5 per cent by 1970. In the first half of the 1960's, it was the decline in the volume of Argentinian meat imports which helped to account for the declining volume of trade through the market. In the late 1960's, the foot and mouth epidemic in the U.K. adversely affected meat imports from South America, with obvious consequences for Smithfield's trade in imported meat. During the 1960's, there was evidence that the trade in beef and mutton declined in relative importance, while that in pork and poultry increased: this can be explained partly by supply factors, but it also fits our expectations, discussed earlier, as to the consequences of rising incomes.

The evidence from the mid-1960's, and forecasts from past trends, suggest some decline in market throughput by say 15–20 per cent by 1980/1. If we ignore the immediate impact of the foot and mouth epidemic, this prediction is in line with the estimates we have been given of the market's own future demand for space, and of present trends in demand for existing space. Again, the factors expected to be important, and already implicit to some extent in recent experience, arise primarily out of general changes in technology and distribution. They include retailing developments already referred to, vertical integration and contract selling (the Fatstock Marketing

364

Corporation, for example, now operates long-term contracts between bacon pig producers on the one hand and bacon owners on the other).

In the mid-1960's, it was expected that the proposed Meat and Livestock Commission would have some effects on market trade. The relevant White Paper (*Marketing of Meat and Livestock*, 1965) stated that one of the Commission's functions should be: 'to bring together producer and producer groups wanting to enter into contracts with buyers wanting to place such contracts' – in other words, to by-pass wholesale markets. The Commission is now established, but it is too early, and too many other changes have occurred, for an assessment of its influence on market trends.

E.E.C. membership, in contrast, might be expected to increase the profitability and hence the volume of U.K. beef output. (See e.g. Cmnd 3274, *The Common Agricultural Policy of the European Economic Community* (*1967*).) But if the result were a reduction in beef *imports*, Smithfield, as the major import market, would lose rather than gain. Equally, the developments in pigs and poultry would be inimical to market trends. Further, if meat import levy schemes are introduced, as is likely, this will also have an adverse effect on Smithfield's import trade.

We would estimate the mid-1960 labour force at some 4,000 persons in the market and extensive market fringe (which of course includes persons in other of our activity groups), and would expect this to decline by about 10 per cent by 1980/81.

In general, foreign meat arrives at the Port of London, and is then transported by road. In the transport of other meat, first indications are that rail transport is declining relative to direct road movement. On average, 200 loaded lorries per day arrive at the market. They are arriving generally from midnight on, and do not generate congestion on the roads in the market area. Distribution is over the London area and surrounding regions, some much further afield. There are some tentative indications that the radius served by the market has been increasing. Departures appear to be bunched at times at which they must contribute to road congestion (e.g. between 8.30 and 9 a.m. and between 2 and 3 p.m.).

Some points of congestion appear to be common, in so far as the results of the questionnaire are representative. Those identified are The Angel, King's Cross, Hackney Marshes, Shoreditch, Farringdon Road to Blackfriars Bridge, Oxford Street, Highbury Corner to Holloway Road and the Vauxhall area. We would draw no policy conclusions from this, since the same points would be identified in a general traffic survey, but they are indicative of the traffic implications of this particular location.

THE PORT OF LONDON

Historically, the Legal Quays between the Tower of London and London Bridge, as well as ancient wharves such as Queenhithe, have been important in the development of the Port of London. The contribution of international trade to the commercial and financial evolution of the City cannot be overestimated; as we have seen in Chapter 1, the growth of the capital as a trading centre has always been closely linked with its functions as a premier port. In 1966, more than 20,000 people employed in the City were still directly dependent on shipping and are crucially interested in its future. They are divided as follows:

Miscellaneous services incidental to transport shipbrokers, shipping and forwarding agents	13,905
Sea transport	5,080
Port and inland water transport	1,962
	20,947

Thousands more are employed in related activities, e.g. wholesaling and warehousing, export and import merchanting, commodity markets and so on. Some of these will be given explicit attention later in this chapter.

In terms of traffic handled, London is the sixth-largest port in the world, serving more than one hundred brokers and shipping lines operating in or through London, a large proportion having at least some of their organization located in the City. The port complex has twenty-nine miles of deep water quays and well over 200 berths and riverside moorings. Some 600,000 sq. ft of associated warehousing is located within the City itself. In 1969, 28 per cent of total value of British exports and 24 per cent of value of imports passed through the Port. These proportions are rather lower than ten years ago, as air freight is taking a larger share of the trade in high-value goods.

The Port and its activities are currently undergoing great change. Decasualization of dock labour has now been achieved – and with it a two-shift system. Great new dock extensions and improvements have been undertaken and are projected at Tilbury. After completion, capacity for containerized traffic will consist of six berths, each capable of handling many times the tonnage of cargo dealt with by conventional berths. In addition there will be two new berths for timber traffic and three for general cargo traffic. Further upstream the story is quite different. At the end of 1969 there were 108 general cargo berths in the enclosed docks exclusive of berths leased to tenants and the specialized container and timber berths at Tilbury. It is estimated that the general cargo remaining after completion of the Tilbury complex could be dealt with by about one-half this number. Already several of the inner docks have been closed. St Katherine's was sold to the G.L.C. in 1963 and there are plans for developing this area into a tourist attraction (with a yacht marina, etc.); 300 acres are also scheduled for high-density housing. In the same year both London and East India dock were closed, while an application for the closure of Surrey dock – which spans 400 acres – is under active consideration.

Innovations in handling and transportation are having, and will continue to have, a considerable impact on traditional methods of warehousing and wholesaling goods entering and leaving the Port. Competition from other ports, both in the U.K. and elsewhere, will change in character and intensity as a result of containerization. Already, these developments are beginning to affect the City's environment: one example is an imaginative new housing scheme which is being considered in order to replace demolished warehouses between St Paul's and the river.

We shall deal briefly with some of these complex developments by considering first the nature of the technical and other changes that have and are occurring, and their general implications for the Port; second, and arising from this, some more detailed consequences for City activities.

Containerization and Other Technological Developments

Containerization is the most recent attempt (following e.g. unitization and palletization) to reduce transport costs by minimizing the costs of handling and bulk-breaking and enabling goods to be shipped directly from manufacturer to final customer. In addition to this main advantage, containerization also offers a much quicker turn-round of ships and a more intensive use of berths.

There will, of course, always be a large variety of shapes and types of cargo, many small units requiring space, and a multitude of origins and destinations.[8] Nevertheless, there are real advantages to

[8] McKinsey and Company, in a report commissioned by the British Transport Docks Board, quote the example of a shipment of fruit from South Africa bound for over 100 different consignees.

367

be gained where suitable cargoes can be shipped, in reducing the turn-round times of ships in ports, in increasing cargo-carrying capacities and in reducing handling costs. Some estimates of potential transportation cost savings are as high as 50–60 per cent per ship – which might make it economic to travel full and return empty. A further example is provided by the handling of timber: formerly dealt with by inland agents, shipments are now being prepacked and dispatched directly from North America and northern Europe for delivery to customers with salesmen as the only essential intermediaries.

As far as regular shipments are concerned, containerization is likely to produce shipping over-capacity or, more likely, an adaptation of shipping patterns. The McKinsey report points out that as few as twenty-five ships with a capacity of less than 2,000 containers each would handle the entire European/North American general cargo trade; over-capacity is in fact already very apparent[9] on the North Atlantic route.

From the viewpoint of the Port of London, these technical changes are likely to result in a need to accept a pattern of trade that shares the U.K. traffic between London and other major U.K. ports such as Liverpool. The McKinsey study suggested an eventual situation in which there is one port for each major trade route or group of routes. This kind of change does not imply any necessary reduction in the value of traffic passing through the Port of London. But it will change in character and in the way it is processed. Containerized traffic will be handled at inland groupage depots rather than at port warehouses, with Customs facilities being handled at the depot instead of the port. Ability to deal with this traffic will depend upon the development of Port facilities. This is already under way. The movement downstream pre-dates the containerization movement: the new investment at Tilbury was initially to cater for conventional cargo, but later developments have been related to the 'container revolution'.

Space is a major requirement for containerized shipments and other modern handling techniques, both at terminal and inland depots. It has been estimated that, per 100 feet of quay, container traffic needs $2\frac{1}{4}$–$2\frac{1}{2}$ acres of handling space compared with $1\frac{1}{4}$–$1\frac{1}{2}$ acres needed by conventional cargo traffic. In the United States, the $24 million Sea–Land Terminal at Elizabeth-Port has 52 acres of paved open area which forms a marshalling yard for over 2,000 containers. Tilbury should, when completed, be able to serve the

9 *The Economist*, March 14, 1970, p. 8.

Port of London in similar fashion so far as terminals are concerned. But the problem of finding inland depots – there were twenty-nine of these at the end of 1969 – may present more difficulties.

Nevertheless, it is clear that containerization will hasten the pronounced changes now taking place in distribution of goods from the Port. This will affect the City in four main ways. First, a smaller proportion of goods will be transported by barge and discharged at City wharves and warehouses. At present, about 60 per cent of the produce entering the enclosed docks is unloaded to barges and then dispatched upstream; this proportion is expected to fall by one-half in the 1970s. Second, there is likely to be some easing of through traffic in the City. This is partly because an increasing proportion of goods originating from Tilbury docks will by-pass inner London, partly because of the closure of several of the inner docks, partly because the average lorry capacity of containerized goods is so much higher than for conventional cargo – and partly because a higher proportion of traffic is now being transported by rail.[10]

Third, important structural changes are likely to take place in the shore-based staff of shipping companies. Sales staff of shipping companies are tending to operate between inland container depots and the manufacturer, so that their number may well decline in the City; furthermore, it is likely there will be more mergers among shipping companies with a consequential contraction of the administrative staff at headquarters into tighter, smaller groupings.

Lastly, it is expected that documentation, which will increasingly be mechanized, will be done outside the City, most probably at inland container depots. Bills of lading, and manifests (which are the consolidated bills of lading for a ship) are the documents primarily involved. Containerization has spurred improvements here, since each container may carry a number of different products for several consignees. The likely outcome is a shift of customs documentation to inland depots, a simplification of the documents themselves, and the evolution of 'container documents' that might well provide a backing for credit facilities of the type that the City has traditionally provided.

In spite of these changes, it is likely that the shipping companies will continue to require a City location if only for a small office. For there are still important advantages of contiguity and centrality to be gained. Our statistical analysis has shown that those employed

10 For example, about one-half of the conventional cargo leaving the Tilbury docks goes by road and the other half by rail. The corresponding percentages for containerized cargo are 10 per cent and 90 per cent.

in sea transport (24) are generally located close to miscellaneous commodity dealers (80), grain brokers and merchants (81), and insurance brokers (43); and that ship brokers and shipping agents (28) usually near to all types of reinsurance brokers (43/4, 46) and to varying kinds of merchants (74, 75) etc. There is also the factor of contingency which draws firms together, and linkages with other shipping companies as a result of the conference system.

As examples of the close links between shipping companies, the container consortia are of interest. These are:

Associated Container Transport (City-based)
Ben Linex
Blue Star Line
Cunard Line (Port Lines)
Ellerman Lines (and five associated lines)
Harrison Line

Overseas Containers Ltd (City-based)
P and O Group
Alfred Holt & Co.
British and Commonwealth Shipping Co.
Furness Withy & Co.

Atlantic Container Line (Stockholm-based)
French Line
Holland America Line
Wallenius Lines
Swedish American Line
Swedish Transatlantic Line
Cunard Line

'Contingency' covers two aspects. First, there is the contingency that arises in normal day-to-day business. A ship has to be chartered, reinsured, cargoes arranged. This is so much easier if it can be done by contacts over the phone to men one has met, with written contracts later. Secondly, in face-to-face contacts, there is always the possibility of meeting new people, hearing of new ideas, promoting new business – the 'contingency of the unexpected'.

Summarizing, it seems likely that containerization, while hastening the destruction of particular City activities such as warehousing, may also generate new functions. It is unlikely that the container trade will be free from uncertainty, and it is reasonable to expect that (e.g.) the Baltic Exchange may find a part to play in the making-up of shipments.

Some Implications for the City

When we turn from global and technical considerations to more detailed problems, account must be taken of port charges and labour relations. In terms of traditional trade, national and international users of the Port of London appear to find its general level of charges high relative to those at outports (e.g. Sheerness, Whitstable, Dover, Shoreham, Felixstowe, Dagenham Dock), not withstanding its generally superior facilities. This does not affect the bulk traffic discussed earlier; but the view (enlarged in the Rochdale Report) that these outports have provided a lead in cost-reduction is not to be ignored.

Again, labour relations must continue to be a matter for concern, though decasualization and the constraints imposed by containerization may operate to reduce any existing differences between the Port of London and other ports.

In this respect, it cannot be ignored that the Port of London continues to have certain clear economic advantages over other U.K. ports. These are primarily associated with the Port's proximity to main market areas. A major study commissioned by the P.L.A. into the Port of London's share of U.K. overseas trade highlighted the advantages. It revealed that in the mid 1960s the Port not only accounted for the dominant proportion of trade entering and leaving London and the South-East, but an important share of trade in the Midlands and South of England as well.

Despite any short-term disadvantages of the kinds instanced then, it must be expected that the Port of London will continue to benefit from its proximity to an important region from the point of view of population (and its anticipated growth) and income. Containerization, and the development of land adjacent to the docks for industry, may introduce the possibility of some loss of Continental traffic to Rotterdam; on the other hand London has reestablished itself as a leading grain terminal in Europe, and plans to develop the oil trade of the Port are well under way.[11] At best, however, such traffic must be destined for a variety of national (European) centres, or must be able to bear the costs of transhipment. It is at least debatable, in the light of the McKinsey findings whether such multinational traffic is likely to be a major element in the development of container traffic.

In respect of existing City activities, the position of public wharfingers and lightermen requires mention. They are faced with a

[11] *The Next Five Years. Outline of Future Policy*, Statement prepared by Director General P.L.A., January 1970.

peculiarly difficult position. The volume of river traffic has been steadily declining in recent years: there are serious labour problems, and the future is uncertain.

Over recent years the total volume of trade entering and leaving the Port of London has declined very slightly.

(Millions of tons)	1965	1966	1968	1969
Total imports	48·3	47·3	49·7	48·1
Total exports	9·5	9·6	8·7	8·6
Transhipments	2·0	2·1	1·7	1·3
	59·8	59·0	60·1	58·0

Of this amount, the total tonnage carried by barges in the Port of London by members of the Association of Master Lightermen has steadily declined:

	Millions of tons
1964	12·6
1965	10·7
1966	9·6
1969	6·9

More cargo is going over the quays and being loaded straight on to road transport while there has been a marked decline in the shifting of cargoes of oil and coal by the lightermen. This is particularly clear in the case of much rough lighterage (i.e. carrying of coal and refuse), but quay lighterage (i.e. general cargoes and oils in bulk) has also been affected. For reasons already argued, these are trends that must be expected to continue.

The decline in throughput handled by lightermen has largely been the result of economic forces, of which three may be mentioned:

(a) a fall in the traffic of the type of goods normally carried by barges;

(b) the decline of the Port of London as an entrepôt port;

(c) strip measures in lighterage charges.

But it is also contended by the lightermen that they are being squeezed by the P.L.A., both by the failure to provide facilities for 'overside' cargo into barges at Tilbury, and by their fear that the P.L.A. may revoke the Free Water Clause.[12]

[12] This Clause originated in the opposition of the Master Lightermen, the Public Wharfingers, and the Waterman's Company to the building of the wet docks in the eighteenth century. They feared a diversion of traffic to the wet docks and a safeguard was introduced in the West India Dock Act of 1799 under Section 138 whereby charges would not be extended to any 'lighters or craft entering into the said docks or basins or cuts to convey, deliver, discharge or receive ballast or goods to or from on board any ships, vessel or vessels'.

It is questionable whether these views have any realistic basis. The nature of technical progress increasingly makes the time-cost of transhipment, rather than landing, prohibitive; it is doubtful whether the practice continues in any other major port.

Labour costs make up about 60 per cent of lighterage companies' total operating expenses. In the course of our inquiry, we found wages were high, at least for those in work. A wage packet of over £28 (now £35) for a four-day week was by no means rare. Prior to decasualization, the National Dock Labour Board levied one-sixth of a lighterage company's total wage bill and thereafter an unknown proportion. Nor will decasualization bring any remarkable short-term advantages to employers of lightermen. Mr B. H. Panton, Managing Director of Thames and General Lighterage Ltd, was reported in *The Times* (August 5, 1967) as saying that his firm had paid 'hundreds of men' a day's pay for doing nothing. (He was appealing against an allocation of 387 men under the decasualization scheme when he has applied for only 300.)

All things considered, it is difficult to be optimistic about the future of lighterage, and in view of this, it is not surprising that some diversification in the activities of lighterage firms has occurred. Lighterage firms are moving into other areas of transport and packing services, and (for obvious reasons) concentrating on produce in which containerization is least likely.

The public wharfingers are in rather a different position, since a fair proportion of the Port's sea-going traffic proceeds straight to the riverside wharves rather than to the docks. In the City, the wharves are situated just south of Upper and Lower Thames Street. The main ones are: *New Fresh Wharf* (just downstream of London Bridge) (handling fresh fruit, tinned goods, dried fruit, nuts, etc.); *Smith's Wharf* (handling 'essential' oils, bristles and fur, dress furs, cotton goods, radios, radio valves, etc.); *Abbey Wharf* (handling tea exclusively); *Brooks Wharf* (handling furs) and *Bull Wharf* (handling tea).

To a greater extent than the lighterage companies, the public wharfingers are fearful of the outcome of nationalization, while the related uncertainties and lack of profitability have gradually inhibited capital investment in some cases. Other wharfingers have been affected by road-improvement schemes, or depend heavily upon trades which might change their location. In recent years, several wharves, including *Hays Wharf* which handled a large proportion of provisions dealt in by the nearby Exchange and consumed in southern England, have been closed. As the Port's main activities have moved downstream, and commodity markets have been dealing increasingly in rights rather than goods, City wharfingers have sought interests elsewhere, not only in other U.K. ports but also abroad (e.g. in Rotterdam). As far as the City itself is concerned, all these trends will make for a further decline of warehousing activities and also, to a limited extent at least, ease the pressure on the City's transport facilities. They will also release land within the City for other uses.

EXPORT AND IMPORT MERCHANTING

Besides the organized markets described earlier, there are a very large number of firms concerned, either as principals or agents, in international trade. Some of these are highly specialized but others range over a very wide area of activities. Our breakdown of the O.S.R.P. data for this sector, based mainly on the three-digit classification of the Standard Industrial Classification, shows 409 firms of export and import merchants employing 6,140 people, and 485 firms in 'miscellaneous services incidental to transport' (including ship brokers and shipping and forwarding agents) employing 13,905 people. There were also about 570 firms employing nearly 8,000 people who described themselves as merchants in a particular commodity; many, though by no means all, of those would be concerned in one or other of the markets previously described. Most of the firms are very small, though a few of the larger ones account for a considerable part of turnover. Among export and import merchants 267 out of 409 firms employed ten persons or fewer and only seven more than 100. In 'services incidental to transport' there were twenty-five firms employing more than 100, but 217 employed ten or less. On the other hand, a survey undertaken by Professor G. M. Sharman among members of the Export Houses Association (and made available to the Invisible Exports Committee) showed that four of the 178 firms surveyed did 25 per cent of the business, while at the other end of the scale 88 firms accounted for only 5 per cent turnover.

On the export side, it is possible to draw a number of broad distinctions in function, though many firms will cut across the borders of different categories. First there is the distinction between activities that are primarily trading and those which are primarily financing. On the trading side, there is the merchant who buys and sells as a principal; the manufacturer's agent or export manager who is the agent, or sometimes a subsidiary company of one or more manu-

374

facturers, and whose primary job is to find markets among overseas buyers; and the buying agent or indent agent, who places orders on behalf of buyers and whose primary job is to find the best source of supply for his clients.

On the financial side, there are the confirming house and the factor. Confirming houses act both on behalf of overseas buyers and on behalf of suppliers, in whatever country they may be. Acting for the buyer they will negotiate contracts, guarantee payment to the U.K. supplier, provide credit, and arrange for shipping, insurance and documentation. When acting for an overseas supplier, they will provide a contract in a form enforceable according to the law of his own country; guarantee payment in his own currency and, in approved cases, arrange credit. They also perform a number of advisory services.

Factoring is a relatively new City activity though it is of fairly long standing in America. The most common arrangement – though there are a number of variants – is for the factor to undertake to purchase from an exporter, for cash, all invoices resulting from orders which the factor has approved, as they come in; the factor then assumes complete responsibility for the collection of the debt without recourse. The exporter thus gets a 'package deal' in which he is paid cash for a credit transaction, thereby avoiding both the credit risk, and the work of collection and accounting.

An interesting feature is the variety of institutions that have participated in setting up factoring firms: these include merchant banks, confirming houses, American banks, hire-purchase finance companies, a firm of East India merchants a shipping line, an insurance company and a firm of insurance brokers. Besides these firms specializing in 'package deals', several other companies have been set up in recent years to provide export finance on a non-recourse basis. Participants are mainly clearing banks, merchant banks and hire-purchase finance companies.

It is impossible to say how much of the mercantile activity of the country is concentrated in London: the Export Houses Association draws over 80 per cent of its members from the London area, but this is not a reliable guide, as the Association is much stronger in London than in the provinces. It is certain that nearly all the firms operating on the financial side are in London; a high proportion of these appear to be in the City, though a few are in the West End.

Firms interviewed stressed the need for proximity to shipping companies, insurance firms and banks, and the importance of the rapid transport of documents by messenger, instead of having to rely on the post. They also emphasized the narrowness of margins and their vulnerability to rising costs, City rents, and selective employment tax. There was a tendency to compromise by seeking locations near the periphery of the City and immediately to the east of it, where there has been considerable redevelopment, and rents are lower than in the financial centre.

Merchants involved in general export, import and entrepôt trade, and those specializing in particular commodities, have found difficulty, because of taxation, in building up sufficient financial reserves to meet the inevitable uncertainties of the trade. They too are working on small margins, and their particular assets have provided no hedge against chronic inflation. Competition from abroad has been increasing for some years, and some British merchants, to escape the financial handicaps here, have left the country and now operate from abroad, e.g. from Switzerland.

The Port of London is regarded as another obstacle to entrepôt trade, not because it is inherently inefficient – on the contrary the turn-round can be quicker than in many European ports – but because the port is too expensive and it is cheaper to ship goods direct to Amsterdam. London's prospects as an entrepôt port are considered to be increasingly less favourable. At present it is still possible to negotiate for terms with private wharf owners. Nationalization would almost certainly remove even that advantage. Containerization might remove some of these present disadvantages: it is more doubtful whether it would do much to improve the situation of the merchants, for reasons already discussed.

The problems of the shipping and forwarding agents are different. The amount of some types of traffic which they might expect to handle will undoubtedly increase: the amount of air freight handled by one firm has recently been growing at the rate of 25 per cent a year. Their main uncertainty is how they will be affected by containerization. This depends partly on what form of document is finally agreed covering door-to-door instead of port-to-port delivery. It also depends upon the stage at which shipping companies will wish to come in – whether they will be content to accept delivery of the loaded containers at the docks, or whether they will also wish to take over, or take part in, loading and unloading the containers at the inland depots.

Container developments will affect the placing of depots. They probably will not greatly affect the location of head offices, which need a central position for the convenience of customers, but also to be near Customs and shipping offices, with which there is a constant messenger service. At least one firm has moved its headquarters to 'L.I.F.T.' – the London International Freight Terminal at Stratford – where Customs have established an office, but this particular firm specializes in road transport and proximity to shipping offices is not therefore a priority.

As in other cases, the need to maintain a messenger service with City offices does not tie the shipping and forwarding agents to a location within the City, and the level of City rents could be an important factor causing a reassessment of their location. Warehouses attached to head offices, which – except in very special cases – are not essential, are especially liable to dispersal.

The Baltic Mercantile and Shipping Exchange, known simply as 'the Baltic', is primarily concerned with providing facilities for the arranging – 'fixing' – of cargoes for merchant vessels. Although its grain and oil-seed markets are still important, chartering constitutes the greatest number of transactions on the exchange.

A tramp-shipowner will let out his ship, voyage by voyage, to trade in any direction where the most profitable cargo is available, the cargo liner on regular service on a regular route will carry whatever cargo is available at the scheduled loading ports. With thousands of deep-sea tramps and cargo liners of all nations constantly seeking employment, and merchants and shippers all over the world in constant need of ships to carry their cargoes, there is a mutual search for the right ship to carry the right cargo. It is the function of the shipping sections of the Baltic Exchange to match one to the other, at rates which fluctuate from day to day in accordance with supply and demand. It is this activity that constitutes the London freight market, still the most important in the world.

There are some 2,500 Baltic members representing about 800 firms. Chartering agents represent the charterers, owners' brokers and the shipowners; but there are many broking firms which have both charterers and shipowners among their clients, who may be in London or anywhere else in the world. Many merchants and shipowners who are members of the Exchange have their own chartering staff.

Since its origins in the seventeenth-century coffee houses, the Baltic has seen, and adapted itself to, great changes, and London brokers have acquired an unrivalled expertise in the complexities of trading by sea. There was a time when virtually all the tramp freight of the world was 'fixed' in London, even though many of the ships and their cargoes never came within thousands of miles of the English coast. Today there are markets in the United States, Japan, Germany and elsewhere; many Scandinavian shippers and shipowners deal among themselves without recourse to London. Nevertheless, London is still the world centre for 'fixing' tramp cargoes and time charters (ships chartered to a company for a given period), and for much other shipping business and information – including the sale of vessels. It is claimed in London that 'whenever anyone gets into difficulties they come to the Baltic'.

Because of the method of transacting business, with each company working privately with others both on and away from the Exchange, there is no means of measuring the amount of business done in any particular field. However, despite the lack of formal statistics, it can be reliably estimated that well over half of the world's tramping freight is 'fixed' on the Baltic and a similar share of time charters. This type of business has been steadily increasing with the growth of world trade, and the tide is thus running favourably for Baltic brokers. London has lost none of its reputation for expertise, enterprise and commercial reliability.

Members of the Baltic were quick to see the prospects offered by air transport. The first steps towards creating a market were taken before the Second World War; the Air Brokers Association, which handles this side of the business, was formally set up in 1949. The market began, understandably, with the chartering of aircraft to fly crews out to vessels. The first charter of this kind on the Baltic was a teleprinter request from a shipowner's office in New York, the first leg of the journey being in an aircraft chartered from an airline office in the same skyscraper as the shipowner. For the first few years, most of the air traffic 'fixed' was freight, only about 30 per cent was for passengers. In 1969 about 70 per cent of the business is believed to have been in passenger charters, while some 60 per cent of all passenger chartering on the Baltic is for 'packaged' tours, which have an obvious growth potential. It has already been suggested that containerization, while diminishing the demand for City space for some existing activities, may in fact create a new role for the Baltic in the selling of container space.

Like the Stock Exchange and Lloyd's, the Baltic is peculiarly a City institution, where a member's word is his bond – without which the functioning of the Exchange would be impossible. As with the other exchanges, the personal relationships of all involved, and therefore their locational links, are necessarily close.

WAREHOUSING AND WHOLESALING

Our estimates show that at least 22,000 people are now employed in wholesaling and warehousing activities in the City. The distributions between these two activities are as follows:

Wholesaling		10,026
Warehousing		
(a) Attached to wholesaling	5,886	
(b) Attached to factories or belonging to owners, trustees, etc., of docks and wharves	1,227	
(c) Miscellaneous storage	2,109	
(d) Other warehousing activities	3,448	12,670
		22,696

Details of wholesaling were obtained from O.S.R.P. and H.M.I.F. data. Our estimate of the total labour force engaged in warehousing was derived from the 1965–6 Employment Survey of the Corporation of London, but the allocation of this figure between (a), (c) and (d) is based on O.S.R.P. statistics. The numbers employed in (b) is a residual between the total of the two sets of data.

For some purposes it is more appropriate to consider wholesaling and warehousing activities as part of the same operation. In the table below, based entirely on O.S.R.P. data, we classify wholesaling establishments according to product group.

	Number of establishments	Number employed
Wholesale distribution:		
Groceries, provisions, confectionery, drinks	112	1,785
Other food	332	4,548
Tobacco	10	107
Footwear and textiles	133	2,044
Paper, stationery, books	114	1,891
Petroleum products	11	595
Other non-food goods	138	2,590
General wholesale merchants	76	2,054
	926	15,614

Wholesaling is a fairly widely distributed activity throughout the City, although there are certain areas of specialization. The more important of these are in the Smithfield, Houndsditch/Billingsgate, Thames Street and Fleet Street districts.[13]

Warehousing has for many years now been of declining importance in the City. In 1939 warehouses occupied 27·3 million sq. ft or 26·4 per cent of all floor-space; by 1962 the area had very substantially

[13] For further details see Chapter 2.

379

fallen to 10·4 million sq. ft or 14·3 per cent of all accommodation, and by 1968 to 10·3 million sq. ft or 13·5 per cent of accommodation.

Both wholesaling and warehousing activities are predominantly the province of small or very small firms. Of the 979 establishments making O.S.R.P. returns (including those classified to miscellaneous services, storage) 620 employed ten or less and a further 233 between eleven and twenty-five. Only twenty-seven establishments had a labour force of more than 100.

Excluding the markets referred to above, there are four main sections of specialized trade:

(a) The riverside warehouses of the Eastcheap merchants.
(b) The clothing and textile trade.
(c) The remnants of the wine and spirit trade.
(d) The P.L.A. Cutler Street warehouses.

There are also a large number of general wholesale merchants, some fairly scattered, but mostly centred in the area to the south and east of the main financial district.

New Fresh Wharf, downstream from London Bridge, handles canned fruit and fish, dried fruit and nuts; the main centre of wholesale trade in canned and dried foods is just to the north in the Eastcheap area. Further upstream, between Southwark and Blackfriars bridges, are a number of general warehouses handling the dried packaged goods of the 'general cargo' trade. Among the great variety of goods handled are tea, furs, bristles, mica, shellac, manufactured drugs, bamboo shoots, lotus nuts and other exotic Eastern produce and essential oils. Just to the north of the wharves are firms in the wholesale fur and paper trades, both reduced in volume but still active.

The warehouses work under severe disadvantages: goods have to be transhipped well downstream and brought up by lighter; the barge beds dry out at low tide; the warehouse entrances are small and only 25-cwt. cranes can be used for unloading, compared to the three- to five-ton ones which are common in the general cargo trade; while stacking on the various floors is done largely by hand. These disadvantages are minimized by the fact that cargoes usually come in small lots and are of high value in relation to their weight. The advantages enjoyed by the warehouse firms are established trade connections, expertise in handling and storing special cargoes, and the care which they can give to goods because they are dealt with in small quantities and largely by hand.

The wholesale trade in textiles and clothing is a good example of the way in which activities which use a comparatively large amount of space for transactions of relatively low value are gradually being squeezed out of the City.[14] The largest remaining group is near the north-east boundary, in Houndsditch, Stoney Lane and Middlesex Street, where similar trades have been carried on since the sixteenth century. Before 1939 there was also a large group in the Barbican area mingling with the book and paper trades around St Paul's, but only a few scattered firms remain.

The ancient trade in wines and spirits of the Coopers Row and Cross Wall area is also much reduced. Besides the high cost of premises in the City, the trade has also been affected by the entry of the brewers, with their own distribution systems, and by the advantages of being nearer to the docks at which imports are now unloaded. As a result the trade has moved eastward to Stepney and Wapping.

Until a few years ago, the Port of London Authority had warehouses near Smithfield and in Commercial Road but both have been closed as uneconomic. The P.L.A. still retain, however, the large warehouse building in Cutler Street, built in 1782 for the East India Company. Carpets are an important trade there, and the many other goods handled include wines and spirits, tobacco, drugs, essences, ostrich feathers and ivory.

It will be apparent from this description that a great deal of the wholesale trade of the City is closely linked with the import trade of the Port of London. Attention was drawn in Chapter 6 to some features in the pattern of London trade that may militate against its rapid growth, though it was also pointed out that closer integration with Europe, and the Channel Tunnel, could shift the direction of trade in favour of London.

Even if this were so, however, there would be no necessary reason why the goods concerned should be handled in the City. Historically, the growth of the wholesale trade of the City depended on the bringing of goods into the City either from abroad or from the provinces, and, as we have shown elsewhere, this is becoming increasingly out of line with modern methods of handling goods and distribution. The possible exceptions are goods of high value where the volume of trade is relatively small, where transport costs are at their lowest, and where the advantages of specialized handling facilities and of concentrating dealings in a few specialized hands are greatest. This is, of

[14] More generally, it is interesting to note that the average space requirements per person in the warehousing trade is 1,000 sq. ft – six to seven times greater than in office activities.

course, the trend of the recent past. Almost all the bulk (as distinct from general cargo) trade that was ever in the City has left, and the goods which still come in are more and more the small-bulk, high-value kind.

Unless goods flow naturally into the City there is little apparent advantage in wholesalers and warehouses being located there. They do not have the same close links with the shipping, insurance and financial world as do import and export merchants and members of the commodity markets. London, at large, must of course remain a great centre of wholesale trade, but firms can be in London without being in the City. The pressure of mounting costs is likely to cause firms which are wholesalers largely of imported goods to move either to the South Bank or to the East End, where they can still be within easy reach of the City, but can enjoy lower rents and closer proximity to the docks. The advantages of such a move are likely to be accentuated with the closure of the St Katherine's dock. Wholesalers of domestic goods have an equally strong incentive to seek lower rents, though no particular reason for going east.

To sum up, wholesaling seems to be one of the traditional activities of the City which has the least strong links with the main financial and commercial centre. It requires a considerable amount of space in relation to the value of transactions and, because of this, is least able to afford the rising costs of space in the City. It is also an activity which is being increasingly dispersed by changes in distribution methods and new advances in technology.

As we have seen, a good deal of wholesaling has already moved out of the City and we should expect this to continue and for the labour force to decline. There are, however, two possible exceptions to these trends. The first is the low-bulk, high-value trades, already mentioned. The second is where goods are sold by description, sample or catalogue and where the seller does not keep a stock on the spot but arranges deliveries either direct from a manufacturer or importer, or from stocks which he may hold elsewhere. Such trade can clearly be conducted from relatively small premises, and firms of this nature may continue to find the advantages of a City location worth the price.

Chapter 11

MANUFACTURING INDUSTRY

PRINTING AND PUBLISHING

Historically, the development of printing as an industry has centred on London, particularly in the central areas. An indication of the importance of printing in the City has been the prominence with which master printers have featured in the roll of honour of former Lord Mayors.

The location of the industry has been subject to two opposing forces: one attracting the industry to central London and the other pushing it out to the suburbs and provinces.[1] The relative strength of these forces has varied from one branch of the industry to another: newspaper and periodical work being more highly concentrated in London and the City. In fact, the attraction to the suburbs and provinces has long been the major force, and this predominance if anything has been increasing in recent years.

The printing industry's concentration within London, and within the City, has been declining over the last hundred years. In 1861, over half the country's printers were in London but by 1951 this proportion was a little over two-fifths. Printing, according to Professor Peter Hall,[2] is a classic example of a trade that developed in a traditional centre and there gathered to itself a select, self-perpetuating group of skilled workers, which then, itself, became a critical factor in location.

Prior to 1850, labour supplies tended to keep the industry tied to London. However, by the end of the nineteenth century, the high cost of London labour began to weigh increasingly heavily upon the publishers. London rates were higher, and the well organized compositors' and bookbinders' unions were more militant than their provincial brethren who, even in the 1890s, were still often non-union

[1] See Peter Hall, *The Industries of London Since 1861*, Hutchinson University Library, 1962.
[2] Ibid.

383

men. Although the provincial work, except in Oxford and Cambridge, was regarded as poorer in quality, this disadvantage was steadily being overcome by increased mechanization. By the 1890s, a great number of London printers were complaining of the competition from low-paid foreign labour. At the turn of the century, work was being put out to Holland, and there was competition from German lithography. A survey in 1930 found that the trade was being rapidly drawn out of London by lower wages and more space. Only newspapers and rapid commercial printing needed to remain.

During the course of a recent manpower survey of the printing and publishing industry conducted by the Department of Employment and Productivity[3] many participating London firms took the opportunity to underline the disadvantages of a London location. The disadvantages given were: obstructions to the economic use of labour, particularly in the casual jobbing system and the associated demarcation issues; higher wage rates; higher overhead costs; and difficulty in obtaining or retaining suitable premises. The report expected the outward movement of firms to continue, except for those such as the national newspapers, that need to remain in London for particular and special reasons.

Despite this outward drift of printing and publishing firms, the industry still remains the biggest employer of non-white-collar workers in the City. In 1966, out of a total of just over 21,000 factory employees, over 16,000 were employed in 'printing and publishing'. An additional 20,000 were shown as employed in the industry under the O.S.R.P. categories. The combined figure of 36,000 represented about 12·7 per cent of total City employment under the eighty-six activities analysed, and 75·8 per cent of factory employment.

Order XV of the Standard Industrial Classification includes paper as well as printing and publishing. Employment in 'paper' is now relatively unimportant in the City. The most important categories are those included under the Minimum List headings 486 – the printing and publishing of newspapers and periodicals – and 489 – other printing, book publishing, bookbinding, engraving, etc. This official classification, combining as it does separate activities, adds to the difficulties of assessing the relative importance of these separate activities, and particularly those parts of them located within the City. However, there is no doubt that the national press is by far the biggest section and, in particular, the biggest employer of 'Factory' labour.

---

[3] 'Printing and Publishing', *Manpower Studies No. 9*, D.E.P., April 1970.

The Economic Development Committee for Printing and Publishing, in its first report in January 1967, emphasized the lack of detailed and comparable information on the industry. A certain amount of information was available, the report said, but some of the larger printers and the majority of the smaller did not publish their results, and only a minority 'collaborate in the collective schemes adopted by specific sectors of the industry'.

In an earlier study of the printing industry, Ronald Brech noted that wages and salaries were rising faster than the national average, whereas output per employee was rising less than both wages and salaries and the national average for productivity.[4] Output in the general printing sector, as a proportion of Gross National Product increased steadily from 2·2 per cent in 1954 to 2·4 per cent in 1958 and remained constant up to the time of Brech's report. Between 1954 and 1958, sales increased at 4·7 per cent per year, but at only 3 per cent per year between 1958 and 1963.

Brech's warning on the dangers of rising wages and salaries coincided with the publication of a report by the National Board for Prices and Incomes.[5] The reference to the Board excluded the printers of the national newspapers which were dealt with under another reference. The Board also referred to the persistent discrepancy between the comparative rises in earnings and productivity. This discrepancy had been reflected in declining profit margins and rising prices. A situation had arisen in which output per man-hour had risen slowly, earnings had risen rapidly, profits had fallen, and prices had risen. The trouble, the Board said, lay 'partly in the structure of the industry, partly in the quality of management, partly in the attitudes of the unions'.[6] Although management has suffered from insularity and been unreceptive to external pressures and ideas, it has had limited room for manœuvre. The nature of the industry, particularly with respect to newspapers, is such that interruption of production must be avoided at all costs. However, the purely commercial printer was not in this extreme position.

The report admitted certain other difficulties facing employers. Besides restrictions on the intake of young trainees and apprentices, a number of union practices were found which acted as a serious deterrent to the introduction of new machinery and methods. On the other hand unions had often demonstrated their willingness to negotiate

[4] Ronald Brech, *Economic Study of the Printing Industry*, 1965, British Federation of Master Printers.
[5] *Wages, Costs and Prices in the Printing Industry*, Cmnd. 2750, August 1965.
[6] Ibid., para. 40.

productivity agreements with progressive employers. Employers, however, often seemed to accept restrictive practices as part of the very character of the printing industry which they could do nothing about.

In a comparison of printing practices in four foreign countries and Britain, an E.D.C. report published in March 1970,[7] concluded that many printing companies would have to amalgamate with other printers and publishers, or with companies in other industries, in order that sufficient capital funds and financial security could be obtained. The ability of British companies to compete in world markets, and even in the domestic market, will depend on raising the level of new investment, following the example of overseas printers. With respect to labour relations, the report also calls for a greater sense of involvement of workers in the running of the industry, and an improvement in communications between management and labour. It further stressed the need for more union amalgamations and elimination of union demarcation. This last point is of particular relevance to the national newspapers, the problems of which we now turn to discuss.

Newspapers

The national press is not located entirely within the City boundaries: *The Sunday Times* and the *Guardian* are in W.C.1 and the *Sun* and the *People* are in W.C.2. A central site, however, remains essential, both for the collection and preparation of news and for the national distribution of newspapers. Paddington, the furthest of the main rail terminals, is about twenty minutes away. If the national press is to survive then it has to be in its present location; nor would their premises be of much use to anyone else.

Again, precise employment figures in the national newspaper industry are not available. However, some data have been supplied by the Newspaper Proprietors' Association:

	Sept. 1966	*July* 1967	*Jan.* 1969
Production workers	14,000		
Maintenance workers		1,000	
Clerical workers	4,000		
Journalists	2,700		3,568[8]

[7] *Printing in a Competitive World*, report of the Printing and Publishing E.D.C. Joint Commission to printing companies in five countries, March 1970.

[8] National Board for Prices and Incomes report on '*Journalists' Pay*', Cmnd. 4077, June 1969.

These figures are approximate and relate to regular employees only – about two-thirds of whom would be employed in the City of London. Comparisons over time are difficult, but there has been an increase in maintenance workers of 200 since October 1961 and an increase of 600, since March 1962, in the number of journalists. Numbers employed in administration have almost certainly increased during the period. A complication in assessing changes in employment is that the machine and publishing rooms employ casual workers and decasualization had decreased the number of workers employed on this basis without any apparent effect on the statistics. The introduction of productivity agreements since 1966 suggests that the trend for employment in production and maintenance has been falling since that date.

Output in the industry, measured in terms of total number of pages published per year, rose by 12·3 per cent between 1960 and 1969. However, total weekly circulation of newspapers fell by 10·9 per cent over the same period. Between 1964 and 1969, the total weekly circulation fell by 5·3 per cent although the decline was almost entirely accounted for by the *Daily Express* and the *Daily Mail*. The National Board for Prices and Incomes in its report on the industry,[9] suggested that this illustrates a polarization of readership towards the popular and quality newspapers. This movement appears to have been strongest towards the quality papers which have been the only group to increase their circulation figures since 1964.

In general, the size of the quality newspapers has increased by more than average, examples of this trend being *The Times* Business News, and Sunday colour supplements. This trend has also been reflected in an increasing share of national press advertising revenue, the most important part of which has been classified advertising. Compared to display advertising, classified advertising is less affected by adverse fluctuations in the economy, and has produced a revenue increase of 65 per cent between 1964 and 1969 compared to 26 per cent for all forms of advertising in the national dailies.

One possible effect of the increased coverage mentioned above, is that duplication in the buying of newspapers has fallen (except for quality Sunday papers which are being bought by readers of popular Sunday papers). The purchase of several newspapers to obtain a variety of viewpoints is no longer so important with increased coverage. However, the most important reason for a fall in duplication of buying is 'probably the rise in newspaper prices. Although

9 *Costs and Revenue of National Newspapers*, Cmnd. 4277, February 1970.

the price per page has fallen for some papers, the absolute price has nearly doubled during the 1960s, against a 40 per cent rise in the retail price index.

The Prices and Incomes Board report stated that the major problem in the industry is that fixed costs form between 54 and 79 per cent of total costs. Hence, in order to spread costs and achieve economies of scale a high circulation is required. To raise circulation may require increased news and content coverage leading to additional costs. The financially strongest paper will often lead in such developments causing the weaker papers to follow. As the circulation break-even point is progressively raised, then the weaker papers become financially weaker.

All the factors mentioned above combine to place a number of newspapers printed in the City in their present financial difficulties. An assessment of profitability is difficult because production facilities are often shared with other newspapers or other activities within the Group. However, the Prices and Incomes Board estimates that four national newspapers do not even cover their direct costs of production which puts their future in doubt. A view often expressed in the industry is that the Government should ensure the continued survival of the present number of papers by whatever means necessary. The report questions whether the present number is in any way a special figure that should be maintained. Newpapers should be considered with respect to a framework including all news media. Any special measures, the report adds, to maintain numbers would discriminate against the efficient in favour of the inefficient.

One popular solution put forward for the industry's problems is that newspaper prices should be raised substantially, allowing less dependence on advertising revenue. No historical data exist of large price changes, hence it is impossible to calculate the price elasticity of demand. The Prices and Incomes Board suggests in its report that the 'price solution' takes insufficient account of available means of cutting costs by raising efficiency. An example given is that newsprint costs, which form 50 per cent of production costs and 30 per cent of total costs, could be reduced by £1·2 million at 1969 prices by means of a reduction in wastage.[10]

The Prices and Incomes Board, in its investigations, found that much negotiation had followed the report on the industry produced by the Economist Intelligence Unit.[11] Between 1967 and 1969, man-

[10] Ibid., paras. 33–5.

[11] *The National Newspaper Industry: A Survey*, The Economist Intelligence Unit, 1966.

ning levels in production departments have been reduced by an average of 5 per cent, while productivity – measured in terms of the number of copies multiplied by the number of pages – has risen by an average of 9 per cent. However, the report states that there still remains considerable room for improvements in manning procedures.

In an industry that is highly vulnerable to stoppages (since revenue, once lost, can never be regained) management has been inclined to make quick concessions to safeguard continued output. Hence, no consistent labour relations policy has been created. It is suggested by the Board that productivity bargains should be introduced more rapidly under Prices and Incomes Board guidelines. The report finally recommends that present work-practices should be further overhauled to reduce overmanning before new methods involving new capital investment are introduced.

The future of the national newspapers is also in jeopardy because of demarcation disputes between the National Graphical Association and the Society of Graphical and Allied Trades, the two major unions in the industry. The National Graphical Association represents the established craft structure of the industry. Although N.G.A. members occupy supervisory positions in the production and publishing rooms, they are able to benefit less than S.O.G.A.T. members from productivity agreements causing erosion in wage differentials. The two unions were able to resolve their differences so that the *Sun* could continue in production. Hopefully they should be able to solve their demarcation problems for the long-term benefit of the industry.

Periodical publishing, now concentrated mainly in or near the W.C.2 area, seem likely to remain largely centralized in London. An important element of this which is still located in the City is provided by the high concentration of the editorial offices of International Publishing Corporation periodicals. A senior member of the I.P.C. Corporate Planning Unit confirmed that I.P.C. had examined the possibility of dispersing periodical editorial staffs from central London; they had, however, made a convincing case for staying.

There are no separate figures to indicate the numbers employed editorially on periodicals within the City. The O.S.R.P. returns showed 12,549 office workers in newspapers and periodicals, but we have no means of allocating them between newspapers and periodicals. The I.P.C. annual report for 1966 notes that the National Trade Press, one of its periodical groups, had a staff of 2,300 serving eighty journals.

There is now very little *periodical printing* in the City of London. Over the years, this has been pushed out into the outer suburbs, the provinces, or even abroad. The high cost of labour is, in most cases, the main reason for the movement. In one exceptional case, wages and salaries, as a percentage of sales less materials, had risen to more than 95 per cent, and charges were 40 per cent higher than those of provincial competitors. But the cost of premises, and the limited scope for expansion in the City, are also important factors in the outward movement.

General Printing

Our statistics show 3,474 factory and 5,537 office workers, i.e. just over 9,000, employed in the City under the Minimum List heading 489. Again no split is available into the various categories, but general 'jobbing' printing is certainly by far the biggest category. In 1969, the British Federation of Master Printers (B.F.M.P.) had twenty-nine City members of whom:

16 were general printers,
1 periodical printer,
6 stationery and finishing firms,
4 typesetters, and
2 machinery manufacturers.

These member firms employed about 2,500. The B.F.M.P. estimates total workers in these categories in the City at about 3,500–4,000.

Present B.F.M.P. membership in the City represents a considerable drop in numbers since 1961 when they had fifty member firms employing about 4,500. Of those who have ceased to be members since that date, eight have moved outside the City – three to the provinces, five to the Greater London area; five (mainly small) have discontinued trading; four have merged or been taken over.

While it is generally accepted that little general printing needs to be done in central London, not everyone agrees that even urgent financial printing – company reports and accounts, offers for sale, allotment letters, dividend warrants, etc. – needs to be located in or near the City. Nevertheless, there are obvious advantages in the case of rush work (copy received in the evening, ready next morning), of being in close proximity to customers. Indeed, there is evidence of a return to central London of some urgent work which had been done further out.

Indeed, there can be few jobbing orders which the customer himself does not consider urgent, and with London one of the world's biggest consumers of print, this is a powerful force against the arguments for dispersal. Many provincial printers maintain London offices. Some of the bigger firms remaining in London are located just outside the City boundary.

The general trend has been illustrated by the movement of all H.M.S.O. activities, except printing, publishing and bookselling, to Norwich in accordance with the Government's dispersal policy. Printing has not been transferred, partly because of investment in existing plants. The main rush-work *Hansard*, has to be printed centrally at St Stephen's Press (employing about 650) in S.E.1, south of the river. H.M.S.O.'s chief wholesale bookshop is also south of the river in Stamford Street, S.E.1. About two-thirds of H.M.S.O.'s print requirements are printed under contract by trade printers. H.M.S.O. is in no way inhibited from expanding its own printing facilities, which it would do for special purposes, but it would not envisage expansion in inner London.

Books

For many years, there has been no book printing in London. Book publishing has also largely moved out of the City. Before the last war, many publishers had offices in Paternoster Row, but bomb damage forced them out. Now, the majority of publishers are located in the Bloomsbury area, the West End of London, or in the outer suburbs. The only major publishing house in the City is the Hodder Group of Companies. There are one or two small publishing firms, but these tend to be combined publishing and bookselling businesses, or the type of publishers that issues one directory, probably a specialized financial directory, annually and nothing else. The Publishers' Association believes that many publishers would like to return to the City but cannot because of the higher rents.

Paper and Board

The paper and board industry is shown as providing employment for approximately 2,000 within the City. This is a small proportion of the total employment in the industry and, even so, the estimate is probably on the high side and does not fully reflect the recent movement of paper warehouses across the south bank of the river as a result of redevelopment around Upper Thames Street.

No paper manufacturing takes place in the City, and our analysis shows that two large firms account for 1,100 of the 2,000, of whom the head office of Wiggins Teape employ 800. Like other large paper firms they require a central position, but again they emphasize that this does not have to be in the City. Reeds and Bowaters, for example, are in the West End.

The remainder of the City employment in the category is made up of a number of small firms employing twenty-five or less. Many are merchants or the head offices of small mills, for whom proximity to other merchants rather than to customers has been the primary factor in location. Service to customers is important – delivery within twenty-four hours is expected – but as no merchant can expect to stock the full range of paper it is more important that he should be close to other merchants, from whom he can expect to obtain items which he has not in stock. It is possible that their numbers will be further reduced if competitive pressures force the big paper companies by vertical integration into this field.

Future Outlook

The future of those parts of the printing and publishing industry still remaining in the City is difficult to predict. There is clear evidence that the historical long-term movement out of the City is continuing; certainly there is no evidence of any movement back, or any expansion, that would balance the observed outward movements.

In the case of the national newspapers, a central location remains a basic requirement both for the preparation of news and for comment on matters of national importance, and for distribution and printing. A central location is also necessary for the editorial staffs of many, if not most, periodicals, though not for printing. The factor which has drawn general printing into, and around, the City and will tend to keep it there, despite labour costs and difficulties, is the tremendous market for print which the City and central London provides.

The future of the newspaper industry within the City centres primarily on the possible demise of certain newspapers. There are continuing hopes within the industry that higher prices for newspapers will solve its financial problems. Whether this will prove so remains to be seen, but the probability is that, within the next few years, there will be a further reduction in the number of national dailies, with at least two or three large printing premises becoming redundant. The downward trend in employment (which has been evident since 1966) would then seem likely to continue and this could be further hastened by technical developments which would enable the printing of local editions to be transferred out of London.

We have no figures for the amount of *periodical printing* still being done in the City, but with the closure of the periodicals section of the St Clements Press in June 1965 (making 250 redundant) and the transfer of the printing of *The Economist* and the *Investors Chronicle* out of London (because of persistent high costs and low productivity) it cannot now amount to very much. It is an advantage to the editorial staffs to have the printing works accessible, and a number of I.P.C. periodicals are being printed at their Southwark Offset plant.

As regards *general printing*, the figures supplied by the London Master Printers' Association showed a recent drop in the number of member firms in the City and the numbers they employed. There is general agreement that little general printing needs to be done in the City. There are even views that urgent financial printing can be done some distance out. It seems possible, however, that this view could change and that there will be a stronger appreciation of the need for closer proximity to customers as competition increases, and as a possible change in the demand/supply position for printing labour eases the labour-cost difficulties. There is evidence of urgent printing which had gone out of the City now returning to inner London. The fact that many of these orders call for close personal attention no doubt helps to account for the large number of small firms (one to ten employees) engaged in this work. The bigger and expanding firms (which the British Federation of Master Printers is more likely to represent) will almost certainly need to move out to find room to expand. The small firms may well find an expanding future in or around the City. Total number employed, however, may well continue to decline.

Among the firms that need to be in close proximity with the newspaper publishing business are the suppliers of duplicate printing plates (usually electrotype and stereotype plates for flat-bed letterpress). These plates are needed mainly for advertising matter in the national press, and in many instances orders are shared and have to be carried out within a matter of hours. Advertisements for goods the day after there has been a change in purchase tax is a case in point. Of the thirty-five members of the Electrotype and Stereotype Federation, the majority are concentrated in the E.C.1 district around Clerkenwell; eight are in E.C.4 around Fleet Street.

OTHER MANUFACTURING INDUSTRIES

This group of activities can be dealt with very briefly. Apart from paper, printing and publishing, there were only 3,020 people employed in manufacturing industry in the City in 1966. Of these 1,919 were in clothing and footwear, 322 in fur and 231 in engineering.[12] In each case there has been a marked fall in the numbers employed even in the last decade; in 1957 these three industries employed 5,239. Perhaps the main reason for this decline is that these industries are largely concentrated in areas subject to redevelopment, viz. Houndsditch/Billingsgate (sub-districts 42, 53 and 54). West of Aldersgate (15, 16) and along Upper Thames Street (12). Since redevelopment is not yet complete in some of these districts, we expect the decline in numbers employed to continue.

There is scarcely an important manufacturing establishment outside printing and publishing left in the City. But there are still a large number of very small specialist firms – 120 in clothing, thirty-eight in engineering and fifty-five in fur. They are mostly family businesses which have been established for many years and are able to remain in the City because they are oriented to either (a) the wholesale or commodity market trade, or (b) the printing and publishing industry. In almost every case, the firms are operating in old premises which they own or are leasing at very low rents. No doubt there will always continue to be a need for a few of these firms for specialized processing and maintenance work, but we do not anticipate these will employ more than a few hundred people when all redevelopment has taken place. Their demise is a perfect reflection of the changing economic character of the City mentioned in Chapter 1.

[12] See Table 2.29, p. 121, for further details.

Chapter 12

TRAFFIC IN THE CITY OF LONDON

INTRODUCTION

This chapter is concerned with assessing the extent and character of the flow of vehicular traffic which directly affects the economy of the City. It is divided into four sections. First, we discuss the movement of all kinds of traffic *within* the City. Second, we analyse the composition of commuting traffic *into*, and *out of*, the City. Third, we discuss the generation of commercial traffic using City roads. And fourth, we look into the future prospects of traffic and road use in the City in relation to its likely economic development.

THE FLOW OF TRAFFIC IN THE CITY 1956–66

In recent years, the volume of traffic flowing through the City has declined slightly. Its composition has also changed: there has been a marked increase in private cars, but a fall in heavy traffic, particularly larger commercial vehicles. The trends since 1956, as extracted from Metropolitan and City Police records, are set out in Table 12.1. It can be seen that they are broadly common to central London; the main exception is the 8 per cent decline in goods traffic in the City (cf. a 9 per cent increase in Central London which reflects both the changing economic structure of the City and the fact that, since November 1964, there has been a ban on goods vehicles of over three tons in weight using certain roads in the City).

Going back further, apart from the interruptions of the two world wars, the volume of traffic in the City has increased from the early twentieth century. The first steep rise came in the 1920s, and by 1935 the traffic flow was 60 per cent greater than thirty years earlier. In 1937, 30,129 vehicles passed through the Bank junction in a twelve-hour period and between 15,000 and 22,000 vehicles at other police census points in the City. The cut-back in traffic during the war was not fully made up until the middle 1950s, when it was rising at the

Table 12.1. Composition of Traffic passing through Census Points in Central London over 12-hour day* 1956-66

| Type of vehicle | 1956 | | 1964 | | 1966 | | Increase (+) or Decrease (−) per cent 1966 compared with | | | |
| | | | | | | | 1956 | | 1964 | |
	All census points	City census points	All census points	City census points	All census points	City census points	All census points	City census points	All census points	City census points
Private cars	12,280	9,896	21,130	14,881	22,630	16,009	+84	+62	+7	+7
Commercial vehicles	8,650	9,529	9,710	9,662	9,390	8,808	+9	−8	−3	−9
Public vehicles	2,400	2,511	2,010	1,918	1,790	1,876	−25	−25	−11	−2
Taxis	1,970	2,651	2,230	2,674	2,200	2,856	+12	+8	−1	+7
Motor cycles/scooters	2,130	1,949	2,450	2,765	1,580	1,983	−26	+2	−36	−28
Total	27,430	26,538	37,530	31,904	37,590	31,532	+37	+19	N/C	−1

* In July of each year.

City census points
14 Blackfriars Bridge/Victoria Embankment
35 Bank
36 Ludgate Circus
37 Monument
53 Holborn Circus
64 Cannon St/Q. Victoria St
66 Tower/Hill/East Smithfield
73 Cheapside/Newgate
83 Blackfriars Bridge
84 London Wall/Moorgate (1962, 1964, 1966 only)
87 Grays Inn/High Holborn
89 Bishopsgate/Liverpool St
93 Cheapside/King St
95 London Bridge
97 Bishopsgate/Cornhill
109 Southwark Bridge

Source: Metropolitan Police Records.

rate of 10 per cent every two years. Thereafter, the rate of increase slowed down to 5 per cent between 1960 and 1962, 4 per cent between 1962 and 1964, and to a decline of 1 per cent between 1964 and 1966. The pattern of traffic trends has varied in different parts of the City. At some points, which are normally dominated by the flow of heavy goods traffic, or which, over time, have been partially by-passed by road improvements, the reduction in traffic has been quite marked. By contrast, those intersections through which an increasing volume of commuting vehicles travels each day have seen a slight increase in their traffic. Table 12.2 presents these trends for the sixteen census points in the City. In general, it would seem that most of the City's new traffic problems since the war, and particularly since 1960, have been caused by an increase in private car traffic. Between 1956 and 1966 there was an increase of 54 per cent of this kind of commuting to Central London at a time when all other vehicular traffic in the City fell by 6·7 per cent.

For its periodic surveys of traffic in Central London, the Metropolitan and City Police use 114 census points, most of which were also used in earlier censuses. Compared with the City, the rest of Central London has, on average, a larger traffic flow, particularly of private cars. There is nothing in the City, for example, to compare with the density of traffic flow at Hyde Park Corner or Trafalgar Square; in any case the roads just could not stand it. On the other hand, there are some very busy intersections in or adjacent to the City. The flow of traffic at the junction of Blackfriars Bridge and Victoria Embankment, for example, was exceeded at only thirteen other of the 114 census points in 1966 and was greater than that observed on the M4 motorway. Within the City, the busiest point was the Bank, which came 35th in the list of the 114 census points. Ludgate Circus was 36th and the Monument was 37th. Table 12.3 presents further particulars.

Finally, in this section, we compare traffic trends in the central area as a whole with those of the inner and outer suburbs of Greater London. Table 12.4 reproduces some data supplied to us by the London Transport Board, which show the average number of vehicles passing through census points in various parts of London for 1966 and the changes which have occurred since 1956. Here the definition of the City is not quite the same as that used in Table 12.1; it excludes the three bridges within its boundaries (which are included in 'River Bridges') but includes one or two census points just outside.

Four points stand out from this table. First, of the ten areas classified, the City ranks 6th in traffic intensity; excluding the river

397

Table 12.2. Composition of Traffic passing through Census Points in the City 1956-66

Census Points	Private cars			Commercial			All vehicles		
	1956	1966	Percentage change 1956-66	1956	1966	Percentage change 1956-66	1956	1966	Percentage change 1956-66
1. Blackfriars Bridge Approach	18,577	28,587	+53·9	17,760	15,886	−10·6	49,295	55,020	+11·6
2. Bank of England Junction	13,119	19,404	+47·9	11,585	9,146	−21·1	40,099	41,019	+ 2·3
3. Ludgate Circus	11,781	18,569	+57·6	13,215	12,945	− 2·0	36,793	40,907	+11·2
4. King William St Junction with Cannon St	12,278	19,017	+54·9	12,226	12,687	+ 3·8	34,906	39,956	+14·5
5. Victoria Embankment with Temple Place	15,284	21,157	+38·4	8,451	8,277	− 2·1	32,551	36,431	+11·9
6. Holborn Circus	10,125	17,176	+69·6	8,421	9,221	+ 9·5	27,510	36,035	+31·0
7. Queen Victoria St with Cannon St	11,878	15,875	+33·7	8,510	8,865	+ 4·2	31,791	33,131	+ 4·2
8. Tower Hill with East Smithfield	8,247	13,427	+62·8	15,287	16,234	+ 6·2	27,789	32,930	+18·5
9. Cheapside with Newgate St	10,667	15,830	+48·4	8,934	8,561	− 4·2	27,796	31,554	+13·5
10. Blackfriars Bridge	8,209	13,996	+70·5	10,712	10,122	− 5·5	26,221	29,494	+12·5
11. Moorgate with London Wall	—	14,476	—	—	8,301	—	—	29,296	—
12. Bishopsgate with Liverpool St	8,172	12,084	+47·9	8,658	8,366	− 3·4	27,747	26,691	+ 7·9
13. Cheapside with King St	7,183	12,833	+78·7	5,893	6,184	+ 4·9	19,571	24,799	+26·7
14. London Bridge	7,940	12,182	+53·4	8,520	6,796	−20·2	24,604	24,714	+ 0·4
15. Cornhill with Bishopsgate	7,354	13,001	+76·8	7,006	6,328	− 9·7	21,290	24,288	+14·1
16. Southwark Bridge	2,829	9,492	+235·5	2,441	4,995	+104·6	7,705	16,941	+119·9

Table 12.3. Census of Traffic 1966. Analysis of Vehicles Recorded at
114 Points in London During 12-hour Day from 8.00 to 8.00 p.m.

Ref. No.	*Point*	*12-hr* total*
1	Hyde Park Corner	136
2	Hammersmith Broadway and Flyover	109
3	Marble Arch	86
4	Western Avenue/N. Circular Rd/Hangar Lane	77
5	N. Circular Rd/Hendon Way/(Brent Cross Flyover)	74
6	Trafalgar Square	73
7	Kennington Pk Rd/ Brixton Rd (Kennington Triangle)	65
8	Elephant and Castle	65
9	Piccadilly Circus	64
10	Parliament Square	60
11	Strand/Wellington St/Lancaster Place	59
12	Knightsbridge/Sloan St	56
13	Shepherds Bush Green	55
14	Blackfriars Bridge/Victoria Embankment	55
15	Barnet By-Pass/Watford Way (Apex Corner)	55
16	Gt West Rd/Gunnersbury Avenue/Chiswick High Rd	54
17	Albert Embankment/Vauxhall Bridge (Vauxhall Cross)	54
18	Gt Cambridge Rd/N. Circular Rd	53
19	Euston Rd/Pancras Rd/York Way/Pentonville Rd	53
20	Eastern Avenue/Southend Rd/Colchester Rd	53
21	Kingston By-Pass (Ace of Spades)	50
22	Eastern Avenue/Cranbrook Rd/Woodford Ave	50
23	Edgware Rd/Marylebone Rd/Praed St	49
24	Grosvenor Rd/Chelsea Bridge	46
25	M4 Motorway	46
26	Uxbridge Rd/Greenford Rd/Windmill Lane	45
27	Uxbridge Rd/Hangar Lane/Gunnersbury Ave	44
28	Brixton Rd/Acre Lane	43
29	Finchley Rd/Belsize Rd/Eton Ave	43
30	Notting Hill Gate/Kensington Church St/ Pembridge Rd	43
31	Kensington High St/Holland Rd/Warwick Gdns	42
32	High Rd Tottenham/Broad Lane/West Green Rd	42
33	Portsmouth Rd/Kingston By-Pass	42
34	Whipps Cross Rd/Leytonstone High Rd/ Cambridge Park Rd	41
35	Bank of England Junction	41
36	Ludgate Circus	41

* Totals in thousands, to nearest thousand.

Table 12.3—contd.

Ref. No.	Point	12-hr* total
37	King William St/Cannon St (Monument)	40
38	Camberwell Green	40
39	Blackfriars Rd/Stamford St	39
40	Euston Rd/Evershott St (St Pancras Church)	39
41	N. Circular Rd/High Rd Finchley	38
42	Seven Sisters Rd/Green Lanes (Manor House)	38
43	Barking Rd/Liverpool Rd/Silvertown Way	38
44	Grays Inn Rd/Theobalds Rd	38
45	Kingston By-Pass/Robin Hood Gate	38
46	Stratford Broadway	38
47	Sidcup Rd/Westhouse Avenue	38
48	Bath Rd/Gt West Rd (Traveller's Friend)	37
49	Old Kent Rd/New Kent Rd/Tower Bridge Rd	36
50	Victoria Embankment/Temple Place	36
51	Whitechapel High St/Mansell St/Commercial Rd/Leman St	36
52	Putney Bridge	36
53	Holborn Circus	36
54	Westminster Bridge	36
55	Old St/Kingsland Rd	36
56	Wandsworth High St/Garratt Lane/York Rd	35
57	Charing Cross Rd/Shaftesbury Avenue	35
58	N. Circular Rd/Chingford Rd (Crooked Billet)	35
59	City Rd/Goswell Rd (Angel, Islington)	35
60	E. Ham and Barking By-Pass/High St South/E. Ham Manor Way	34
61	Grove Rd/Southend Rd/High Rd, S. Woodford	33
62	Old St/City Rd	33
63	St George's Circus	33
64	Queen Victoria St/Cannon St	33
65	Morden Rd/Kingston Rd, S. Wimbledon	33
66	Tower Hill/E. Smithfield	33
67	Waterloo Bridge	33
68	Kingston Bridge	33
69	Clapham High St/The Pavement/South Side	32
70	Ilford Lane/High Rd, Ilford/Cranbrooke Rd	32
71	Streatham High Rd/Mitcham Lane/Tooting Bec Gardens	32
72	Clerkenwell Rd/Farringdon Rd	32
73	Cheapside/Newgate St	32
74	Kew Bridge	31
75	Hampton Court Bridge	31
76	Cricklewood Broadway/Cricklewood Lane	31
77	Lewisham Way/New Cross Rd (Marquis of Granby)	31

* Totals in thousands, to nearest thousand.

Table 12.3—contd.

Ref. No.	Point	12-hr* total
78	Vauxhall Bridge	31
79	Sutton By-Pass/Rose Hill/Bishopsford Rd	30
80	Ripple Rd/Heathway/New Rd, Dagenham	30
81	Kingsland Rd/Balls Pond Rd	30
82	London Rd/Thornton Rd (Thornton Heath Rd)	30
83	Blackfriars Bridge	29
84	Moorgate/London Wall/Fore St	29
85	Borough High St/Luke St Hill	29
86	Lordship Lane/Dulwich Common	28
87	Grays Inn Rd/High Holborn	28
88	Gt South West Rd/Staines Rd	27
89	Bishopsgate/Liverpool St/Houndsditch	27
90	Shooters Hill Rd/Rochester Way	26
91	Chelsea Bridge	26
92	Twickenham Bridge	26
93	Cheapside/King St/Queen St	25
94	High St/North St/South St, Romford	25
95	London Bridge	25
96	Holloway Rd/Archway Rd (The Archway)	25
97	Cornhill/Bishopsgate	24
98	Hammersmith Bridge	24
99	Staines By-Pass Bridge	23
100	Harrow Rd/Bridgewater Rd	23
101	High St, Harlesden/Station Rd/Manor Park Rd	22
102	Bromley Rd/Beckenham Hill Rd (Peter Pan Pool)	22
103	Chiswick Bridge	21
104	Tower Bridge	20
105	Blackwall Tunnel	20
106	Lambeth Bridge	18
107	Wandsworth Bridge	17
108	Staines Bridge	17
109	Southwark Bridge	17
110	Battersea Bridge	15
111	Richmond Bridge	14
112	Rotherhithe Tunnel	14
113	Albert Bridge	14
114	Woolwich Free Ferry	2

* Totals in thousands, to nearest thousand.

bridges only the outer suburbs south of the Thames ranks lower. Second, the greatest increase in the flow of vehicles since 1956 has occurred in outer London; the increases in the various parts of Central London have been much less and of the same order as each other. Third, this substantial rise in outer London traffic is explained almost entirely by the increase in private car traffic. Fourth, the City still has a higher proportion of commercial traffic of one kind or another than any other part of London.

Table 12.4. Average Number of Vehicles passing through Census Points by Zones 1966

Zone	All vehicles			Private cars only				
	1966	Increase per cent compared with		1966	Increase per cent compared with		Per cent of all vehicles	
		1956	1964		1956	1964	1956	1966
Central Area								
City	34,970	24	−3	17,560	68	7	37	50
West End	62,250	24	−4	34,540	59	—	43	55
River bridges	25,630	24	−3	13,860	74	5	38	54
South of river	43,080	18	−2	24,670	69	10	40	57
	41,300	23	−3	22,150	65	4	40	54
Inner Suburbs								
North of Thames	45,310	49	1	28,630	102	7	46	63
South of Thames	39,670	30	—	24,380	86	9	43	61
River bridges	20,220	50	4	13,720	92	8	53	68
	36,070	43	1	22,900	95	8	46	63
Outer Suburbs								
North of Thames	40,590	57	6	26,660	100	11	51	66
South of Thames	30,370	60	4	21,320	105	10	55	70
River bridges	20,550	88	5	15,350	136	9	60	75
	33,960	60	5	23,040	105	11	53	68
All points	37,590	37	—	22,630	84	7	45	60

Source: London Transport Board.

THE ORIGIN OF TRAFFIC − COMMUTING

Road traffic in the City is used to carry both people and goods. Most of the former type of traffic is closely associated with two things; (a) the level and structure of commuting; and (b) the level and structure of intra-City or intra-Central London business visiting. Goods traffic is either delivering goods to or from City institutions, or passing through the City to other destinations. We propose to look at these origins of traffic movement separately.

Compared to the volume of traffic generated outside its boundaries by the commuting labour force, that generated within the City (at least above ground) is comparatively small. But it is, in the form of the private car, of growing significance and involves not only the use of City roads but also car parking space, certain servicing facilities, e.g. petrol stations, and manpower, e.g. car-park attendants, police, traffic wardens, etc.

Table 12.5 presents the broad picture of passenger traffic entering Central London during the morning peak over the last ten years. It reveals a steady rise in the use of rail transport up to 1962 in the case of the underground, and up to 1964 in the case of British Rail, after which there was a slight decline. The use of public road transport has fallen throughout the period, as has that of two-wheeled private transport. Moreover, in terms of *numbers* of road vehicles entering the City (as opposed to people carried by these vehicles), the increase in motor cars has far outstripped the fall in buses. A London Transport Board survey shows that there were 70,500 cars entering the Central Area between 7 a.m. and 10 a.m. on a July day in 1966, of which about a third entered the City. It was estimated that these cars contained about 100,000 occupants and that 67·4 per cent carried only the driver, between 1957 and 1966, the average occupancy per car fell from 1·50 to 1·42 persons.

The rapid decline in two-wheeled traffic since 1962 is symptomatic of national trends. If we look simply at the various forms of motorized bicycles, we find that new registrations in Great Britain rose to an all-time peak in 1959, declined to a trough in 1962, turned upwards to reach a secondary peak in 1964, and have since fallen again. For the three years 1958–60, new registrations totalled 813,000; in the period 1962–4 they were only 497,000. It is possible to explain this fall and the related rise in motor vehicle traffic in terms of growing national affluence. But it is also noticeable, from the way in which the various types of road traffic are distributed at different census points in Central London, that the proportion of two-wheel traffic is less where the traffic is the most dense. This would suggest that as roads become more crowded people become less willing to ride motor and pedal cycles on them.

The more gradual reduction in bus and coach traffic entering

403

Table 12.5. Passenger Traffic into Central London (Inner Cordon) during the Morning Peak (7 a.m.–10 a.m.) 1956–66
(thousands)

	1956	1957	1958	1959	1960	1961	1962	1963	1964	1965	1966
By Public Transport											
British Rail	414	426	440	438	453	475	473	477	492	482	484
Underground	480	471	486	501	520	529	545	527	520	524	519
Total (excl. double counting)	791	791	816	830	860	885	900	885	889	886	882
Road Services	259	258	234	222	215	209	215	191*	191	180	175
Total	1,050	1,049	1,050	1,052	1,075	1,094	1,115	1,076	1,080	1,066	1,057
By Private Transport											
Private car	65	69	79	83	85	89	94	95	98	99	100
Motor cycle/scooter	11	11	17	18	21	20	20	18	16	13	11
Pedal cycle	13	9	14	12	11	10	9	7	6	5	4
Total	89	89	110	113	117	119	123	120	120	117	115
Grand Total	1,139	1,138	1,160	1,165	1,192	1,213	1,238	1,196	1,200	1,183	1,172
By rail	791	791	816	830	860	885	900	885	889	886	882
By road	348	347	344	335	332	328	338	311	311	297	290

* Affected by the ban on overtime and rest day working.

Source: London Transport Board.

Central London reflects a variety of factors, including rising living standards. For as the bus has become a less popular means of transport, both the private car and the taxi have become more popular. On the other hand, the growing congestion of Central London roads and unreliability of bus services has tended to favour the underground for intra-London travelling; while, because of the decline in short-distance commuting, less people are now coming to work by bus or coach. As mentioned in Chapters 2 and 6, the occupational structure of the City's labour force is changing. This partly explains why the fall in bus traffic in the City has been particularly noticeable in the early hours of the morning, i.e. before 9 a.m.

A *Social Survey* conducted by the Corporation, in 1966 based upon a 5 per cent sample of the working population in the City, revealed that rail travel was by far the most usual form of transport by commuters. Not allowing for double counting – i.e. some people use more than one mode of transport in their journey to work – the *Survey* revealed the following results.

Journeys to Work in the City on a Particular Day, 1966

Journeys to work using main line railway stations	198,573
Journeys to work using underground stations	134,116
Journeys to work using buses	40,901
Journeys to work using motor cycles or scooters	2,997
Journeys to work using bicycles	916
Journeys to work using motor cars	
(i) commuting	7,917
(ii) business	6,947
Total	392,367
Total persons estimated to be working in City	316,836
Discrepancy due to persons using more than one of transport	75,531

It will be noted that the use of motor cars recorded in this survey is very much lower than the net figure of approximately 23,000 cars entering the City between 7 a.m. and 10 a.m. according to the London Transport Board survey.

Table 12.6 shows the destination of B.R. travellers by London termini. The importance of Cannon Street, Broad Street, Liverpool Street and London Bridge is clearly seen. These four termini serve three in five City commuters. On the other hand, the stations serving the west and north of London – Paddington through to King's Cross – are used by only 6 per cent of the commuting traffic. Of the underground stations, the Bank with 39,305 passengers accounts for

Table 12.6. Estimated Number of Passengers using Main Line London Termini and Working in the City 1966. (Based on morning arrivals)

		Per cent
1. Stations serving areas north-east and east of City		
(a) Broad St and Liverpool St	48,057	
(b) Fenchurch St	19,238	
	67,295	33·8
2. Stations serving areas south-east of City		
(a) Cannon St	42,653	
(b) Blackfriars	12,490	
(c) Holborn Viaduct	9,306	
(d) London Bridge*	32,060	
	96,509	48·5
3. Stations serving areas south and south-west of City		
(a) Waterloo	23,447	
(b) Victoria and Charing Cross†	3,006	
	26,453	13·5
4. Stations serving areas west and north of City		
(a) Marylebone and Paddington	2,913	
(b) King's Cross, St Pancras and Euston	5,403	
	8,316	4·2
	198,573	100·0

* Also serves areas to south of City.
† Charing Cross also serves areas to south-east of City.
Source: Social Survey 1966.

nearly one-third of all underground users, of whom nearly three-fifths travel on the Bank/Waterloo route. The pattern of arrivals and departures by time of day, reveals that there is a marked concentration of commuter arrivals between 8.45 a.m. and 9.30 a.m. and departures between 5 p.m. and 5.45 p.m. Probably three-quarters of all the City commuters arrive and depart at these times. Another survey (unpublished) undertaken by British Rail, shows that of the 88,000 travellers on Southern Region into the stations serving the City in March 1966, 74 per cent were due to start work between 9 and 10 a.m. Table 12.7 sets out the ranking of arrival times, by number of passengers involved, of three underground lines and the average of the main lines into City termini. The fact that passengers on the main lines tend to arrive rather earlier is very evident. There

Table 12.7. Ranking of Arrival Times of Railway Passengers into the City by Route Used 1966

	Metro-politan Line	Central Line	District Line	Northern Line	B.R. Line
7.00–7.15 a.m.	1	1	1	2	1
7.15–7.30 a.m.	2	2	2	1	2
7.30–7.45 a.m.	3	3	3	4	4
7.45–8.00 a.m.	5	4	4	7	5
8.00–8.15 a.m.	6	6	5	6	7
8.15–8.30 a.m.	7	7	7	5	8
8.30–8.45 a.m.	9	8	8	9	11
8.45–9.00 a.m.	12	10	12	11	12
9.00–9.15 a.m.	11	12	11	10	10
9.15–9.30 a.m.	10	11	10	12	9
9.30–9.45 a.m.	8	9	9	8	6
9.45–10.00 a.m.	4	5	6	3	3

Source: Social Survey 1966.

does not appear to have been any significant change in the time profiles of arrivals over the last ten years; save that the proportion of passengers travelling at the height of the peak has increased slightly.

The *Social Survey* also classified commuters arriving at various London termini and underground stations according to their final destination. While it is clear that passengers arriving at underground stations worked in establishments near to these stations, there is no such obvious spatial relationship between main line termini used and place of work. To take two examples from Table 12.8, quite a large proportion of people from the South-Eastern Division of the Southern Region work in the west of the City, while an above-average proportion from the Central Division travel to the east of the City.

407

We have made an approximate assessment of journey times into the City for Southern Region commuters. For stations on main lines and principal branch lines, we noted the time taken at the peak hour to reach London Bridge in May 1964. Minor branch lines were not treated station by station: we took an average time from an approximately central station on the branch. According to these time-estimates the stations (or groups of stations) were then divided between five time-bands, each of twenty minutes duration. Stations close to London Bridge were in the first, those involving between twenty and forty minutes were in the second, and so on. The last band represented a journey exceeding eighty minutes. These bands were then divided into zones, according to the broad direction of travel. In all, there were thirty-seven zones.

Table 12.8. Passengers Travelling from the Sub-divisions of the Southern Region to Different Parts of the City 1966

| Sub-Division of S.R. | Part of City of London | | | |
	Western part	Central part	Eastern part	Total
South-Eastern	14·2	19·0	11·6	44·8
Central	9·2	15·5	10·8	35·5
South-Western	5·7	7·7	4·4	17·8
Total	29·1	42·2	26·8	98·1

Notes:
1. Eastern part includes:
   zones 716, 717, 719, 722 (as defined in London Traffic Survey).
2. Central part includes:
   zones 720, 721, 728 (as defined in London Traffic Survey).
3. Western part includes:
   zones 727, 729, 730, 731, 732 (as defined in London Traffic Survey).
   Source: Southern Region, British Rail.

The broad results of this survey are presented in Figure 12·1 and Table 12·9: this latter table also sets out the findings of the Shell International Company of a similar survey of its Central London employees in 1960. Clearly about two-thirds of those commuting by train spend under half an hour on their journey. One suspects, however, that the total travelling time of the commuters would be between forty minutes and an hour.

The impact of day commuting on rail services varies from area to area. On British Rail, the most critical sector is the South-Eastern

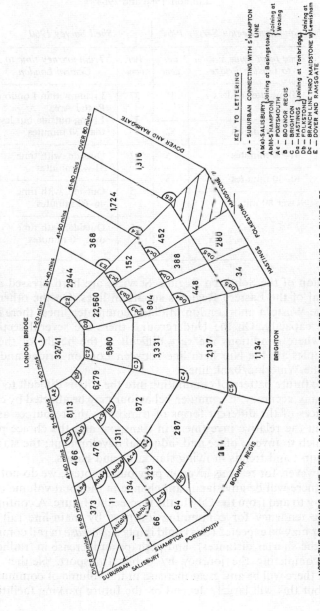

FIGURE 12.1 DISTRIBUTION OF COMMUTERS TRAVELLING ON SOUTHERN REGION TRAINS BY ZONES
MAY 1964. TOTAL COMMUTERS: 98,176

KEY TO LETTERING

Aa - SUBURBAN CONNECTING WITH S'HAMPTON LINE
Ab(a)-SALISBURY } Joining at Basingstoke
Ab(b)-S'HAMPTON } Joining at Woking
Ac - PORTSMOUTH
B — BOGNOR REGIS
C — BRIGHTON
Da — HASTINGS } Joining at Tonbridge
Db — FOLKSTONE } Joining at Maidstone w/Lewisham
Dc — BRANCH LINE THRO' MAIDSTONE w/Lewisham
E — DOVER AND RAMSGATE

NOTE: THE 37 ZONES HAVE BEEN CLASSIFIED ACCORDING TO THE AVERAGE TIME IT TAKES TO REACH LONDON BRIDGE FROM ALL STATIONS IN THE GROUP.

409

Table 12.9. Rail Travelling Times of Commuters into Central
London 1960 and 1964

Southern Region Survey 1964			Shell Survey 1960
Time from home station to London Bridge	*Per cent*	*Per cent*	*Train journey time to Central London*
20 minutes or less	35	37	Living within London Postal Area
21–40 minutes	52	35	Living outside but less than 30 minutes
41–60 minutes	5	17	Outside, with time 31–45 minutes
61–80 minutes	5		
Over 80 minutes	8	5	Outside, with time 46–60 minutes
		5	Outside, with time over 60 minutes

Division of the Southern Region. Services are hard pressed also on several of the Eastern Region's suburban lines. On the other hand, on the Western and London Midland commuter lines, there is some spare capacity. On the Underground there are several sections of line where conditions are very difficult at the height of the peak. Examples are the Northern line between London Bridge and Bank, and the Waterloo/Bank line.

The future pattern of commuting into the City is difficult to predict with any accuracy. Commuter behaviour may be affected by changes in prices of the different forms of transport; the resources as available in the relative investment in transport and the choice projects in which to invest; office and industrial development; the staggering of hours; and trends in living standards and habits.

However, for reasons given in previous chapters, we do not anticipate there will be any significant change in the total volume of commuting to and from the City in the foreseeable future. A continuation of the tendency for commuting journeys by main-line rail to get longer may be expected (this could imply a *decrease* in rail commuting over the shorter distances); and perhaps an increase in 'railheading' and completing the journey by public transport. Neither do we think there will be any great increase in the volume of commuting by car, but this will largely depend on the future parking facilities and traffic management in the City – a subject which is worth exploring in a little more detail.

CAR-PARKING IN THE CITY

At the time of the 1965–6 land-use survey, there was accommodation in off-street car-parks for 9,873 cars. More than half of these places were in private car-parks inaccessible to the public. Those attached to offices accounted for 1·8 million sq. ft – about one-fifth of the site area on which the offices are situated. 146 buildings in the City had their own car-parking facilities which were fully operational. Of these, only seven had no public off-street car-park (either permanent or temporary) within 400 yards. There were 1,170 places available in temporary public car-parks, and 2,947 places in permanent public car-parks. The location of these parks is largely peripheral but few places in the City are more than a quarter of a mile from one or other of them. Since the survey was completed, rather more than 1,000 additional spaces have been created in new buildings, and permanent car-parks, but there are fewer places available in temporary car-parks. In the Autumn of 1969, there were 6,409 private off-street parking spaces and 3,609 public off-street spaces. In addition some 1,400 street parking meters were in operation, and there was a small amount of residential parking. The total provision was thus sufficient to accommodate about 12,000 cars. In addition to this there are several sizeable car-parks just outside the City.

If we take a working population in the City of about 350,000, and assume a car occupancy of 1·42 persons, then the car-parks and meter spaces actually within the City can at present accommodate just over 6 per cent of its work force; however, about a seventh of these would have to park at meters, and would be commiting offences if they did not move their cars after two hours. In the Shell survey mentioned earlier, car and cycle users formed about 6 per cent of the company's Central London work force. This is about the same as the percentage of the City's day population which can currently park within the City if they make full use of on and off-street facilities and takes no account of the needs of the business callers.

In 1965, the City Corporation estimated that, at any moment of the working day, about 20 per cent of its street parking bays were unused. This is an estimate which has to be treated with some caution as it is based on the addition of several overlapping sets of observations. This means that some meters were counted more than once. The Ministry of Transport publication *Parking – The Next Stage*

411

(1963), written before the City became a completely restricted zone (which it did in August 1965) gives a higher utilization figure. For weekday observations between 10 a.m. and 2 p.m. in the Guildhall area, sixteen observed meters showed 100 per cent utilization. In the Smithfield area, 121 meters were observed and showed 98 per cent utilization. According to a senior member of the City Police, meter bay utilization is, currently, well above 90 per cent.

It is possible to obtain some confirmation of this view by looking at the number of excess charge tickets issued by traffic wardens and fines levied for parking in a restricted area in recent years. The former rose from 26,236 in 1963 to 40,222 in 1966; the latter from 16,000 in 1964 to 28,000 in 1966. But part of the explanation for these figures lies in the extension of the restricted area in March 1963 and again in August 1965.

It would be interesting to know the extent to which street parking is used by business callers rather than by people who work in the City. According to the Ministry of Transport,[1] business visitors account for about 75 per cent of meter use in Central London, but the extent to which 'musical cars' is played in the City suggests that there the business caller is more frequently frustrated by the commuter. In his 'Traffic in Towns' Professor Colin Buchanan estimated that in the West End Central Area there were 750 meters, spread out over an area of 148 acres to meet the needs of a working population of 50,000. To provide comparable street facilities for short term parking on an area basis, the City should have over 3,000 meters: on a *working population* basis it should have nearer 5,000 meters. Although these calculations do not take account of public car-park facilities, such figures as are available, suggest that these cater for the commuter who wishes to leave his car there all day rather than for the business caller. On the other hand, the business caller is well served by taxis and the City is a more compact pedestrian area than the West End.

The Corporation's survey of off-street parking, completed in 1965, suggested a utilization rate of about 80 per cent for both public and private parks. The public parks charge widely different rates, ranging from 25p to 55p per day for the open temporary parks up to between 10p and £1·075 per day for the covered permanent parks. The percentage of these facilities in regular use varies between location and, to some extent, according to charge; although the more centrally located car-parks are fully subscribed and occupied for most of the day. Since about four-fifths of the space in these parks is taken up

[1] *Ministry of Transport Parking Meter Traffic in Towns Inquiry* (The Buchanan Report, S.I.G.M.A. 1966), H.M.S.O., 1963, pp. 127–8.

by those who work in the City, the casual visitor has only about 2,000 bays at which he may compete with other drivers for accommodation. This falls well short of West End standards, but of course takes no account of parking facilities just outside the City.

It would be wrong to suggest that limited parking is the only, or even the main, deterrent to the use of the car for commuting. The experience of the Shell Company suggests that, if there are adequate private parking facilities, one can expect the use of the car to increase, but no less important is the distance travelled and the conditions of the roads. For people living in Central London and the inner suburbs a car journey is not too tedious, but for those living further out it can be a deterrent. At the same time, a variety of studies have shown that improvements in roads leading into London lead to greater use of cars. As the journey becomes easier, more people make it.

There is only limited provision for coach parking in the City. Tourist organizations claim that they have considerable difficulty in organizing tours because of this. There is provision for thirty coaches in the Tower Hill park, but on an average day in the tourist season, between 10 a.m. and midday, and from 2 p.m. until 4 p.m. there may be as many as forty coaches visiting the Tower at any one time. The recently completed Minories scheme will help to some extent; it offers forty-six spaces for lorries and coaches, and 590 spaces for private cars. However, unless there are loading and unloading facilities near to the buildings which are to be visited, the organization of tours, which is quite an important foreign currency-earning activity, is bound to be hampered.

Another area with a similar problem is St Paul's Churchyard. Provision is planned for about twelve spaces of coach parking here, but estimates of the coaches now parked as close as they can get to the Cathedral, at peak tourist times range from twenty-five to forty. Most of the coaches that visit the Tower also visit the Cathedral. One possible solution to this problem is for some of the car-parking spaces in the Paternoster development scheme which are unused by people working in those buildings to be converted into coach spaces.

Lorry parking is a different problem, and becomes at times indistinguishable from that of loading and unloading. Part of the Smithfield Market area is in an unrestricted zone for lorries, and there is a lorry park just north of it, outside the City, which is used for overnight parking. Lorry meter bays which were provided by the Corporation on the Embankment were poorly utilized and are to be turned over to cars. On the whole, the police and wardens are lenient in their treatment of lorry drivers whose loading and un-loading activities cause them to exceed the specified maximum waiting times, but in many areas collection and delivery is still very difficult.

THE ORIGIN OF TRAFFIC – GOODS VEHICLES

Some information about goods traffic in Central London is to be found in the publication *Better Use of Town Roads*.[2] It is based largely on the G.L.C. 1962 *London Traffic Survey*. Measured in passenger car units, about 24 per cent of peak hour traffic across the Central London river bridges consisted of goods vehicles. Half of this consisted of heavy vehicles (i.e. vehicles of over 3 tons unladen weight). During an average twenty-four hours, goods vehicles formed 36 per cent of the traffic, of which about three-fifths were heavy vehicles.

The London Traffic Survey showed that between 8 a.m. and 7 p.m. on a normal weekday in 1962, about 250,000 vehicles entered the Central London area. Forty-two per cent of these were private cars going to destinations within the area, 25 per cent were buses, taxis and motor cycles, 18 per cent were goods vehicles delivering to points *within* the area and the remaining 15 per cent – some 37,000 vehicles – were cars and goods vehicles passing *through* the area.

For the Survey area as a whole – which was slightly larger than Greater London – 56 per cent of the total journeys recorded by goods vehicles were for retail deliveries, 10 per cent for wholesale deliveries and 10 per cent for services, maintenance and repairs. Goods vehicles journeys which originate *outside* the area amounted to only about 5 per cent of the journeys excluding retail deliveries originating *within* the area. Unfortunately, the report does not say how many of these latter journeys were for destinations outside London; nor does it take account of goods carried long distances in several stages.

Some idea of the goods traffic in City streets is obtainable from the Metropolitan Police censuses. For example, in 1966, 5,137 light vans, 3,629 heavier two-axled commercial vehicles, and 380 larger commercial vehicles passed through the Bank junction over a period of twelve hours. Together they accounted for 22 per cent of the total number of vehicles recorded there.

The numbers of goods vehicles, and their proportion to the total traffic, passing through other census points in the City, is shown in Table 12.10. This distribution is clearly a function of (a)

[2] *Better Use of Town Roads*, Ministry of Transport, 1967, p. 9.

Table 12.10. Goods Vehicles passing through Census Points in the City 1966

Census points	Light vans	Class 1	Class 2	Class 3	All vehicles	(Percentage of all vehicles)			
						Light vans	Class 1	Class 2	Class 3
Blackfriars Bridge/Victoria Embankment	8,036	5,828	573	1,449	55,020	14·6	10·6	1·0	2·6
Bank of England Junction	5,137	3,629	128	252	41,019	12·5	8·8	0·3	0·6
Ludgate Circus	6,607	4,927	416	995	40,907	16·2	12·0	1·0	2·4
King William St/Cannon St	6,309	4,938	447	993	39,956	15·8	12·4	1·1	2·5
Victoria Embankment/Temple Place	4,468	2,963	274	572	36,431	12·3	8·1	0·8	1·6
Holborn Circus	6,390	2,354	154	323	36,035	17·7	6·5	0·4	0·9
Queen Victoria St/Cannon St	4,365	3,158	422	920	33,131	13·2	9·5	1·3	2·8
Tower Hill/East Smithfield	4,059	6,680	1,592	3,900	32,930	12·3	20·3	4·8	11·8
Cheapside/Newgate St	5,133	2,912	123	393	31,554	16·3	9·2	0·4	1·2
Blackfriars Bridge	5,097	3,043	233	847	29,494	17·3	13·4	0·8	2·9
Moorgate/London Wall	5,100	2,644	231	326	29,296	17·4	9·0	0·8	1·1
Bishopsgate/Liverpool St	4,979	2,601	309	477	26,691	18·7	9·7	1·2	1·8
Cheapside/King St	4,096	1,824	47	217	24,799	16·5	7·4	0·2	0·9
London Bridge	3,478	2,823	204	291	24,714	14·1	11·4	0·8	1·2
Cornhill/Bishopsgate	3,750	2,284	76	218	24,288	15·4	9·4	0·3	0·9
Southwark Bridge	2,940	1,716	120	219	16,941	17·4	10·1	0·7	1·3

415

the structure of economic activity in the City, (b) the road system of the City – particularly as it affects west/east through traffic, and (c) the role of the Port of London. We deal with these last two points first.

The road system in the City has remained basically unchanged for many years. It was described succinctly in the Corporation's own publication *The City of London – A record of destruction and survival* published in 1951. We repeat the two relevant paragraphs here:

The City is curiously served in the distribution of its existing roads. The most southerly route, Thames Street, is blocked during part of the day by Billingsgate traffic and other warehouse vehicles. The next route (Queen Victoria Street, Cannon Street and Eastcheap) has difficult crossings at the Mansion House and London Bridge. The next west–east route (which is Holborn, Newgate, Cheapside, Cornhill, Leadenhall Street and Aldgate) is the most direct way through the City, and also, because of the narrowness of the road in some parts and the frequency of its crossings, the slowest. North of this cross-route there is practically no main thoroughfare going from west to east, and it is one of the proposals in the plan that a new road should be provided between Gray's Inn Road and Liverpool Street on the northern boundary of the City, and that there should be a new circulating street approximately midway between this and Cheapside. This new street would be a general distributive channel opening up new business frontages in the devastated area north-east of St Paul's, and it would follow generally the line of London Wall.

'The north-south routes all come to bridgeheads. The most important from the traffic point of view are those which cross Blackfriars and London Bridges. The former is relatively broad, the only difficulty being the approach at Blackfriars where there is no continuous traffic flow owing to the levels and the confluence of so many streets. Far more intractable is the other main north–south crossing which uses London Bridge. . . . This route, which passes east of Liverpool Street Station, comes down through Bishopsgate and Gracechurch Street to a very difficult traffic knot at London Bridgehead. The roads cannot be widened except at great expense; and the only alternative is to sink a road for the through-traffic in a cut or tunnel, leaving the existing level for local traffic. This, however, is an improvement which cannot be carried out for some time. Meanwhile proposals are made for a roundabout at London Bridgehead to distribute the traffic and maintain a continuous movement of vehicles.'

Despite various road improvement schemes notably the Blackfriars underpass and the construction of new highways in the re-developed areas of the City – especially London Wall – the conges-tion problem which faced the City seventeen years ago remains today to a greater or lesser degree.

Undoubtedly, one of the largest generators of goods traffic is the Port of London. In the year ending March 1969, its total trade was 58·0 million tons, a quarter of the national tonnage. Much of this trade does not touch inner London: indeed it has been estimated that only about 2 million tons of imports and the same quantity of exports are actually transferred 'between land and water transport within the enclosed docks of the built-up-area of London'.

At the same time, the *London Traffic Survey* revealed that about two-thirds of the heavy lorries going to or from the dock gates made journeys of less than two miles. Although the Port serves the country, the 6–7 million tons of cargo transported to or from it by road each year may do so in several stages. The daily journeys labelled 'whole-sale to the docks' in the *Traffic Survey* have to be augmented by those that go to or from intermediate destinations. Even the goods which are discharged into barges probably complete their journey by road, sometimes from wharves and warehouses within the City.

In the course of our inquiry we obtained new information about the quantity of traffic generated by the activities of a group of wharfingers. Collectively, the wharves we examined had a river frontage of over 3,000 feet in 1967, and occupied an area of almost 100,000 sq. yd.[3] Each group has premises comprising multi-storey warehouses, cold stores, cool-air stores and offices.

The volume of commodities arriving by river at these wharves shows a marked downward trend since 1960. This is in line with our findings in Chapter 10. Nevertheless, over 500,000 tons of produce was unloaded each year to be transported inland by road. These wharves are on the south bank of the river adjoining the City. Un-fortunately, we do not have direct estimates of the proportion of this traffic that goes north of the river by way of the City bridges. How-ever, if we assume the proportion of northbound traffic originating from other wharfingers to be fairly representative, these wharves could be responsible for up to 370 vehicles per day travelling on City roads.

On the one day in 1967, for which we have information, about 700 vehicles called at these wharves for loading or unloading. Not all loading and unloading is carried out within the premises of these

---

[3] Since that date a number of the wharves have been closed.

o

wharves. Some vehicles are dealt with in the surrounding streets. Some calling at wharves were dealt with in as little as five minutes; others had to wait for up to eleven hours. The average waiting time for vehicles appears to be about 2¾ hours, but this varies considerably from wharf to wharf, and from one group of wharves to another. In one case, 55 per cent of the vehicles that arrived and were 'booked in between 7 a.m. and 8 a.m. were still waiting to be dealt with by noon. At 3 p.m., 28 per cent of them had still not been dealt with. It is not unknown for vehicles arriving at wharves at 7 a.m. to be turned away unloaded after 4 p.m. when labour declines to work overtime. The longest waiting periods appear to be experienced at cool-air stores, some of which show *average* waiting periods of nearly six hours.

Vehicles waiting to be loaded or unloaded do not necessarily remain in the immediate vicinity of the wharves. They may be unable to park in this area, and it is known that vehicles, having 'booked-in', do move away and return before they expect to be dealt with. In this way it is likely that congestion is exported from the immediate area surrounding wharves. There does, however, appear to be at least a prima facie case to be made for timed deliveries and timed collections at wharves.

Almost certainly, the trade generated by the Port of London, which passes through the City, will fall further in the future. This is not because of the closure of some of the inner docks and the smaller proportion of goods which will be shipped upstream to be discharged at City wharves and warehouses; but because, as we saw in Chapter 10, developments in the structure of inland distribution and the nature of commodity trading in the City are tending to diminish the need for wholesaling and storage activities to be located in the vicinity of the Port.

When we turn to look at the wider pattern of economic activity in the City, we see there are two main sectors which account for the bulk of goods traffic generated from *within* the City. These are (a) the wholesale food markets and (b) the newspaper publishing industry. The demands made on City roads by the wholesale goods markets have been dealt with in Chapter 10. We now pay brief attention to the goods traffic arising out of the newspaper and publishing trade in Fleet Street.

The distribution of morning or weekly papers does not seriously interfere with day time traffic in the City, but evening papers are a different proposition. For example the *Evening News*, which has a daily printing of almost two million copies, uses over 300 vans.

About 45 per cent of the print is distributed by road, the rest goes by road to railway stations. A very rough statement of the time profile of van departures from the office is:

9.30 a.m.	about	300 vans
11 a.m.	about	75 vans
1.30 p.m.	about	300 vans
2 p.m.	about	220 vans
3 p.m.	about	150 vans
4 p.m.	about	130 vans
5 p.m.	about	75 vans

The same newspaper receives about 35 lorries of newsprint a day. Most of these deliveries are made at night to avoid interference with distribution, but at 4.30 p.m. on a day in July 1967, of the eight lorries parking in adjoining streets awaiting access to the loading bays, two were carrying newsprint for the *Evening News*.

Distribution of *The Times* and *The Observer* does not present any problems of any concern to us, but we may note that each weekday *The Times* receives seven or eight large lorries of newsprint. There are two collections of waste in a week, and three lorry-loads of printers' ink. Each day there are three G.P.O. collections from the building. There is a weekly delivery of stationery, and every lunch-time about five vans deliver to the canteen.

We do not foresee that the volume of goods traffic originating from the newspaper industry will greatly change in the near future – certainly not as much as it has done in the last ten years. It is possible, of course, that the size of papers (in terms of numbers of pages) will further increase, and supplements, of one kind or another, become more frequent and ambitious. If this is so, transport requirements, both for inward and outward delivery, will increase. On the other hand, rationalization and mergers within the newspaper publishing industry and the gradual shifting of the magazine industry westwards would tend to have the reverse effect.

TRAFFIC AND THE CITY IN THE FUTURE

It is time for us to summarize the situation that exists, and to consider the adequacy of present policies to cope with the present and future problems. The City has crowded roads, with a substantial, though declining, volume of through-goods traffic. Only a small proportion of the commuters arrive by private vehicle, but those who do, add significantly to road congestion, especially at peak periods.

Some of these commuters use their cars during the day for business purposes, especially if trips to the Home Counties, or the rest of London, are involved.

The use of the car is still growing. Commuting by bus is declining, and arrivals by underground and rail have, for some years, been more or less stable. Commuter journeys by rail are getting longer. The growth of population is largely an outward growth. Electrification and other improvements have made travelling into London relatively easier and more comfortable, even though other factors, including a tendency for an increased proportion of people to travel during the peak period, have worked in the opposite direction.

Volume II of the *London Traffic Survey*, published in July 1966, makes some predictions of future traffic and travel characteristics in Greater London. They are based on the forecast that the population of the Survey area will increase by 4 per cent between 1962 and 1981, the number of households will rise by 6 per cent, employment by 10 per cent, and average household income by 3·25 per cent per annum. It is also assumed that basic land-use patterns in the area will remain unchanged. Clearly some of these assumptions are already being made improbable, the closure of some inner docks, and the imaginative redevelopment proposed in their place is a case in point, but the forecasts, are still amongst the best we have.

In the traffic districts nearest to the City (Nos. 202 and 204) the Survey estimates the resident population will rise from 6,240 in 1962 to 12,050 by 1971, and then fall by about 300 in 1981. Particulars are given in Table 12.11. This population growth, however, is likely to be a negligible factor in determining the rate of growth of employment in the City, which is expected to be slower in the 1970s than in the 1980s.

It is also predicted that the City will attract about 520,000 work trips from other areas in 1971, compared with 530,000 in 1962, but that by 1981 the decline will be reversed and there will be about 540,000 trips. Other trips (non-work) to the City are expected to increase from 100,000 in 1962 to 122,000 in 1971 and to 137,000 in 1981. The detailed forecasts are given in Tables 12.12 and 12.13. They show that there is likely to be a continued decline of bus usage, an increase of travel by rail, and an increased use of cars for non-work trips.

The City Corporation has used the detailed results of the Survey in order to examine the likely pattern of vehicle journeys across the City boundaries. More precisely they have looked at the extended boundary of the City defined to be the two traffic districts. Their results are summarized for the year 1981 in Table 12.14. The predicted total number of trips across the boundary is 432,300 in an average twenty-four-hour day. Of these, 249,390 or 57·5 per cent are expected to originate or end beyond this radius.

It shows an average daily flow of 88,700 vehicles over Blackfriars Bridge (compared with 41,000 in 1962), Farringdon Street will carry 61,500 vehicles, and Newgate Street 12,900. Much of the traffic over Blackfriars Bridge will flow along Ludgate Hill, which will carry 47,000 trips, of which 38,000 will flow past the east end of St Paul's Cathedral, reducing to 29,800 in St Martin's-Le-Grand. There it joins London Wall, running east–west, with a load of 37,100, turning into Moorgate with a slightly increased load and passing north out of

Table 12.11. Estimated Future Employment in Selected Traffic Districts
(in Central London)
(Traffic Districts 202 and 204)

	Total employment		Employment in services other than retail and wholesale distribution	
		Change from previous figure		Change from previous figure
1962	384,500		255,840	
1971	434,660	50,160	309,080	53,240
1981	454,310	19,650	327,530	18,450

Source: London Traffic Survey, Vol. II, p. 194

the City. The main link with the area to the east will be through Aldgate (23,000 vehicles), leading to 19,000 vehicles along part of what is now Camomile Street and to 14,300 along Fenchurch Street. London Bridge will carry 20,900 vehicles, which is less than its 1962 load of 36,000.

These are projections which must not be taken too literally. They are intended to give an idea of the sort of thing that might happen if car-ownership and usage, and through-traffic of all kinds, grow in the way that they may, and if the proposed road programmes go through. But they take no account of such factors as road pricing, new ring road schemes, and so on.

Containerization is also likely to have a substantial effect on the volume of goods traffic – not only for reasons given earlier but also because, when completed, Tilbury will be the only major deep-sea

Table 12.12. Estimated Internal Future Work Trip Generations and Attractions by Mode of Travel and Traffic District

Traffic district	Year	Generations					Attractions				
		Driver	Bus	Rail	Others	Total	Driver	Bus	Rail	Others	Total
202	1962	745	2,186	947	189	4,067	11,604	81,355	195,690	10,244	298,893
	1971	836	1,831	836	210	3,713	9,248	75,306	194,937	10,949	290,440
	1981	903	1,598	755	229	3,485	7,186	76,613	205,939	12,134	301,872
204	1962	246	427	216	55	944	11,228	67,241	142,240	9,688	230,397
	1971	1,563	2,748	1,315	407	6,033	11,820	61,414	147,548	9,592	230,374
	1981	1,506	2,784	1,304	405	5,999	12,339	59,253	156,092	9,559	237,243

Source: London Traffic Survey, Vol. II, p. 205.

Table 12.13. Estimated Internal Future Non-work Trip Generations and Attractions by Mode of Travel and Traffic District

Traffic district	Year	Generations					Attractions				
		Driver	Bus	Rail	Other	Total	Driver	Bus	Rail	Other	Total
202	1962	19,090	10,779	7,919	7,323	45,111	18,356	14,663	21,127	8,083	62,229
	1971	21,823	8,152	4,812	6,556	41,343	24,058	12,682	19,135	12,183	68,058
	1981	23,795	3,452	2,509	12,225	46,981	28,389	11,795	19,368	16,346	75,898
204	1962	9,439	6,042	2,700	4,752	22,933	8,383	10,646	10,315	9,113	38,457
	1971	15,025	6,873	2,076	8,751	32,725	16,998	10,734	13,153	13,540	54,425
	1981	16,104	7,813	1,217	10,887	36,021	21,815	9,470	14,550	15,351	61,186

Source: London Traffic Survey, Vol. II, p. 211.

Table 12.14. Traffic Forecasts in the City for 1981

Area	Trips occurring wholly within this area and crossing the City boundary	
	With origin or destination inside the City	With neither origin nor destination inside the City
City and immediately adjacent districts	64,378	20,941
Ring of districts within an approximate radius of 3 miles	110,323	60,619
Ring of districts within an approximate radius of 5 miles	137,135	112,255

Source: Corporation of London.

container port in the U.K. linked by railway with all principal rail centres.[4]

Another innovation envisaged is containerized delivery service to shops. A firm of stockbrokers explained to us how this might affect the traditional pattern of distribution.

'In the case of multiple retail chain the central distribution warehouse would fill small containers with merchandise. The containers would be roughly comparable in size to a filing cabinet; these would be put on to a lorry or flat trailer with an automatic loading and unloading device. On arrival at the shop, the required number of containers, at the push of a button, would be unloaded and then wheeled into the premises on a special trolley; empty containers being taken back from the shop on the return journey. The entire operation could be operated by one old man or boy, and the period during which the vehicle was stationary would be cut dramatically.

'The containers themselves, although of identical dimensions, might be fitted out with trays to hold such things as confectionery or be cleared of any shelves so as to carry dresses. Furthermore, they could be designed to open out to display units, so that the merchandise would be sold directly out of them.

'Whereas the suggestion is for this system to operate on an internal basis, the overall dimensions of these small containers would be such

[4] As we have seen 90 per cent of container traffic to and from Tilbury is carried by rail, compared with about 50 per cent of conventional goods traffic.

as to enable them to be fitted into an international container – a large box taking a set of smaller boxes – thereby enabling the system to be extended as required, dovetailing in with the larger road, rail and seaboard container and also, in the future, aircraft.'

Such technical changes are bound to have some effect on transport flows, and the cost of congestion will, for a long time, stimulate innovation in the carriage of goods and people. Nevertheless, the growth of population and rising incomes will both add to the total volume of goods which must be transported by one means or another. For the City commuting and through-traffic will remain the principal problems.

The public transport authorities are attempting to tackle the commuting problem in a variety of ways, some of which will directly impinge upon the City. The extension of the Victoria line to Brixton, for example, which will be completed in the near future, may well lead to increased arrivals in the City from the south on the District line, via Victoria, rather than on the Northern Line at London Bridge. The proposed Fleet Line, from Baker Street to Lewisham, via Green Park, Aldwych and Fenchurch Street, would certainly make the City more easily accessible from both north and south; it would also considerably affect the pattern of journeys to work.

Another significant development is the rapid expansion of station car-parks at London Transport stations. By the end of 1968, seventy-one stations provided over 11,000 spaces, compared with the 4,500 which existed in 1965; but a vast expansion of these is necessary if they are to cause a significant reduction in the number of people driving into Central London.

A scheme which is being considered for the South Region of British Rail would involve running trains from the southern through stations which are now termini, and on to the northern suburbs. The logic behind this is that double the number of trains that can be brought to a station and then turned round can be run through it. Schemes of this kind, with adequately designed marshalling yards, and reversing facilities, could undoubtedly increase the number of trains that could be operated, but it would mean a very considerable expenditure on additional rolling stock, and other forms of investment, chiefly to meet peak hour demand.

Against this background we have to note the attitude of the public authorities towards car-parking. The policy of the Ministry of Transport is clear enough – it is that car commuters should be discouraged from entering Central London, that where practicable parking should be off-street, and that there should be some control over the use of

private car-parks. Though the City Corporation is planning an extension of public car-parks in the City, it is primarily interested in
ensuring that there are adequate private parking facilities for the
business visitor. Between 1952 and 1956, the minimum standard
was one car space for every 5,000 sq. ft of floor-space. It was then
altered, against the wishes of the Corporation, to one space for every
2,500 sq. ft. Since 1960 it has been one car space for every 2,000 sq. ft
of floor-space. The Corporation assesses the 'ultimate' floor-space in
the City as 80 million sq. ft which in time would lead to the provision of parking space for something approaching 40,000 cars,[5] but
this is a figure which is far away, and would be achieved only if all
existing buildings were adapted to the same standards, or replaced
by new ones incorporating them. When one considers that in 1965
only 146 buildings in the City had their own car-parks (averaging
one space per 3,500 sq. ft), the remoteness of the provision for
40,000 cars is perfectly clear.

Some idea of costs involved can be obtained from the figures for
the Minories scheme. Here a multi-storey car-park for 590 cars and
46 lorries is now being provided at a net annual cost to the Streets
Committee of £11,000, after allowing for receipts of £40,640. Without
these receipts the gross annual cost (including management and
maintenance) is estimated at about £80 per vehicle. This is a figure
for providing car space in a specially designed car-park below another
building, and so is probably fairly representative of the kind of cost
that would be incurred if similar provision were made in newly built
office blocks, although each building and site can present problems
of its own. When an existing building is adapted, the cost can vary
from much less to much more than this figure.

The City is a business area, well served by public transport and
taxis, to which few people *need* to commute completely by car. But
people do commute by car, and consider it to be worth several
shillings a day in parking fees, as well as the trouble of driving. Why
is this? We do not know, but a few points may be made rather tenta-
tively.

First, there is the question of the inadequacy of parking facilities
at suburban stations. We have already seen that efforts are being
made to improve this situation.

Second, some people working in the City feel that they need their
car during the day to make business calls and, perhaps, to return
home by a different route. It may be recalled that, according to our

---

[5] I.e. if the present standard were continued to be applied.

Communications Survey,[6] over three-quarters of the visits to meetings outside the building in which the respondent worked, but still in the City, were made on foot, and only a very small fraction of them by private car. But the private car was still the most favoured method for reaching other parts of Outer London and the suburbs on business trips which started from the City. And it must be remembered that decentralization will often involve a frequent exchange of visits of senior executives between central and branch offices and these will usually be made by car.

There is one obvious answer to this. Cars are useful. If they are useful enough, people pay enough for their use. The man who uses his car to move from place to place need rarely park it long in one spot. A highly progressive system of parking charges, on-street and off-, can help to secure a reduction in commuting by car in a way which will not heavily penalize the man who needs to drive from place to place. But such a scheme should preferably be accompanied by the increased provision of first class public transport facilities.

We advocate this attempt to discourage commuting for two reasons. One is that we feel, at the moment, cars parked by commuters may be hindering that business of the City which depends on callers from more remote places, who have difficulty in finding convenient parking places with reasonable speed. The other is that the provision of more and more off-street parking means the expenditure of a great deal of money pursuing a policy which is likely to add to the volume of unnecessary road traffic. We would doubt that this is desirable.

The provision of better parking facilities at suburban stations, and the construction of new underground or other fast public transport systems from a wide catchment area can do a great deal to reduce commuting by car. Yet the development of the town car, and increasing affluence, along with the increased residential population of the City, may lead to a greater use of cars. Even for the commuters, one can envisage a day when the City worker may arrive by public transport and then, after getting to work, take his mini-car out of his private garage beneath his office and drive round to meetings in the City and elsewhere. Such a practice would reduce peak-hour travel by road, but might well increase the off-peak traffic.

The final question we must ask, is: What kind of traffic do we want to see on City roads? There are the following principal claimants:

[6] See Chapter 3 for further details.

1. commuters to work in the City,
2. goods traffic making collections and deliveries in the City,
3. people making business calls from elsewhere in the City,
4. people making business calls to or from places outside the City,
5. shoppers,
6. residents,
7. tourists,
8. through-goods and private traffic.

Not all of these can be simultaneously satisfied. One extreme forecast of the future is that each of the 350,000 or more workers converging on to the City will commute in their own cars. It is a prospect which takes us into the realm of science fiction, with multi-tiered roads and towering car parks. It is a prospect which we can dismiss. But even if, at another extreme, there was no commuting by private vehicle it seems likely that the combined claims of other users would still lead to certain congestion and parking problems. Congestion does not exist simply at peak hours, nor would the removal of commuters' cars from parking places necessarily ensure an adequate provision for other road users. The problem of not being able to stop more or less outside the door of the building from which goods, documents or money have to be collected, or to which they have to be delivered, is an important one. A business journey across the City may consume more time than is spent in subsequent discussion. It is true that, in many areas, goods can be collected or delivered in the evening, even though this may lead to increased costs on the part of the person whose premises are involved, but a large part of City business, including the tourist trade, involves movement in the City of a kind which can take place only in the daytime. This is the essential daytime traffic of the City to which, from the City's point of view, all other traffic should be subordinated unless the cost of doing so is too high.

The City is part of London and we cannot look at its traffic problem in isolation to that of the capital as a whole. Obviously anything which encourages through-traffic – particularly goods traffic – to avoid the roads of the City would be a welcome relief to the City's own difficulties. Whether it would simply increase the problems in other parts of London would depend on the means used to redistribute the traffic. On the other hand, a major new road project in the City, e.g. an elevated road from London Bridge station to north of Liverpool Street, might well help to alleviate traffic congestion in neighbouring boroughs as well as the City itself. It is well outside our terms of reference to attempt a cost–benefit study of alternative policies of solving the through-traffic prob_ems of the City or even to appraise the best way of dealing with them under certain assumptions.

But this much might be said. Viewed purely from an economic standpoint, any traffic policy of the City Corporation should be directed to ensuring that, in so far as it is within its power, the flow of goods and people entering and leaving the City should do everything to enhance and nothing to interfere with its efficient working. We know that some forms of transport *do* add to the value of the City's activities,[7] and others, by the congestion and delays they cause, lessen the value of this traffic. If the full price of this dis-economy was paid by its originator, well and good. But this is not usually the case. Therefore the level and pattern of traffic flowing through the City today is not at its optimum. Under the normal operation of the pricing system, the problem would largely solve itself, assuming that one could properly evaluate the costs and benefits of different forms of road traffic. But in this particular sector of the economy, the mechanism of the market is not always acceptable. Alternative policies have to be devised. But we do not know of any urban study which has seriously sought to relate the control of road use in a town, city or region to its economic needs – or indeed to establish what sort of relationship exists between road use and other forms of space use.

Sixteen years ago the following words were written:

'the first great planning problem of the City is to obtain a good balance between the amount of circulation space and accommodation space, an equilibrium which existing forms of control have failed to maintain'.[8]

In our view this problem still remains but with a different emphasis. As far as we have been able to establish from our researches, the City's *accommodation* space problems have been, and are beitng realistically and efficiently tackled. In this study, we have suggested, further lines on which policies in this direction might be pursued.

The problem of the use of *circulation* space had not been so successfully resolved, simply because of the difficulty of finding an

[7] Most pedestrian traffic falls into this category. This is why the provision of pedestrian ways and zones free of vehicle traffic is so important for the City. We understand that the Corporation is planning to build a thirty-mile net of 'pedways' in the next ten years. These will be pavements built at first-storey level, which when complete will enable pedestrians to cross most of the City without having to compete with the traffic. (See R. Hartley, *No Mean City*, 1967, p. 109.)

[8] *County of London Development Plan*, 1950, L.C.C.

429

effective means of traffic control.[9] Maybe none is possible but we are inclined to think otherwise. We also believe that because space – accommodation and circulation – is, next to its labour force, the most precious commodity which the City possesses, the time is both opportune and urgent to undertake a full-scale study of the uses (and abuses!) of circulation space and its effects on the economy of the City.

[9] Similar to the plot-ratio, use-zoning and pricing mechanism controls in the use of accommodation space.

Chapter 13

MISCELLANEOUS ACTIVITIES

CENTRAL OFFICES OF MANUFACTURING COMPANIES

The definition of the group of offices to be discussed in this section is largely imposed by the nature of our statistical sources. As was mentioned in Chapter 2, employment in offices attached to factories is separately recorded from employment in independent offices. A City Corporation investigation of these offices revealed that there were 6,750 people employed in the former category in 1964–6 almost all of whom were within the printing and publishing industry. Chapters 8 to 10 have dealt with independent offices in banking and finance, insurance, and the main trading activities of the City. We are left with offices of industrial companies which are separate in location from their manufacturing plants. We now briefly discuss their activities.

The O.S.R.P. returns show that there were 450 offices of manufacturing companies in 1964–6 with a total employment of over 12,000 people. More than 300 of these establishments employed over 100 and a further eighteen between 5 and 100. The group includes the head offices of some major national and international companies but also a great number of offices of smaller firms and small specialized departments of firms whose main office activities are elsewhere. The large number of tiny units shown by the O.S.R.P. returns suggests that this last category must be numerous.

We examined a list of 335 large firms including 'The Times 300' for 1966, and found that fifty-two of them had head offices either in the City or immediately adjacent to its boundaries. However, the registered head office of a company is not always the place where its main office activities are carried on, and some firms which nominally have their head offices in the City maintain only a small staff there and do most of their office work elsewhere. We also examined similar lists for earlier years in order to ascertain the extent of movement, but the position is complicated by the large number of mergers and changes of name

431

which have taken place. But in general we found very little evidence of movement into the City, but at least six large firms have moved out since 1950. We know too that there are at least twice the number of head offices of manufacturing firms in the West End than are in the City.

Interviews with firms which had moved, as well as those remaining in the City, suggested that, while they had strong reasons for being in London, links with the City itself were not particularly strong, and that the City had little advantage over the West End. In such cases, location is often the result of past history, since moving a big office is a complicated and costly operation, and once a firm is established in a satisfactory location it rightly stays there until a major change of circumstances arises. Such changes reported to us by firms moving out included mergers with other firms having office premises outside the City; the expiry of leases and/or the desire to acquire freehold premises; and the difficulty of finding space in the City big enough to accommodate large increases in staff. Rents become important as leases expire, and one large company at present in the City said that while its rent was now reasonable, it would consider moving if the rent was raised.

We expect, therefore, that there will be a continued, though gradual, movement of the large offices of manufacturing companies out of the City. Some may move their whole office, others only part. On the other hand many firms may have good reason for maintaining small offices in the City to deal, for example, with exports or with the employment of short-term funds in the market, and the number of these small specialized offices will probably continue to grow. On balance, however, we think that the trend of total employment in this type of office activity is likely to be downward.

PROFESSIONAL SERVICES

Legal and Accountancy Services

Both legal services and accountancy provide a substantial volume of employment in the City. The relevant O.S.R.P. figures for the 1964–6 period are:

	No. of establishments	No. employed		
		Total	Male	Female
Legal services (64)	297	6,766	3,220	3,546
Accountancy (62)	370	11,407	8,085	3,322

Since these figures do not include the Inns of Court, it may be presumed that firms under the heading of 'legal services' are virtually all solicitors. Even so, the O S.R.P. returns are not quite comprehensive, for a check in a classified directory revealed rather more than 300 firms with addresses in the City. There is, as one would expect, a large number of small firms in both professions; 4 per cent of the accountants and 4 per cent of the solicitors had ten people or less, including both partners and employees. At the other extreme, however, there were twenty firms of accountants and fifteen firms of solicitors each employing more than a hundred.

A number of the largest firms of solicitors in financial and commercial transactions, either on the side of company finance (new issues, amalgamations, take-overs, etc.) or commercial documents (acceptance credits, bills, shipping documents, etc.) have offices in the City. These naturally have close links with banks and merchant banks, and have their offices in or very near the main financial centre. A large number of other firms specialize in conveyancing, both for leasing and for investment in property, and these tend to develop close associations with property companies and with financial institutions such as insurance companies and pension funds which are big investors in property. There is also, of course, a large volume of private client work for people in the City who find it more convenient to handle their legal business from their place of work than from their home. Some of the leading firms also get a substantial volume of business from other parts of the U.K. and from overseas.

A large part of the 'bread and butter' work of accountants is, of course, auditing, advising on tax problems, and negotiating with the Inland Revenue. City firms are, however, also concerned with schemes for the financial reorganization of companies and with amalgamations and takeovers, while some of them also manage investment trusts. A significant amount of business has also come, in recent years, from the Monopolies Commission, the Prices and Incomes Board and the Restrictive Practices Court, and from firms and associations appearing before them; most of this seems to go to a small number of firms, nearly all of which are in the City. The big firms of accountants have developed their connections with the provinces in a rather more formal way than have the solicitors, taking provincial partners and establishing provincial offices. Some of them also have associate firms overseas.

It has been shown in Chapter 6 that demand at the national level both for legal and accounting services has been growing rapidly. There are obvious links between these services and the financial

433

work which, as shown in Chapter 8, is likely to be the most rapidly expanding of the City's activities. The advantages of a City location are strong – proximity to major clients, ready contact with other centres in the U.K. and overseas, and proximity to one another. All these are important since financial negotiations often call for consultations between bankers, lawyers and accountants, and also between members of the same profession acting for different clients. Both types of service employ mainly highly-trained people and produce output of high value in relation to the space occupied. Finally (though accountants make extensive use of computers for some purposes) neither profession is likely to feel the full effect of office automation. It seems likely, therefore, that the expansion of both these professions within the City will take place at least as fast as in the country as a whole.

RETAILING AND CATERING

Retailing

According to the O.S.R.P. figures, retail distribution employs 5,072 persons in 901 establishments, 808 of which employed ten people or less and only one employed over 100. Broadly, though not strictly comparable, data, and more detail, can be obtained from the Censuses of Distribution for 1950 and 1961.

City retailers have to cater for a very small resident population, a very large working population and a small amount of casual and tourist trade (largely around St Paul's). They have to pay dearly for their space and also for their labour. Recent figures of relative wages are not available, but the 1950 Census showed average wages of £344 in the City, compared with £246 for Greater London and only £192 for Great Britain. The characteristics of the industry follow very much the pattern that one would expect from these supply and demand conditions.

The proportion of establishments of various types is very different from the national average, as is shown in Table 13.1.

The concentration on the kind of things likely to be bought (particularly by men) on their way to or from work, or in the lunch hour, is obvious. Adaptation to the high cost of space and labour is reflected in a high turnover per establishment. As Table 13.2 shows, City shops had an average turnover, according to the 1961 Census, of over £38,000, compared to £13,000 for Greater London and only £9,000 for Great Britain.

434

Turning to the changes revealed by the Census figures, the number of shops fell from 995 in 1950 to 880 in 1961, though the decline appears to have been checked since. Employment increased between the two Censuses, but at well below the national average rate. Although the O.S.R.P. returns showed a slightly larger number of shops, they showed nearly 2,000 less workers. In view of the differences in the way the figures have been compiled, they are not strictly comparable, but they leave little doubt that there has been a quite sharp decline in employment. The Census returns also show that, between 1900 and 1961, total turnover in City shops was rising less fast than the

Table 13.1. Proportion of Different Kinds of Retail Outlets in the City and Great Britain 1951

	Percentage of total establishments	
	City	Great Britain
Food	10·8	49·2
Household goods	7·0	12·7
Confectioners, tobacconists and newsagents	24·7	12·2
Shoes	3·8	2·5
Men's clothing	11·9	2·4
Women's clothing	13·0	11·0
Books and stationery	8·2	1·1
Chemists and photography	6·4	3·2
Jewellery, leather and sports goods	9·9	3·3
Other	4·3	2·4
	100	100

Source: Census of Distribution, 1961.

national average, but that turnover per establishment was rising considerably faster (by 86·9 per cent against 66·7 per cent). Finally the use of part-time labour, though still below the national average, was rising considerably faster.

The demand for retailing services in the future will depend on the growth of population and income, and on changes in shopping habits; these again will be influenced, among other things, by changes in the working week, and in the hours at which shops are open.

We have given reasons elsewhere for predicting that there will not be a big rise in the working population. The Barbican scheme may rather more than double the residential population, but even if these

435

Table 13.2. Characteristics of Retail Trade in the City, Greater London and Great Britain 1950 and 1961

	City of London			Greater London			Great Britain		
	1950	1961	Percentage change	1950	1961	Percentage change	1950	1961	Percentage change
Number of establishments	995	880	−16·4	78,364	84,071	+7·3	531,143	577,307	+8·7
Turnover (£ thousand)	20,386	33,691	+65·3	1,033,233	1,773,405	+71·6	4,922,931	8,918,860	+81·2
Persons engaged:									
Full time	5,561	5,665	+1·9	325,497	318,744	−2·1	1,811,329	1,858,240	+2·6
Part time	661	1,240	+87·6	85,822	120,933	40·9	453,962	665,844	+46·7
Wages and salaries (£ thousand)	2,028	n.a.	—	90,793	n.a.	—	392,070	n.a.	—
Turnover per establishment (£)	20,488	38,285	+86·9	13,185	21,094	+60·0	9,269	15,449	+66·7
Wages per employee* (£)	344	n.a.	—	246	n.a.	—	192	n.a.	—

* Part-time employees are counted as one-half of full time ones.
Source: *Census of Distribution*, 1950 and 1961.

new residents brought new shops in the national average proportion of shops to population, which is unlikely, this in itself would only create about 300 extra jobs in retailing.

Average incomes of people working in the City are likely to rise at more than the average rate, while the fact that some of them are coming from further afield may lead them to do more shopping in the City. On the other hand, the five-day week, already very widespread in offices, is likely to become even more so, and an extension of the hours in which shops are open (for which the Consumer Council is pressing) would give City workers more opportunity of shopping elsewhere.

In none of these trends is there any dynamic influence which could counteract the disadvantages of high rents and high labour-costs with which City retailers have, and will have, to contend. Greater freedom of movement, resulting from the diversion of heavy traffic and the building of pedestrian walks, may give some stimulus to shopping. It is likely, however, that City shops will maintain their specialized character, and there may well be a further reduction in their number as that of their employees.

We conclude this brief survey with particulars of the results of two surveys conducted by the Corporation in recent years. Table 13.3 sets out the spatial distribution of the main types of retail activities in the City in 1967. The figures for this table were obtained directly from retailers, and the corporation estimated the coverage was about 95%. The data reveal that there are considerable variations in the type of facilities offered by the various centres – compare, for example, Moorgate/London Wall with Leadenhall Market, and Tower Hill with West Fleet Street. Since 1960, the main area of growth has been in non-food shops and public houses in the primary centres, and the main locational development has been that of the new shopping precincts, e.g. Paternoster and a growing connection between retail outlets and railway stations. The average size of the shopping unit has also increased. The survey concluded that a more rational policy should be adopted towards the future siting of shops and that expansion should be largely concentrated in the four main centres and the Ludgate Hill and Fleet Street secondary centres.[1]

The second survey, conducted in 1969, was that concerned with assessing shopping needs in the City.[2] Of the 23,000 persons questioned, all of whom worked and/or lived in the City, 54% claimed

[1] Corporation of London, *Report of the Shop Survey* (unpublished), 1968.

[2] *Interim Shop Policy*, Report of the Planning and Communications Committee to the Court of Common Council, 11/6/70.

Table 13.3. Location and Types of Retail Establishments in the City 1967

	Food Shops		Non Food Shops		Department Stores		Service Establishments[1]		Public Houses		Other[2]		Total	
	A	B	A	B	A	B	A	B	A	B	A	B	A	B
*Primary Centres**														
Moorgate/London Wall	13	15.8	44	58.0	—	—	22	36.0	5	20.8	8	7.3	92	137.9
Cheapside/Bow Lane	10	12.3	51	69.1	1	35.2	44	77.9	9	40.4	6	15.9	121	250.8
Liverpool Street	28	14.5	70	58.7	—	—	43	53.8	6	29.7	4	2.9	151	159.6
Leadenhall Market	32	55.4	53	50.8	—	—	39	78.4	7	24.0	6	5.9	137	214.5
Total	83	98.0	218	236.6	1	35.2	148	246.1	27	114.9	24	32.0	501	762.8
*Secondary Centres**														
Paternoster	4	2.2	11	18.5	—	—	5	9.8	2	8.6	29	37.4	51	96.5
Tower Hill/Byward Street	3	1.0	8	9.9	—	—	5	3.2	1	10.6	12	23.2	26	47.8
Holborn	—	—	7	24.9	1	441.1	5	8.5	—	—	1	0.5	14	475.0
Royal Exchange	2	0.5	12	9.4	—	—	5	3.6	—	—	—	—	19	13.5
West Fleet Street	10	6.0	30	48.0	—	—	29	55.8	11	42.0	4	6.7	84	158.5
Poultry/Bucklersbury	4	1.6	33	59.9	—	—	8	9.8	3	8.8	3	8.1	51	88.2
Ludgate Hill	6	5.4	25	34.8	—	—	18	38.8	3	10.9	11	21.3	63	111.3
Podwin/London Wall	1	0.4	2	0.9	—	—	6	8.9	3	23.1	13	6.6	25	39.9
Total	113	115.1	346	442.9	2	476.3	226	384.5	50	218.9	97	155.8	834	1793.5

A = Number of Shops.   B = Floor space area (000's sq. ft)

1 Including laundries and dry cleaners, hairdressers, restaurants, shoe repairers, tourist and travel agencies.

2 Including unoccupied establishments.

* Primary Centres are defined by the Corporation as those which are large enough to attract the general shopper. Secondary Centres are those which have an attraction to a limited number of shoppers but because of their size and other features make them more important than a third category, the local centre, which is generally no more than a grouping of a few shops for the convenience of the employer working in the vicinity. No separate analysis was made by the Corporation for this third category of shops.

Source: Corporation of London.

that there was a shortage of grocers and 32% wanted more restaurants; there was also a big demand for more department stores. An earlier investigation by the Corporation had found that three fifths of the working population in the City considered the shopping facilities in the City as 'adequate' and 30% that they were unsatisfactory. The most pronounced shortages were noticed in food shops of all kinds, in ladies' clothing and in hardware.

Catering

Like the shopping facilities, the catering facilities of the City are directed very much towards the male working population. The 'pub lunch' is a City institution and pubs, old and new, abound throughout. Pubs are one of the more successful ventures in the newer developments – Paternoster, Barbican, Milk Street. In the survey conducted by the Corporation in 1967, the two pubs in the Paternoster development indicated that turnover was adequate whereas the two restaurants in the precinct indicated that it was far from adequate.

The Social Survey throws some light on the canteen facilities provided by firms within the City. It shows that 34 per cent eat within their employer's building, 11 per cent bring their own lunch and the remainder eat outside. Unfortunately the latter is not split down by the type of lunchtime facilities used. However, it does mean that about 190,000 people (based on our employment estimate of 350,000) seek some sort of catering facility outside their own building in the City at lunchtime.

The main difficulty faced by catering firms is that they must rely solely upon the lunchtime trade for their survival. In the evening the City is very quiet. A few restaurants are open, but most rely on their lunchtime trade and close in mid-afternoon. A Persian restaurant (well-known for its cabaret), and a Turkish restaurant opened in 1967 have attracted some publicity, but these are quite expensive. Some of the public houses do a fair trade. Around Fleet Street there is a good deal more activity, but it is quieter than one might expect.

Moreover, the City, once the main provider of overnight accommodation for visitors to London, had only five hotels by 1951 and two by 1961. In 1961, the hotels represented under 1 per cent of the hotel population of the Central Area. Two hotels still remain: the Great Eastern, Liverpool Street Station and the Three Nuns, Aldgate High Street. It is possible that, when the Barbican scheme is completed, the City will be enlivened in the evening, but there is some considerable way to go before one can see this happening. More promising is the planned development of the St Katherine's dock area as a tourist attraction. This coupled with other improvements to the City's environment, e.g. the redevelopment of parts of the waterfront, and the possibility that the main rail and road terminal to the third London airport may be at King's Cross, could have quite fascinating repercussions. These we believe are to be commended as the charm and character of the Square Mile have much to offer the visitor in preference to an increasingly crowded West End.

Chapter 14

CONCLUSIONS: THE FUTURE SHAPE OF THE CITY

INTRODUCTION

The time has now come for us to sum up. Previous chapters have shown that the most significant change which has occurred in the City in recent years has been the gradual shift in its trading activities from 'goods' to 'rights to goods'. This chapter, in bringing together the results of our researches into the various activities carried on in the City, examines the more important implications of this change. More particularly it tries to answer the question: What (on certain assumptions) is likely to be the shape of the economy of the City of London in the near- or medium-term future, i.e. up to 1981 or thereabouts?

THE FUTURE: (A) PROJECTING FORWARDS ON PAST TRENDS

We start, first, with a résumé of the likely future demand for the products and services at present supplied by the City. Chapter 2 showed not only that the City has above its share of growth industries, but that these industries are becoming more important to the City's economy. Chapter 6 attempted to project the likely labour force up to 1981 in the six most important groups of industries in the City, assuming three alternative patterns of growth. In each case, we saw that the pressures of demand were likely to raise the level of employment in the City. If we take our estimate of 350,000[1] as the labour force in 1966 (see Chapter 2) and apply our three predictions in Chapter 6 to this figure, then the *average* of these predictions would give us a labour force in the City of around 390,000 by 1971, 430,000 by 1976 and 475,000 by 1981. It is interesting to note that only the forecast for 1981 is around the target envisaged by the Holford/Holden report in 1947, which was then thought to be within the capacity of the City's space. We believe this still to be the case,

[1] These are different from those contained in Table 6.10 since the initial employment is assumed to be 350,000 not 322,708.

assuming the absence of restrictions on office development. A more important physical constraint, in our opinion, is the pressure on circulation and car-parking space likely to arise from a rapid expansion of commuter car traffic into the City (see Chapter 12).

Our projections, based upon past trends, also show a continuation of the movement towards an increasing specialization of activity in the City, with insurance, banking and finance, and professional services increasing their share of total employment from around two-fifths to one-half. It is quite clear that apart from (i) printing and publishing and ancillary industries, e.g. maintenance and repair shops, and (ii) specialized processing activities associated with whole-saling and commodity trading, there will be virtually no manufacturing industry in the City by 1980. The numbers employed in wholesaling activities are also expected to fall by up to 2,000; on the other hand, past trends suggest an increase of up to 20 per cent in postal and telecommunication employment in the City.

The *actual* level and structure of employment achieved in the City by 1981 will obviously depend on certain considerations, e.g. the rate at which national output grows, which are outside the control of the City. Likewise crucial are developments in international trade and finance. As far as we have been able to judge, most of these, e.g. the possible entry of the U.K. into the European Economic Community, will work in favour of the City although we believe international, and particularly Continental, competition will undoubtedly become stronger in a number of fields in which the City has had a dominant position in the past (see Chapter 8). Similarly, the discriminatory and restrictive actions taken by some developing countries towards foreign insurance operations is acting to the detriment of U.K. insurance companies. We do not consider attempts by these same countries to evolve their own commodity brokerage and terminal markets will prove competitively serious to commodity trading in the City in the next decade or so, but we do think that the City will be faced with a situation in which the Port of London faces competition from other ports, particularly in respect of containerized traffic, and in which the new international trade patterns and techniques require adaptation to new functions.

On national trends, we also expect the productivity of City firms, and incomes of City workers, to expand faster than the average. This is because the value of the output, in relation to space and labour inputs, of the activities in which the City is increasingly specializing, is likely to rise more quickly than that of other activities.

So much for predictions based on *past* trends. What is the likelihood of these being accomplished? Basically there are two reasons why they may not be. First, our estimates of the demand for the type of products and services produced by the City might be wrong. Second, the City's share of any additional output produced may be different to its share of the present output produced. It is this latter question which is our main concern here.

In Chapter 5, we expressed our scepticism in making precise forecasts about employment trends in the City. We said instead we would look into a number of the more important factors likely to affect the City's ability to develop in certain directions and how particular industries viewed their own growth prospects. What then are the constraints to growth in the City? Are its resources likely to be sufficient to meet all the demands likely to be made of it?

THE FUTURE: (B) SUPPLY CONSTRAINTS

We may say immediately that we do not think the City's labour force will expand to the level projected on the assumptions of Chapter 6, although its share of the national output may well be maintained or even increase. We now examine the reasons for this statement in terms of the three crucial variables likely to affect the City's future.

1. Labour Supply

The material in Chapter 6 quite clearly suggests that the City, in common with other parts of Central London, is likely to be faced with quite a serious problem of labour supply up to 1981, and particularly in the next five years. This is simply because of the expected decline in the size of the working population in the regions traditionally supplying the City with its labour force. In saying this, we have taken into account the new residential schemes planned in the Barbican, adjacent boroughs and the 'twilight' areas. The implication of this forecast is that if the City is to maintain, let alone expand, its labour force – particularly its clerical and junior managerial labour – it will either have to draw a larger share of the working population from its existing areas of supply or recruit from further afield. In either case, we cannot see how this could be accomplished without a relative increase in wages and salaries (or other forms of employee compensation) in the City.

In the course of our work, we obtained some information on wages and salaries in the City and in other areas. The data show that, in 1966, labour costs in the City and West End were generally 10–15 per cent above those in the rest of London[2] and 20–40 per cent above those in other parts of the country. It would seem too that these differentials have increased in recent years, and we think this trend will continue, making it more expensive for labour-intensive activities to maintain their operations in the City. Both labour shortages and rising costs will, then, make for increasing mechanization and decentralization of activities and a reduced labour force. They have certainly been the most important reasons for the movement of part of the insurance and printing industries out of the City in recent years.

2. Rents

The main conclusions to be drawn from Chapters 4 and 6 are, first, that City rents have risen very steeply in recent years, and generally faster than the national average, and second that, within the City, there has been a tendency for rents to equalize as office activities have spread outwards from the financial and trading nucleus. We also said that, in our opinion, recent government measures and particularly the operation of O.D.P.s have tended to force rents up faster than would otherwise have been the case.

Rents are largely determined by the pressure of demand for accommodation and the availability of land and buildings. The difficulties in obtaining labour militate against an increase in demand to accommodate more people, but technological developments, e.g. automatic data processing, closed-circuit television, etc., and the desire to improve standards of accommodation, work in the opposite direction. Given the existing plot ratio and use-zoning controls of the Corporation, we believe that, unless there is some relaxation in office development policy, rents in the City will continue to rise, particularly in the peripheral areas of the City, and in older properties as they are modernized.

We believe that the general trend in rents is likely to operate as a decentralizing force for space-intensive activities, although our observations of rents in districts near London, e.g. Croydon, suggest that the cost attractiveness of these areas will decline. But we foresee that those activities, which have a very high 'accommodation' productivity will continue to find a City location attractive.

Both the trend in labour costs and rents – and these are by far the most important costs incurred by firms operating in the City – make

[2] One exception is the older male clerical worker who appears to be better paid in both Outer London and many of the provinces than in the City.

for a reduction in the level of employment and a change in its pattern. Those activities which remain will be those for which a City location is more important than it is at present. We have explained at very considerable length, both in Chapter 3 and in the case studies, the nature and importance of the external economies of contiguity and accessibility to quick knowledge. We foresee these advantages of spatial linkages becoming more, rather than less, important in the future.

3. Technology

Changes in technology both affect and are affected by rents and labour costs. Whatever their cause, their results are far-reaching. We have seen that the application of automatic data processing to office activities is still very much in its infancy and will undoubtedly increase in the next ten to fifteen years. No less important are technological innovations in newspaper printing. We believe these will have a profound effect on the structure of industries, on the labour and space requirements of particular firms and on their locational patterns.

In general, we expect that trends in office mechanization will reduce the demand for labour in the City both by encouraging mergers of firms to take advantage of these techniques, and by making it economic for individual firms to substitute machines for labour in routine and regular operations. On balance, we believe it will encourage decentralization. Advances in telecommunications will have the same effect. On the other hand, these developments will in no way lessen the need for personal contact between the top decision-takers and specialists in e.g. insurance, stock exchange, commodity broking and foreign exchange transactions. Indeed, by speeding up the processing of data, computers may well tend to increase the need for a close contact between the providers and the users of information.

Whether these centralizing forces will outweigh the costs of centralization remains to be seen. We have been given evidence that the present generation of computers are considerably less space demanding than their predecessors, and we know of at least one firm which is planning to move its facilities back to the City.

Changes in the methods of handling and distribution of goods are likely to affect both the organization of traditional produce and commodity markets, and the trading function of the City. Not only are these varied activities very space- and labour-intensive; develop-

445

ments in food processing and preservation, containerization and palletization, and new methods of dispatching goods to and from the docks, which by-pass the Port wholesaler, will also lessen the need for trading activities in the City. We feel sure that these activities will continue to be important but that the volume of *goods* handled by them will fall, and consequently their demands for space and labour.

SOME RESULTS OF THESE CHANGING CONDITIONS

1. On the Structure of Firms

These changes in supply conditions which, on the whole, work in the opposite direction to the demand trends earlier forecast, will affect firms in the City in various ways. It has not been our brief to look into the efficiency of the City firms or markets as they are now organized. From recent trends, however, it is quite clear that the *number* of firms in many activities is falling and the average size is increasing. There have been a significant number of mergers in all the important activities in the City, notably insurance, newspapers, stock jobbers, merchant banks, commodity brokers, and it seems more are likely to come. Our expectancy is that increasing international competition and government legislation will accentuate this trend.

The other possible effect of changing demand and supply conditions is on the structure of organized markets. Here, apart from the continued trend towards a market in rights in commodity dealing and samples in produce markets, we do not anticipate any major change. The three central Exchanges – Lloyd's, Stock Exchange, and the Baltic are likely to continue much the same way in the future as in the past; in general, we think the organization of these markets is efficient, and they are meeting the needs required of them.

On the other hand, because of the growing concentration of the decision-taking and policy-making functions in the City, we expect that the size of the typical establishment will remain small. In fact, we foresee a decline in the large establishment, employing 1,000 or more people. At the other end of the spectrum, mergers and government legislation (see Chapter 8) will tend to work against the very small firms. Perhaps the other most rapid growth will be in firms employing more than ten but less than a hundred people.

2. Employment and Space Needs

What, then, is likely to be the net effect of all these trends on the size of the labour force and demand for space in the City? When we turn

446

to look at the opinions given to us by a large number of people engaged in a wide variety of activities, and the results of our own researches, we see that very rarely is an increase in employment envisaged. It is generally felt that the City will not be as favourable a location for large-scale office employment as in the past. In insurance, a small decline of the labour force in the insurance companies is forecast up to 1971 and then, possibly, a small increase up to 1975. Little change is expected in the employment of insurance brokers. At Lloyd's, the number of underwriting agents may increase slightly but, due to mechanization, they are likely to fall elsewhere.

In banking, the only activities likely to need more space and labour in the City are the head offices and overseas departments of clearing banks and some of the merchant banks. We anticipate little change in employment in other financial activities; for example, we expect that mergers and improved productivity among stockbrokers and jobbers will enable more business to be done with the same or a slight fall in numbers. We do, however, expect a continued rise in the employment of ancillary services in the City, e.g. accounting, legal services, and of business services, e.g. computer firms. We also foresee an increase in the number of international financial and trading companies wishing to set up offices in the City.

In the trading sector, we expect a further decline in traditional wholesaling and warehousing activities. We anticipate further integration of firms in commodity markets with a possible decline in their labour force. As shown in Chapter 10, we also foresee that mergers and technical trends will affect the structure of the shipping industry. We expect the numbers of shipping agents and brokers to fall, and a possible shift in their location upstream. We also foresee a decline, to varying degrees, of the space and labour of produce markets.

In manufacturing, we would expect the numbers employed in newspaper publishing to decline slightly for reasons given in Chapter 11, and also a further decline in newspaper and general printing. Most book publishers have already decentralized from the City. A continual rise in labour costs and difficulties with unions over the introduction of new production methods is now forcing some of the weekly and monthly publications to print outside London. In other manufacturing industries, we predict a further fall in the labour force.

We do not foresee any substantial growth in the head offices of companies outside finance and trade. There has been a gradual movement westwards and outwards from the City for several years now, and we would expect this trend to continue.

447

In the tertiary sector, we anticipate an increase of some hundreds in the numbers employed in retailing and other income-absorbing activities consequent upon the completion of the Barbican scheme, and various shopping precincts in key tourist areas. Moreover, with the building of the London museum, and a concert hall and theatre in the Barbican area, and the possibility of the St Katherine's dock area being redeveloped as a tourist attraction, we would expect an increase in international tourism and also of evening and weekend activities. The need for new hotel accommodation would be further enhanced if King's Cross became the main road and rail terminal for the third London airport. The character of shopping needs will also change as a higher proportion of the labour force will be managerial and executive rather than clerical. The further development of the City University and City of London Polytechnic will lead to an expansion in educational personnel; there is also likely to be an associated rise in medical and local government facilities.

When we add up all these various forecasts, *it would seem that the level of employment in the City is not likely to expand significantly in the next ten to fifteen years and in the next five years may even contract very slightly.* It is difficult to predict the exact timing of these trends. Our study has indicated that there are a complex number of counter-acting forces at work. On the one hand, official policy towards office decentralization, technological and institutional changes, trends in labour costs and rents, all combine to make for a reduction in the labour force; on the other, increases in national and international demand for the type of output produced in the City will make for an expansion in employment. We think these forces will compensate each other, at least up to the mid 1970s, after which it is possible that the expansionary forces will outweigh the contracting forces.

Our reasons for thinking this are that, in the next few years, dispersal policies, redevelopment and the pace of mergers and mechanization will keep any increase in labour force in check. After a decade or so – or possibly less – any dispersal which is worth while will already have been accomplished; redevelopment will be virtually complete and most of the important institutional changes will have been made. But the forces of expansion will continue. It is at this point that we would expect some increase in the City's labour force.[3]

At the same time, we would expect the pressure for new building

[3] The timing is very difficult to predict. If national output rises faster than in the past and/or mechanization is slower, the labour force in the City could rise in the immediate future. If the reverse is the case, the labour force would fall only to rise at an earlier date in the future.

448

accommodation in the City to be maintained throughout the period. There are still quite a large proportion of old premises in the City unsuitable for conversion to modern requirements. There will be an increasing demand for premises suitable for the needs of up-to-date office methods. Mergers will encourage this trend. Since, too, we envisage an increasing proportion of highly skilled administrative and professional workers in the City's labour force, the standard of accommodation will need to rise. We can thus foresee a need for continued growth of office building in the City.

Official policies towards office development are important here. We have shown in Chapter 6 that the present policy of O.P.D.s probably militates against the efficient allocation of resources in the City. Neither are we convinced that it keeps the level of employment lower than it would otherwise be if the pricing mechanism and existing local planning controls were allowed to operate freely.[4] We consider that the Selective Employment Tax, while probably leading to a reduction in the numbers employed in certain activities in the City, insufficiently takes into account the contribution of these activities and others like them – both to the national output and the balance of payments.

We believe that the City is likely to be faced with a period of much more intensive international competition than it has been used to in the past. Its activities are also likely to be subject to more scrutiny by Governments at home. Its past record in adapting itself successfully to changing conditions speaks for itself. It is important that nothing should interfere with this adaptability in the future.

The most noticeable feature of the City of London in the future will be 'specialization within specialization'. Not only will the type of activities carried out be almost entirely in 'rights to goods'; *within* each activity only those functions involving decision-taking and close contacts with people – clients, customers or competitors – will remain. The first of these specializations has been going on for many years now: the second we regard as the most significant development likely to come. The net result will be a labour force, more highly skilled in expertise, judgement and experience, and land and buildings better utilized. The interrelated network of activities will be even more closely associated with each other.

All this will have implications on circulation space. If our predic-

---

[4] This is because, as we have shown in Chapter 14, in certain cases, a move to a new office sparks off a chain of moves. If each move results in a reduction in the labour force – save the last one where a new firm comes into the City, the final outcome may be a lower employment in the City.

tions about the trading function of the City are right, we may expect a fall in goods traffic originating and terminating in the City or passing through the City from the Port of London. We believe that the plan to 'box in' the City by building a network of major carriageways (two running north/south and two east/west) on the City's boundaries will aid through-traffic. The most pressing problem in the future is that of the private car. With rising living standards and a more highly skilled labour force in the City, we would expect the proportion of City workers who own their cars to increase. Whether or not these cars are used for travelling to work will depend on the availability of good public transport arrangements and the distance commuters have to travel: we have indicated in Chapter 4 that we think long-distance commuting will increase.

In Chapter 12, we suggested that very careful thought needs to be given to the control of commuting car traffic into the City to allow adequate road and parking space for business callers and a free pedestrian traffic. Some of the Corporation's plans for pedways and for large-scale car-parks on the periphery of the City show that this problem is being taken very seriously. We see the extension of pedways as essential characteristics of a City whose intra-City traffic is largely pedestrian.

We have observed that several new national transport developments are likely to directly or indirectly affect the flow of commuter traffic in the City, notably the two new tubes – the Victoria and Fleet Lines. It is, of course, possible that an easier access to the City from both north and south will tempt more residents in Outer London to work in the City. The building of new office accommodation close to main line termini would help to reduce the walking distance of commuters at the end of their train journeys. Furthermore, due to the likely shortage of labour from the traditional supplying areas (e.g. Essex, Surrey and Kent), we consider that attention might well be given to ways and means of improving access to the City from the west and north main line termini into which there is some surplus 'commuting' capacity on British Rail.

In summary, we do not anticipate there will be any substantial change in the *level* of the City's labour force in the next decade or so, although we do expect there will be a continual pressure on new accommodation for office building and, to a lesser extent on retail and catering facilities. The more far-reaching changes will take place in the *composition* of the City's employment. Already now largely concentrated in financial and trading activities we believe that further functional specialization will take place *within* these activities, that gradually only those involving more highly skilled manpower will remain in the City. We expect that these changes will reduce the proportion of female labour to all labour. They will involve more dealing with people, and linkages will become increasingly important. We foresee that the City will become an even more tightly-knit complex of complementary activities than it is today.

One final point. We believe that the developments forecast in this chapter will be the outcome of changes in national and international economic circumstances. We further believe if the City is in any way restricted from making the necessary adaptations to its institutions and markets to meet these changes, it and the nation will be the losers. It has not been our brief to analyse whether or not the City is operating as efficiently as it might be: we have attempted neither to condemn nor to praise, but rather produce the facts.

Three things, however, cannot be denied. First the labour productivity and activities carried on in the City are considerably higher than the national average in all branches of industry; second the balance of payments contribution of City firms, per worker employed, is very much greater than the average in manufacturing industry (see Chapter 3); third, because of the widespread national and international activities of firms represented in the City, the success or failure of the decisions and judgements taken in City offices affects many times the number of people that are actually employed in these offices. For these three reasons alone, we strongly believe that any policy or planning programme of public authorities should recognize the distinctive contribution of the City's economy and encourage rather than hinder its capacity to meet the changes and challenges of the future.

Index